INTERNATIONAL HELICOPTER THEORY

Navigation Theory
for Helicopter Pilots

Copyright © 1998-2016 International Helicopter Theory Pty Ltd

Navigation Theory
for Helicopter Pilots

First Edition – 1998
Second Edition – 2003
Third Edition – 2008
Fourth Edition – 2010
Fifth Edition – 2013
Sixth Edition – 2015
Seventh Edition – 2016

Author
Captain Mike Becker

Published by
    International Helicopter Theory Pty Ltd
    21 Friendship Avenue
    Marcoola
    QLD 4564, Australia

Copyright
The contents of this manual are protected by copyright throughout the world under the Berne Union and the universal copyright convention.

All rights reserved. No part of this publication may be reproduced in any manner whatsoever - electronic, photographic, photocopying, facsimile, or stored in a retrieval system - without the prior written permission of the author.

Disclaimer
Nothing in this text supersedes any operational documents issued by any civil aviation authority or regulatory body, aircraft, engine, and avionics manufacturers, or the operators of aircraft throughout the world.

The Publisher and the Author make no representations or warranties with respect to the accuracy or completeness of the contents of this work and specifically disclaim all warranties, including without limitation warranties of fitness for a particular purpose. No warranty may be created or extended by sales or promotional materials. The advice and strategies contained herein may not be suitable for every situation. This work is sold with the understanding that the publisher is not engaged in rendering legal, accounting, or other professional services. If professional assistance is required, the services of a competent professional person should be sought. Neither the Publisher nor the Author shall be liable for damages arising herefrom.

The fact that an organisation or website is referred to in this work as a citation and/or a potential source of further information does not mean that the author or the Publisher endorses the information the organisation or website may provide or recommendations it may make. Further, readers should be aware that internet websites listed in this work may have changed or disappeared between when this work was written and when it is read.

Table of Contents

1. Introduction to Navigation 1-1
2. Maps and Charts 2-1
3. Track, Distance, Time and Speed 3-1
4. Flight Computer Front Side 4-1
5. Flight Computer Back Side 5-1
6. Vertical Measurement 6-1
7. Advanced Calculations 7-1
8. The 1 in 60 Rule 8-1
9. Calculating the Effect of Wind on a Runway 9-1
10. Equal Time Point (ETP) 10-1
11. Calculating Rates of Climb And Descent 11-1
12. Point of No Return (PNR) 12-1
13. Radio Navigation 13-1
14. Creating a Flight Plan 14-1

Detailed Table of Contents

1 Introduction to Navigation 1-1
- VFR and IFR 1-2
- Dead Reckoning 1-4
- Radio Navigation 1-6
- Categories of VFR Navigation 1-6

2 Maps and Charts 2-1
- Difference between a map and a chart 2-4
- Properties of an Ideal map 2-6
  - Conformity (Angles correct) 2-7
  - Constant Scale 2-7
  - Great Circles 2-7
  - Small Circles 2-9
  - Rhumb Lines 2-10
- Imaginary Lines on the Earth's Surface 2-11
  - Latitude 2-12
  - Longitude 2-13
  - Degrees, Minutes and Seconds 2-14
- Map Scale 2-17
  - Large scale vs Small scale 2-18
  - Finding a maps scale 2-19
- Map legend 2-21
  - Heights 2-22
  - Cultural features 2-24
  - Specialised information 2-24
  - Validity 2-24
- Map Projection Classifications 2-25
  - Mercator's Cylindrical Projections 2-26
  - Lamberts Conformal Conical Projections 2-27
- Summary of Map/Chart Properties 2-28

3 Track, Distance, Time and Speed 3-1
- Track 3-1
  - Tracks and Headings 3-1
  - Variation, Wind and Deviation 3-2
  - Deviation 3-14
  - Summary 3-15
- Distance 3-16
- Time 3-17
  - The Date/Time grouping of numbers 3-17
- Use of Time 3-19
  - Time as a concept 3-20
  - Time as a unit of measurement 3-25
  - Time as a Tool 3-28
- Speed 3-38
  - Groundspeed 3-39
  - Airspeed 3-41
  - Summary 3-49

4	**Flight Computer Front Side** 4-1
	Front Side Markings 4-2
	Beginners Rules 4-3
	Finding Time 4-4
	Finding Distance 4-5
	Finding Speed 4-6
	Flight Fuel 4-7
	Fuel Burned 4-8
	Fuel Consumption Rate 4-9
	Calculation of TAS 4-10
5	**Flight Computer Back Side** 5-1
	Back side scales 5-2
	Beginners rules 5-4
	Definitions 5-5
	Understanding Wind on the Back Side 5-6
	Triangle of velocities 5-6
	Heading and Groundspeed Calculations 5-9
	Wind Velocity Calculations 5-15
6	**Vertical Measurement** 6-1
	Definitions 6-1
	Altimetry Problems 6-3
	Variations Mean Sea Level Pressure 6-4
	Effects of variation in MSL Pressure 6-7
	The Effect of Temperature on Pressure 6-8
	Adjusting the Subscale of an Altimeter 6-9
	Pressure Height (Altitude) 6-9
	Density Heights (Altitude) 6-9
7	**Advanced Calculations** 7-1
	Introduction 7-1
	The 1 in 60 Rule 7-1
	Runway crosswind components 7-2
	Climbs and Descents 7-2
	Equal Time Point 7-3
	Point of No Return (PNR) 7-3
8	**The 1 in 60 Rule** 8-1
	What is the 1 in 60 Rule 8-2
	Extending the 1 in 60 Rule of Thumb 8-3
	Applying Ratios to the 1 in 60 Rule 8-4
	Applying the 1 in 60 Rule 8-5
	Applying the 1 in 60 Rule: A Simple Example 8-6
	Calculating Track Error 8-6
	Applying the Track Error Correction 8-7
	Calculating the Closing Angle 8-7
	Heading Correction Amount 8-8
	Heading Correction Amount 8-9
	Intercept and Regain the FPT 8-10
	Different Methods of Applying the 1 in 60 Rule: 8-12
	Using 1 in 60 Formulas 8-14
	Using 1 in 60 Formulas: An example 8-15

The Flight Computer method 8-16
1 in 60 Summary 8-21
Definitions Summary 8-22

9 Calculating the Effect of Wind on a Runway 9-1

Introduction 9-1
Wind 9-2
      Wind components 9-3
      Calculating the effect of wind on a runway 9-5
      Wind Component Tables 9-5
Calculating Head Wind Component (HWC) 9-6
Calculating Cross Wind Component (XWC) 9-8
Calculating Tail Wind Component (TWC) 9-10

10 Equal Time Point (ETP) 10-1

11 Calculating Rates of Climb And Descent 11-1

Introduction 11-1
Calculating the Rate of Climb or Rate of Descent 11-1
      Revision of the variables to calculate ROC or ROD 11-3
Climb and Descent Gradient 11-7
Airspace Protection 11-12
      Review of CTA Steps 11-14
Calculating a ROC/ROD to Maintain CTA Protection 11-17
      Climbs 11-17
      Descents 11-19

12 Point of No Return (PNR) 12-1

Calculating Time to the PNR 12-4
Calculating Distance to the PNR 12-6

13 Radio Navigation 13-1

Introduction 13-1
What is a Radio Navigation Aid 13-2
How the Information is Displayed 13-3
      Written Information 13-3
      Multi-Function Display (MFD) 13-5
      Azimuth Indicator 13-5
      Course Deviation Indicator (CDI) 13-7
The NDB 13-9
      The VFR Pilot Needs to 13-10
      Finding the Right Frequency 13-10
      NDB Summary 13-16
The VOR 13-17
      The VFR Pilot needs to 13-18
      VOR Summary 13-23
      Position Fix Using the VOR/NDB 13-24
The GPS 13-25
      The VFR Pilot needs to 13-27
      GPS Summary 13-30

14 Creating a Flight Plan 14-1

Introduction 14-1
Tools Required 14-1

Introducing the Flight Log 14-6
    Becker Helicopters Flight Log 14-7
    The Front Side 14-8
    The Back Side 14-12
Creating a Flight Plan 14-18
Transposing information onto the topographical map 14-32
        Summary 14-35
Map Reading 101 14-36
        Map to Ground and Ground to Map 14-36
Rules 14-38
    1. Use the clock code 14-38
    2. Select the right features 14-40
    3. Map to Ground 14-42
    4. Ground to Map 14-42
Flight Notification via NAIPS 14-42

1 Introduction to Navigation

In order to fly from one place on the earth to another place on the earth, the pilot will need to know how to "*navigate*".

The art of "*navigating*" is the ability to use the navigation tools and collate all the relevant planning information that may be available about the route and the destination in order to accurately plan and then travel from one place to another.

This travelling from one place to another in aviation is commonly called a "*Cross Country*" flight. It is called this because you are travelling across new country that you may never have seen or been over before.

The tools and planning information we use and that have been developed over time include the clock, magnetic compass, weather reports, navigation flight logs, Planning Check Lists, Notices to Airmen (NOTAMS), maps, ruler, protractor, manual flight computer (commonly called a "wiz wheel"), and in modern aircraft GPS, electronic computer based applications (such as Oz-Runways and NAIPS) and any other modern aid or device that is appropriate and can be used to assist in navigating the aircraft.

VFR and IFR

The techniques used to plan and execute a navigational flight plan, will depend on which *rules* the pilot is operating under.

There are two different sets of rules used in aviation, they are:

1. The **V**isual **F**light **R**ules referred to as the **VFR** and
2. The **I**nstrument **F**light **R**ules referred to as the **IFR**

VFR

If the pilot is operating under the VFR then the pilot will use "**Dead Reckoning**" (**DR**) and "**Pilotage**" techniques with reference to topographical maps to navigate. Of course if the pilot also knows how to use some of the radio navigation aids and they are installed in the aircraft then they can also be used to assist or supplement VFR navigation.

The fundamental rule for navigating under the VFR is that the pilot is able to visually look outside the cockpit and determine the helicopter's position every 30 minutes with reference to a map.

If flying **below 2000 feet AGL** then the pilot must also remain in sight of the ground or water at all times and clear of any cloud.

If flying **at or above 2000 feet AGL** then the pilot may occasionally lose sight of the ground or water as the helicopter may be flying on top of the cloud.

2000 feet AGL or less

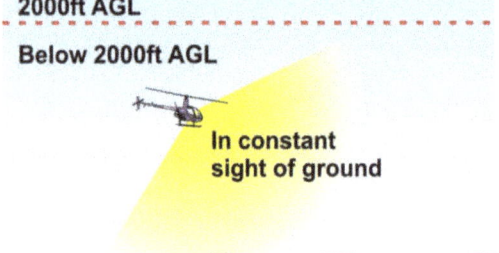

2000 feet AGL or more

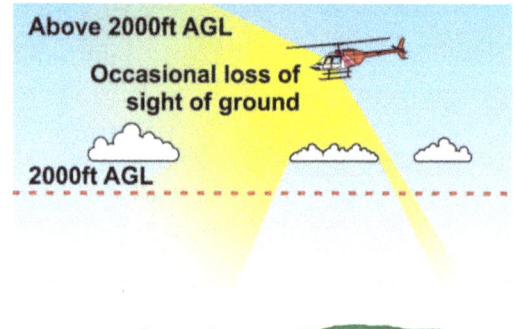

IFR

If the pilot is operating under the IFR then it is normal to exclusively use instruments in the aircraft and radio navigation aids such as the GPS, VOR, and NDB or be directed by ATC in order to navigate. IFR navigation can be done by day or night and the pilot is able to fly into the cloud. There is no longer a need to be able to see outside and fix the helicopters position on a map with reference to the ground as navigation is accomplished by reference to the Radio Navigation aids.

IFR flight

IFR navigation will be covered in detail later in the Instrument Rating course.

Dead Reckoning

The term "Dead Reckoning" comes from abbreviating the term "Deduced Reckoning". The word deduced simply means to calculate or reason or figure out.

Historically the term Dead Reckoning originated with maritime (sea) navigation where a ship's navigator had to figure out (reason or reckon) the position of the ship relative to something stationary or *dead* in the water.

By pure definition then, Dead Reckoning is the process of estimating your position over the surface of the earth by moving from a known position, steering a course (compass heading) maintaining a constant speed for a particular amount of time to give a distance travelled.

It is the pilot figuring out where the helicopter will be at a certain time if maintaining a particular speed for a particular time on a particular heading.

The three most important factors to consider in Dead Reckoning navigation are:

Time – Distance – Heading

For example, if the helicopter leaves Gympie Airport at 10am and travels on a heading of 270 degrees magnetic at 100kts for 30 minutes, then by Dead Reckoning you can calculate the helicopter should be 50NM along track and over a small cross road.

This is Dead Reckoning or DR Navigation.

---

[1] Cole 2008, CC by 2.0, Replica sailing ship Niña leaving Morro Bay Ref: https://www.flickr.com/photos/kevcole/3040887411

Pilotage

The term "Pilotage", sometimes referred to as "Track Crawling" or "Post to Post" refers to the pilot flying from one ground based reference point to another. The pilot or navigator has to identify landmarks such as rivers, roads, mountains, towns, airports, wires and buildings etc. on a map, then sight them on the ground and then fly to each reference point before flying to the next one.

Instead of pre-planning a navigation using time distance and heading, pilotage navigation is more about flying from one known point (post) on the ground to another known point (post).

Pilotage relies on good *map interpretation* skills and in a lot of cases good local knowledge of the area.

Pilotage navigation becomes more difficult in low visibility or over areas with very few features. It is also not a very efficient method of navigating over longer distances. Pilotage navigation is usually reserved for operations below 500 feet where the pilot is required to terrain fly and navigates in and around terrain and obstacles.

Radio Navigation

Radio navigation refers to the use of Radio Navigation aids including the NDB, VOR and GPS to use radio signals received from ground or space based stations. These signals are translated in a receiver unit then displayed on an instrument in the cockpit which then must be interpreted by the pilot to determine the aircraft's position.

The most accurate and commonly used Radio Navigation aid in modern aircraft is the GPS which sends radio signals from space to a receiver in the aircraft.

Radio Navigation is the primary means to navigate for IFR operations, but may be used to help or supplement VFR navigation if they are on board the aircraft and the pilot knows how to use them.

This course will focus primarily on Dead Reckoning and Pilotage navigation information and techniques with a small chapter on the very basic use of the Radio Navigation aids to supplement VFR navigation.

The bulk of information for Radio Navigation under the IFR will be taught in the Instrument Rating course.

Categories of VFR Navigation

VFR navigation is divided into several different categories depending on what height above the ground the helicopter is being flown, the categories are:

Category	Height above the ground
High Level Navigation	10,000 – 18,000 feet AMSL
Medium Level Navigation	500 – 10,000 feet AGL
Low Level Navigation	500 AGL and below
Terrain Navigation This includes terrain flying and time on target	Nap-of-the-earth (NOE) (not above 360ft AGL) Note: In Australia an obstacle, tower or structure that is no higher than 360 feet does not need to be marked on a map or lit. For this reason then, any flight below 360 feet comes with an added level of risk and is why NOE is considered to be not above 360 feet.

---

[2] Engineerography Blog 2009, CC by 2.0, Artists rendition of a GPS satellite in orbit Ref:
https://www.flickr.com/photos/engineerography/3567109693/sizes/m/

Diagram

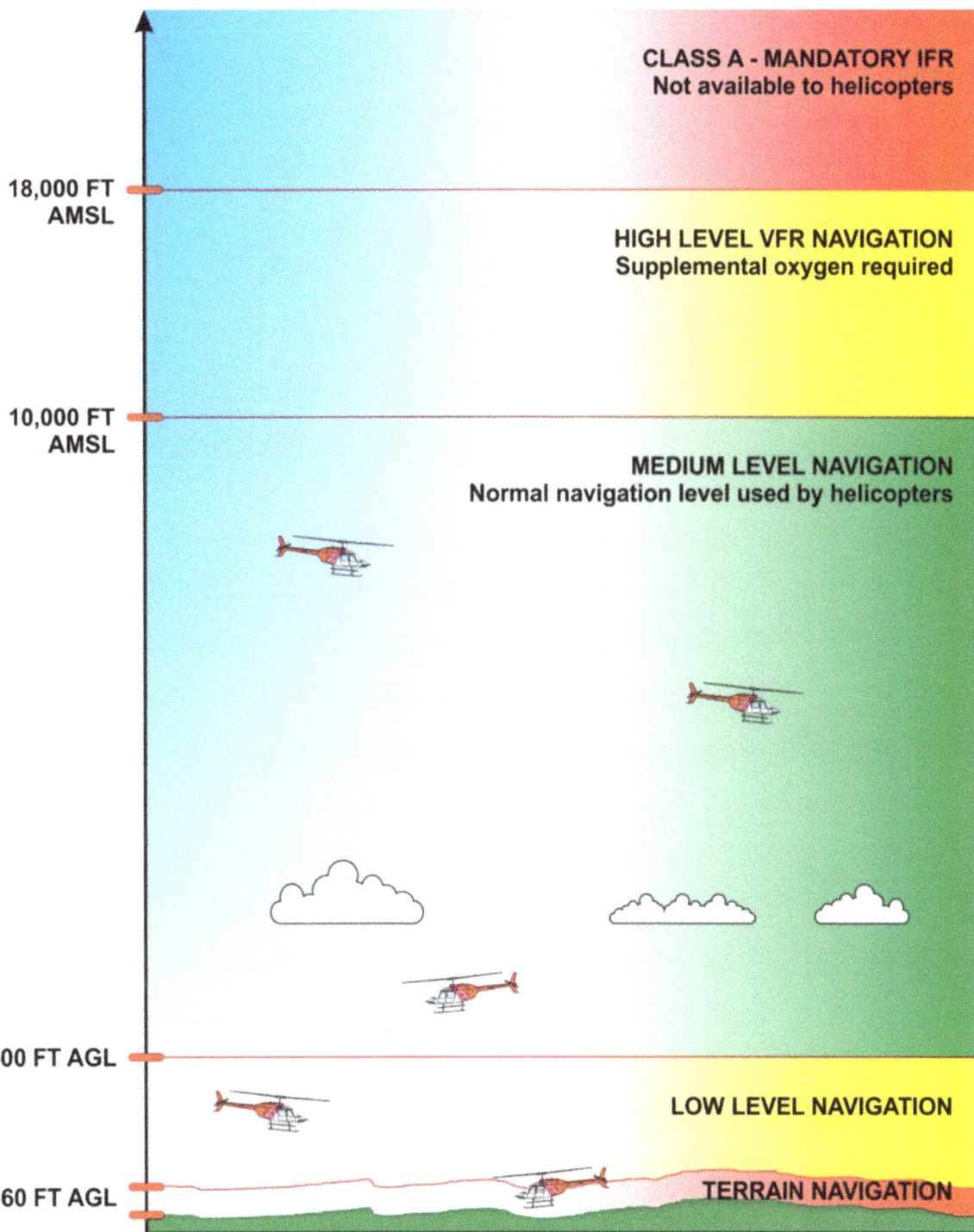

Each category of navigation can use different tools and techniques to assist the pilot and may also lead to changing how the cockpit dynamics between Pilot Flying (PF) and Pilot Monitoring (PM) operate if navigating as part of a Multi Crew operation.

For example:

Category	Technique	Multi crew operation
High Level Navigation (Not normal for helicopter operations)	More suited to the use of radio navigation aids and IFR	Crew function more as an instrument flight
Medium Level Navigation (Normal helicopter operating levels)	Suited to both dead reckoning and instrument navigation	Pilot Monitoring (PM) will navigate and direct the Pilot Flying (PF)
Low Level Navigation (Normal helicopter operating levels)	Suited to both dead reckoning and pilotage navigation	Pilot Monitoring (PM) will navigate and direct the Pilot Flying (PF)
Terrain Navigation This includes terrain flying and time on target (Specifically suited to helicopter operations)	Suited to pilotage navigation	Pilot Monitoring (PM) will navigate and direct the Pilot Flying (PF)

Preparation

Being properly prepared is essential for successful navigation and this all starts with the ground preparation.

The ground preparation requires a pilot to gather all of those items that can affect the flight including the wind, weather, NOTAMs, aircraft performance details etc. and creating a navigation flight plan. Once the planning is completed the crew can then carry out the flight by actioning the plan.

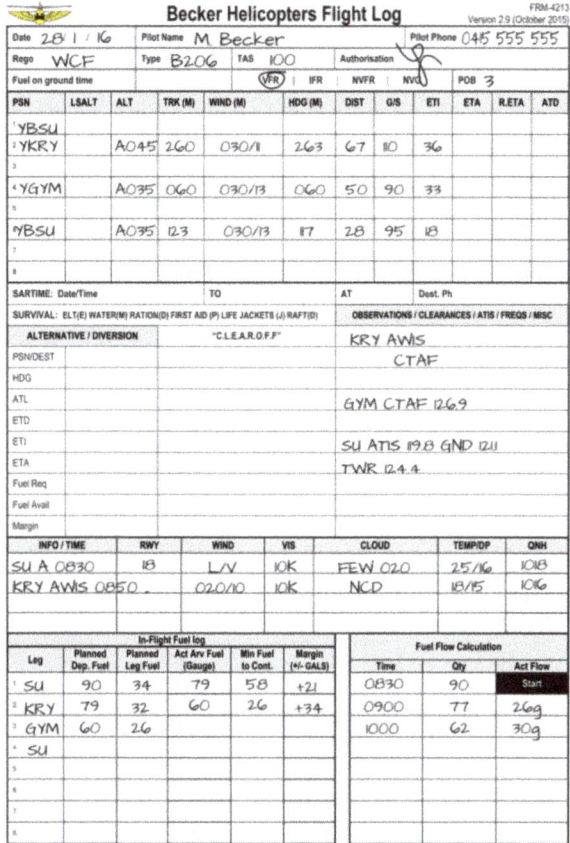
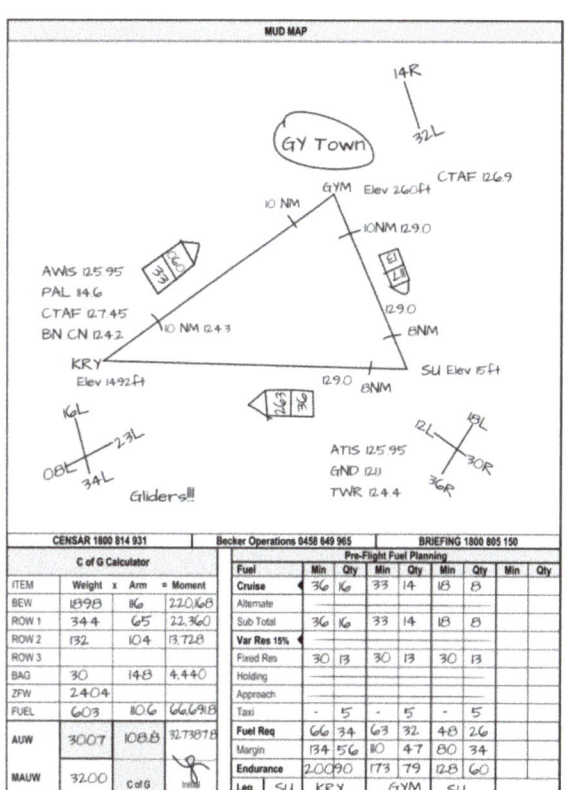

The information in the following chapters is considered "Foundation Theory" for Visual Flight Rules (VFR) navigation and is fundamental knowledge you will have to apply later when planning a real VFR flight and knowledge you will need to know to pass a navigation theory exam.

The *practical* aspects you will need to apply on a real flight will be covered later in the Pilot Handling Notes (PHNs) for the specific helicopter type you are flying.

2 Maps and Charts

Although the earth is not a perfect sphere (ball shape) with its many valleys, oceans, mountains and volcanoes forever changing shape, for practical navigational purposes and the production of aeronautical charts it is assumed that the earth is a perfect sphere. Probably the most accurate representation of the earth, at a reduced size, would be a globe.

The true shape of the earth is known as an **Oblate Spheroid**. The earth's rotation causes it to bulge out at the equator and become flatter at the poles and, therefore, become slightly oblong in shape.

Traditional Globe shape   **Oblate Spheroid (earths real shape)**

---

[3] FreeImages.com / Ove Topfer / Content License / globe-1-1415571
[4] FreeImages.com / Barun Patro/Content License / planet-earth-3-1356447

With advances in technology, the use of a traditional paper based map is reducing and maps are now displayed on electronic tablets and moving map displays in the cockpit.

iPad

Moving Map on a Multi-function Display (MFD)

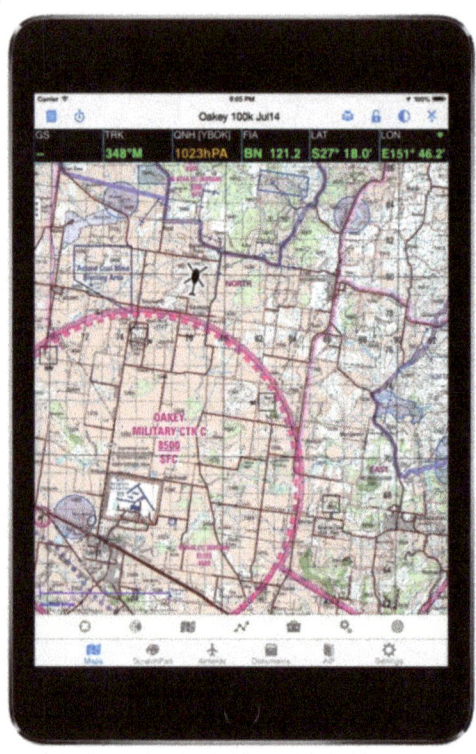

Who knows, in the future we may be able to project a 3-D holographic image coupled with GPS in view of the pilot instead of having a simple map.

For training purposes, there is still the need for suitable paper based maps and charts that can portray any area with any desired level of detail and can be folded for convenient carriage and use.

No flat map or chart can truly represent all or even part of the earth's surface exactly. Distortion will always be a problem when converting the curved shape of the earth on to a flat surface.

This fundamental problem in map construction can be illustrated by cutting a globe (or round ball) in half, and trying to press one of the halves flat on a table.

It is impossible to flatten the half sphere without stretching, distorting tearing or cutting it.

When it is cut there will be voids so the flat globe will no longer give a true representation.

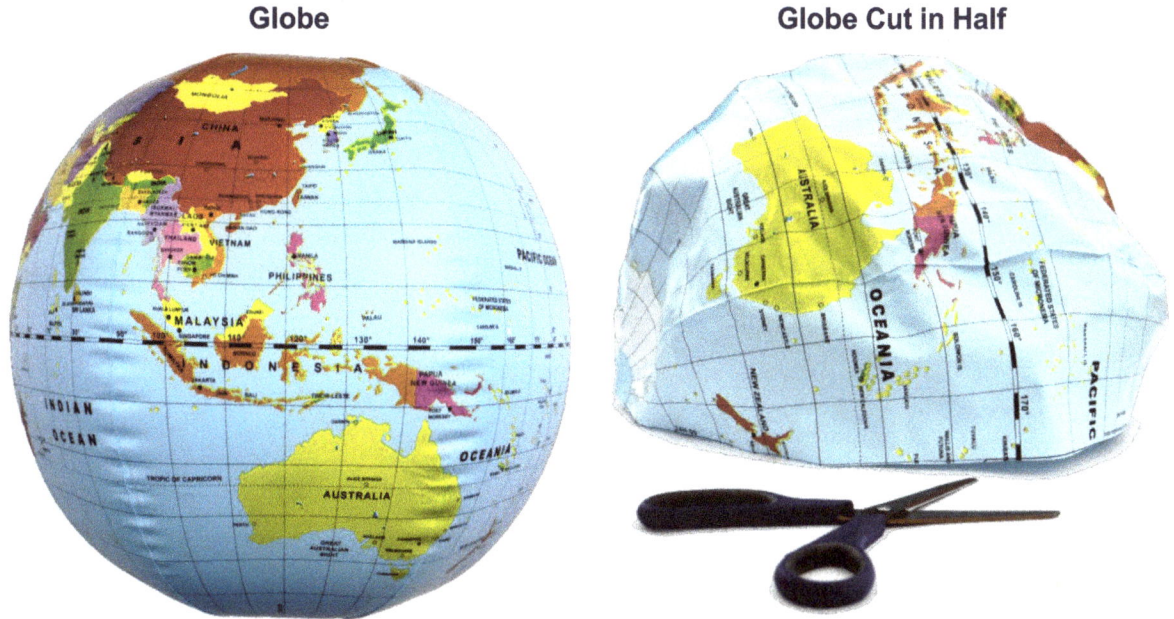

Globe   **Globe Cut in Half**

Globe cut down the edges. Lays flat but now the map is distorted.

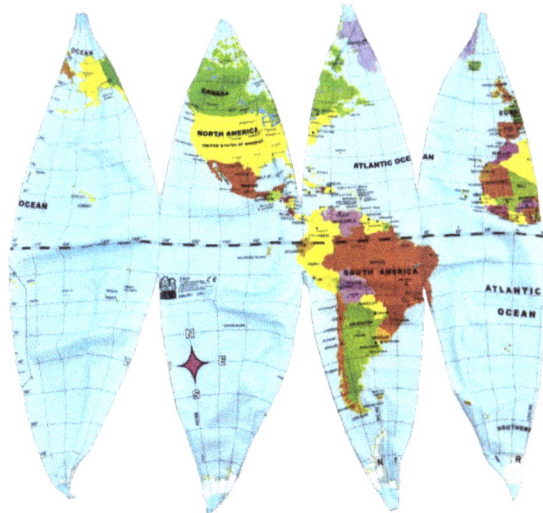

The transfer of details from a globe to a chart will result in distances, angles, shapes and areas always being distorted to some extent.

Cartographer (Chart maker)

The challenge facing the chart maker (referred to as a cartographer) is how to minimise the distortions and at the same time produce a chart that can be used for navigation. This is done by the cartographer using special mathematical formulas (which, fortunately, we don't have to worry about), in conjunction with different projection processes to produce a usable map or chart, not just an image of a globe on a piece of paper.

Difference between a map and a chart

The earliest charts made by man were of the stars and can be dated back more than 8000 years ago.

Maritime Navigation Charts

In the modern exploration age between roughly 1500AD and 1900AD navigation charts were created for maritime (ocean) navigation showing depths of water and heights of land (topographic map), natural features of the seabed, details of the coastline, navigational hazards, locations of natural and human-made aids to navigation, information on tides and currents, local details of the Earth's magnetic field, and human-made structures such as harbours, buildings and bridges in order for a ships navigator to plot a safe course.

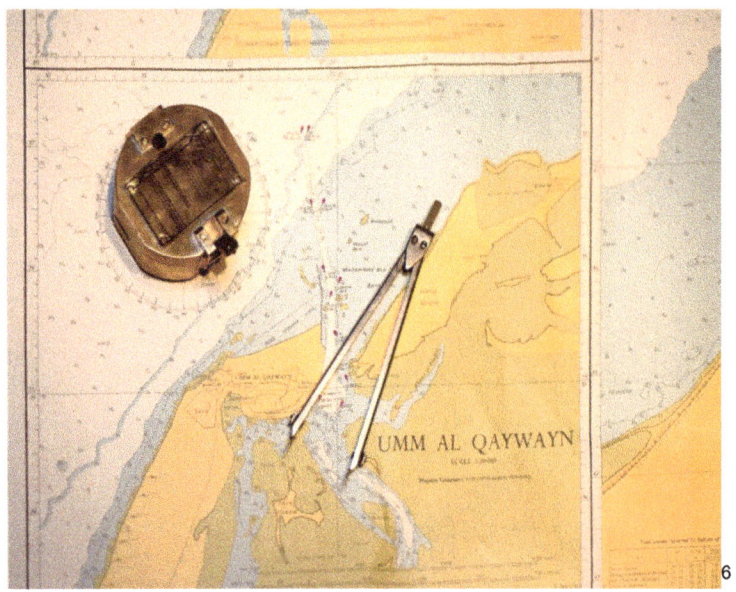

---

[5] Funk 2005 / CC by 2.0 / New Boston the Cartographer / Ref: https://www.flickr.com/photos/cindyfunk/2843079059/sizes/o/
[6] FreeImages.com / Krzystof Sxkurlatowski / Content License / old-maritime-map-1156710

Aeronautical Sectional Chart

On December 17th, 1903 the Wright brothers officially conducted the first flight in an aircraft, so aviation charts were not in existence or required prior to that time, with the first official aeronautical sectional chart being printed in the USA in 1930.

It was called a "sectional chart" because it showed a section (or part) of the continent of the USA. In Australia we refer to these as Visual Navigation Charts (VNCs) or Visual Terminal Charts (VTCs).

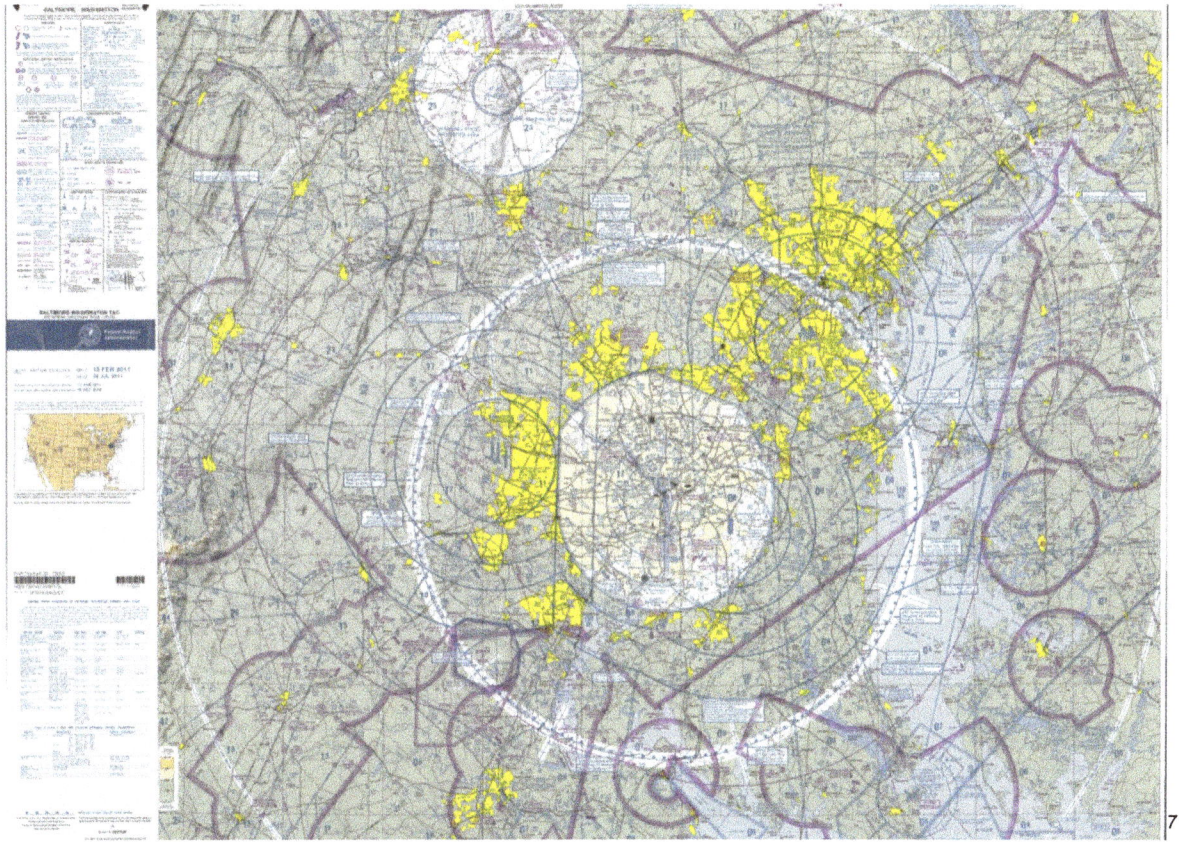

Aeronautical charts then had information that was important for a pilot to know which was different to what a navigator on a ship needed to know.

---

[7] By US Department of Transportation, Federal Aviation Administration, National Aeronautical Navigation Services [Public domain], via Wikimedia Commons / https://commons.wikimedia.org/wiki/File%3ABaltimore-Washington_TAC_82.png

Difference between Chart and a Map

Chart	Map

A chart is a *working* document used to plot courses allowing a navigator (or pilot) to draw lines and determine a safe path to a particular destination.

It aids the navigator (pilot) in determining their position, safe altitude, best route to a destination, navigation aids along the way, alternative landing areas in case of an in-flight emergency, and other useful information such as radio frequencies and airspace boundaries.

A map is a *static* document which serves as a reference guide.

A map is not, and should not be used to plot a course.

Rather it provides a predetermined course, usually a road, path, or in aviation, a predetermined safe route as found on the En-Route Chart (ERC) or Terminal Area Chart (TAC), to be followed.

The difference in charts and maps in modern times is less pronounced so the terms are both commonly used to mean the same thing.

Obviously, by pure definition in aviation we can use both maps and charts, however, for ease of communication and throughout the rest of this course we will simply refer to them all collectively as "**Maps**".

Properties of an Ideal map

The ideal map or chart would portray the features of the earth in their true relationship to one another. Directions would be true and distance would be represented at a constant scale over the entire chart. This would result in equality of area and true shape throughout the chart. Such a relationship can only be represented on a globe. A flat chart, however that is made, will always suffer some distortion in its creation.

As far as aeronautical maps are concerned, the most desirable and important properties with the least amount of distortion are as follows:

Conformity (Angles correct)

The correct angular relationship between all surface features should be preserved. This means that all the parallels of latitude and meridians of longitude must intersect at right angles, as they would on the actual earth. Maps that possess this property are known as **conformal** or **orthomorphic**.

Constant Scale

A constant scale allows distances measured anywhere on the chart to correctly represent distances on the full-scale earth.

Great Circles

A great circle is any circle on the earth whose plane passes through the earth's centre. The plane of a great circle must therefore bisect (cut in half) the earth.

The smaller arc of a great circle (which is any smaller part of the whole) which passes through two places on the earth represents the shortest distance between those two places.

Only one great circle can pass through any two places on the earth's surface unless the two places are diametrically opposite.

- Because the earth is a sphere (or globe) any lines we draw on the globe will actually be a large curve, which we call a great circle.

The diagram below shows what a great circle looks like when the map is laid out flat.

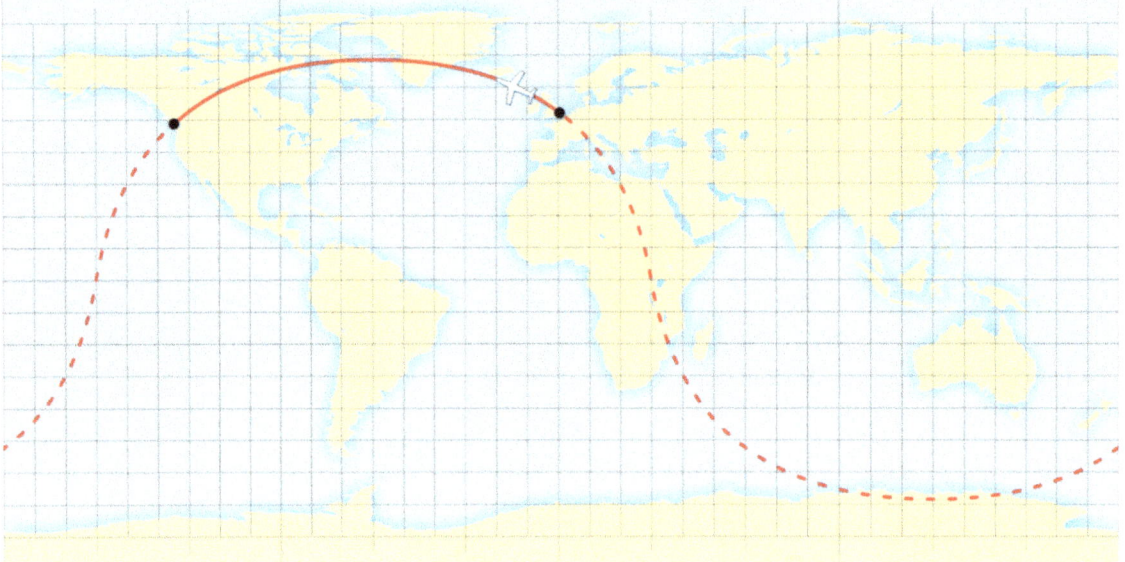

Small Circles

A small circle on the earth's surface is any circle (or line) whose plane does not pass through the earth's centre.

Summary

- A great circle drawn on the earth's surface is one whose plane passes through the centre of the earth.
- A great circle is the largest circle that can be drawn on the surface of the earth.
- The arc of a great circle is the shortest distance around the surface of the earth between two points.
- All meridians of longitude are great circles.
- All other parallels of latitude are considered small circles except for the equator as it is the only parallel of latitude considered a great circle.

Rhumb Lines

A Rhumb line is a curved line on the earth that will cut all the meridians of longitude at the same angle.

When navigating from one place on the earth to another over long distances following a great circle may be the shortest distance between those two places but to fly the great circle you will periodically have to alter course as the direction of the great circle changes.

Example

When flying from 'A' located at 30°S, 150°E to 'B' located at 30°S, 120°E on a constant track of 270° True, the helicopter will fly along a parallel of latitude which is a track that crosses each successive meridian at the same angle. The helicopter will be flying a Rhumb line which is represented in the diagram below by a dotted line.

To fly the shortest distance, and therefore, the quickest path between 'A' and 'B' the helicopter would need to fly a great circle track. This would mean the track would initially be less than 270° True, and gradually changing to a track of more than 270° True which is represented in the diagram below by the solid line.

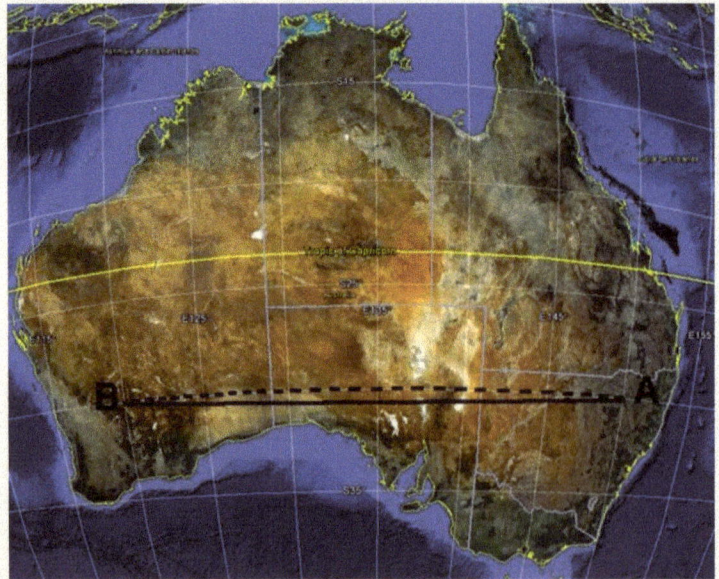

For this reason then, Rhumb lines are widely used in navigation because its direction (track) is constant between the two places even though it is not the shortest distance between two points.

Summary

A Rhumb line is a curved line over the earth that will cut all meridians of longitude at the same angle and therefore give a constant direction from one place to another even though the distance travelled may be greater.

Imaginary Lines on the Earth's Surface

The usual method of specifying the exact position of any point on the earth surface is by reference to imaginary lines forming the latitude and longitude grid.

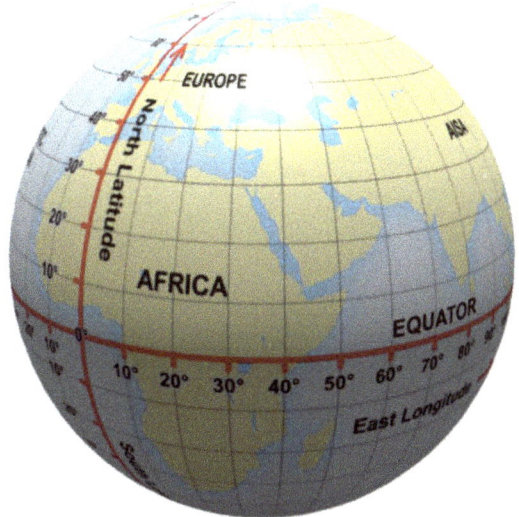

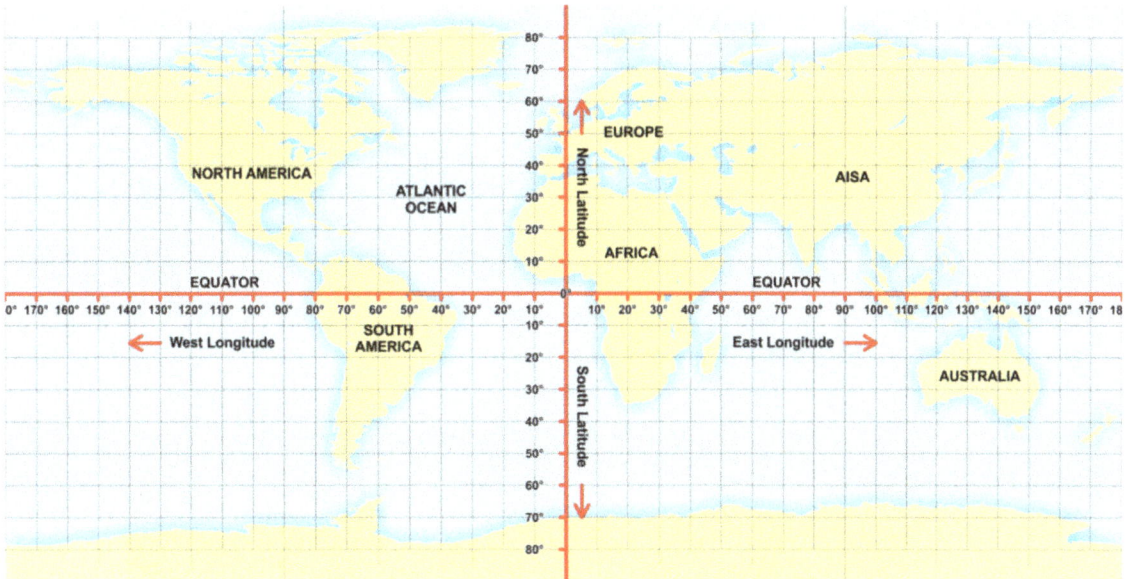

Latitude

The reference for latitude is the equator referred to as Latitude 0°.

The Latitude of any place on the surface of the earth is its angular distance, in degrees, from the equator, measured at the centre of the earth and designated either north or south.

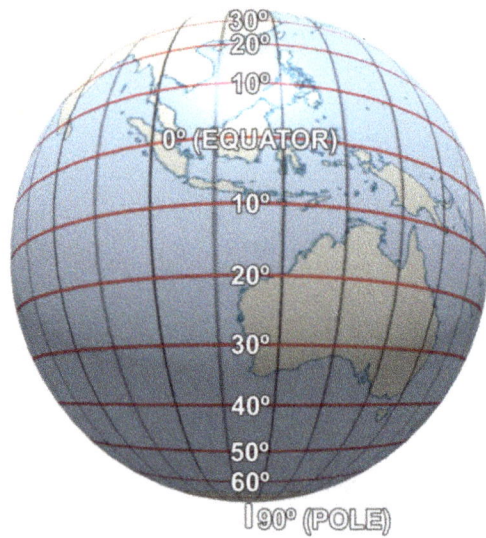

Latitude can be easily remembered as the lines that run "laterally" (horizontally) around the earth parallel to the Equator.

A Latitude position can be displayed in several different formats.

The most common format is Degrees, Minutes and Seconds.

Other formats include Degrees, Minutes and decimals of minutes or a topographical grid system which will not be covered in this course.

Example
The Latitude of the Sunshine Coast Airport is 26 degrees, 36 minutes and 00 Seconds South of the Equator. It is written as 263600S or S263600.

Facts about lines of latitude

- Lines of latitude are referred to as parallels as each successive line of latitude is parallel to the next and never meet
- They run in an East-West direction
- Measure distance North or South from the Equator
- Cross the Prime Meridian at right angles
- Lie in planes that cross the Earth's axis at right angles
- Get shorter toward the geographic poles with only the Equator being a Great Circle.

Longitude

The reference for Longitude is the **Greenwich Meridian,** which is also known as the **Prime Meridian** and is designated as longitude 0° E/W.

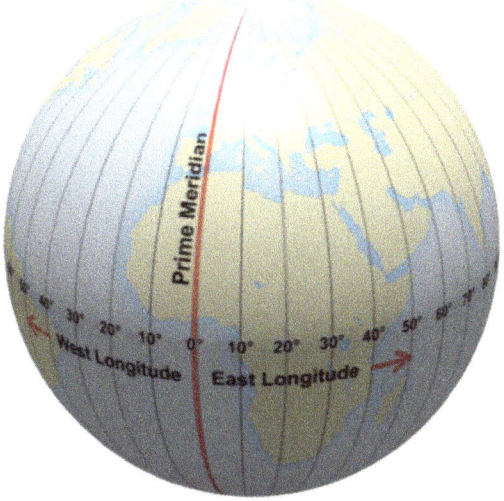

Each meridian of longitude passes through both the North and South geographic poles and are also **Great Circles.**

The longitude of any place on the surface of the earth is its angular distance between the Meridian of longitude it is on, measured either East or West of the Prime Meridian.

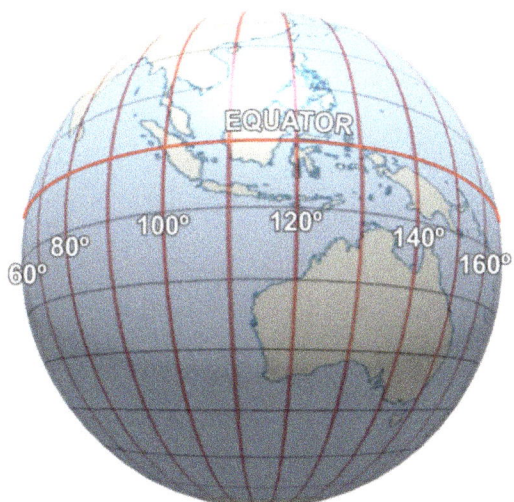

It is important to note that although there are 360° in a full circle, Longitude is only measured up to 180° either East or 180° West.

Longitude can be easily remembered as the lines that run "long ways" (vertically) up and down the earth and all meet at the North and South Poles.

A Longitude position can be displayed in several different formats.

The most common format is Degrees, Minutes and Seconds

Other formats include Degrees, Minutes and decimals of minutes or a topographical grid system which will not be covered in this course.

Example
The Longitude of the Sunshine Coast Airport is 153 degrees, 05 minutes and 00 Seconds East of the Prime Meridian. It is written as 1530500E or E1530500.

Facts about longitude

- Lines of longitude are referred to as meridians
- They run in a North-South direction
- Measure distance East or West of the Prime Meridian
- Are furthest apart at the Equator and meet at the Poles
- Cross the Equator at right angles
- Lie in planes that pass through the Earths centre
- Are equal in length
- Are halves of great circles

Degrees, Minutes and Seconds

The Latitude of a place is its angular position North or South of the Equator.

The Longitude of a place is its angular position East or West of the Prime Meridian.

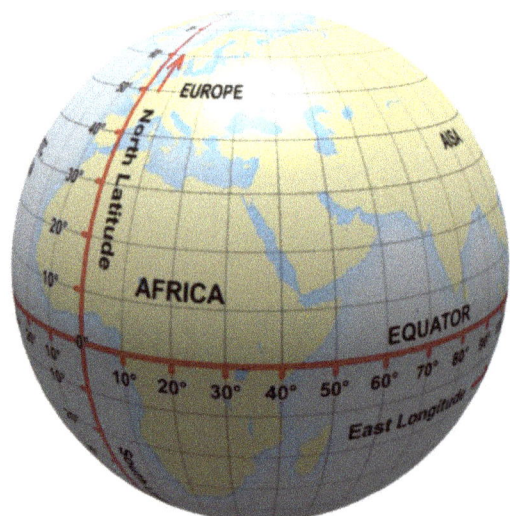

To pinpoint the exact position of a particular place on the earth the Latitude and Longitude grid system is normally expressed in **Degrees (°), Minutes (') and Seconds (") where**

60 minutes make up **one degree**

60 seconds make up **one minute**

> **Example**
>
> The Sunshine Coast VOR is located at S26°35'51" E153°05'25"
>
> For ease of writing these references down, typically, the degree (°), minute (') and second (") symbols are deleted and the S, E, N or W cardinal point is placed at the end or beginning of the reference number.
>
> Therefore the Latitude and Longitude for the Sunshine Coast VOR could be written down as 263551S1530525E or S263551E1530525.
>
> Additionally it is acceptable to write the reference with no seconds shown. This will mean the reference is not as accurate but when flying to a waypoint and getting within several feet of the waypoint, this sufficient for air navigation. In this case the references may be written as 2625S15305E or S2625E15305. Either method is acceptable.
>
>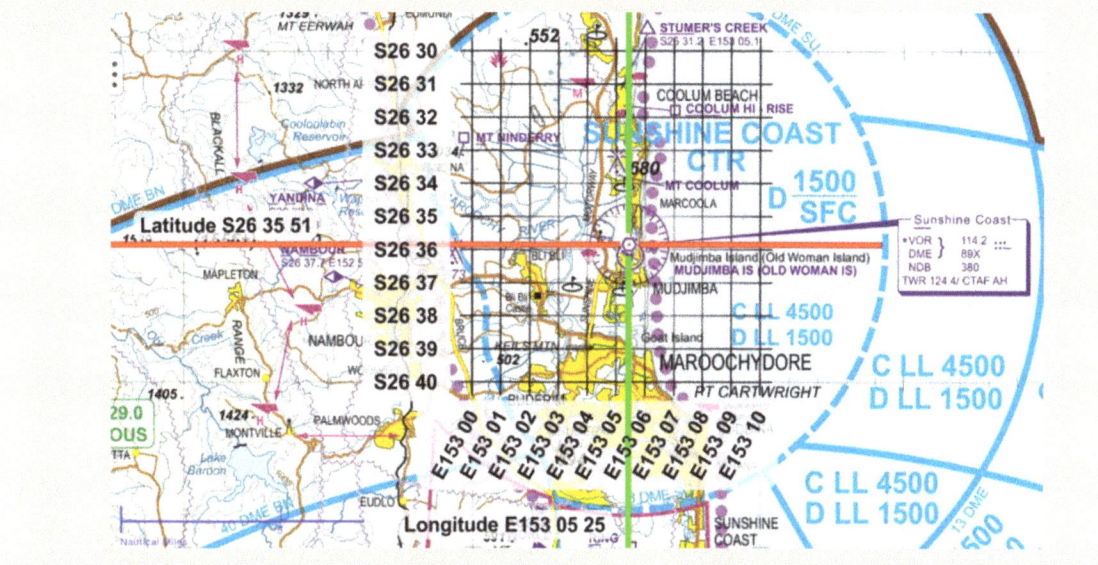

With the introduction of computers and GPS it has also become common to use Degrees, Minutes and *Decimals* of minutes.

This simply means that the seconds has been converted into a decimal of a minute by dividing the seconds by a factor of 60.

> **Example**
>
> Consider the Gympie Airport, with a Latitude of; South 26 degrees 17 minutes 20 seconds and a Longitude of East 152 degrees 42 minutes 08 seconds. This can be written as S261720 E1524208 but also written as S2617.333 E15224.133 if using decimals of minutes.
>
> If converting degrees minutes and seconds, to degrees, minutes and decimals of minutes simply divide the seconds by 60 to realise the decimal equivalent.
>
> Conversely if wanting to convert decimal minutes back into seconds simply multiply the decimal portion by 60 and round up to the nearest whole number.

Example
Consider a reference of S261720 E1524208. Taking the last two (2) numbers of east reference divide them by 60
20 divided by 60 equals .333 (the decimal equivalent of 20 seconds)
08 divided by 60 equals .133 (the decimal equivalent of 08 seconds)
Conversely consider a reference of S2617.333 E15224.133: Taking the last numbers to the right of the decimal place within the reference multiply them by 60 and then round up to the nearest whole number
.333 multiplied by 60 equals 20 (the seconds equivalent of .333 of a decimal minute)
.133 multiplied by 60 equals 08 (the seconds equivalent of .133 of a decimal minute)

This can become important when entering a user waypoint manually into a GPS as the GPS will be setup to read a particular Latitude and Longitude format. If the pilot enters a different format to that programmed into the GPS when creating the user waypoint, the GPS may take the helicopter to a different location.

The pilot has the option in the GPS setup menu to decide what format is preferred so understanding how each individual GPS unit works is going to be important.

Map Scale

Maps represent a *"scaled-down"* or reduced view of the earth's surface.

A maps scale is defined as the ratio of a given distance on a map compared to the actual earth distance that it represents and can be stated by the following formula:

$$\text{Scale} = \frac{\text{Map Distance}}{\text{Earth Distance}}$$

Example
A World Aeronautical Chart (WAC) with a scale of 1:1,000,000 would be described as $$\text{Scale} = \frac{1}{1,000,000}$$

In simple terms 1 unit or increment on the Longitude grid of the particular map equals the corresponding number of the same units on the earth.

Example	Image
The VTC has a scale of 1:250,000 so 1 unit on the map equals 250,000 of the same units on the earth's surface.	GOLD COAST — BRISBANE SUNSHINE COAST — VISUAL TERMINAL CHART Scale 1:250,000
The VNC has a scale of 1:500,000 so 1 unit on the map equals 500,000 of the same units on the earth's surface.	VISUAL NAVIGATION CHART VNC BUNDABERG ROCKHAMPTON 1:500 000
The WAC has a scale of 1:1,000,000 so 1 unit on the map equals 1,000,000 of the same units on the earth's surface.	WORLD AERONAUTICAL CHART ICAO 1 : 1 000 000

Large scale vs Small scale

A large-scale map portrays a small area in great detail, whereas a small-scale map portrays a larger area in less detail.

A World Aeronautical Chart (WAC) with a scale of 1:1,000,000 means that one unit on the map represents 1,000,000 of the same units on the earth. This would be considered a small scale map.

A Visual Terminal Chart (VTC) with a scale of 1:250,000 means that one unit on the map represents 250,000 of the same units on the earth. This would be considered a large scale map.

Example Small Scale Chart

A map of the entire earth on one map would be deemed a small-scale chart compared to a WAC (1:1,000,000).

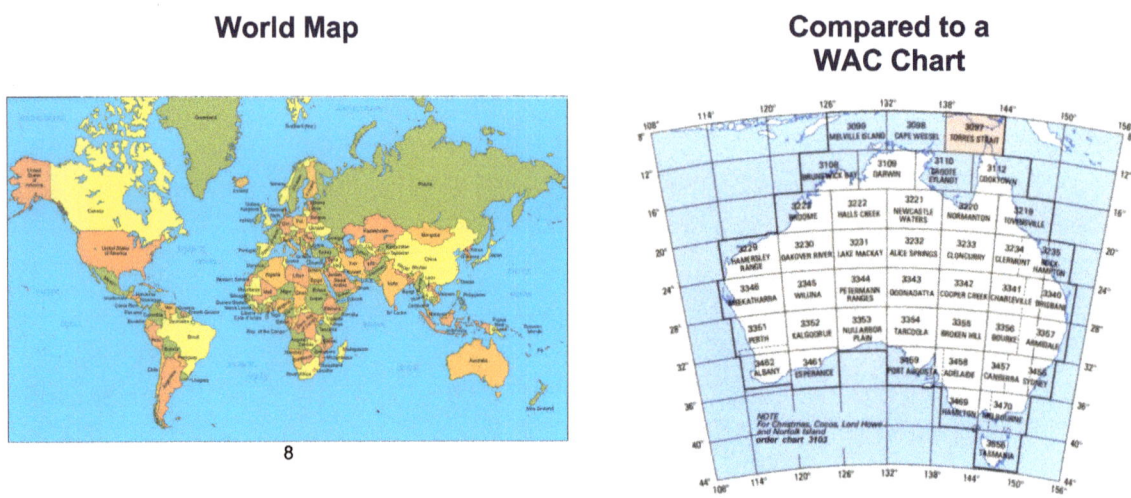

World Map | Compared to a WAC Chart

WAC compared to a VTC

A WAC with a scale of 1:1,000,000 is deemed to be a small scale map when compared to a VTC with a scale of 1:250,000 and so on.

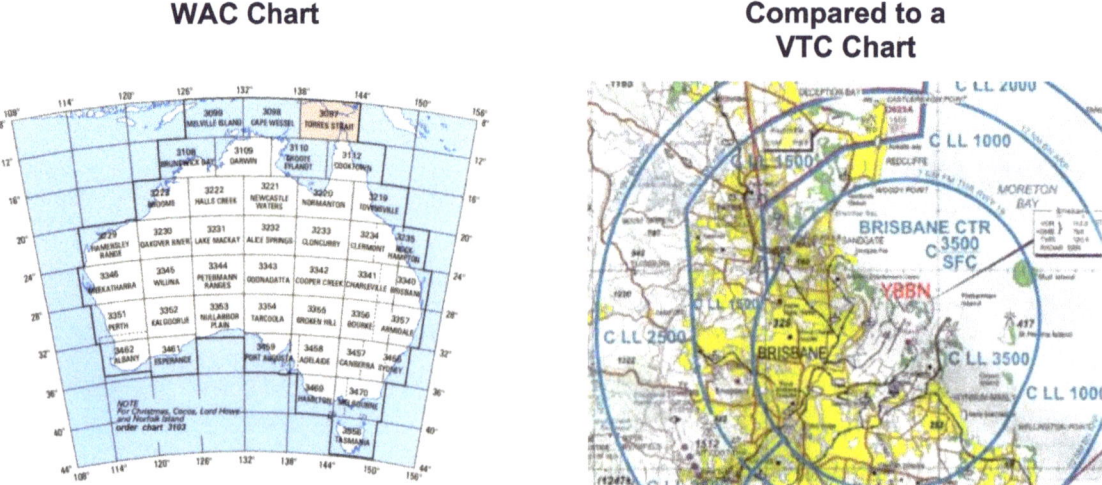

WAC Chart | Compared to a VTC Chart

---

[8] Day Donaldson 2014 / CC by 2.0 / World Map Ref: https://www.flickr.com/photos/thespeakernews/15371421002/sizes/o/

Finding a maps scale

The scale of a map can be indicated on a map in the following ways:

A simple statement of scale

This can be a statement made on the bottom of the map simply stating what the scale is.

For example:

The map scale is 1 inch equals 25 miles.

This means that a distance of 1 inch on the map represents 25 miles on the earth's surface.

One inch equals 25 miles

scale 1:25000

Scale as a representative fraction

Such as 1:500,000 or 1/500,000. This means that any unit on the map equals 500,000 of the same units on the surface of the earth.

For example:

Visual Navigation Chart (VNC)

1:500,000 scale

- Used for planning and in flight
- It show less detail than a VTC, but covers the east coast and other major centres

Graphic scale

This is a graphic ruler used for measuring distance and is usually found printed along the bottom border of a chart. A measurement may be taken from the chart and then compared directly to the graphic scale. The distance is then read off the scale.

For example:

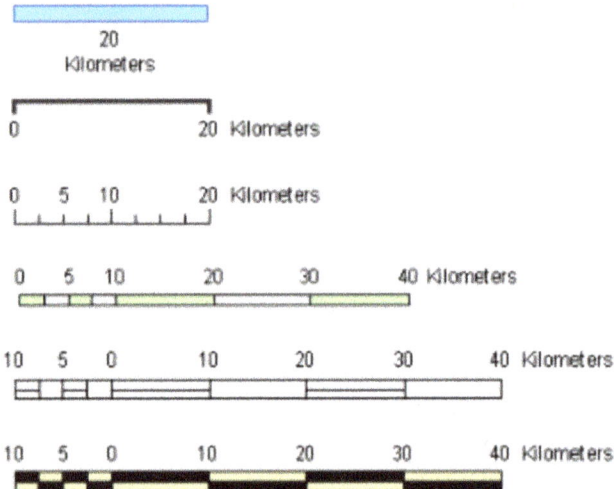

As an exercise, refer to each of the aviation maps available with this course and identify the scale on each individual map.

Map legend

Each map will have a legend describing each of the different methods used to describe features, lines, heights, spot heights etc displayed on the map. The legend is a very useful tool and should be referred to often when interpreting features and marks on the map.

VNC legend

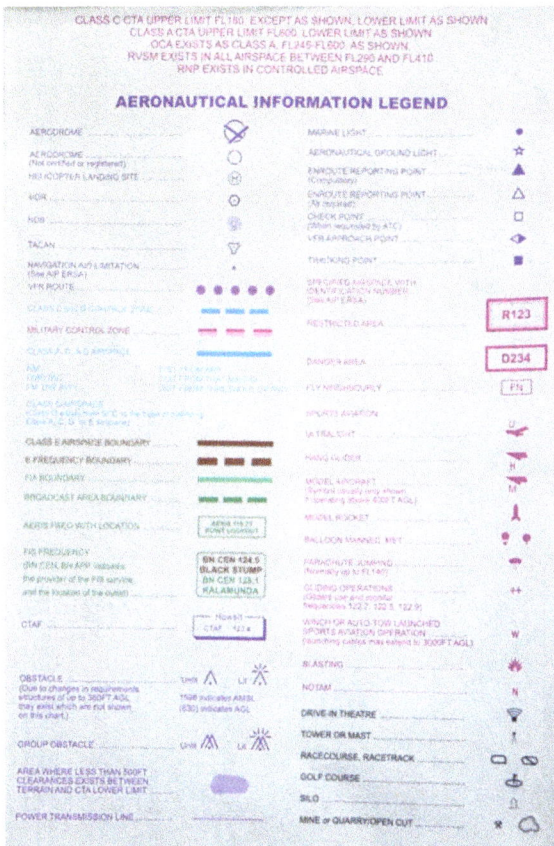

ERC Low legend

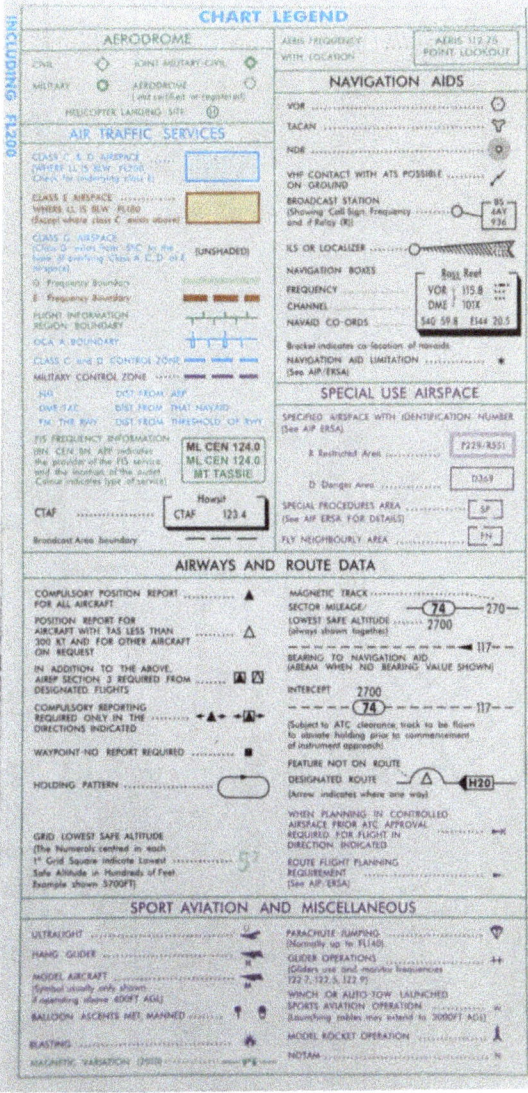

Heights

Heights on a map can be given as contour lines (lines joining areas of equal height) hypsometric tints (coloured areas), spot heights, or surveyed heights.

Contour Lines

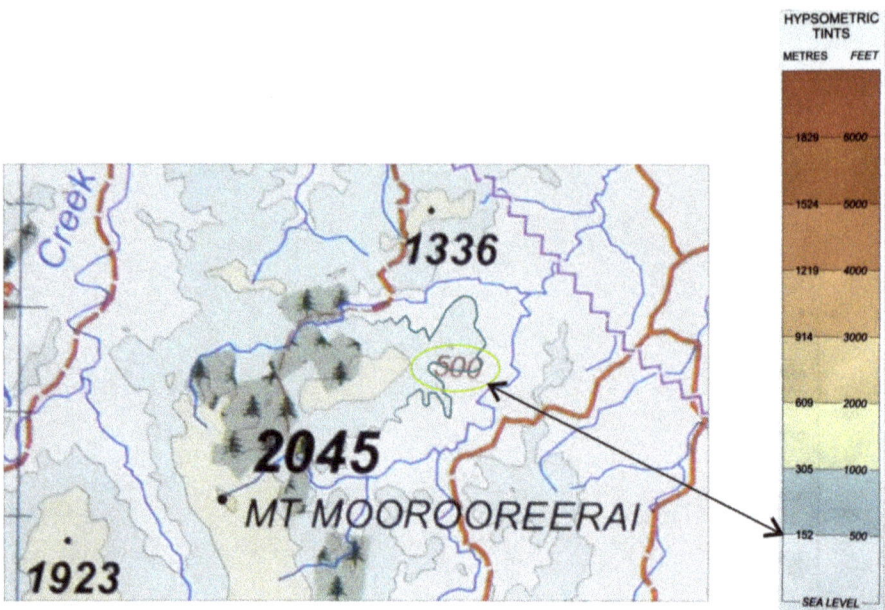

Hypsometric Tints

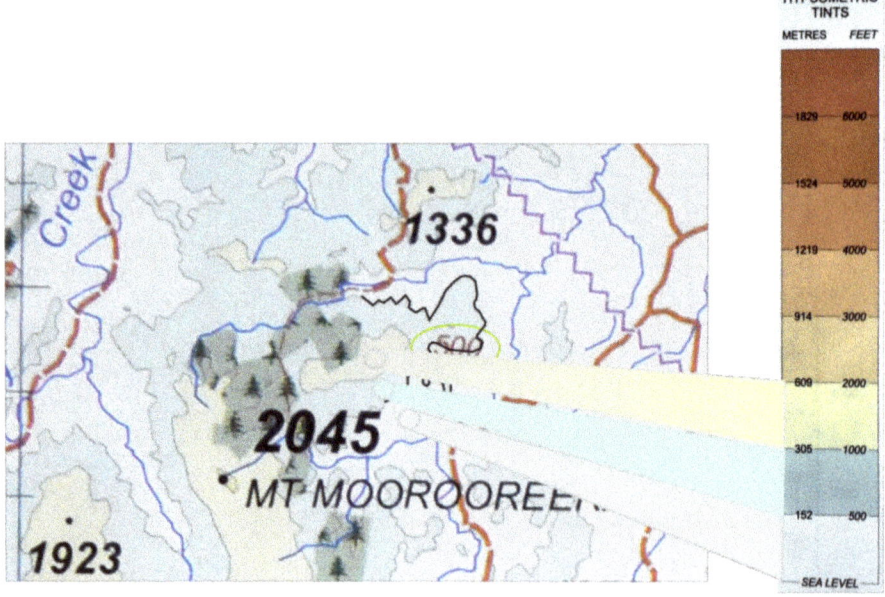

Spot heights

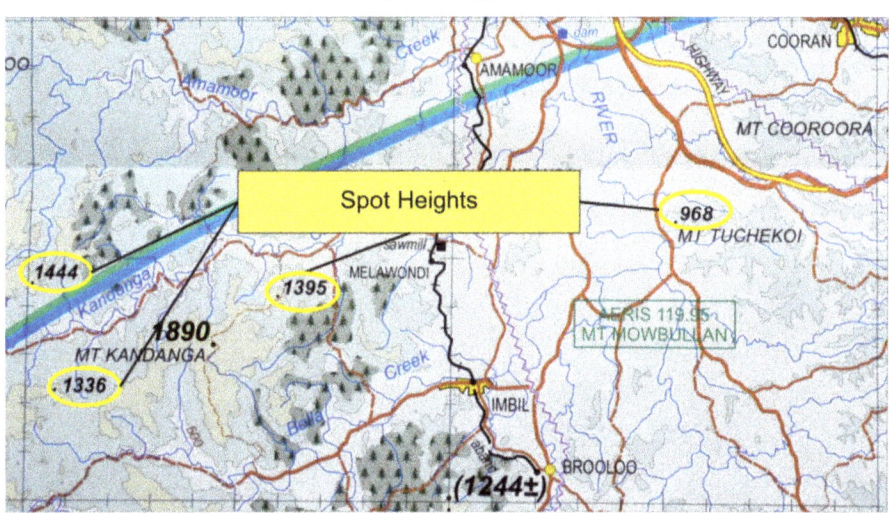

Accurate heights (Surveyed)

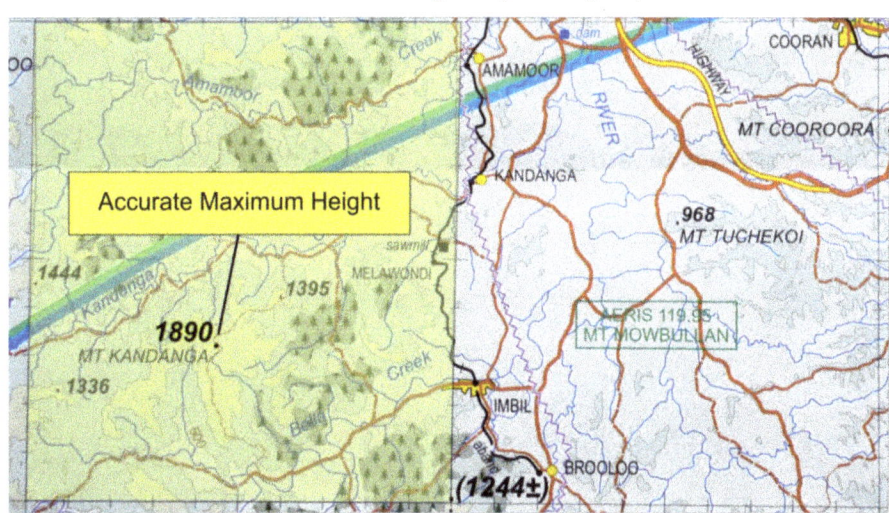

Calculated heights (Estimated)

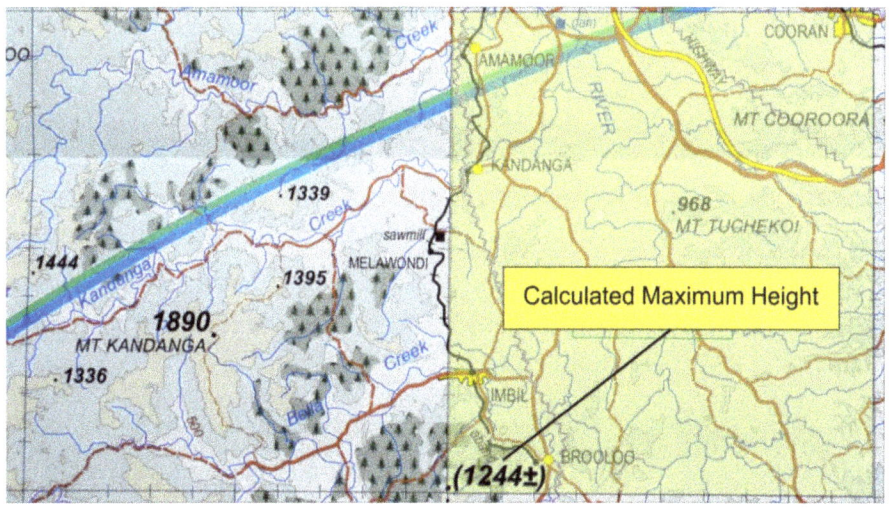

Cultural features

Cultural features such as towns, airports, roads, power lines, railway lines, towers, etc will all be depicted on the legend and marked on the map in their correct positions.

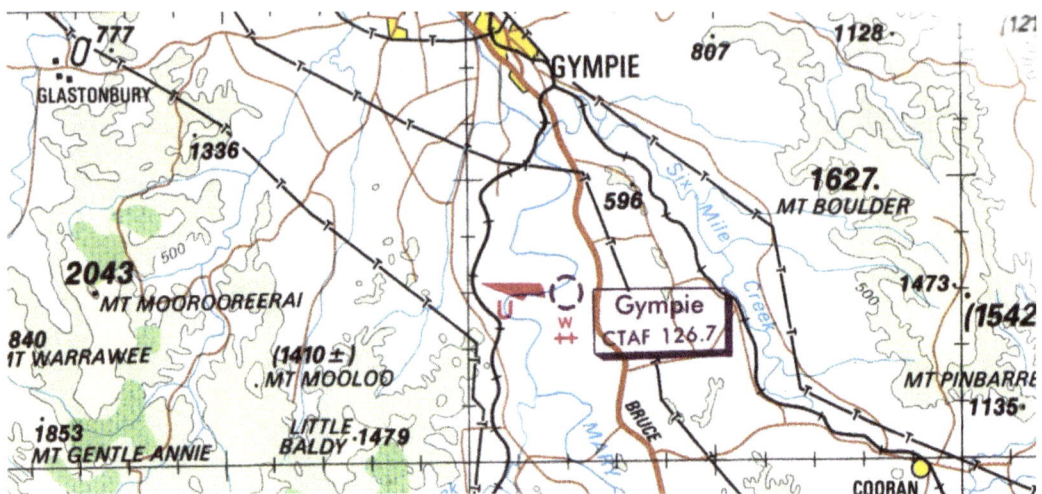

Specialised information

Specialised information includes control zone boundaries, danger and restricted areas, VFR routes and other information that we specifically require on aviation charts will also be depicted on the legend and marked on the map in their correct positions.

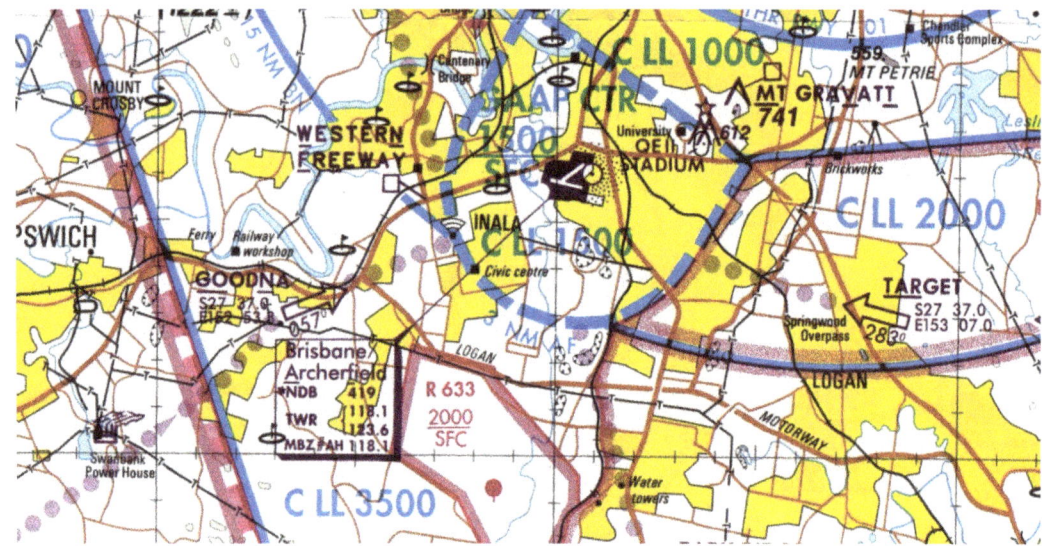

Validity

Specialised information, especially in the aviation environment is constantly changing. Because of this each map or chart will have a validity date printed on the front.

Flight Crews may only use those maps and charts that are within their validity date otherwise use of the map may be giving false or old information. This could lead to a serious safety issue if planning using old information.

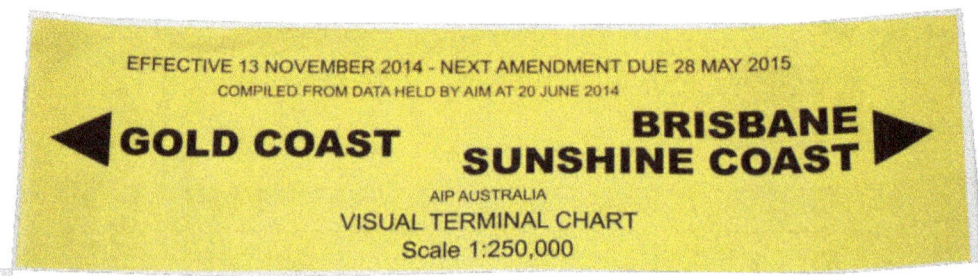

Map Projection Classifications

The following information is no longer relevant due to the widespread use of computers however it is still core knowledge that is sometimes tested in aviation exams.

For trainees at Becker Helicopters this is foundation knowledge that is "nice" to know but not mandatory.

Before a chart is produced it must go through four (4) stages of production.

Stage	Description
1	**Correction of the spheroid:** The Earth is known as an Oblate Spheroid because it is not a perfect spherical shape. Before the map process is begun the cartographer must use complicated mathematical calculations (which is obviously done by a computer in modern times) to take out these inconsistencies and correct the oblate spheroid to a perfect sphere.
2	**Reduction to a suitable size:** The cartographer then reduces the size of the sphere to a workable form known as the Reduced Earth (RE)
3	**Projection of the graticule:** Lines are drawn on the reduced earth. This network of lines (graticule or grid) dividing the reduced earth's surface is known as meridians of longitude (up and down lines) and parallels of latitude (horizontal lines). These lines are then projected onto a surface (map) by either of the following methods. Perspective Projection: A light source from inside the reduced earth projects a shadow of the lines onto a flat surface, which is then copied to form a chart. Mathematical Projection: The cartographer uses mathematical calculations to plot the lines from the reduced earth onto a flat surface. Computer simulation. A computer program applies the lines to the reduced earth
4	**Survey and Plotting of Features:** Various land features are determined by surveys and plotted onto the projection with reference to the lines (graticule or grid)

The most commonly used projections used to make charts are the conical and cylindrical projections however because of the advent of computers mathematical projections are obviously becoming more common. Other methods such as the Polar Stereographic or Azimuth Projection are not commonly used and will not be discussed.

Mercator's Cylindrical Projections

A cylindrical projection is a simple system of transferring a grid representing latitude and longitude of the earth onto a cylinder of paper, which is then opened out flat. A small-scale model of the earth is enclosed in a cylinder. Imagine a point source of light at the centre of the model earth. The shadow of the graticule on the earth would be projected onto the cylinder and traced, resulting in a grid, which represents parallels of latitude and longitude meridians as straight lines at 90 degrees to each other.

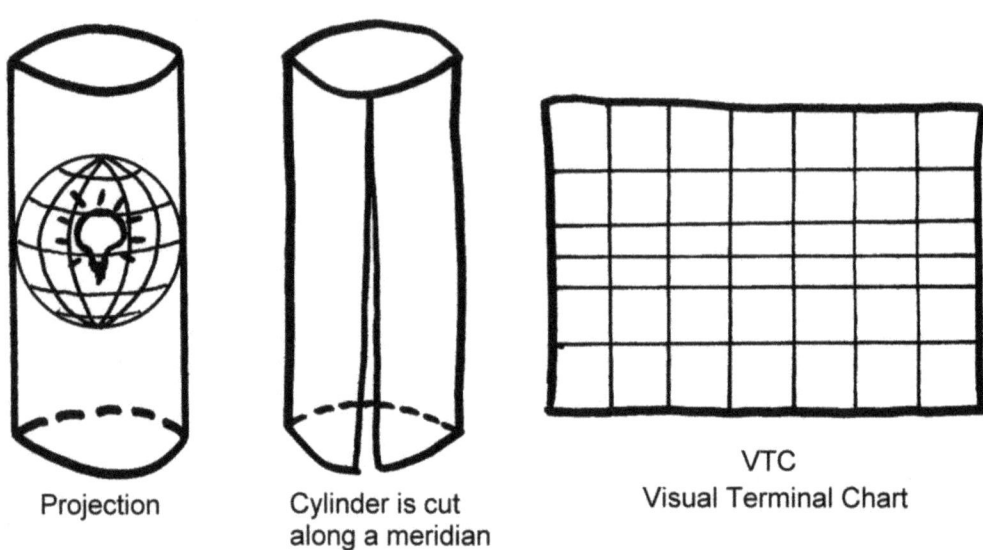

Projection | Cylinder is cut along a meridian | VTC Visual Terminal Chart

In the diagram above you will note that the cylinder is wrapped vertically around the globe. If the cylinder is wrapped horizontally around the globe then it is known as a Transverse cylindrical projection.

Lamberts Conformal Conical Projections

A conical projection is another method of projecting a grid from a reduced earth onto a cone placed over the reduced earth. The cone is then opened out, showing a grid, which represents parallels of latitude as concentric circles radiating from the pole, and longitude meridians as straight lines passing through the pole.

- All Lambert charts are conformal, i.e.: all angles and bearings between features on the earth are correctly represented over the whole of the chart.
- Meridians of longitude are straight lines radiating from the nearer pole, while the parallels of latitude are circles concentric to the same pole.
- Great circles are straight lines.
- Rhumb lines are curved lines, concave to the nearer pole.
- Scale is effectively constant over the whole of an individual chart.
- Adjacent individual charts may be lined up East/West.

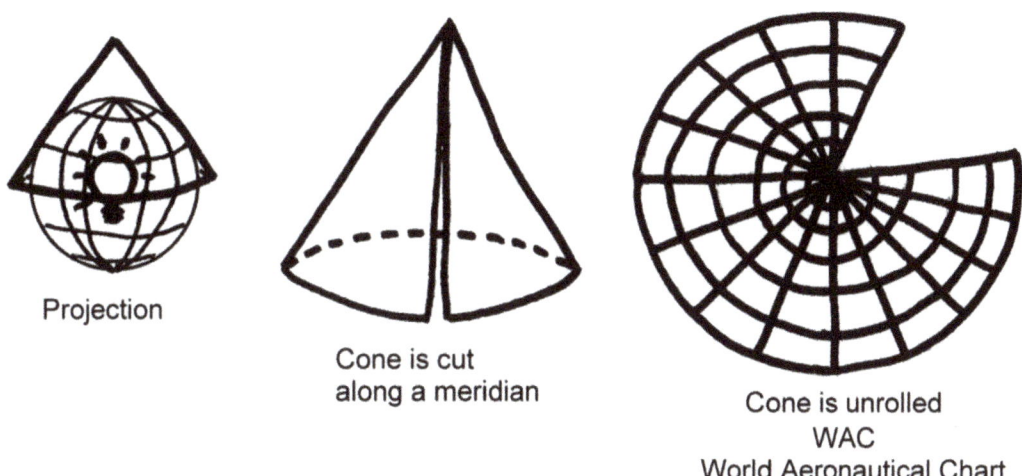

Projection

Cone is cut along a meridian

Cone is unrolled
WAC
World Aeronautical Chart

The type of projection used to make a map will be noted somewhere on the chart itself.

 The VTC is actually a Transverse Mercator which means the cylinder wrapped around the globe is lying horizontal instead of vertical. Draw it on the board

Summary of Map/Chart Properties

Characteristic	Polar Stereographic	Mercator	Lambert Conformal	Polyconic
Parallels	Concentric circles Unequally spaced	Parallel straight lines Unequally spaced	Arcs of concentric circles nearly equally spaced	Arcs of non-concentric Circles equally Spaced on mid-meridian
Meridians	Straight lines radiating from the pole	Parallel straight lines equally spaced	Straight lines Converging at the pole	Mid-meridian straight Other curved
Appearance of grid				
Angles between Parallels and Meridians	90°	90°	90°	Variable
Straight line Crosses meridians	Variable angle (Approximates a great circle)	Constant angle (Rhumb line)	Variable angle (Approximate great circle)	Variable angle (Approximate great circle near mid-meridian)
Great circle	Approximated by Straight line	Curved line (Except equator and meridians)	Approximated by Straight line	Approximated by Straight line near mid-meridian
Rhumb line	Curved line	Straight line	Curved line	Curved line
Distance scale	Nearly constant Except on small Scale charts	Mid-latitude	Nearly constant	Constant for small areas Variable for larger areas
Illustration				
Origin of projectors	Opposite pole	Centre of sphere	Centre of sphere	Centre of sphere
Distortion of Shapes and areas	Increases away from pole	Increases away from equator	Very little	Increases away from mid-meridian
Method of production	Graphic or mathematical	Mathematical	Graphic or mathematical	Mathematical
Navigational uses	Polar navigation, all types	Dead reckoning and celestial (Suitable for all types)	Pilotage and radio (Suitable to all types)	Ground forces map
Conformity	Conformal	Conformal	Conformal	Not conformal but is used as such on very large scale maps

3 Track, Distance, Time and Speed

Track

A *Track* is a line drawn on a map joining two or more waypoints. All the waypoints joined together represent the route to be flown.

Tracks are usually **straight lines** however they could be curved, but these would be more difficult to fly as the heading of the helicopter would have to be constantly altering. It is much easier to break up a long leg into smaller straight lines in the planning stages of a flight.

Tracks and Headings

A **Track**, either true or magnetic is a plotted line with reference to a map.

A **Heading** is the way the nose of the helicopter is pointed in order to fly the planned track.

A **Track Made Good** is simply the actual path of the helicopter over the ground where the pilot is flying a particular heading in an attempt to maintain a planned track.

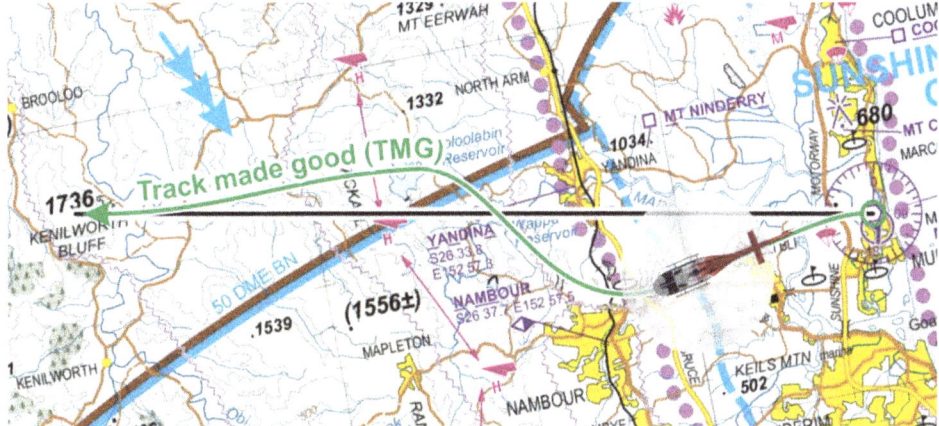

By definition:

The **True Track** is the angular difference of individual lines between each waypoint compared to the True North Pole and is the same as the lines drawn on a map.

The **Magnetic Track** is the True Track corrected for the variation in the earth's magnetic field which has its origin at the Magnetic North Pole. The Magnetic track must be calculated by adding or subtracting the known "*magnetic variation*" which is found on the same map.

The **Magnetic Heading** is the magnetic track corrected for any wind.

The **Compass Heading** is the Magnetic Heading corrected for any compass deviation errors.

Variation, Wind and Deviation

True North

The North and South geographic Poles are located on the axis about which the earth rotates.

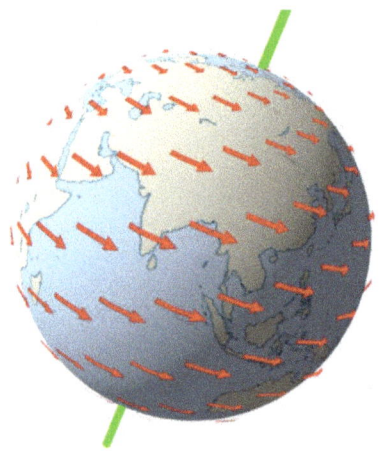

Magnetic North

The North Magnetic Poles is located at the point a magnetic compass orientates to and it is in a different location to True North.

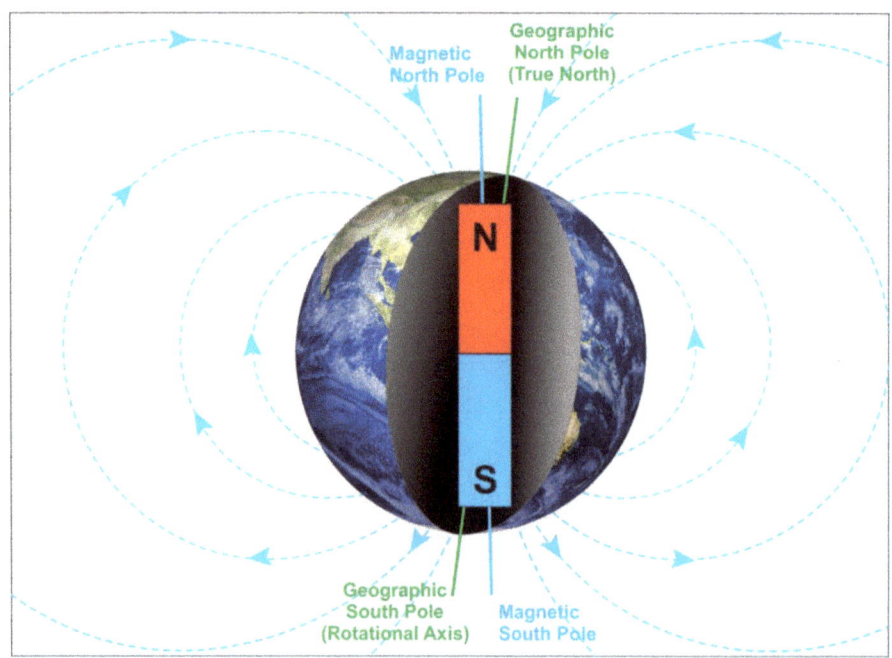

The centre of the earth is filled with iron which acts as a huge magnet.

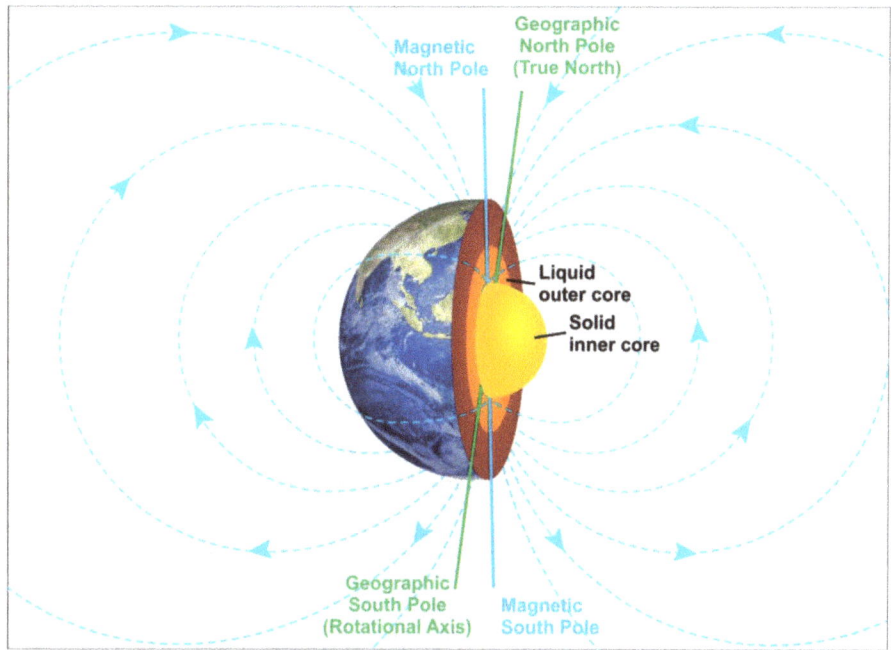

This large magnet generates lines of magnetic forces of various strengths acting all around the earth and ultimately protects us from solar radiation.

---
[9] NASA Artist's rendition of Earth's magnetosphere 2005 / Public Domain/ http://sec.gsfc.nasa.gov/popscise.jpg

Another advantage is the Earth's magnetic field can be detected by using a magnetic compass (simply a small piece of metal pivoting on a needle and floating in fluid that is affected by the magnetic field) with a pointer that will always give an indication of where the North or South Pole of the earth is and therefore can be used by pilots for navigation purposes giving an indication of direction.

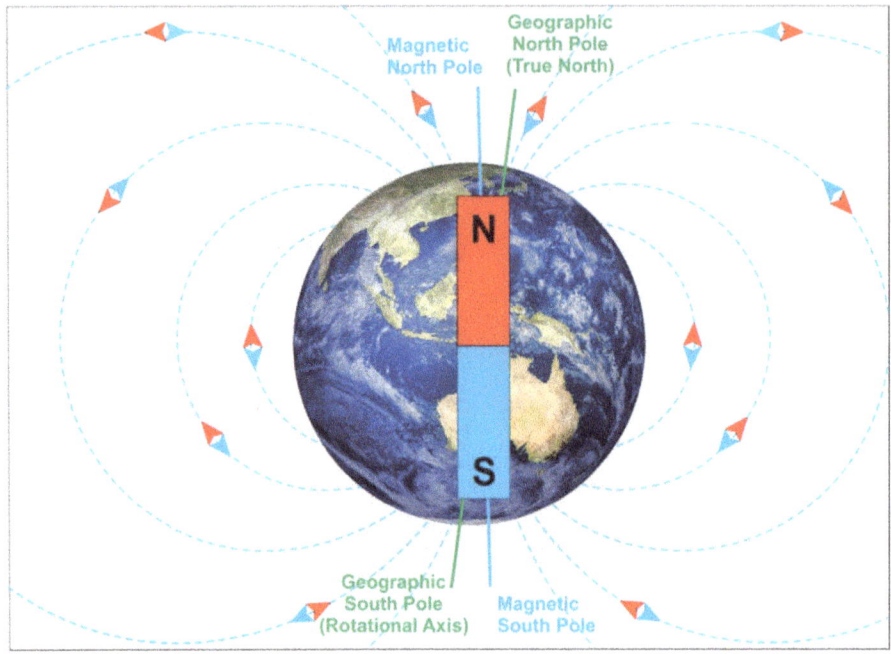

The magnetic compass may be a simple standalone unit set away from the other cockpit instruments. It may form part of a complicated Horizontal Situation Indicator (HSI)

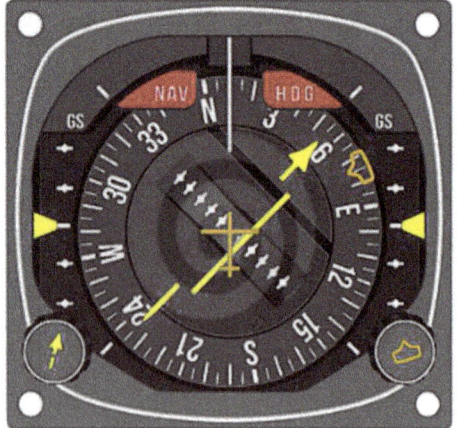

It may form part of an Electronic Flight Information System (EFIS)

Compass rose

The **North Magnetic Pole** and the **South Magnetic Pole** will be constantly moving over thousands of years as the Earths inner core independently rotates.

The difference in physical location of the North and South Geographic Poles about which the earth rotates and the North and South Magnetic Poles is referred to as ***"Variation"***.

This means that when the pilot calculates the True Track to a destination on a map by using the protractor it must be converted to a Magnetic Track for use with the Magnetic Compass within the aircraft.

Variation

The angular difference between **True North** and **Magnetic North** at any given point on the earth is called **Magnetic Variation**.

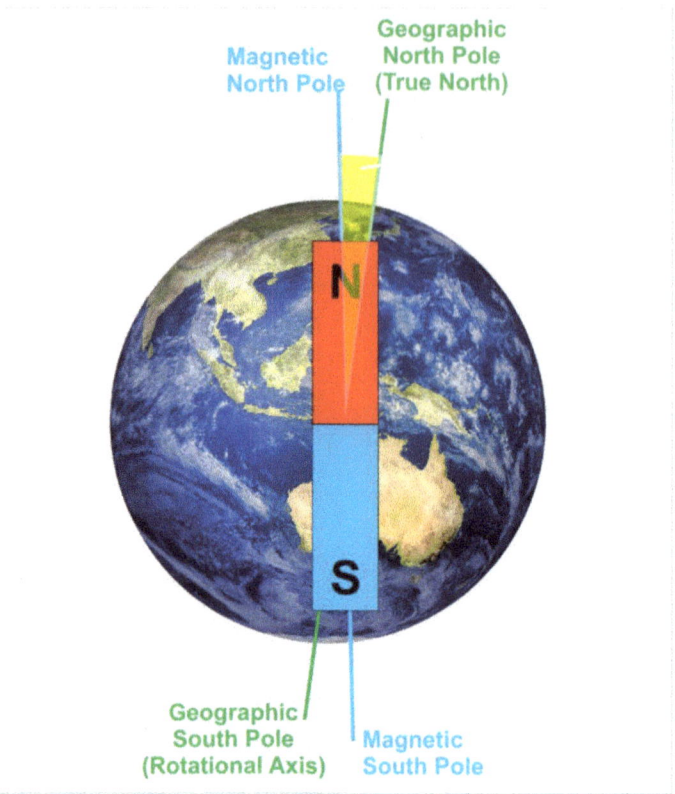

Lines joining places on a map with the *same magnetic variation* are called *Isogonal lines.*

A line joining places on a map with *zero magnetic variation* is called an *Agonic line*.

In the image below, all of the light purple coloured lines are Isogonal lines. The dark purple line is the Agonic line.

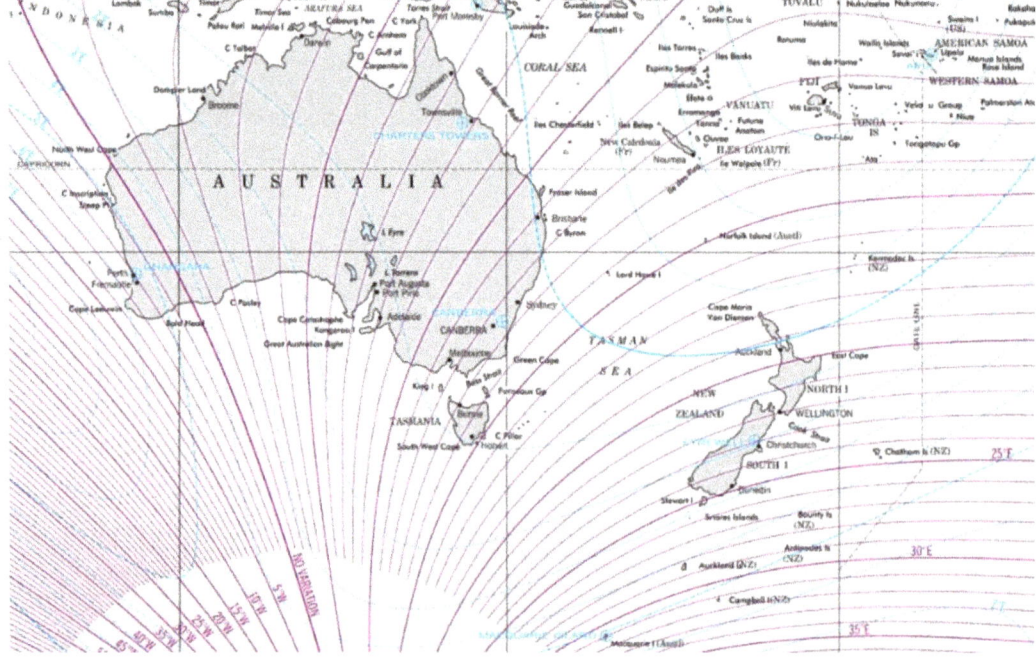

As a guide to variation on the 1:1,000,000 scale World Aeronautical Chart (WAC) lines of equal magnetic variation are identified as a dotted purple line.

TRACK, DISTANCE, TIME AND SPEED
NAVIGATION

In the image below the Magnetic Variation is 10.5 degrees East.

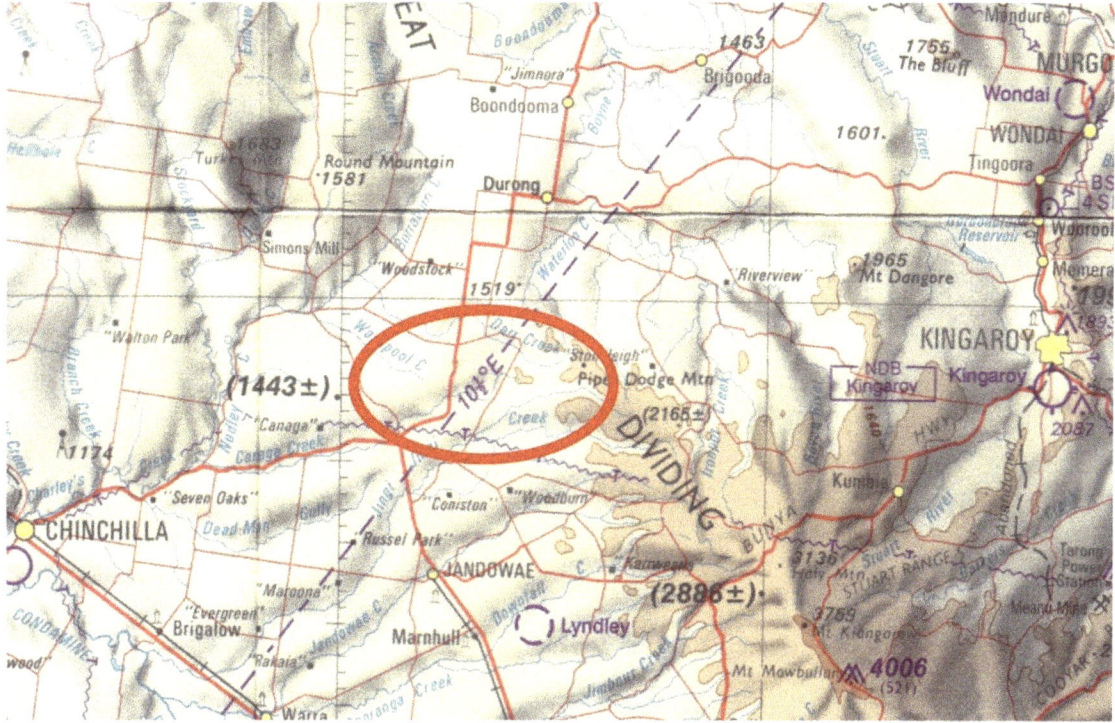

The Visual Navigation Chart (VNC) and Visual Terminal Chart (VTC) state the magnetic variation applicable to the entire area being covered by these larger scale maps as a written statement on the top of each map.

BEARINGS ARE MAGNETIC
MAGNETIC VARIATION 11°E (2010)
LOCAL STANDARD TIME = UTC+10

Convert True Track to Magnetic Track

To convert a True Track to a Magnetic Track the following rules apply

If the Variation is East, then the magnetic track is least

(Subtract the variation away from the true track to calculate the magnetic track)

If the Variation is West, then the magnetic track is best

(Add the variation to the true track to calculate the magnetic track)

Example
If the True Track is 010°, and the variation is 10°W, then the magnetic track is **020°M**
010°T **+** 10°W = **020°M**
If the True Track is 010°, and the variation is 10°E, then the magnetic track is **000°M**
010°T **−** 10°E = **000°M**
If the True Track is 010°, and the variation is 0° then the magnetic track is **010°M**
010°T **−** 0° = **010°M**

Wind and Drift

Wind will always affect the helicopter as it flies through the air. This is because the helicopter is not attached to the ground like a car. Instead it will be influenced greatly by the air (wind) that it is flying through.

Car

Helicopter in flight

As we know wind on the nose will slow the helicopters groundspeed and wind on the tail will increase the helicopters groundspeed for the same indicated airspeed.

Any wind blowing across the helicopter, commonly referred to as a "**crosswind**" will cause the helicopter to be blown off the **Planned Magnetic Track**. This is referred to as "**Drift**" and the new track that the helicopter actually flies over the ground is referred to as the "**Track Made Good**".

---

[10] Fotos GOVBA 2011 / CC by 2.0 / Stock Car 2011 / https://www.flickr.com/photos/agecombahia/6113293076/sizes/o/
[11] Kobel Feature Photos (Frankfort, Indiana) / State Archives of Florida, Florida Memory /c1940 / Jess Dixon's flying automobile / Public Domain/
https://www.flickr.com/photos/floridamemory/3983331817/in/set-72157622396753151/

Track Error

The difference between the **"Planned Magnetic Track"** and the **"Track Made Good"** is referred to as the **"Track Error"**.

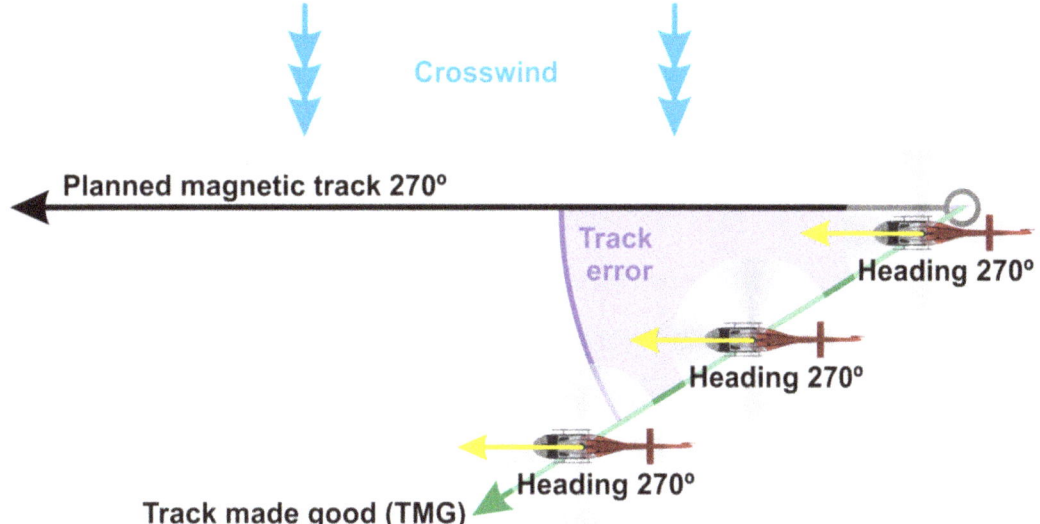

Drift

Any wind from the right will cause the helicopter to drift *left* of the desired track. This is referred to as "**left drift**".

Any wind from the left will cause the helicopter to drift *right* of the desired track. This is referred to as "**right drift**".

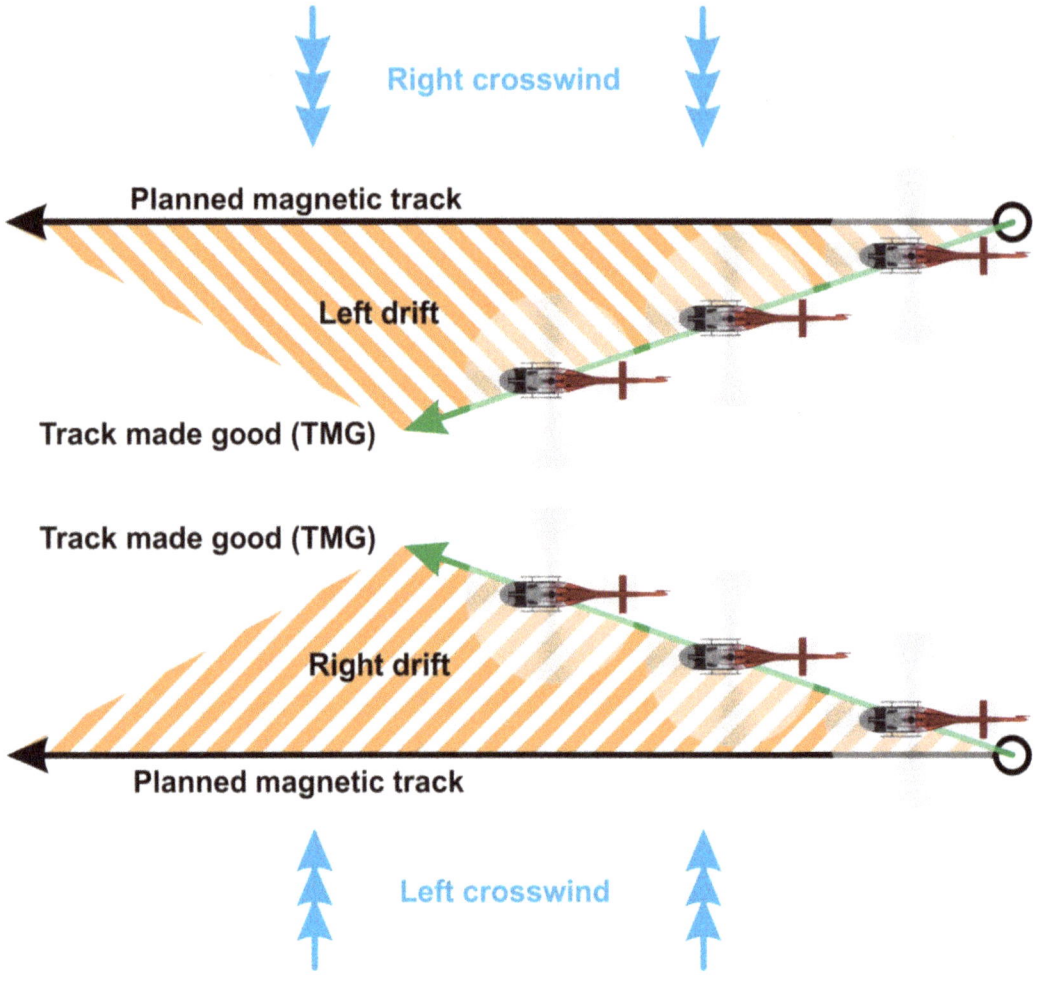

To counter any drift the pilot will need to turn the helicopter so that it is pointing into the wind by a small amount.

This adjustment to the magnetic track is now referred to as the new **Magnetic Heading** because this is the way the helicopters nose will be pointing (heading) in order to maintain the planned **Magnetic Track** with reference to the **Compass**.

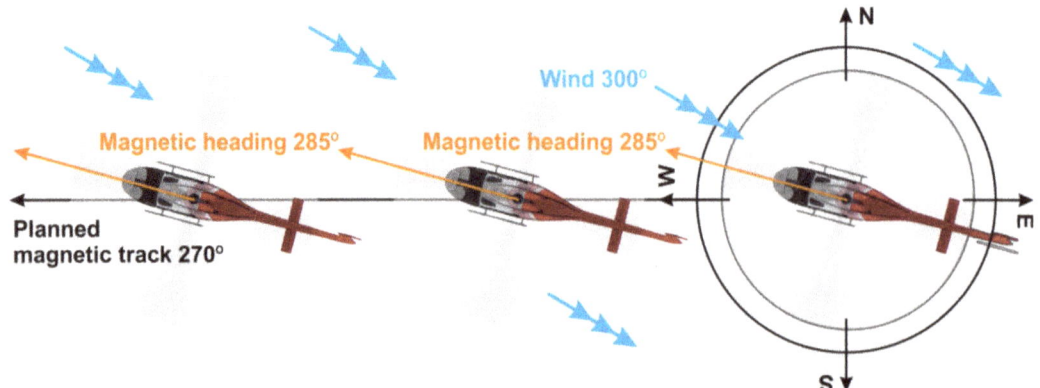

The calculation of how much to turn the helicopter into the wind to counteract the drift is done by drawing the wind triangle of velocities on the Flight Computer (wiz wheel) which will be covered in another chapter.

When countering for right drift and now maintaining the planned track, the magnetic track will always be on the right of the heading (nose of the helicopter).

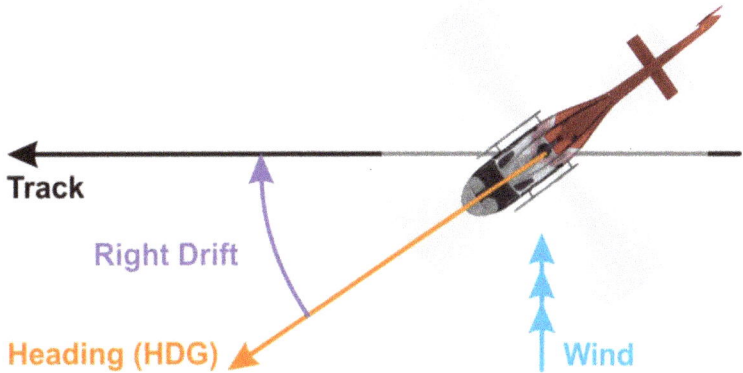

When countering for left drift and now maintaining the planned track, the magnetic track will always be on the left of the heading (nose of the helicopter)

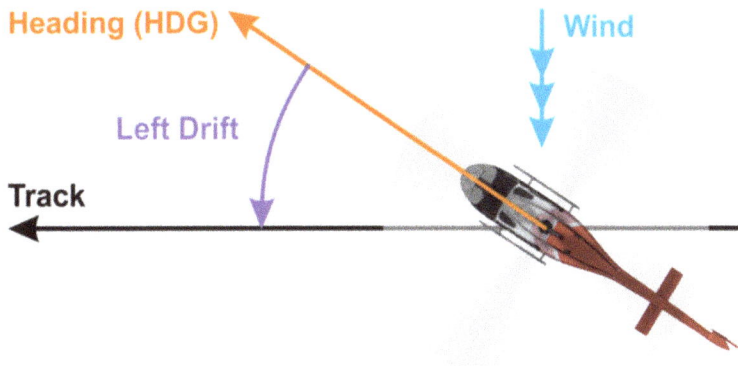

**Drift is always measured
from the Magnetic Heading on the Compass
to the Track Made Good (TMG)**

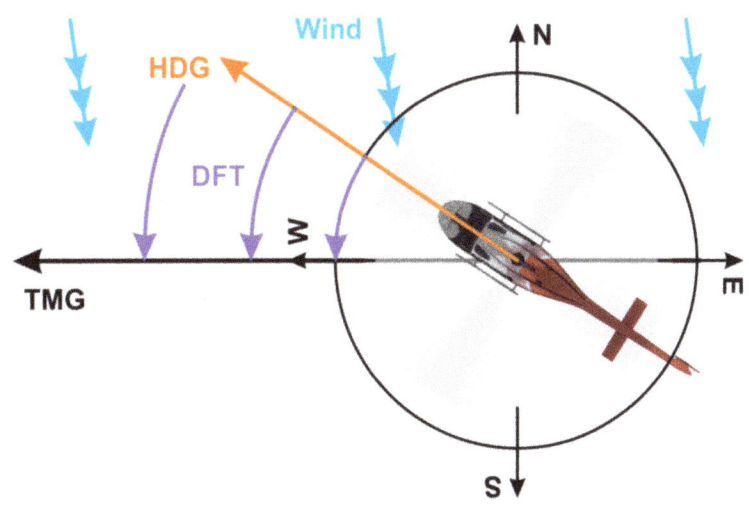

If the wind has blown the helicopter away from the planned track (drift) then a one in sixty (1 in 60) calculation may be used to determine the new heading to regain the original planned track. This can be done manually or by using the Flight Computer and will be covered later under the **1 in 60 Rule** in the "Advanced Calculations" chapter.

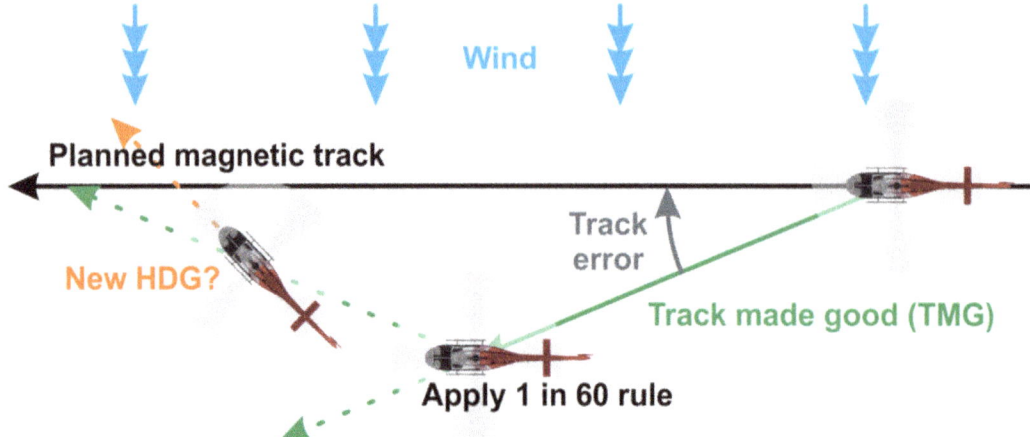

Referencing wind

When referencing the wind it is given as a direction it is blowing from and a strength. Together, a direction and strength is referred to as the "wind velocity".

If the wind is blowing from East to West at 10kts it will be written as 090/10.

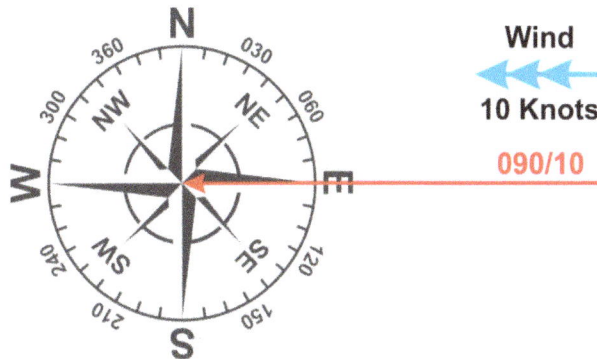

If it is blowing from the 210 direction at 12 knots then it will be written as 210/12.

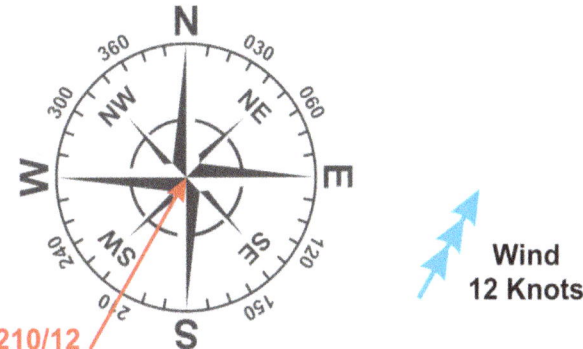

When the wind is calculated in the aircraft it is done so with reference to the magnetic compass so any result will be a magnetic wind direction where the local variation will already be accounted for.

When the wind is obtained from a printed weather forecast such as that taken from NAIPS the local variation where you may be flying will not be accounted for in the weather information. This means that when making calculations for the magnetic heading and using wind from a printed forecast the pilot will have to add or subtract the local variation to the wind. This will result in a magnetic wind that can be used to calculate accurately a magnetic heading.

To convert a True Wind to a Magnetic Wind the following rules apply:

If the Variation is East, then the magnetic wind is least

(Subtract the variation away from the true wind to calculate the magnetic wind)

If the Variation is West, then the magnetic wind is best

(Add the variation to the true wind to calculate the magnetic wind)

Example

Consider the following wind taken from NAIPS:

```
WIND:
2000      5000      7000      10000          14000          18500
230/15    240/20    240/15    240/20 PS07    260/25 PS02    260/30 MS06
```

At 2000 feet the wind is blowing from 230 degrees True at 15 knots.

If the local variation is determined to be 10 degrees East, then the pilot will have to subtract 10 degrees (East is least) from 230 degrees to calculate a magnetic wind direction of 220 degrees magnetic at 15 knots wind.

$$230°T - 10°E = \textbf{220°M/15}$$

If the True Wind is 240/20 and the variation is 10°W, then the magnetic wind is **250/20**

$$240°T - 10°W = \textbf{250/20}$$

If the True Wind is 260/30 and the variation is 0° then the magnetic wind is **260/30**

$$260°T - 0° = \textbf{260/30}$$

Deviation

Deviation is the difference between the calculated Magnetic Track and the Magnetic Compass Heading taking into account any errors in the compass itself.

Often the Magnetic Compass in the helicopter is affected by surrounding electrical devices and any metal that is placed close to it. Additionally there are often design errors or manufacturing faults in each individual magnetic compass which need to be accounted for.

An engineer or avionics technician will have to swing (calibrate) the compass with reference to a master compass positioned outside the helicopter and then write up any errors on individual compass headings and place on a placard inside the helicopter for the pilot to reference.

These errors are called "**deviation**" because it is a compass deviation away from the actual magnetic heading desired.

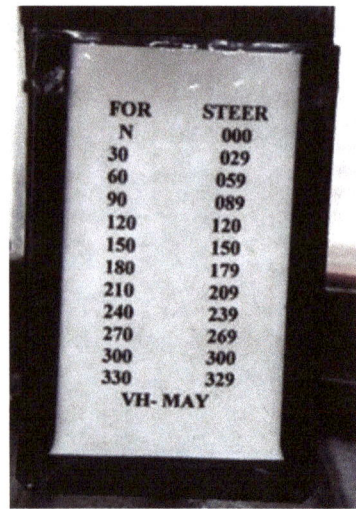

Once the pilot has taken into account the deviation of the compass the "actual" desired heading can be maintained and accurately flown.

Example
Consider the Deviation Card above.
If the pilot has calculated on the map by determining the True Track and then accounting for the Magnetic Variation that in order to fly from A to B a Magnetic Heading of 270 degrees is required. On referencing the Deviation Placard it states that to fly an actual heading of 270 degrees then the compass should display and the pilot should fly a compass heading of 269 degrees.
The pilot will, therefore, fly 269 degrees in order to maintain an actual heading of 270 degrees because of the compass deviation.
Using the same deviation card above, if the Magnetic Heading calculated was 150 degrees then there is no Deviation error so the compass heading would also be 150 degrees and so on.

Summary

To determine the compass heading to accurately navigate the aircraft, the pilot will need to:

1. Draw a line on a map
2. Use the protractor to calculate the True Track relative to True North
3. Add or Subtract the Magnetic Variation to calculate a Magnetic Track
4. Add or subtract for any known wind to account for any drift and calculate the Magnetic Heading
5. Use the Compass deviation card in the helicopter to take into account any errors in the Compass and determine the Compass Heading.

$$\text{True Track} \pm \text{Variation} = \text{Magnetic Track}$$

$$\text{True Wind} \pm \text{Variation} = \text{Magnetic Wind}$$

$$\text{Magnetic Track} \pm \text{Magnetic Wind} = \text{Magnetic Heading}$$

$$\text{Magnetic Heading} \pm \text{Deviation} = \text{Compass Heading to fly}$$

Pull out a map, draw some tracks, use the protractor to work out the True Track and use a ruler to measure distance. Calculate the Compass heading by adding or subtracting Variation and Deviation to the True Track.

Distance

Distance is a measurement of how far apart each waypoint is from the next waypoint.

Distance can be measured against many different scales including

- Kilometres (1000 meters)
- Statute miles (5,280 feet)
- Nautical miles (6,076 feet)
- Meters (1000 millimetres) and
- Feet (12 inches)

When measuring distance in aviation it is typical to use **N**autical **M**iles (**NM**) to measure distance on a map because one NM equates to one (1) knot of speed in the same manner as one (1) statute mile equates to one (1) mile per hour and one (1) kilometre equates to one (1) kilometre per hour.

To calculate distance, use a ruler that has the same scale as the map in use.

Different maps can have different scales so knowing which scale to use is important and should be confirmed prior to attempting to measure the distance.

Most scaled rulers will have at least three different scales incorporated within their design so that they can be used on several different scaled maps at the same time.

It is important that the correct scale is used on the correct map when measuring the distance.

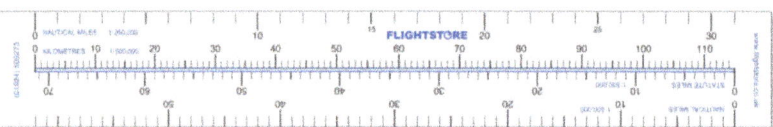

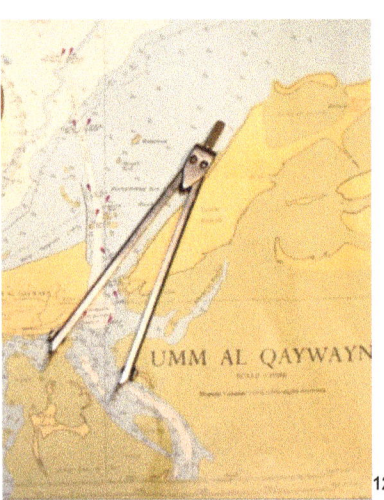

If a ruler is not available, then use a reference line or set of dividers and compare it to the reference scale on the map to obtain the distance.

---

[12] FreeImages.com / Krzystof Sxkurlatowski / Content License / old-maritime-map-1156710

Time

Time is measured in years, months, days, hours, minutes and seconds. Years, months and days are counted and viewed on a calendar and typically referred to as *"dates"*. Hours minutes and seconds, are viewed on a clock and are typically referred to as *"time"*.

Date

Time

The Date/Time grouping of numbers

There are several different ways to write calendar dates and clock time. When put together it is referred to as the **Date/Time group** and is commonly used on weather reports and when creating a flight plan.

Traditionally calendar dates are written long hand in either, the Day, Month and Year (DD/MM/YY) format or in the USA as the Month, Day and Year (MM/DD/YY) format.

Example
If having to write the 10th of May 2016 it can be written as 10/05/2016 or if in the USA 05/10/2016

When clock time is written down it can either be in a 12 hour or 24 hour format.

12 hour format

If clock time is written in the 12 hour format the letters AM or PM follow the number to designate whether the time is before noon or after noon.

- The abbreviation **AM** stands for "**A**nte **M**eridiem" which is Latin for "before noon"
- The abbreviation **PM** stands for "**P**ost **M**eridiem" which is Latin for "after noon"

Example
11AM is 11 o'clock in the morning whereas 11PM is 11 o'clock in the evening.

24 hour format

If clock time is written in the 24 hour format it progressively increases once past midnight so that each hour incrementally increases from 00:00 to 24:00 throughout the day.

Example
00:00Hrs is exactly midnight. 01:00Hrs is 1 o'clock in the morning, 10:00Hrs is 10 o'clock in the morning; 1300Hrs is 1PM, 18:00Hrs is 6PM and so on.

In aviation, the 24 hour clock format is used both orally (spoken) and when written and shall be memorised.

Combining calendar and clock time into the Date/Time Group

When combining the calendar dates and clock time into the Date/Time Group it is simply a matter of running the numbers together in one sequence in the 24 hour format.

Example						
10:30:05PM on the 10th of May 2016 would be broken down as follows					
Year	Month	Day	Hour	Minutes	Seconds
2016	05	10	22	30	05
It would then be written into the Date/Time Group as **20160510223005**.					

Another example could be the 8th of July 1963 at 5 minutes and 10 seconds past 5AM would be written as 19630708050510.

This number can be abbreviated for convenience by deleting some of the numbers. Typically the year and the seconds are not used as we assume the year and often do not need the seconds.

Example
The 8th of July 1963 at 5 minutes and 10 seconds past 5AM could be abbreviated to 7080505.

Each aircraft normally has its own clock or multiple clocks that may be integrated into other aircraft systems such as the ADF, GPS or EFIS display. Additionally, the pilot can use a personal watch.

Aircraft clock

Pilots watch

ADF timer

GPS timer

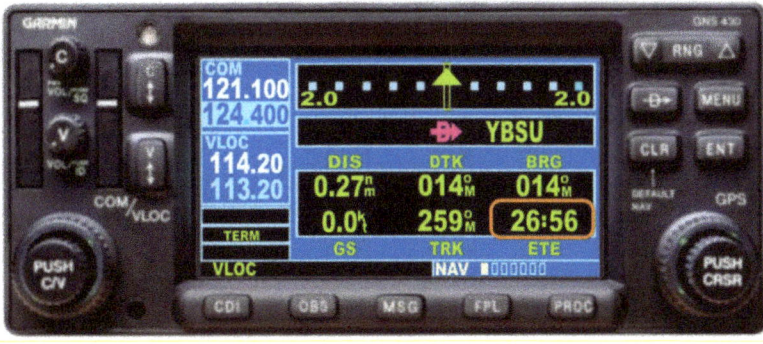

Use of Time

Time can be thought of in three different ways.

1. Time as a **concept**
2. Time as a **unit of measurement** and
3. Time as a **tool**

When navigating time is one of the *most* important tools you will use. It is *vital* that you have a solid understanding of the relationship between Time, Distance and Speed (covered in more detail later) in order to navigate accurately.

Time as a concept

The Earth rotates on its axis from West to East and does a full 360° rotation in relation to the Sun in (approximately) 24 hours. At the Equator this equates to a rotational speed of approximately 1770 kilometres per hour reducing to almost zero at the poles because they do not have any distance to travel.

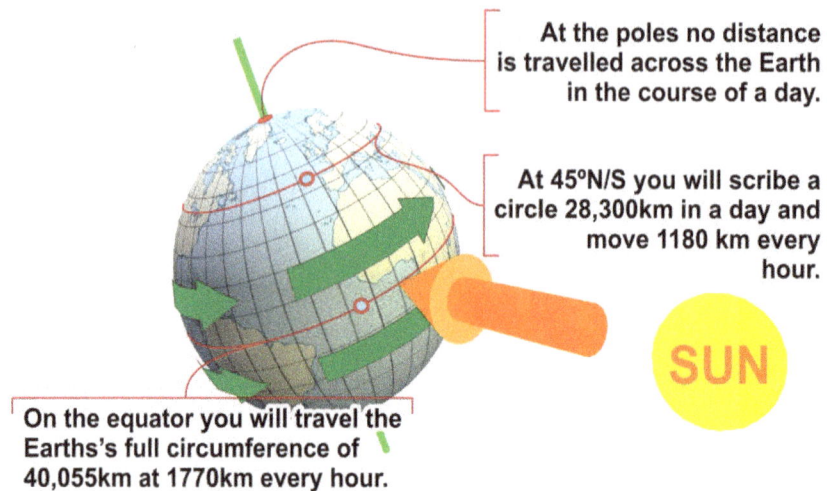

At the poles no distance is travelled across the Earth in the course of a day.

At 45°N/S you will scribe a circle 28,300km in a day and move 1180 km every hour.

On the equator you will travel the Earths's full circumference of 40,055km at 1770km every hour.

If the 360 degrees of rotation is divided by 24 hours it can be calculated that the Earth rotates 15 degrees of Longitude every hour.

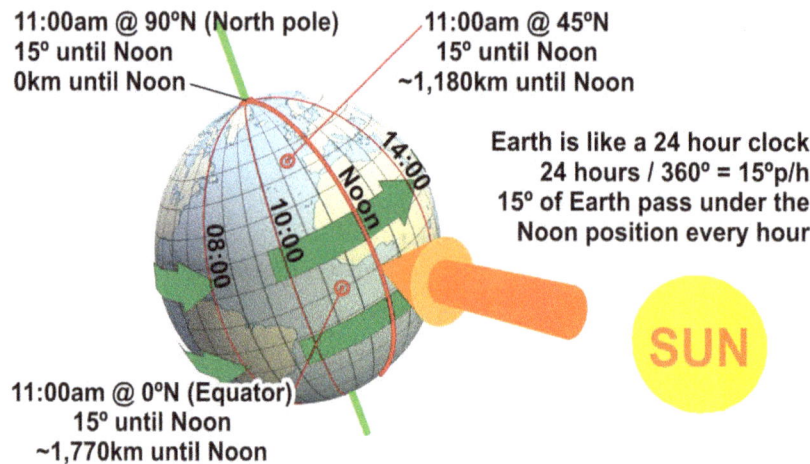

11:00am @ 90°N (North pole)
15° until Noon
0km until Noon

11:00am @ 45°N
15° until Noon
~1,180km until Noon

Earth is like a 24 hour clock
24 hours / 360° = 15°p/h
15° of Earth pass under the Noon position every hour

11:00am @ 0°N (Equator)
15° until Noon
~1,770km until Noon

Additionally, the Earth also orbits the Sun completing one full orbit in 12 months.

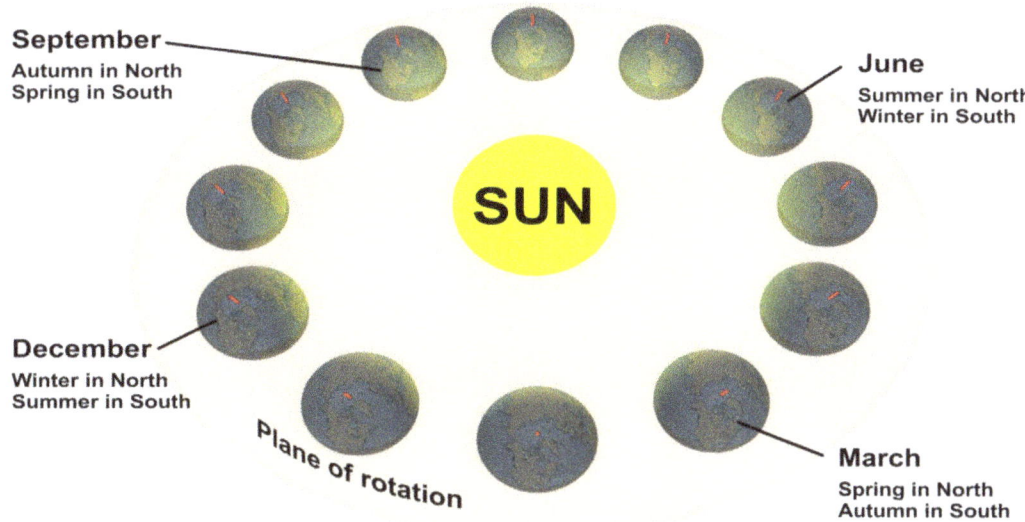

Because of this repeating pattern humans have developed a concept called "*time*" allowing us the ability to count the progress of time and measure our existence on a calendar and a clock in order to help predict the future.

As we know, meridians of Longitude are measured from Zero degrees from the Prime Meridian to 180 degrees East and West with both 180 degree meridians sharing the same line running through the Pacific Ocean and New Zealand. (180 E/W).

When it is 1200Hrs (noon) on a particular meridian then 15° to the **East** the time is 1300Hrs because that is the meridian which faced the Sun an hour ago.

If the meridian is 15° to the **West** the time is 1100Hrs because in an hour's time, **that** meridian will face the Sun and then experience noon. This reasoning can then be used for all the remaining meridians.

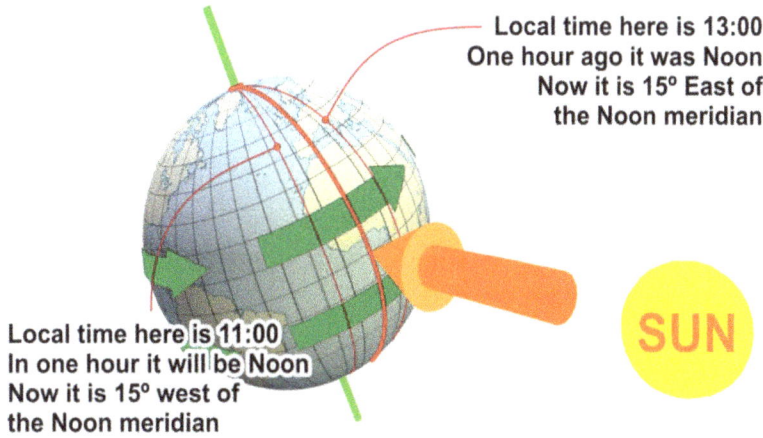

Summary

As the earth rotates from West to East (or anti-clockwise when viewed from above the North Pole) then:

Meridians of longitude further **East** are **ahead** in local time
Meridians of longitude further **West** are **behind** in local time

What does it all mean?

Time is represented in a number of different ways all based on various references around the world.

By now you may have heard time being expressed as Local **M**ean **T**ime **(LMT), UTC, ZULU, GMT,** Eastern Central or Western Standard Time just to name a few. If daylight saving is in effect in a particular area then Eastern Daylight Time or summer time etc.

When operating locally we use whatever the local time is. In Aviation because we can travel long distances it is better to use one **Universal** time.

UTC

Universal **T**ime **C**o-ordinated **(UTC)**, or **Z**ulu Time (Military description), or formerly **G**reenwich **M**ean **T**ime **(GMT),** is the Local Mean Time at the Meridian of Longitude that runs through the observatory at Greenwich, a city near London in the UK.

The Greenwich Meridian is located on Longitude 0° East and West and is known as the **Prime Meridian**. Greenwich was chosen as the Prime Meridian because this was where the first mechanical clock ever made was located and was a centre for worldwide shipping and exploration from the UK.

---

[13] Christine Matthews / Meridian Line, Greenwich / CC by SA 2.0 / http://s0.geograph.org.uk/geophotos/01/69/88/1698855_57d55573.jpg

The aviation industry across the world uses UTC so pilots need to be able to convert quickly and accurately to UTC from whatever time zone that is currently being referenced.

Any Country located East of the Prime Meridian will be in a time zone ahead of UTC.

Any Country located West of the Prime Meridian will be in a time zone behind UTC.

Each time zone can therefore be displayed on a map showing their difference to the Prime Meridian.

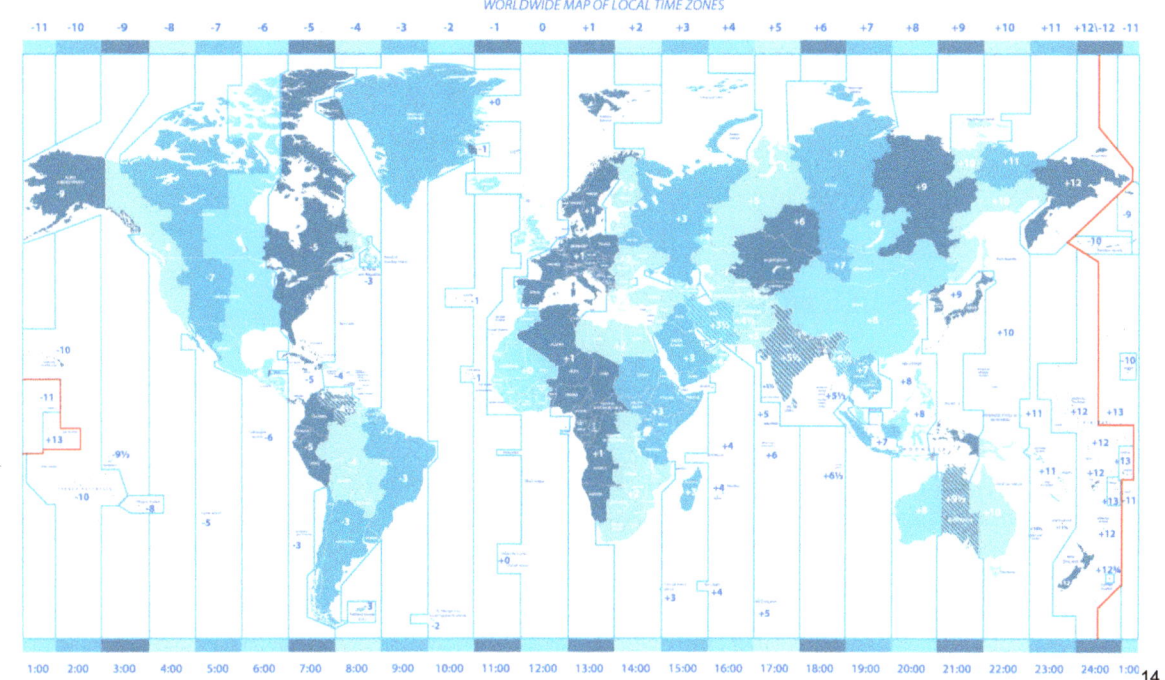

LMT

Local **M**ean **T**ime **(LMT)** (or more appropriately, *Local Meridian Time*) uses the local meridian of longitude of that particular place as a reference for time. This means that all points along the same meridian of longitude will have the same LMT.

Obviously with different Meridians of Longitude, the LMT on each meridian will be different. This difference will equal the change in longitude expressed in units of time.

LMT is important to us as Day VFR pilots when having to determine the times for the beginning and end of daylight.

The problem with LMT is if it is used exclusively in everyday life there would be multiple times in close proximity making it difficult for us all to work together. For this reason areas of commonality are grouped into a common time zone.

For example:

Australia is placed into three common time zones referred to as **E**astern **S**tandard **T**ime (**EST**), **C**entral **S**tandard **T**ime (**CST**) and **W**estern **S**tandard **T**ime (**WST**).

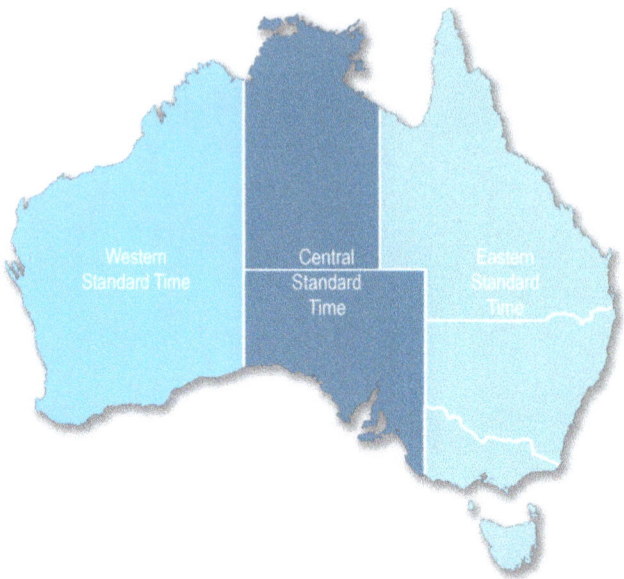

Eastern **S**tandard **T**ime **(EST)** or more correctly Australian Eastern Standard Time (AEST) covers the Eastern states of Australia, using the 150°E meridian as a reference; therefore EST is **10 hours** ahead of UTC.

Central **S**tandard **T**ime **(CST)** or more correctly Australian Central Standard Time (ACST) covers South Australia and the Northern Territory using the 142°30'E meridian as a reference; therefore CST is **9.5 hours** ahead of UTC.

Western **S**tandard **T**ime **(WST)** or more correctly Australian Western Standard Time (AWST) is used in Western Australia using the 120°E meridian as a reference; therefore WST is **8 hours** ahead of UTC.

For any questions relating to time, it is a good idea to convert everything to UTC, which you can think of as 'Universal Time', then relate it back to LMT or the Standard Times.

Daylight saving

Many Countries implement a daylight saving time so that during the summer month's people are able to finish work but still enjoy hours of daylight for recreation. When a particular part of the country is operating under a daylight saving time then the abbreviation is altered to include **D** for **D**aylight

For example:

Eastern Standard Time (EST) becomes Eastern Daylight Time (EDT) or Australian Eastern Daylight Time (AEDT).

Central Standard Time (CST) becomes Central Daylight Time (CDT) or Australian Central Daylight Time (ACDT) etc.

Countries

Each country depending on its size may have their own unique names for each of its various time zones and also for daylight saving.

For example:

CET is Central Europe Time and CEST is Central Europe Summer Time.

PDT is Pacific Daylight Time.

GST is Gulf Standard Time

Military

Instead of using a time zone in a particular Country, Military organisations simply add or subtract time from UTC and then give it an alphabetical letter designator from Alpha (A) through to Zulu (Z).

For example:

Alpha Time (A) zone is UTC plus 1 hour

Bravo Time zone (B) is UTC plus 2 hours

Charlie Time zone (C) is UTC plus 3 hours

Quebec Time zone (Q) is UTC minus 4 hours

Romeo Time zone (R) is UTC minus 5 hours

Sierra Time zone (S) is UTC minus 6 hours

Zulu Time zone (Z) is actual UTC time and why we sometimes refer to UTC as Zulu.

For more information visit http://www.timeanddate.com/library/abbreviations/timezones/

Time as a unit of measurement

Typically society is used to working in a decimal world or working with numbers based on the number 10.

When working with time we deal with numbers based on the number 6. This makes for some interesting mental gymnastics as instead of a one (1) whole being made up of ten equal parts it is made up of 60 equal parts. (60 minutes)

For example:

1 hour is made up of 60 minutes; 1 minute is made up of 60 seconds.

1 hour (or one whole) is 60 which is the equivalent to 1.0 in the decimal system.

Half an hour (or one half) is 30 minutes which is the equivalent to 0.5 (half of a whole) in the decimal system.

Three quarters of 1 hour is 45 minutes or 0.75 in the decimal system and a quarter of an hour or one quarter is 15 minutes or .25 in the decimal system.

TRACK, DISTANCE, TIME AND SPEED
NAVIGATION
INTERNATIONAL HELICOPTER THEORY

The following is a conversion table of minutes (base 6) to decimal time (base 10):

Minutes	Decimals	Piece of pie
60	1 (whole)	
45	0.75 of an hour (3 quarters)	
30	0.50 of an hour (half)	
15	0.25 of an hour (1 quarter)	
0	0.00 of an hour (nothing, zip, zero, nada!)	

Thankfully we do not have to work out time, as the flight computer was created to do this automatically for us.

TRACK, DISTANCE, TIME AND SPEED
NAVIGATION

Maths revision using base 6

If you already have a good understanding of how to use base 6 to add and subtract skip this section. If (like me) you need some revision complete this section.

When adding or subtracting times it is important to remember to work in Base 6 (as opposed to how we normally work in Base 10).

A whole now equals 6 equal parts not 10 equal parts.

One (1) year equals three hundred and sixty five (365) days

One (1) month equals between twenty eight (28) to thirty one (31) days

One (1) day equals twenty four (24) hours

One (1) hour equals sixty (60) minutes

One (1) minute equals sixty (60) seconds

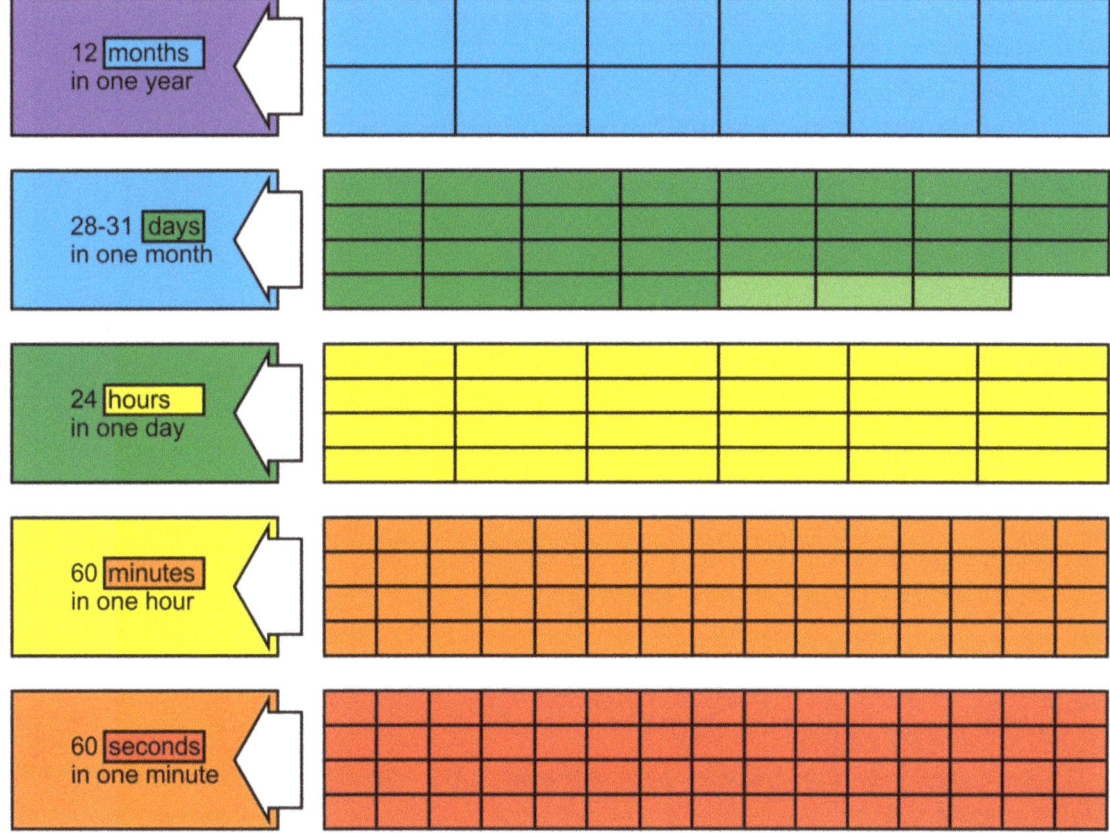

Knowing the above and understanding how each of the units work now allows numbers to be added and subtracted.

Example
(1) Given a UTC time of 22:00 on the 10th of May what will the date and time be in another 10 hours? 2200 + 10 = 32 32 – 24 = 0800 plus 1 day (24 hours) added to the 10th to arrive at the 11th of May Therefore the answer is 0800 11th May This is then written as 05110800
(2) Given a UTC time of 01:50 on the 10th of July what was the date and time 10 hours previously? 01:50 - 10:00 does not work so mathematically therefore we add a day (24 hours) 01:50 to come up with 25:50, at the same time we then have to take 1 day away from the date so that the 10th now becomes the 9th The calculation would therefore look as follows 01:50 + 24:00 = 25:50 25:50 – 10 = 15:15 The answer is 15:50 on the 9th of July and is written as 07091550

Time as a Tool

A clock, as we know measures the passage of time. As a pilot it is vital that this is done accurately and regularly as the safety of the helicopter relies on it for a multiple of tasks including but not limited to:

- The management of fuel
- Navigation
- The awareness of weather restrictions
- First and Last light
- Airspace activation and restrictions, start and slot times etc
- The management of SAR times
- Maintaining mission parameters and charge time
- Maintenance time on the engine and airframe

Time is a vital tool to the pilot so having a good clock either in the helicopter or on the pilot's wrist is essential.

Noting time

As a pilot you will write various times down so it is recorded and then add time to the base number to project forward.

This can be required for many reasons.

For example:

- The pilot will have to write down the helicopters start time so that at the end of the flight they know how long the flight has lasted and can put this in their log book or add the airframe and engine maintenance hours into the maintenance log. Assuming the helicopter started at 1300 and landed at 1430 the pilot will add 1 hour and 30 minutes to the aircraft log.
- The pilot will be required to note the start time and then add the time available to fly based on how much fuel is available. This will give a time the helicopter should be landed back on the ground prior to running out of fuel. Assuming the helicopter started at 0800 and has enough fuel for 2 hours and 20 minutes the fuel on the ground time would be 10:20.
- The pilot will be required to note the departure time on a navigation flight so that they can project forward to the anticipated arrival time over the next waypoint assuming they are maintaining a constant compass heading and speed.

The use of the clock is important but just as useful is a stop watch or a countdown timer as both measure time and can be used if available. It is common for ADF receivers and GPS units to have stopwatches, countdown timers and a clock integrated into their circuitry.

A stopwatch will always count up from zero (0) to whenever it is stopped.

A countdown timer will start at a pre-determined number set by the pilot and count down to zero (0).

ADF stop watch
(Counts up from 0)

GPS Countdown timer
(Counts down from Estimated Time)

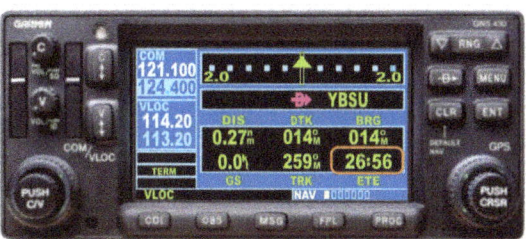

TRACK, DISTANCE, TIME AND SPEED

Time as a tool for Navigation

The most important relationship to understand when navigating is the relationship between Time, Distance and Speed.

When navigating, the pilot needs to be able to calculate the current position of the helicopter and also be able to project forward into the future where the helicopter is going to be.

There are three pieces of information that are required in order to calculate this. They are:

1. The Magnetic Compass Heading (HDG) which will indicate to the pilot the direction the helicopter is travelling
2. The speed that the helicopter is travelling across the ground and most importantly
3. Time

Having the above information allows the pilot to calculate the Distance travelled by dividing the speed by 60 and then multiplying it by the time. This will result in a distance travelled.

Example
Consider travelling across the ground at 100Kts per hour for an elapsed time of 6 minutes. The distance travelled will be 10NM.

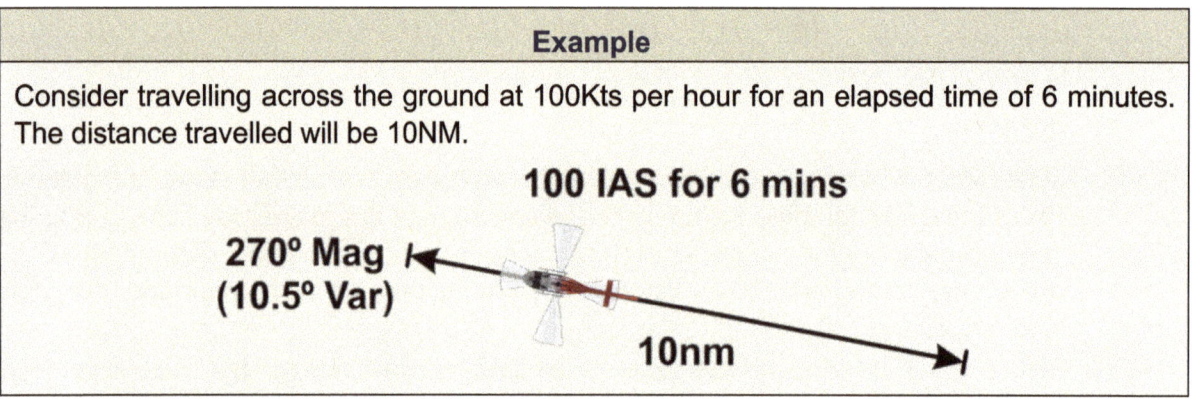

With a known distance in a particular direction from a known starting point the pilot can then plot the position of the helicopter onto a map.

Example
If departing the Sunshine Coast at 08:30 on a magnetic heading of 270 degrees at 100kts for 6 minutes the pilot can now plot on a map their current position as 10NM West of the Sunshine Coast Airport.

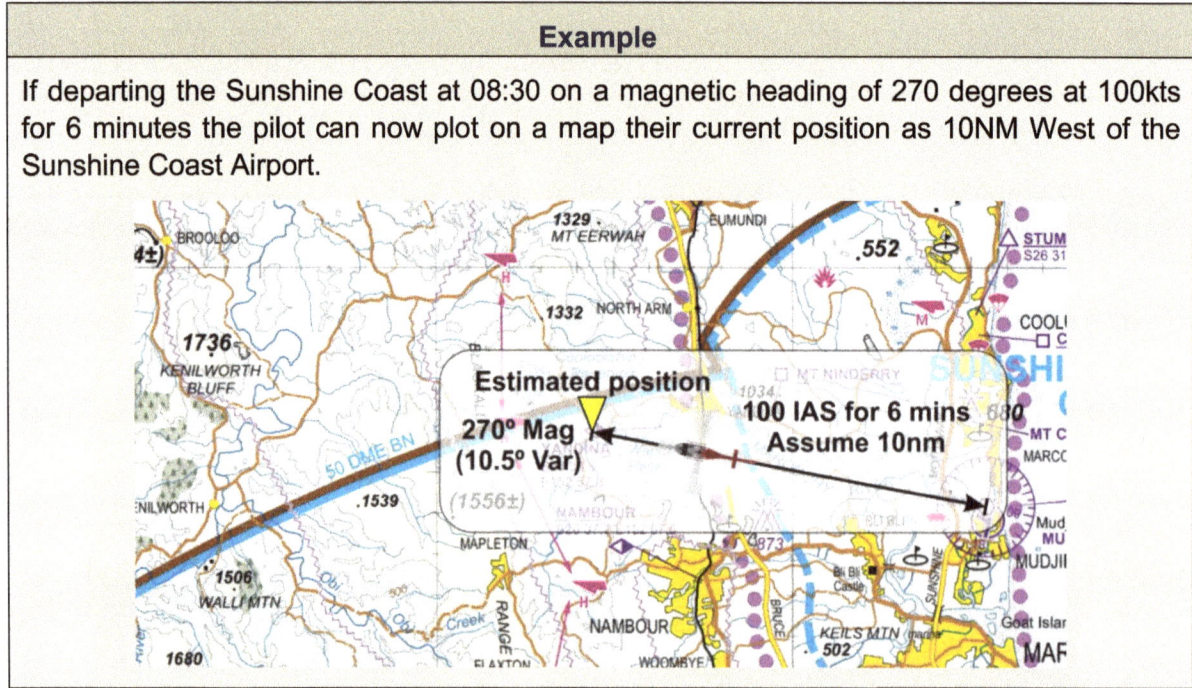

Additionally, once at least two (2) positions are plotted onto the map the pilot can also calculate the groundspeed and therefore the wind by determining how far the helicopter has travelled (Distance) in a given amount of time.

Example
If departing the Sunshine Coast at 08:30 on a magnetic heading of 270 degrees at 100kts for 6 minutes the pilot can now plot on a map their current position as 10NM West of the Sunshine Coast Airport.
If the pilot now continues for another 10 minutes and can plot their position on a map by identifying a feature on the ground and then calculates the distance travelled from the last known position in 10 minutes was 18NM it can be calculated that the groundspeed was 108kts. (We will cover how to do these calculations with a Flight Computer in the next chapter.)

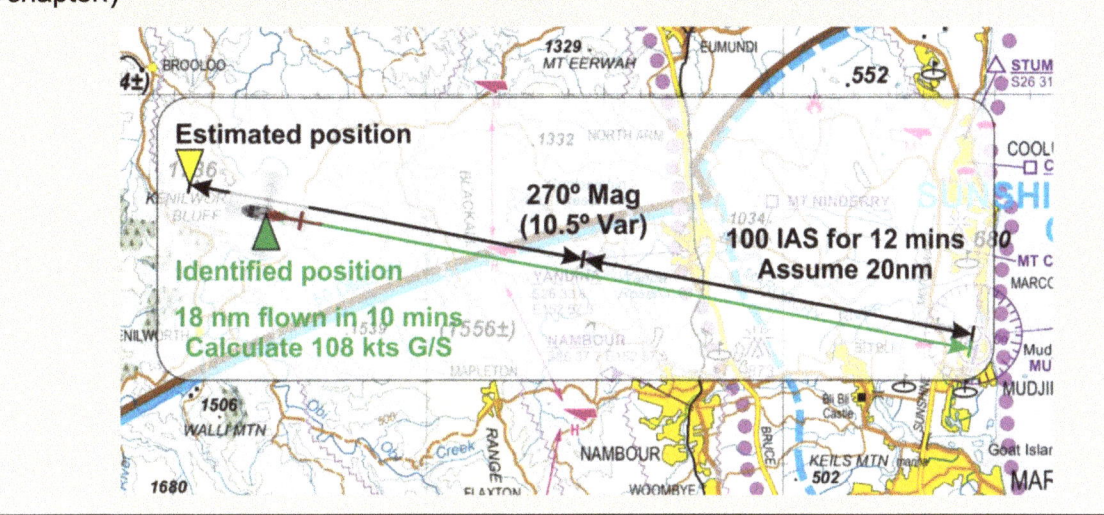

Being able to use time accurately is essential for accurate navigation

Calculating Beginning and End of Daylight

A pilot will have to be able to calculate the beginning and end of daylight. This is particularly important if the pilot is only qualified to fly during daylight hours and therefore needs to know what time the helicopter should be on the ground before it gets dark or, alternatively, the pilot may need to know what is the earliest time to depart in the morning before the sun rises.

[15] By NASA / E. James (Great Images in NASA: Home - info - pic) [Public domain], via Wikimedia Commons / https://upload.wikimedia.org/wikipedia/commons/a/a2/Cobra_Helicopter_at_Sunrise_-_GPN-2000-001555.jpg

The beginning and end of daylight can be different to sunrise or sunset. The sun can still be below the horizon and give enough light to fly by; this is because the sun will still give some reflected light for a short period of time. This is referred to as "**twilight**".

The further North or South the aircraft is away from the equator the longer the twilight period between sunrise and sunset and actual daylight and darkness.

The closer to the Equator the shorter the twilight period between sunrise and sunset and actual daylight and darkness.

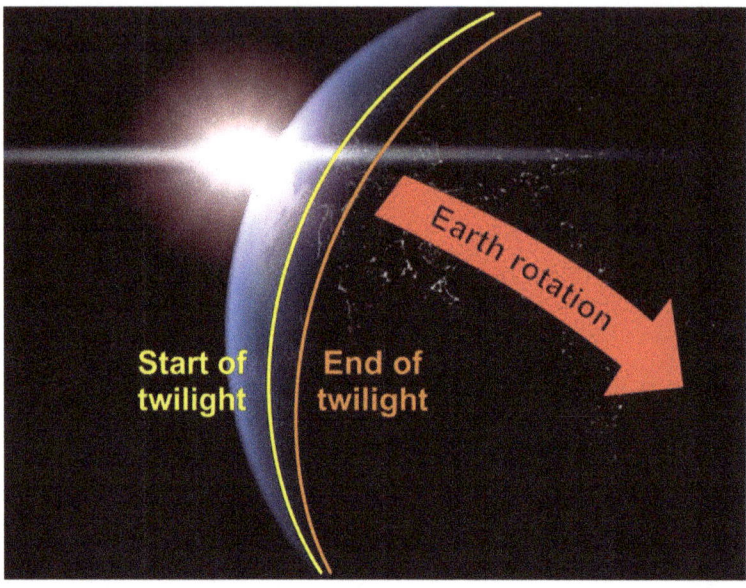

To calculate the beginning and end of daylight there are several methods available:
1. The old method using graphs and tables often referred to as an Almanac (which is still commonly assessed during theory exams) and
2. The new method using computers, the internet, smart phone and tablet applications.

The Old Method

This can be calculated by using graphs and tables printed in the **A**eronautical **I**nformation **P**ublication (**AIP**).

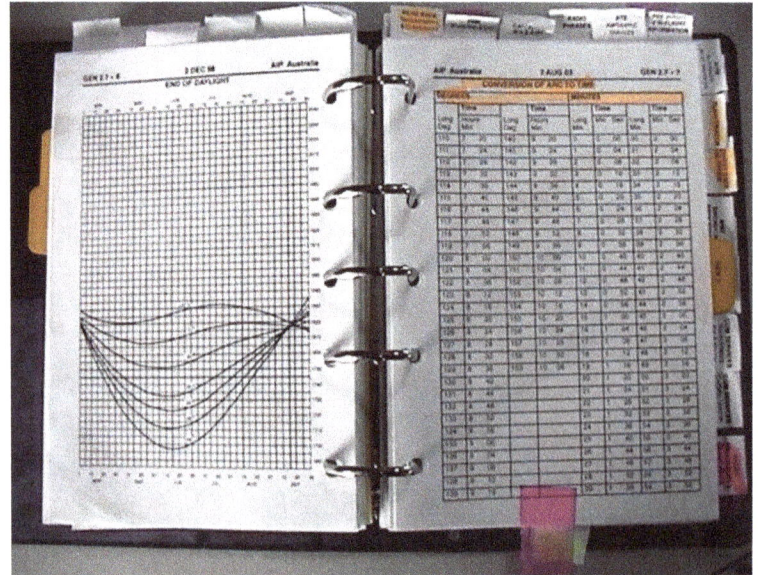

The following table lists the steps to follow if using the paper based graphs and tables.

Step	Action
1 Calculate the LMT	(1) Select the appropriate graph: ■ **B**eginning **o**f **D**aylight (**BOD**) or **E**nd **o**f **D**aylight (**EOD**) (Both can be found in the AIP GEN section 2) (2) Enter the top or bottom of the scale at the appropriate date (3) Move vertically up or down until intersecting the curved line at the correct latitude for the location required. (This may require interpolation for intermediate latitudes) *(4) Move horizontally across to the right or left and read off the Local Mean Time (LMT) on the vertical scale at the side.* ■ If the question asks for LMT stop now. ■ If the question asks for UTC continue to Step 2
2 Calculate the ARC TIME	(1) Refer to the Conversion of Arc to Time Table (2) Slide down the DEGREES Table until identifying the Longitude that relates to the location required and note (write down) the time (3) Slide down the MINUTES Table until identifying the Longitude that relates to the location required and again note the time (4) Add these two times together for the Total Arc Time
3 Obtain UTC	Subtract the Total Arc Time from the LMT to obtain UTC
4 Convert UTC to Standard Time	■ To convert to AEST add 10 hours to UTC ■ To convert to ACST add 9 1/2 hours to UTC ■ To convert to AWST add 8 hours to UTC

TRACK, DISTANCE, TIME AND SPEED

For Example:

Find the Beginning of Daylight (BOD) in UTC for YBSU (26:36S 153:05E) on the 7th of February.

Step	Action
1 Calculate the **LMT**	(1) Select the appropriate graph: BOD (2) Enter the top at the appropriate date 07th Feb. (3) Move vertically down until you intersect the curved line at the correct latitude 26:36S 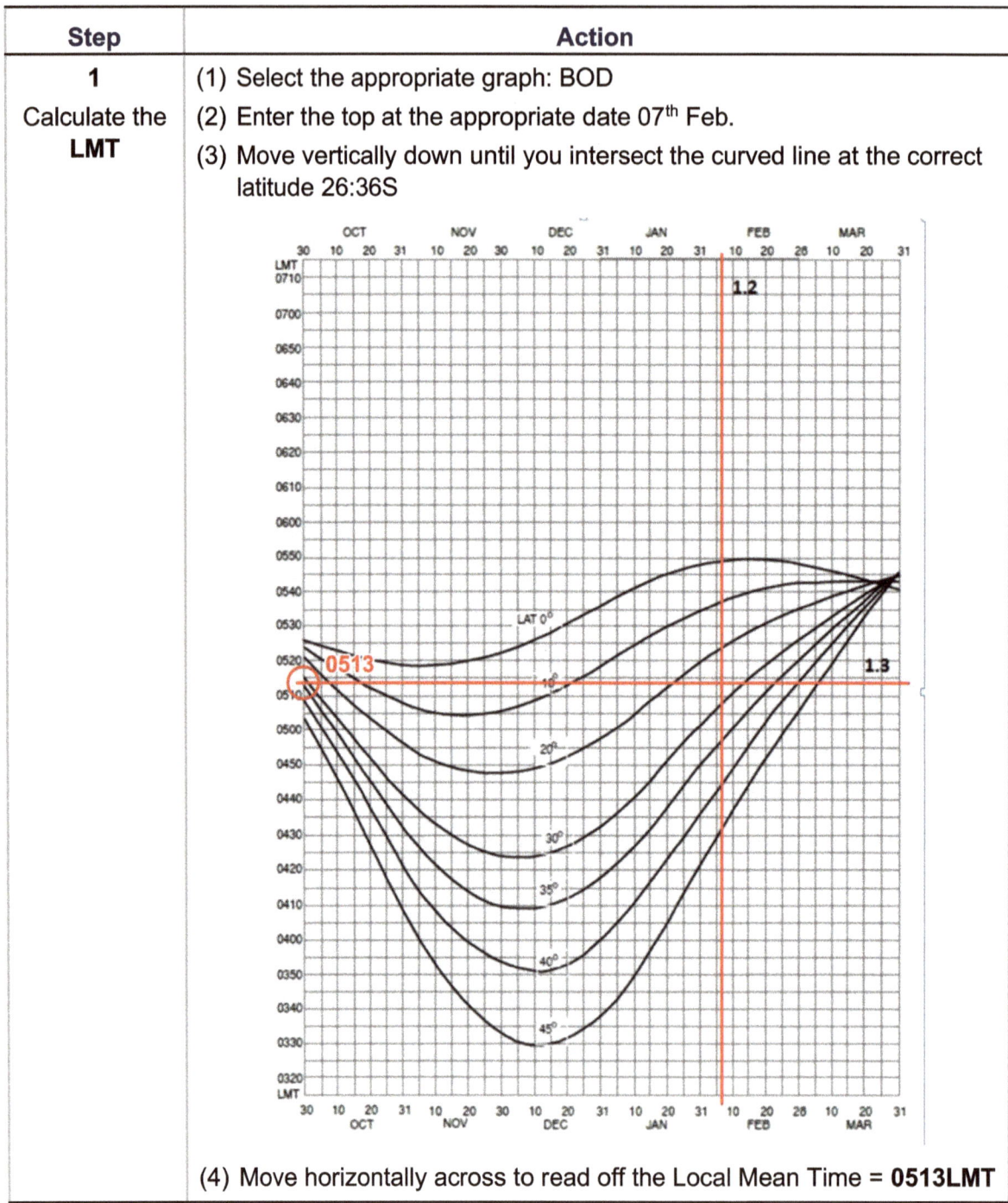 (4) Move horizontally across to read off the Local Mean Time = **0513LMT**

TRACK, DISTANCE, TIME AND SPEED
NAVIGATION

Step	Action
2 Calculate the ARC TIME	(1) Refer to the Conversion of **Arc to Time Table** (2) Slide down the Longitude DEGREES 153 = 10hrs 12min (3) Slide down the **Longitude MINUTES (05) = 0mins 20sec** (*less than 30 sec round down*) **CONVERSION OF ARC TO TIME** | DEGREES				MINUTES			
---	---	---	---	---	---	---	---
Long Deg	Hours Min	Long Deg	Hours Min	Long Min	Min Sec	Long Min	Min Sec
110	7 20	140	9 20	0	0 00	30	2 00
111	7 24	141	9 24	1	0 04	31	2 04
112	7 28	142	9 28	2	0 08	32	2 08
113	7 32	143	9 32	3	0 12	33	2 12
114	7 36	144	9 36	4	0 16	34	2 16
115	7 40	145	9 40	5	0 20	35	2 20
116	7 44	146	9 44	6	0 24	36	2 24
117	7 48	147	9 48	7	0 28	37	2 28
118	7 52	148	9 52	8	0 32	38	2 32
119	7 56	149	9 56	9	0 36	39	2 36
120	8 00	150	10 00	10	0 40	40	2 40
121	8 04	151	10 04	11	0 44	41	2 44
122	8 08	152	10 08	12	0 48	42	2 48
123	8 12	153	10 12	13	0 52	43	2 52
124	8 16	154	10 16	14	0 56	44	2 56
125	8 20	155	10 20	15	1 00	45	3 00
126	8 24	156	10 24	16	1 04	46	3 04
127	8 28	157	10 28	17	1 08	47	3 08
128	8 32	158	10 32	18	1 12	48	3 12
129	8 36	159	10 36	19	1 16	49	3 16
130	8 40			20	1 20	50	3 20
131	8 44			21	1 24	51	3 24
132	8 48			22	1 28	52	3 28
133	8 52			23	1 32	53	3 32
134	8 56			24	1 36	54	3 36
135	9 00			25	1 40	55	3 40
136	9 04			26	1 44	56	3 44
137	9 08			27	1 48	57	3 48
138	9 12			28	1 52	58	3 52
139	9 16			29	1 56	59	3 56	 (4) Add these two times together for the Total Arc Time **10hrs:12mins + 00mins:00sec = Total Arc Time 10:12:00**
3 Obtain UTC	Subtract the Total Arc Time from the LMT to obtain UTC 		Days	Hours	Mins	Seconds
---	---	---	---	---
LMT	07th	:05	:13	:00
- ARC	0	:10	:12	:00
= UTC	06th	:19	:01	:00	

Step	Action				
4 Convert UTC to Standard Time	• To convert to AEST add 10 hours to UTC • To convert to ACST add 9 1/2 hours to UTC • To convert to AWST add 8 hours to UTC				
		Days	Hours	Mins	Seconds
	UTC	06th	:19	:01	:00
	+ 10 (for AEST)	0	:10	:00	:00
	= BOD AEST	07th	:05	:01	:00

The New Method

Access a computer with internet access and using the **N**ational **A**eronautical **I**nformation **P**rocessing **S**ystem (**NAIPS**) found at https://www.airservicesaustralia.com/naips/

Simply go to the home screen, log in then follow the prompts to get to the correct screens.

It is easy to use and self-explanatory.

Remember that after you have the answer it will be given in UTC so you may have to convert it to Local time to be useful.

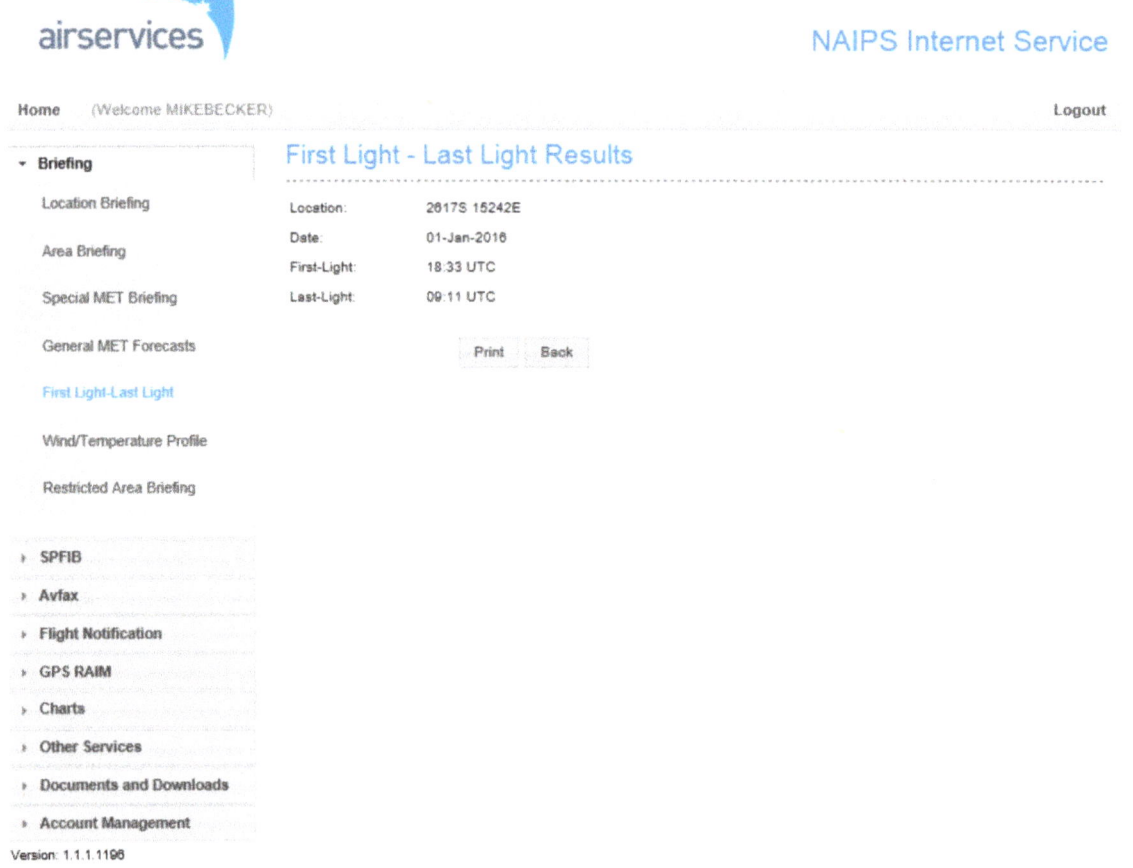

Alternatively, smart phones and tablets have applications (APPS) that can access NAIPS to get the same information.

NAIPS APP

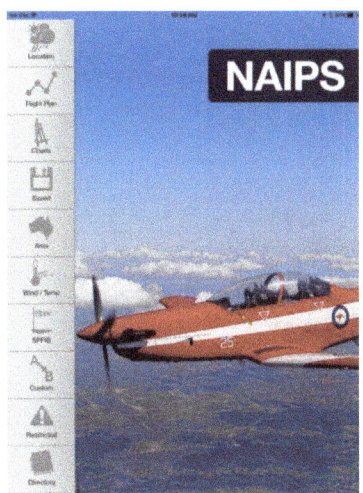

Light Page

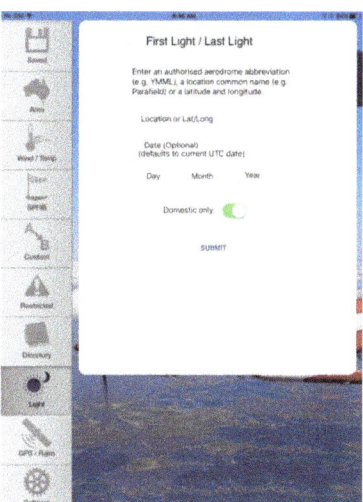

Your instructor will demonstrate how to use both systems.

Speed

There are two speeds that are important to Aviation, they are Airspeed and Groundspeed. Both are measured in "**knots**" which relates to the Nautical Miles per hour travelled.

A **N**autical **M**ile (**NM**) is the average length of one minute of longitude (or latitude at the equator) which is equal to 6080 feet.

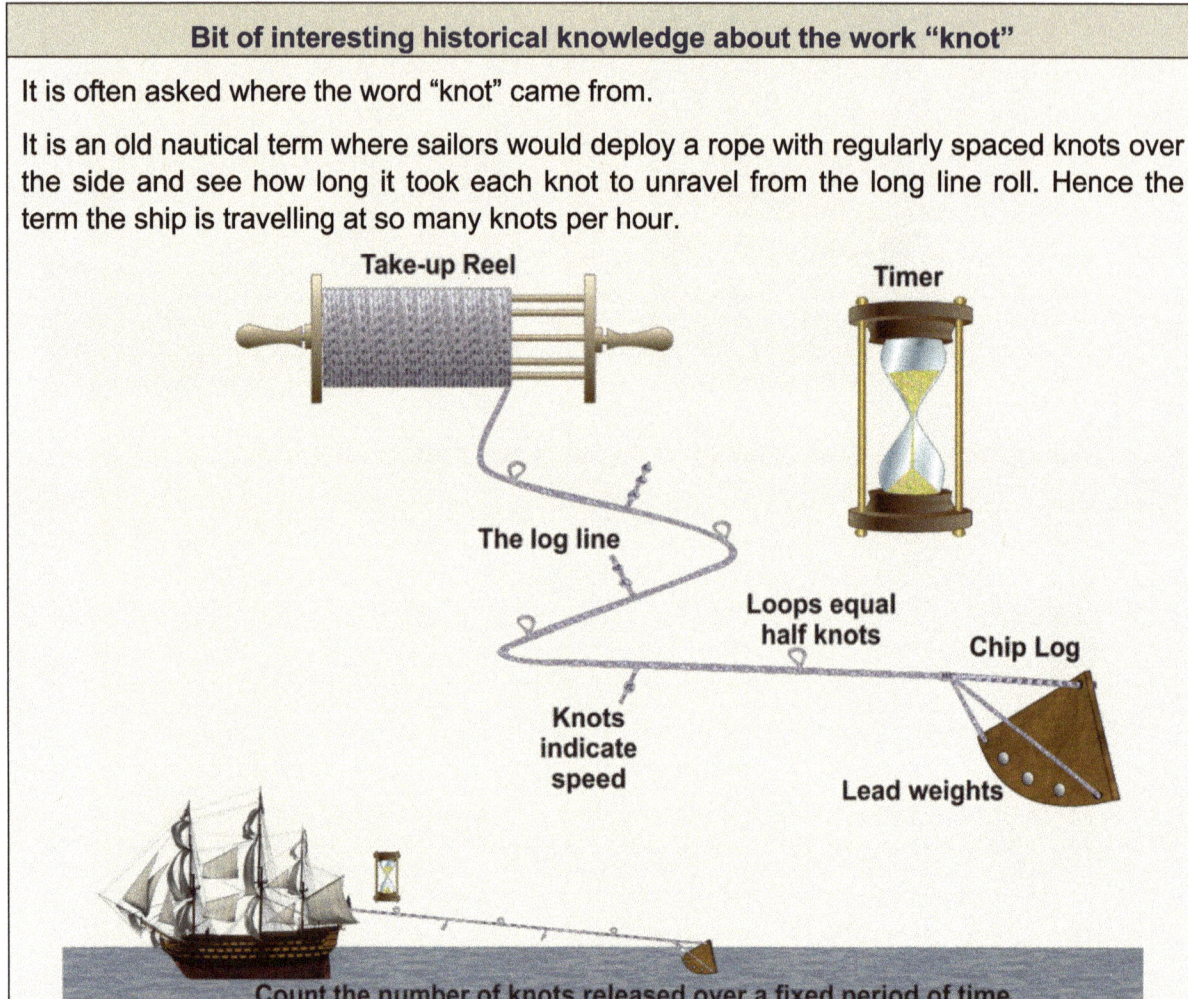

Bit of interesting historical knowledge about the work "knot"

It is often asked where the word "knot" came from.

It is an old nautical term where sailors would deploy a rope with regularly spaced knots over the side and see how long it took each knot to unravel from the long line roll. Hence the term the ship is travelling at so many knots per hour.

Count the number of knots released over a fixed period of time.

Speed

Groundspeed

Ground**s**peed (**G/S**) is the actual speed of the aircraft over the ground irrespective of its speed through the air and is influenced by altitude, power and wind.

Groundspeed is defined as the distance travelled over the ground over a certain period of time.

Example
If a helicopter travels 60NM in 1 hour (60minutes) the Groundspeed (G/S) will equal 60 knots or 60 NM per hour. 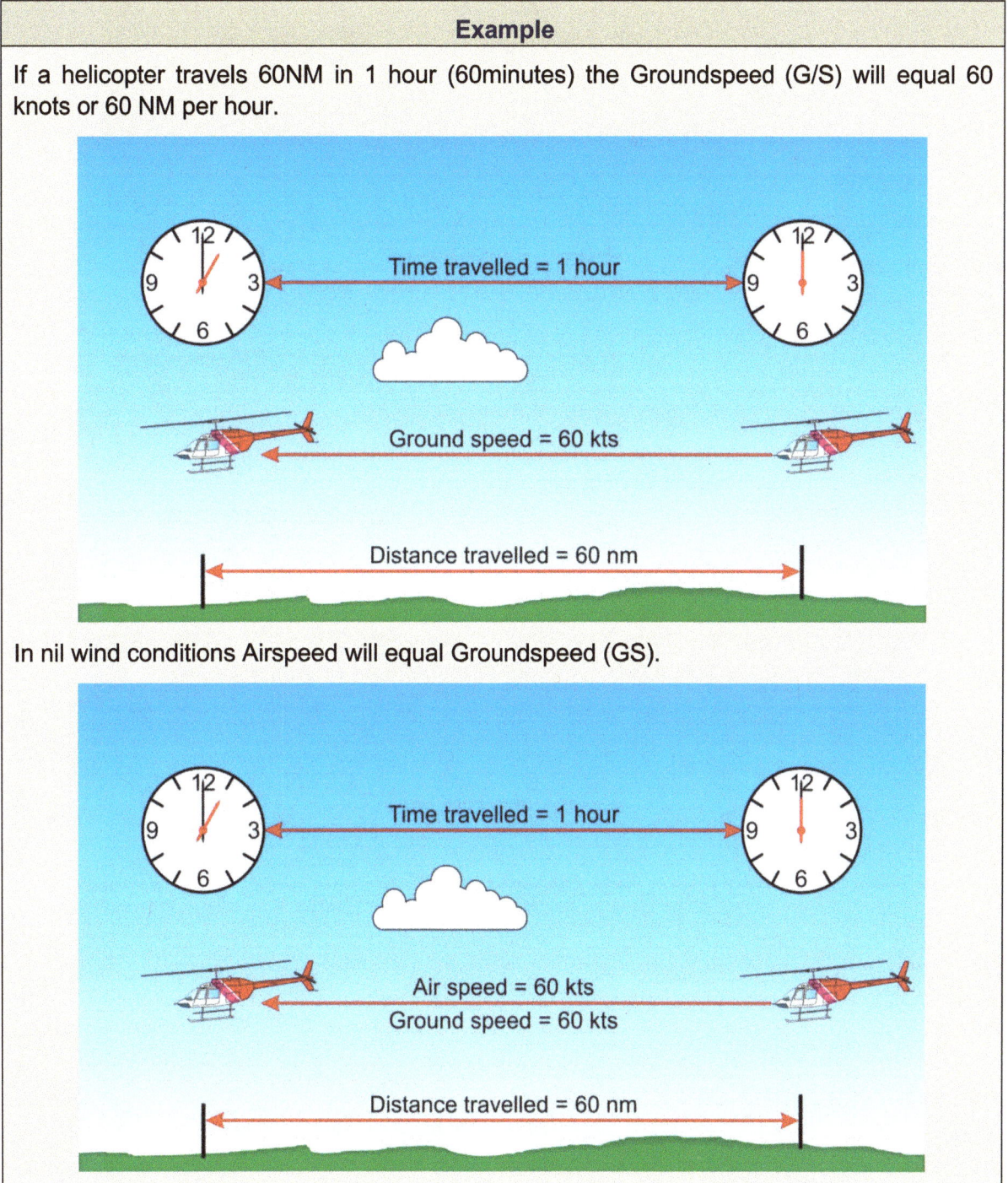 In nil wind conditions Airspeed will equal Groundspeed (GS).

TRACK, DISTANCE, TIME AND SPEED

When there is a wind blowing it will have an effect on the groundspeed depending on whether it is a headwind, a tail wind or a crosswind (or any combination)

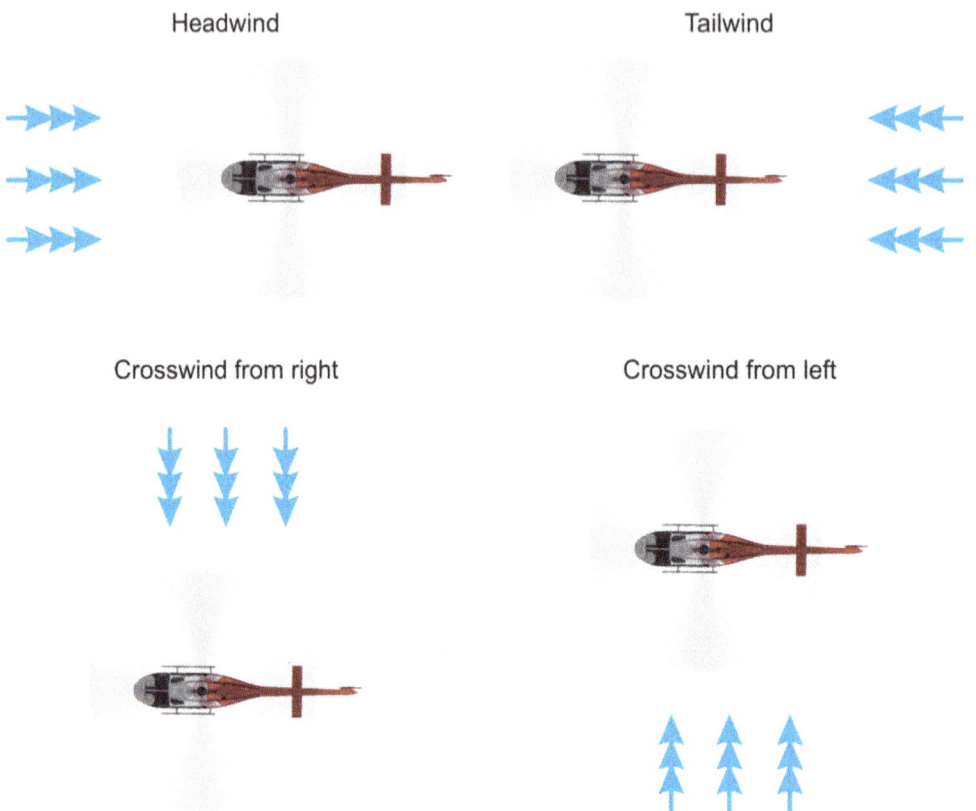

With a constant airspeed any headwind or headwind component will reduce the groundspeed and any tail wind or tail wind component will increase the ground speed.

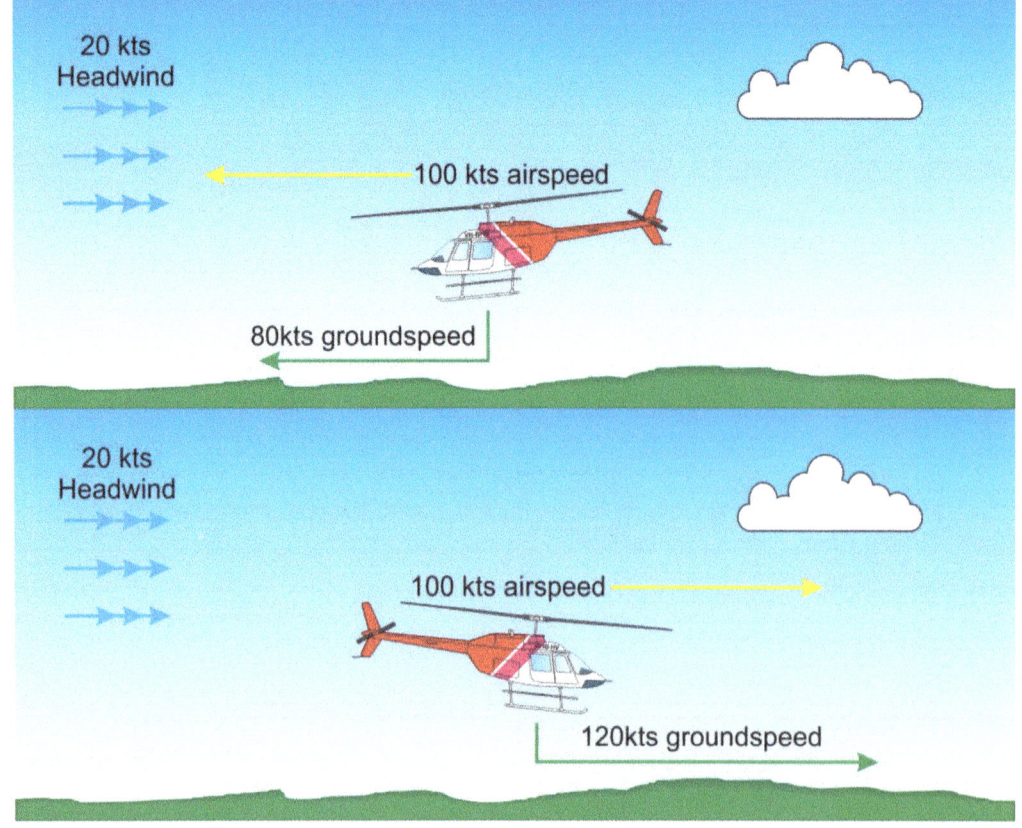

To calculate Groundspeed during the planning stages of a navigation, it is important to obtain the wind direction and strength. This can be found on a weather report taken from the NAIPS system, calculated in flight using the Flight Computer or it may even be displayed in the cockpit on the EFIS display if available.

TAS/GS (true air speed ground speed)

Airspeed

Airspeed is the actual speed of the helicopter through the air irrespective of its speed across the ground and is influenced by temperature, atmospheric pressure and power.

The helicopter is a flying machine; it is not influenced by the ground in flight. It is only the pilot that is concerned with the ground as he tries to get from A to B as quickly and efficiently as possible.

Airspeed is *independent* of wind and can be the same whether the helicopter is flying into wind, downwind or cross wind. What will be different will be the sight picture observed by the pilot as the ground moves underneath the helicopter at differing speeds.

When flying a helicopter in a particular air mass, the helicopter moves within it.

If the helicopter is going in the same direction as the air mass then it would appear to be moving faster with reference to the ground.

If the helicopter is moving in the opposite direction as the air mass then it would appear to be moving slower with reference to the ground but in both cases the airspeed would be the same.

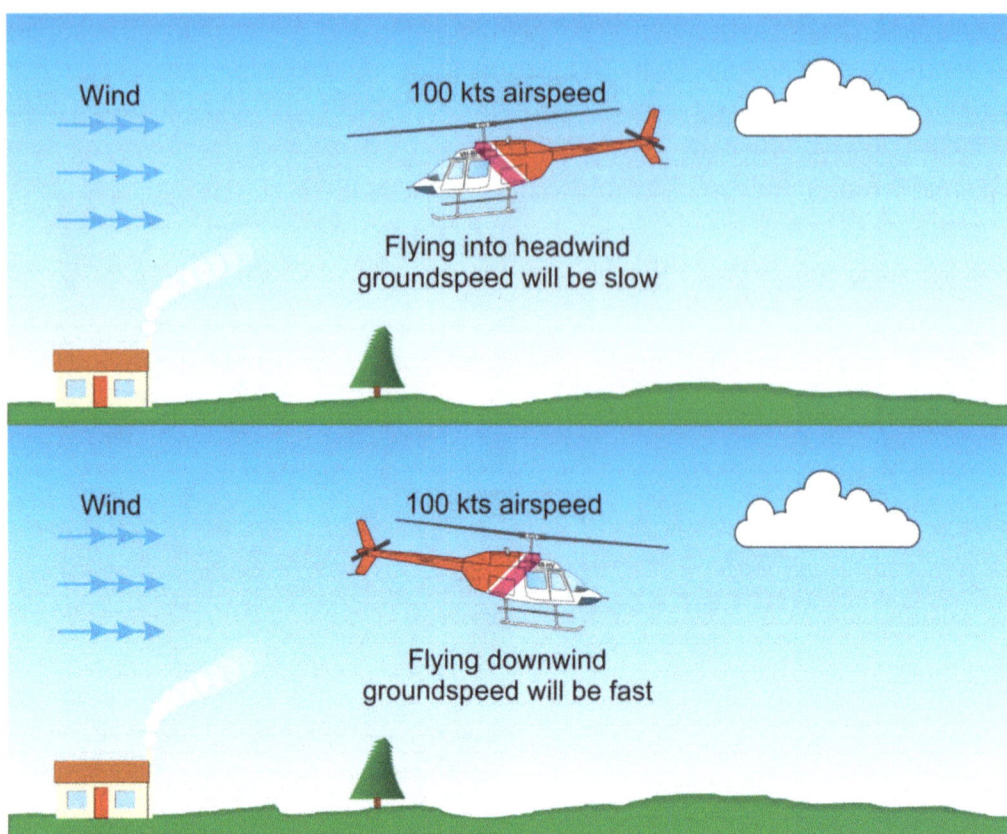

If the air mass was not moving, then Airspeed would equal Groundspeed.

The easiest way to understand this is to consider a boat on water.

If the water is moving, then the boat would go with it.

If the water was not moving, then the boat would not move.

---
[16] By Bob Heims, U.S. Army Corps of Engineers [Public domain], via Wikimedia Commons / https://upload.wikimedia.org/wikipedia/commons/c/cc/Drift_boat_aka_Mckenzie_River_dory.jpg

In order for the boat to move independently of the water it would need power.

Once moving under power, if it went up the river it would appear to be going slow because of the movement of the water. If it went down river it would appear to be going faster because of the movement of the water. The exact same principle applies in the helicopter while in flight.

Airspeed can be divided into three categories:

1. Indicated airspeed (IAS)
2. Calibrated airspeed (CAS) and
3. True Airspeed (TAS)

---

[17] By Pseudopanax at English Wikipedia (Own work) [Public domain], via Wikimedia Commons /
https://upload.wikimedia.org/wikipedia/commons/c/c7/Shotover_Jet_boat_in_Shotover_Canyon_at_Arthur%27s_Point.jpg

Indicated Airspeed

Indicated Airspeed (**IAS**), often referred to as **KIAS**, (**K**nots **I**ndicated **A**ir**s**peed) is the value displayed on the **A**irspeed Indicator (**ASI**) located in the cockpit.

Analogue ASI

Digital EFIS tape ASI

It shows the difference between the dynamic (moving) air entering the Pitot tube due to the helicopters forward movement and the stationary air pressure measured by the static vents. (refer to the Aircraft General Knowledge course). It shows the airspeed value based on the helicopters movement and an assumed air density and temperature calibrated to the **I**nternational **S**tandard **A**tmosphere (**ISA**) at sea level.

Because a helicopter will change its altitude and because the density (thickness) and temperature of the air can vary from day to day, the ASI will not accurately measure the true speed of the helicopter through the air at all times and therefore is not an accurate instrument to use for navigational planning.

Indicated **A**irspeed (**IAS**) is used to measure performance of the helicopter and shall be relied upon by the pilot as an indication for any speed limitations as stated in the Flight Manual.

Calibrated Airspeed

The ASI suffers from two errors

- Instrument error and
- Position error

Instrument error is the result of poor design or construction, wear and tear and internal friction of any internal mechanical mechanism.

Position error is a result of where the pitot and static vents are in relation to the airflow which can disrupt the readings on the ASI. In helicopters being out of balance, in an autorotation or flying sideways all have an adverse effect on the ASI indication.

Calibrated Airspeed (CAS) is the IAS corrected for instrument and position error.

The Flight Manual of some (not all) helicopters will have a table or graph that is produced by the manufacturer that will show what the real CAS is for a given IAS.

If available, the CAS is more accurate that the IAS but the error is generally very small so it does not have to be considered. In the case of the Bell206BIII assume that IAS and CAS are equal.

Table 4-1. Airspeed installation correction table

INDICATED A/S — MPH	CALIBRATED A/S — MPH	INDICATED A/S — (KNOTS)	CALIBRATED A/S — (KNOTS)
40	40.5	(35)	(35.5)
45	45	(40)	(40)
50	50	(45)	(45)
60	59.5	(50)	(49.5)
70	69	(55)	(54.5)
80	79	(60)	(59)
90	88.5	(70)	(69)
100	98.5	(80)	(79)
110	108	(90)	(88.5)
120	118	(100)	(98.5)
130	128	(110)	(108.5)
140	138	(120)	(118.5)
150	148	(130)	(128)

Indicated Airspeed (IAS) corrected for position and instrument error equals Calibrated Airspeed (CAS). Determine Calibrated Airspeed (CAS) from the above table.

True Airspeed

True Airspeed (**TAS**), often referred to as **KTAS** (**K**nots **T**rue **A**ir**s**peed) is all about the density of the air and is important to know for accurate navigation.

The TAS must be calculated based on the temperature and pressure of the day, as these will affect the actual speed the helicopter can move within a given air mass. This can be done on the Flight Computer (wiz wheel) or by use of an APP on a smart phone or tablet.

Flight Computer **MyE6B APP**

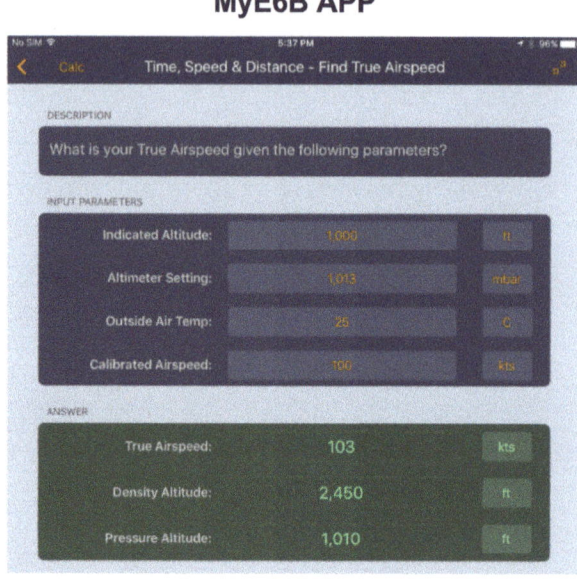

Alternatively, in modern helicopters the TAS may be displayed on the EFIS display

TAS/GS
(true air speed
ground speed)

To understand TAS consider a helicopter moving through the air where all the air molecules are very close together. Flying from one air molecule to another the helicopter will have an actual speed through the air. If these molecules are collected in the Pitot tube then the ASI will display a speed. Let's say that speed is 100 KIAS.

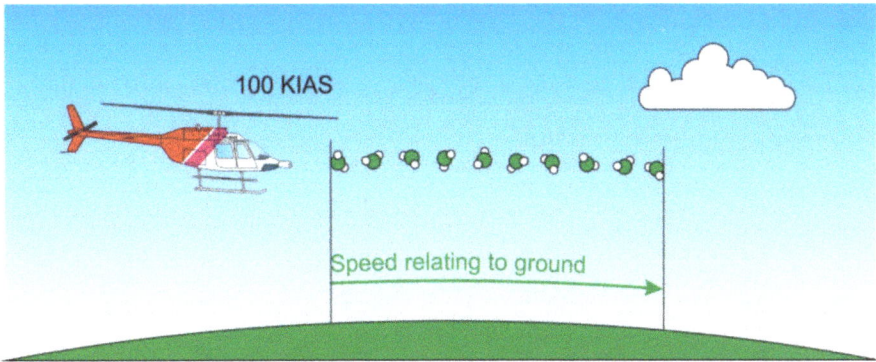

Now let's assume that the helicopter is still doing 100 KIAS but on a different day and the air molecules are much further apart. In order to maintain 100 KIAS the true speed through the air (and therefore over the ground) will be much higher.

This proves that IAS and TAS can in actual fact be different.

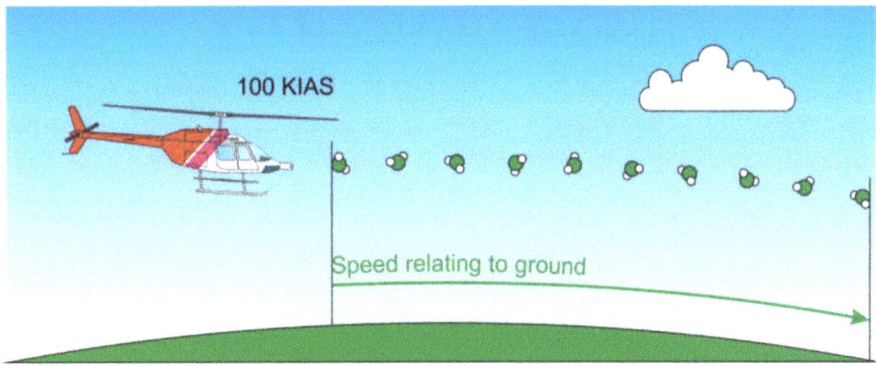

The two variables that can affect TAS are temperature and pressure.

Temperature effect

Cold air is denser (thicker) that warm air. On a warm day the helicopter will travel faster through the air to collect the same number of molecules per second in order for the ASI to give the same reading as it would on a cold day when it collects the same number of molecules but at a slower speed.

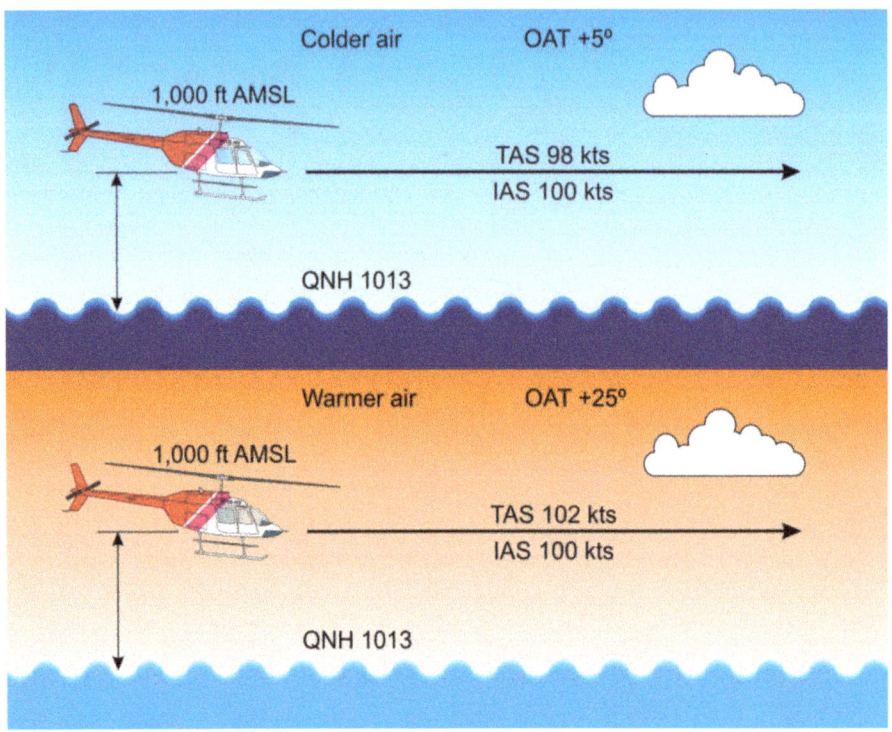

Pressure effect

The higher the altitude the lower the air pressure, and the further apart the air molecules.

If maintaining a constant IAS an aircraft that is flying at a higher altitude will have a greater TAS compared to an aircraft flying at a lower altitude.

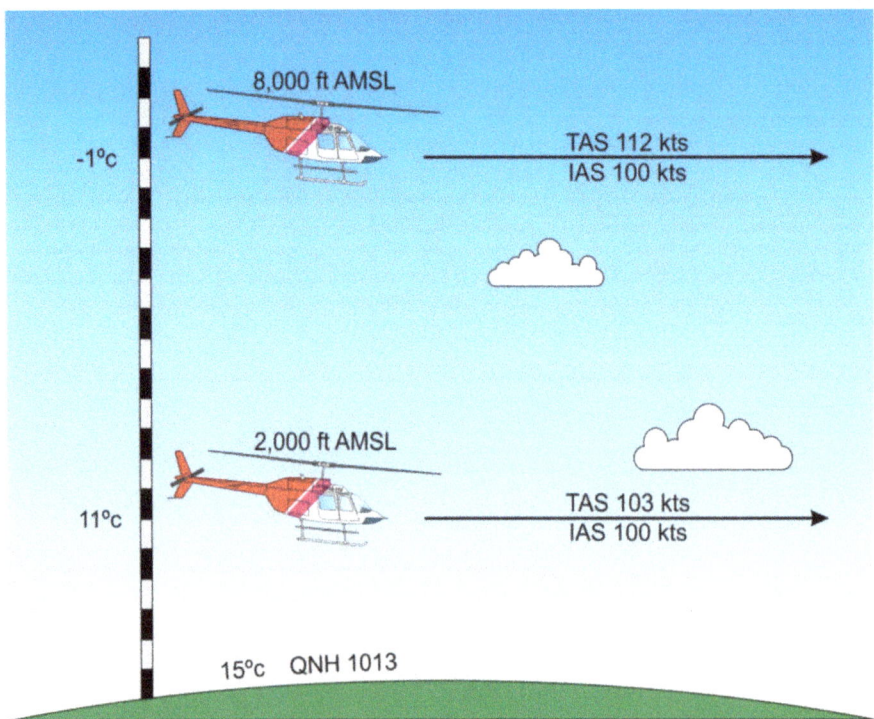

Summary

Indicated Airspeed (IAS) is that speed displayed on the airspeed indicator (ASI) and shall be used to measure the helicopters performance and limitations

Calibrated Airspeed (CAS) is tabulated data provided by the manufacture to account for errors in the ASI installation. The errors are very small and can be ignored in smaller helicopters operating below 5000 feet AMSL.

True Airspeed (TAS) is the actual speed of the helicopter through the air when taking into account temperature and pressure and shall be used for flight planning and navigation purposes.

4 Flight Computer Front Side

The Front Side of the Flight Computer is simply a detailed manual slide rule able to do addition, subtraction, division, multiplication and unit conversions.

In this chapter we will only cover some of the basic calculations including:

- Time
- Distance
- Speed
- Flight Fuel
- Fuel Burned
- Fuel consumption rate, and
- TAS.

FLIGHT COMPUTER FRONT SIDE

NAVIGATION

INTERNATIONAL HELICOPTER THEORY

Front Side Markings

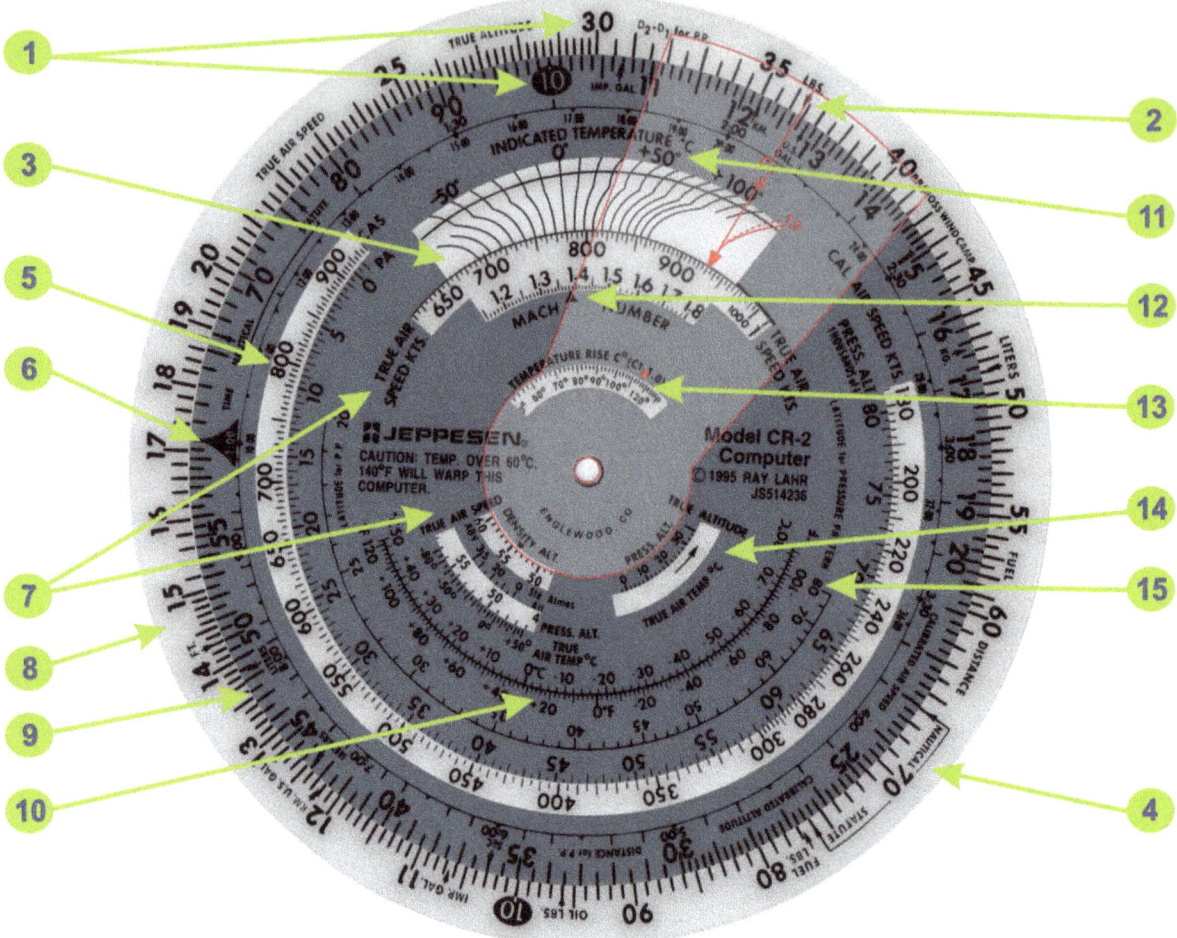

Item	Description	Item	Description
1	Unit index	9	Top Disc - **Scale B and Scale C**
2	Cursor Hairline	10	Temperature Conversion Scale
3	Recovery Coefficient 1.0	11	Indicated Temperature Window
4	Nautical-Statute Conversion Arrows	12	Mach Number Window
5	Calibrated Air Speed Window	13	Temperature Rise Scale
6	Time Index	14	True Altitude Window
7	True Air Speed Windows	15	Latitude for Pressure Patern Scale
8	Base Disc - **Scale A**		

Beginners Rules

Prior to using the Flight Computer, there are three (3) basic rules to remember:

1. The arrow head indicator (referred to as the true index) always points to the rate
2. The outer scale always represents quantity
3. The inner scale always represents time

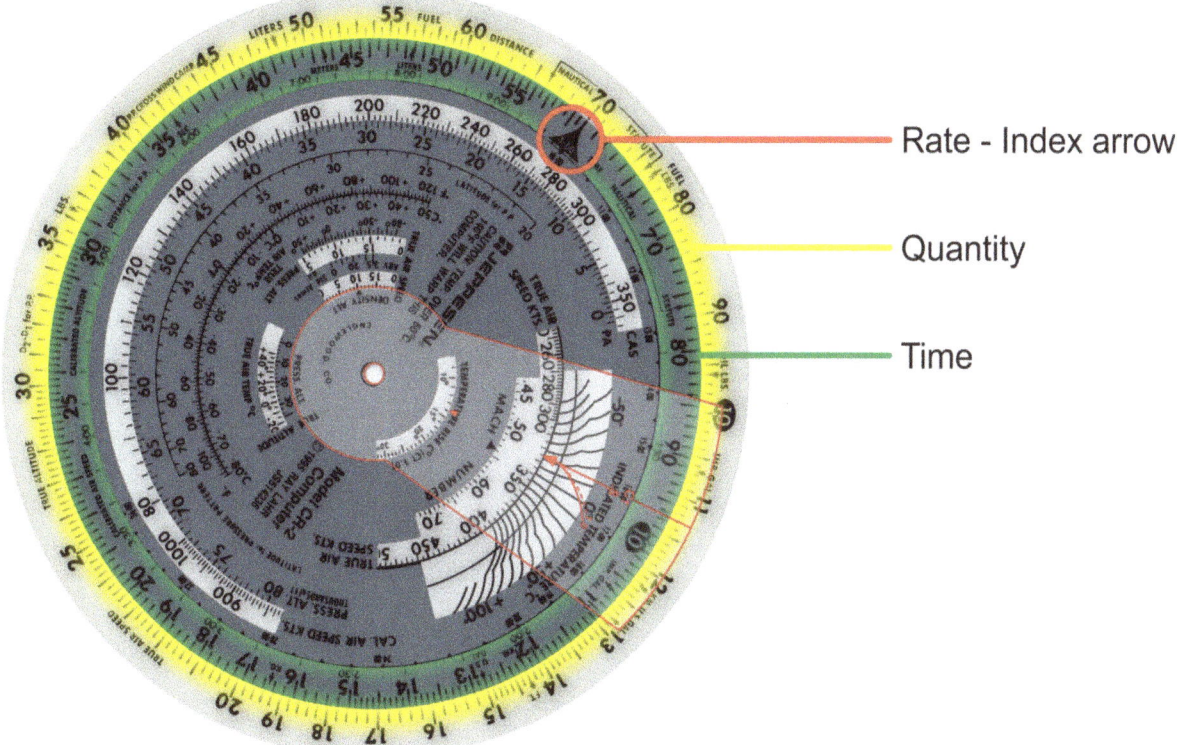

- Rate - Index arrow
- Quantity
- Time

Finding Time

If an aircraft is flying at 100kts how long will it take to fly 150 nautical miles?

Step	Description
1	Turn to the calculator side of the computer.
2	Rotate the inner disc until the time index (big black triangle) is located directly under the 10 which represents 100kts.
3	Follow the outer 'A' scale to 15 which represents 150 nautical miles.
4	Look directly below the 15 to the inner 'B' scale and read off the time which is 90 minutes or 1 hr 30 minutes on the 'C' scale.

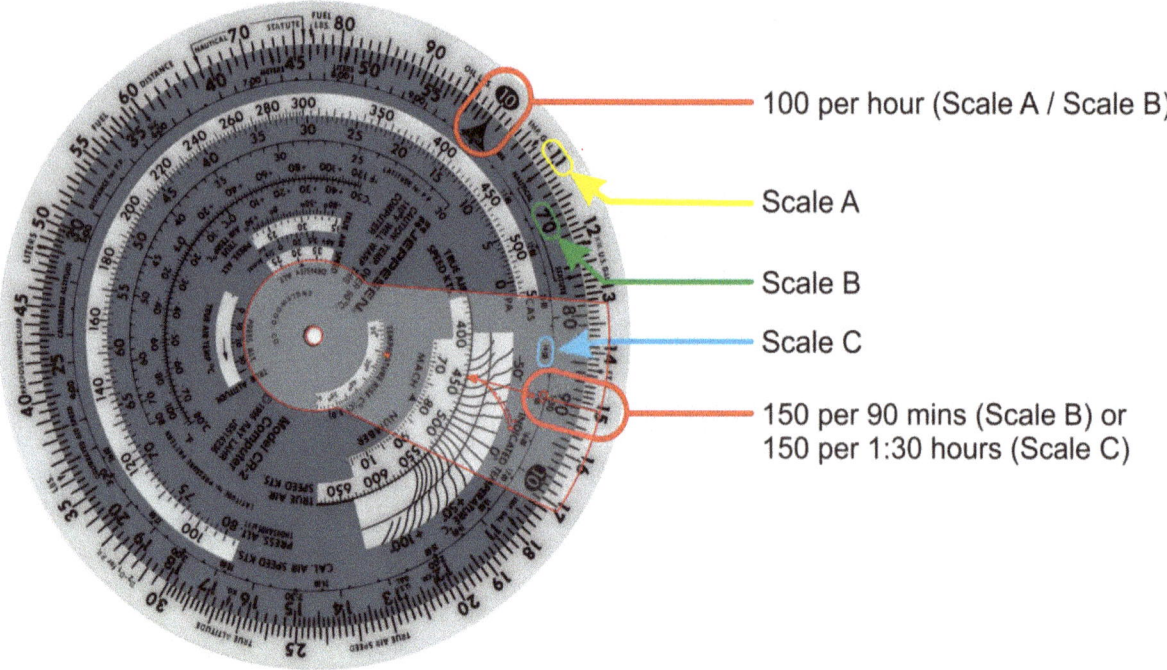

- 100 per hour (Scale A / Scale B)
- Scale A
- Scale B
- Scale C
- 150 per 90 mins (Scale B) or 150 per 1:30 hours (Scale C)

Finding Distance

If an aircraft flies at 77kts how far will it go in two hours?

Step	Description
1	Turn to the calculator side of the computer.
2	Rotate the inner disc until the time index (big black triangle) is located directly under the 77 which represents 77kts
3	Follow the inner 'B' scale to 120 minutes or the inner 'C' scale to 2.00 hours
4	Look directly above the 'B' scale and read off 154 on the 'A' scale which represents 154NM travelled

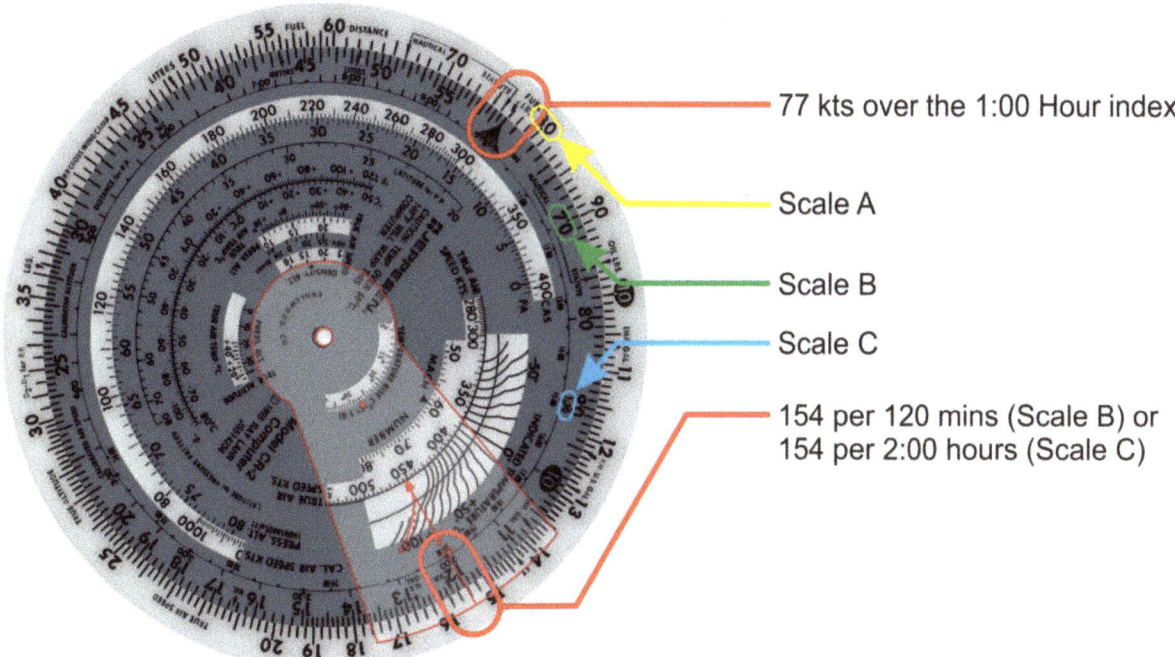

- 77 kts over the 1:00 Hour index
- Scale A
- Scale B
- Scale C
- 154 per 120 mins (Scale B) or 154 per 2:00 hours (Scale C)

Finding Speed

If an aircraft travels 230NM in 50 minutes how fast is it going?

Step	Description
1	Turn to the calculator side of the computer
2	Rotate the inner disc until the 50 on scale 'B' (which represents 50 minutes) is located directly under the 23 on scale 'A' which represents 230NM
3	Look now directly above the speed index (big black triangle) and you will find 27.6 which represents 276kts

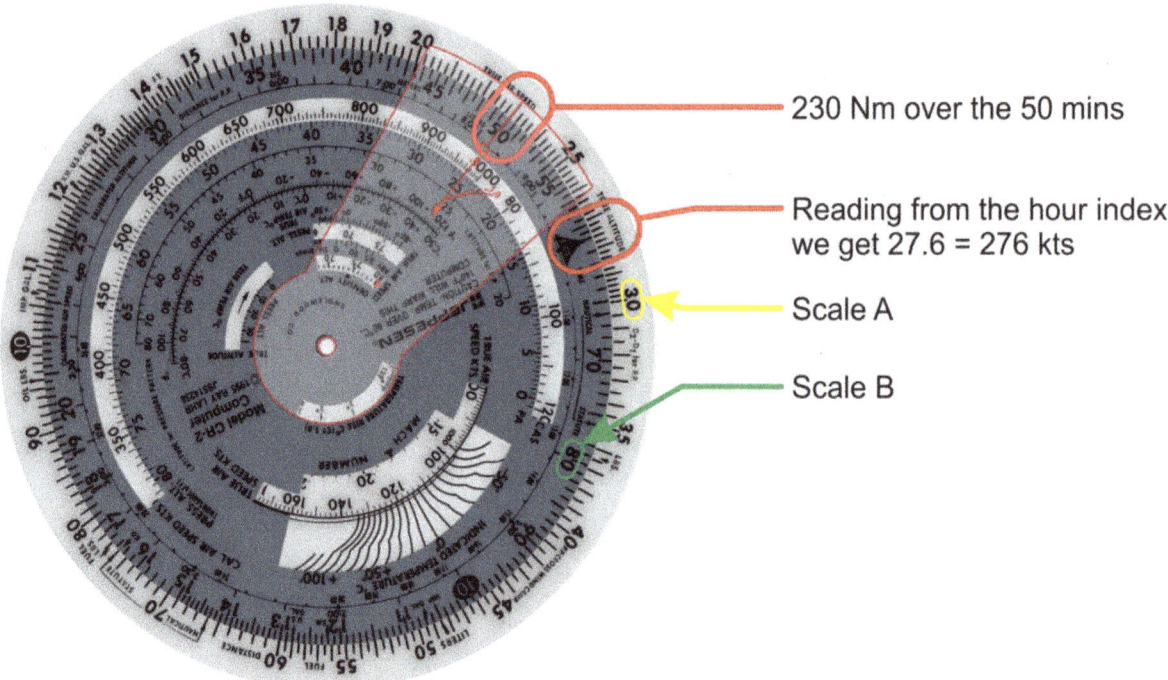

- 230 Nm over the 50 mins
- Reading from the hour index we get 27.6 = 276 kts
- Scale A
- Scale B

Flight Fuel

If an aircraft burns fuel at the rate of 55 litres per hour and has 120 litres of usable fuel onboard how long can the aircraft fly for?

Step	Description
1	Turn to the calculator side of the computer.
2	Rotate the inner disc until the time index is directly under the 55 which represents 55lts per hour (note that the measurements do not matter e.g.: litres, gals, lbs, grams, buckets etc.)
3	Follow the outer 'A' scale and locate 12 which represents 120lts of usable fuel.
4	Directly under the 12 on the 'B' scale is 13.1 which represents 131 minutes or on the 'C' scale 2 hours eleven minutes.

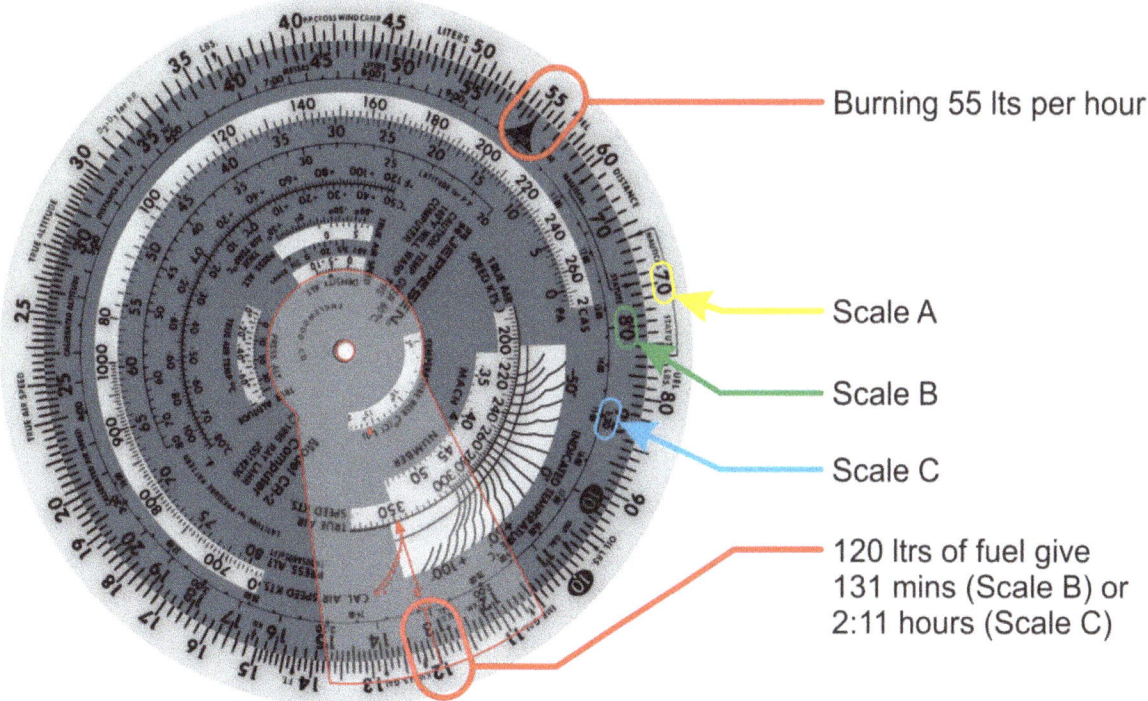

Burning 55 lts per hour

Scale A

Scale B

Scale C

120 ltrs of fuel give 131 mins (Scale B) or 2:11 hours (Scale C)

Fuel Burned

If an aircraft burns fuel at the rate of 7.5 gals per hour and flies for 2 hours how many gallons were burned?

Step	Description
1	Turn to the calculator side of the computer.
2	Rotate the inner disc until the time index is directly under 75 which represents 7.5gals per hour. Because 70 and 80 represent 7 and 8 respectively for this problem 7.5 is half way between.
3	Follow the 'B' scale to 12 or the 'C' scale to 2:00 which represents 2 hours.
4	Look directly above the 12 to the 'A' scale and the answer 15 which represents 15gals burned.

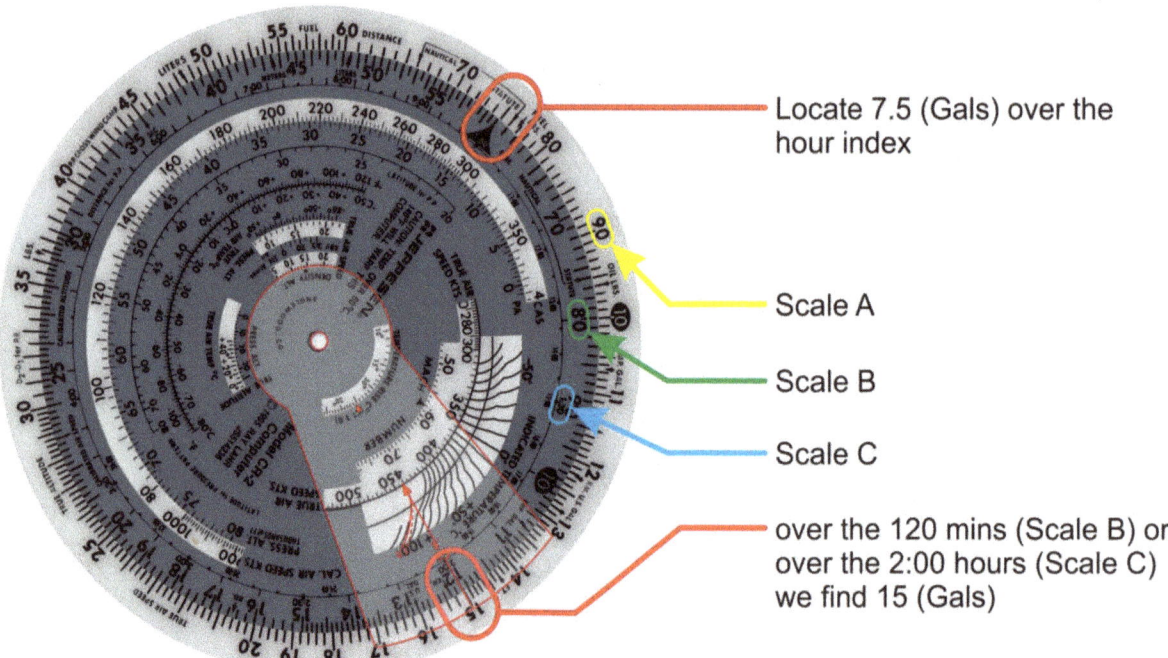

Locate 7.5 (Gals) over the hour index

Scale A

Scale B

Scale C

over the 120 mins (Scale B) or over the 2:00 hours (Scale C) we find 15 (Gals)

Fuel Consumption Rate

If an aircraft burns 85lbs of fuel in 75 minutes, what was the consumption rate?

Step	Description
1	Turn to the calculator side of the computer.
2	Rotate the inner disc until 75 minutes on the 'B' scale is directly under 85 on the 'A' scale which represents 85lbs.
3	Turn the whole computer until you locate the time index which will be pointing to 68 which represents 68lbs per hour.

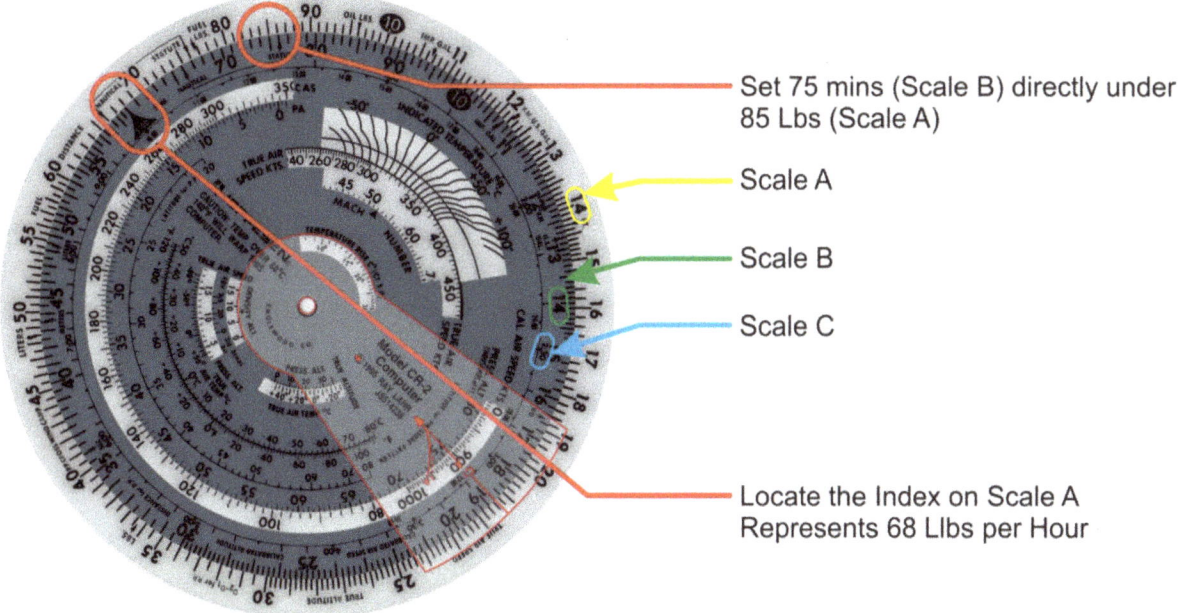

Set 75 mins (Scale B) directly under 85 Lbs (Scale A)

Scale A

Scale B

Scale C

Locate the Index on Scale A Represents 68 Llbs per Hour

Calculation of TAS

Before we get started, let's review some of the many abbreviations we are going to be using:

Abbreviation	Meaning	Description
ASI	Air speed indicator	The airspeed indicator in the cockpit
IAS	Indicated airspeed	Aircrafts speed through the air
CAS	Calibrated airspeed	IAS corrected for instrument and position error
TAS	True airspeed	CAS corrected for temperature and pressure
Pht	Pressure height	Height using QHN of 1013Mb
OAT	Outside air temperature	Ambient temperature outside

Quick Review

The **Airspeed Indicator (ASI)** shows **Indicated Airspeed (IAS)**, which is not calibrated to consider outside air temperature and pressure, therefore, will vary at altitude for the same **TAS**.

Calibrated Airspeed (CAS) is IAS corrected for instrument and pressure errors.

True Airspeed (TAS) is defined as our actual speed through the air considering temperature and pressure.

This section will explain how to convert IAS (CAS) to TAS for a given outside air temperature and Pressure Height (Pht).

Given a Pht of 7000ft, an OAT of +5°C and a CAS of 110kt find the TAS.

Step	Description
1	Turn to the calculator side of the computer
2	In the 'True Airspeed Window', set Pressure Altitude against the OAT
3	Against CAS on the 'Inner Scale' of the whiz wheel, read TAS on the 'outer scale' 7000ft and OAT +5°C with a CAS of 110 equals a TAS of 123kts

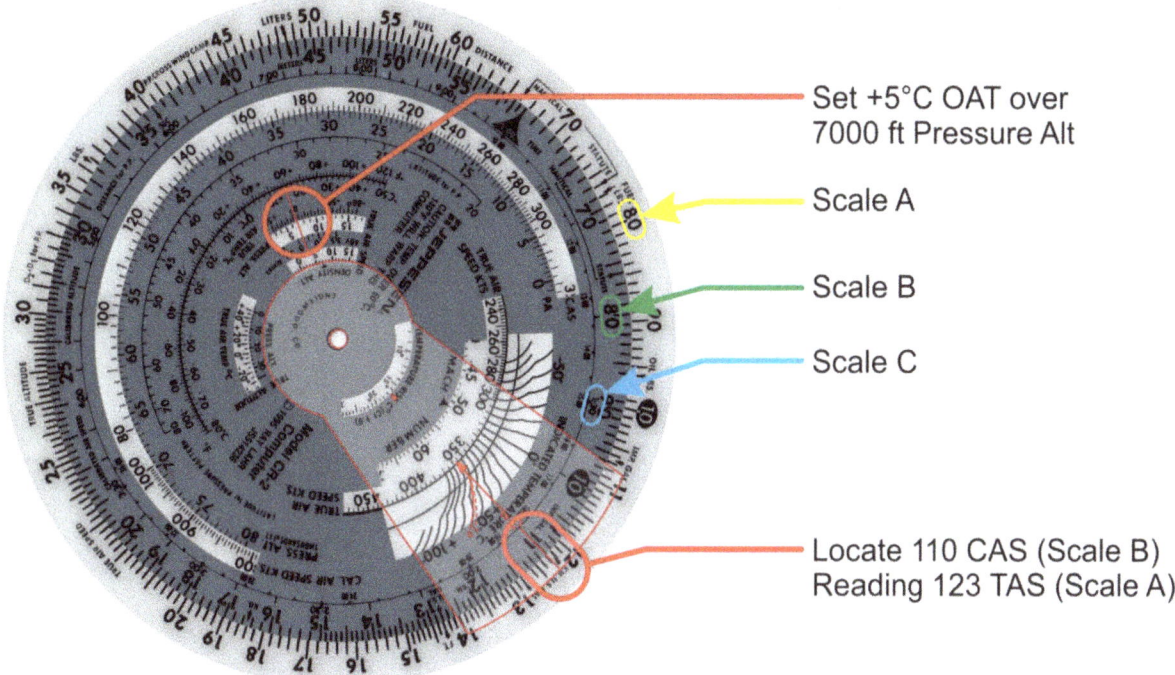

 The words Calibrated Air Speed and True Air Speed appear between 25 and 30 on both scales

5 Flight Computer Back Side

The Back Side of the Flight Computer is all about calculating wind and how that wind will affect the magnetic heading of the helicopter and its speed across the ground.

The backside of the Flight computer is often referred to as the "wind side".

This chapter will then continue on to explain the basic wind calculations including:

- Heading
- Groundspeed
- Drift
- Unknown Wind velocity

Back side scales

There are three scales on the back side of the Flight Computer with two (2) of them being able to independently turn. Each scale radiates outwards from the "*Centre Grommet*".

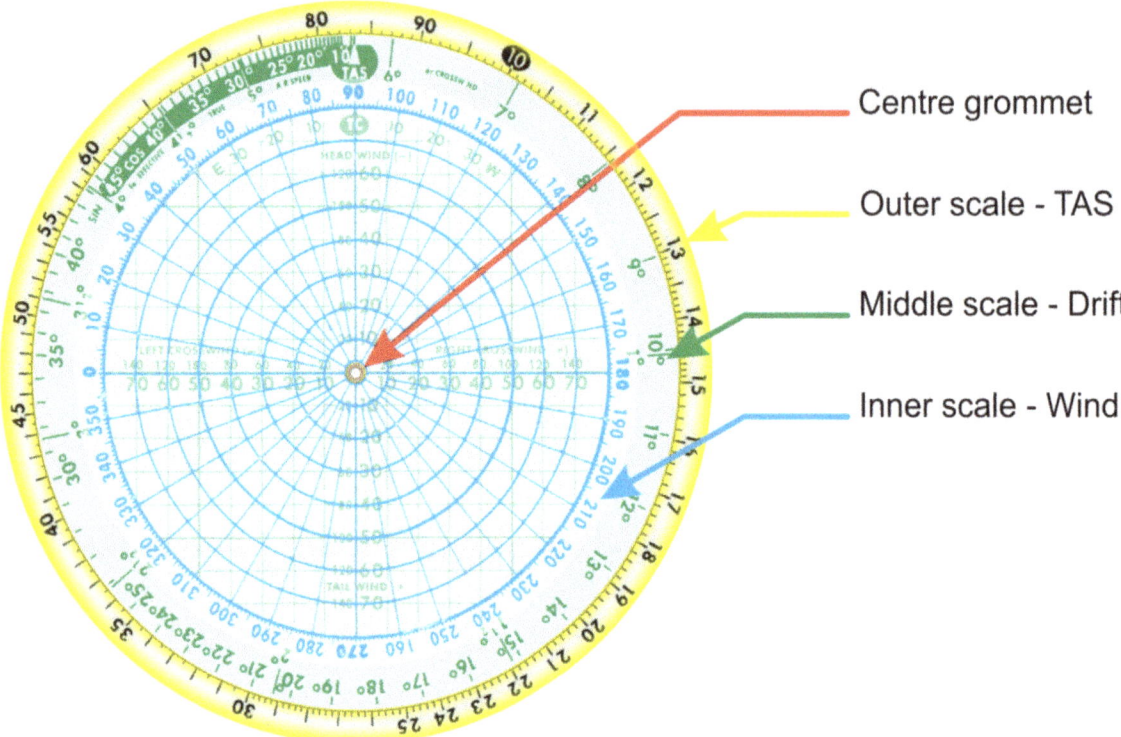

1. The *Outer* scale displays TAS. The outer scale is fixed in place and cannot be moved.
2. The *Middle* scale displays drift. It can be rotated so that the TAS index can point to a selected TAS or a wind speed can be compared to a drift angle in degrees.

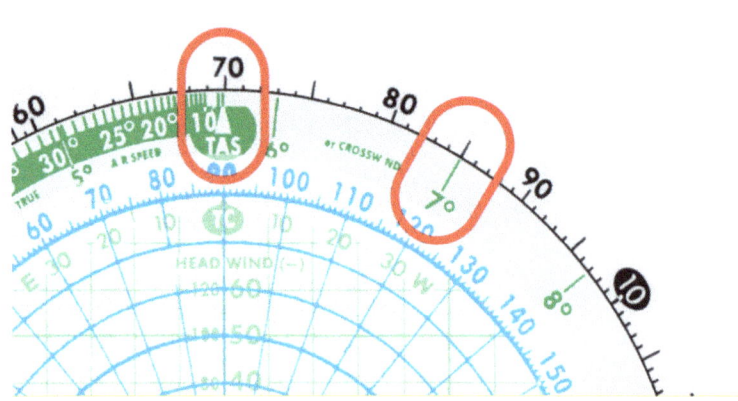

3. The *Inner* transparent scale displays the wind grid. It can be rotated so that wind components and wind speed can be calculated.

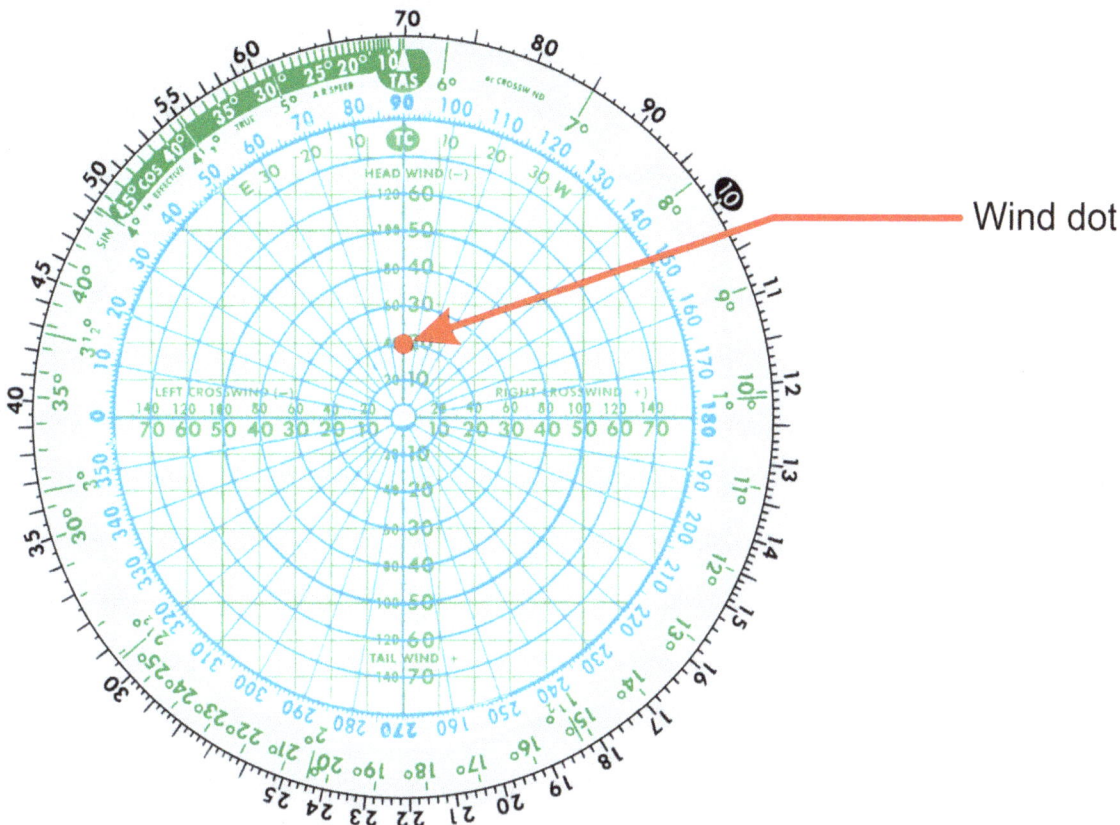

Wind dot

Underneath the Inner transparent scale is a "2-value" scale system to accommodate wind calculations either below or above 100kts. This means that when using the Flight Computer the pilot needs to be very careful on which scale is actually being used.

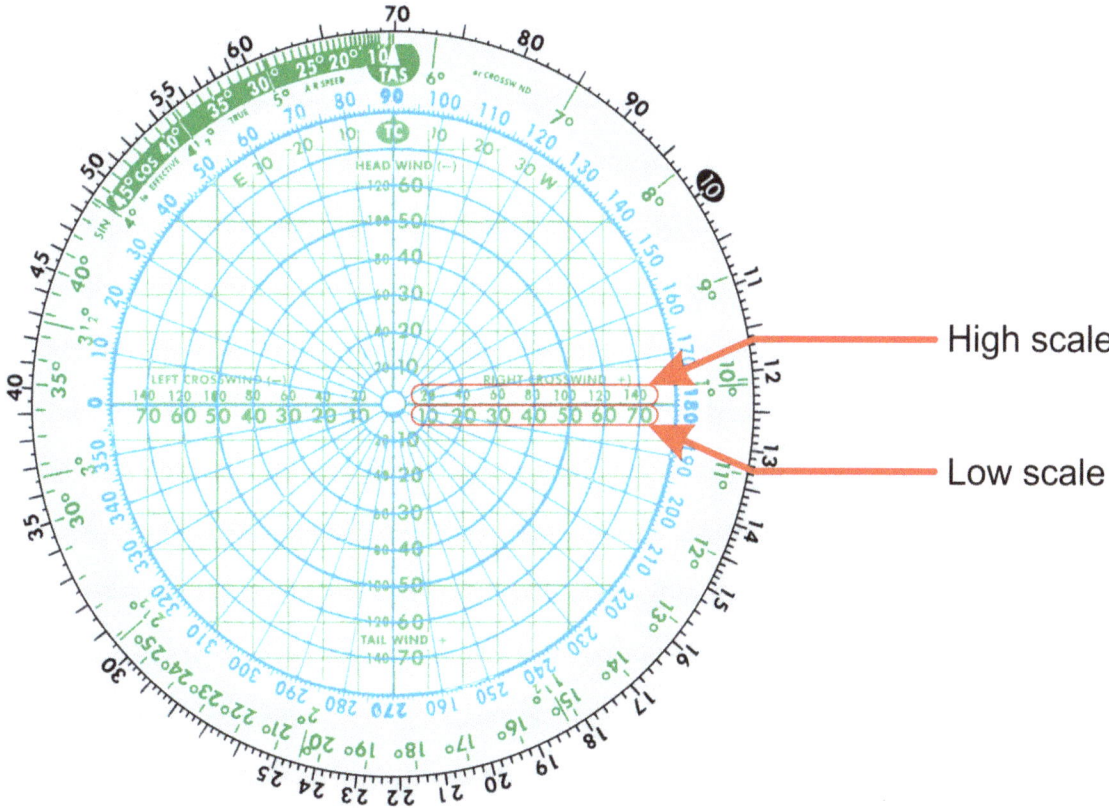

High scale

Low scale

Beginners rules

Prior to using the Flight Computer, there are six (6) basic rules to remember:

1. Always start with a clean transparent slider.
2. Draw a rough picture on a piece of paper *before* you mark the Flight Computer so you understand what information you have and can get a mental picture of what the result is going to look like.

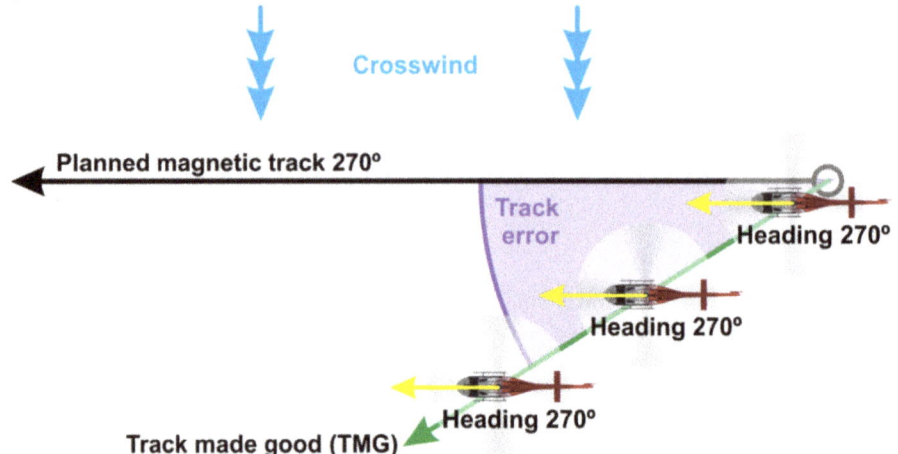

3. When marking the transparent slider with a pencil or felt tip, be accurate in how you place the wind mark. This is usually done as a small **X** or ●.

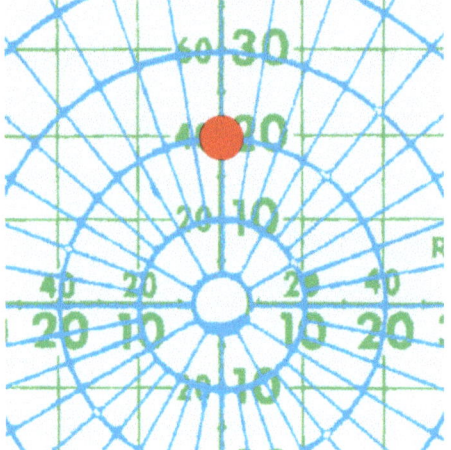

4. The Outer scale calculates TAS.
5. The Middle scale indicates drift.
6. The Inner transparent scale is where the user marks the wind direction and speed (wind velocity).

Definitions

Listed below are some definitions to review that will be used in this chapter.

Term	Abbreviation	Description
Flight Planned Track	**FPT**	Often referred to as just 'Track' or if you are in America it is often referred to as 'True course'. This is the planned track of the helicopter over the ground and represents the line drawn on the map.
Track Made Good	**TMG**	The actual track that the helicopter has flown over the ground. The TMG in a perfect world would exactly match the FPT but due to wind, pilot choice or pilot error the helicopter may not match the FPT. Where the TMG does not match the FPT there will be a Track Error (TE).
True Airspeed	**TAS**	The actual speed of the aircraft through the air. TAS and IAS are the same under ISA conditions at sea level. TAS and IAS may be different due to variations in temperature and pressure when not in ISA conditions and not at sea level.
Heading	**HDG**	It is the way the nose of the aircraft is pointing displayed on the magnetic compass.
Groundspeed	**G/S**	The actual speed of the aircraft over the ground.
Drift	**DFT**	The difference in degrees between HDG and TMG. Drift is *always* measured from the HDG to TMG in degrees Left or Right.
Track Error	**TE**	The angular difference in degrees between FPT and TMG. Measured *from* FPT to TMG. It is expressed in degrees left or right of FPT.

Understanding Wind on the Back Side

The Back Side of the Flight Computer is all about understanding wind and how it affects heading and groundspeed.

Conversely, while in flight, if the pilot already knows the heading and ground speed then unknown winds can be calculated.

An understanding of the wind triangle of velocities and the convention for writing and describing vectors is needed as foundation knowledge.

Triangle of velocities

The basis of dead reckoning navigation is the understanding of the wind triangle or more commonly referred to as the triangle of velocities.

The wind triangle is made up of three vectors. Knowing any two of the vectors allows the pilot to calculate the third.

The three vectors that make up the wind triangle are:

1. Heading and True Airspeed (HDG and TAS)
2. Flight Planned Track and Ground Speed (FPT and G/S) and
3. The Wind Velocity (W/V)

In some Countries (the USA in particular) the Heading (HDG) is sometimes referred to as the "*True Course*" and the Flight Planned Track (FPT) is sometimes referred to as the "*True Track*".

Revision of vectors

A vector is simply a graphic representation of velocity which is something that has speed and direction.

By convention, all plotted lines (or vectors) are designated by lines and arrow heads.

Heading

The heading vector is made up of the heading (the way the helicopter's nose is pointing) and the TAS (the actual speed of the aircraft through the air) and is identified by a line having a single arrow head indicating direction and the length of the line indicates speed.

Track

The track vector is made up of the track across the ground (Track Made Good - TMG) and the ground speed (the actual speed of the aircraft over the ground) and is identified by a line having a double arrow head indicating direction and the length of the line indicates speed.

W/V

The W/V or wind velocity vector is made up of the winds direction and speed and is identified by a line having a triple arrow head indicating direction and the length of the line indicates speed.

When the three vectors are put together they form the "**Triangle of Velocities**".

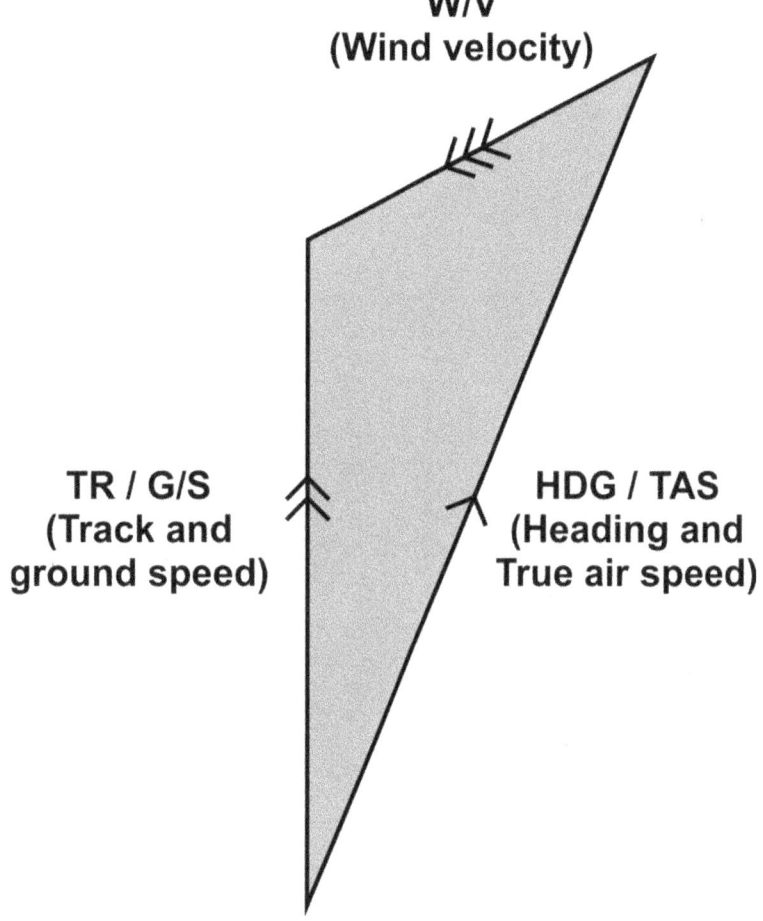

By convention, the triangle of velocities is drawn with the HDG/TAS as the primary vector, the W/V vector is always drawn from the top of the HDG/TAS vector and joins the top of the TR/GS vector.

Modified triangle

The backside of the flight computer is not big enough to fully draw the triangle of velocities. Instead the triangle of velocities is slightly modified.

By drawing a line from the HDG/TAS vector straight across to the top of the TR/GS vector a smaller triangle will be created on top of the original.

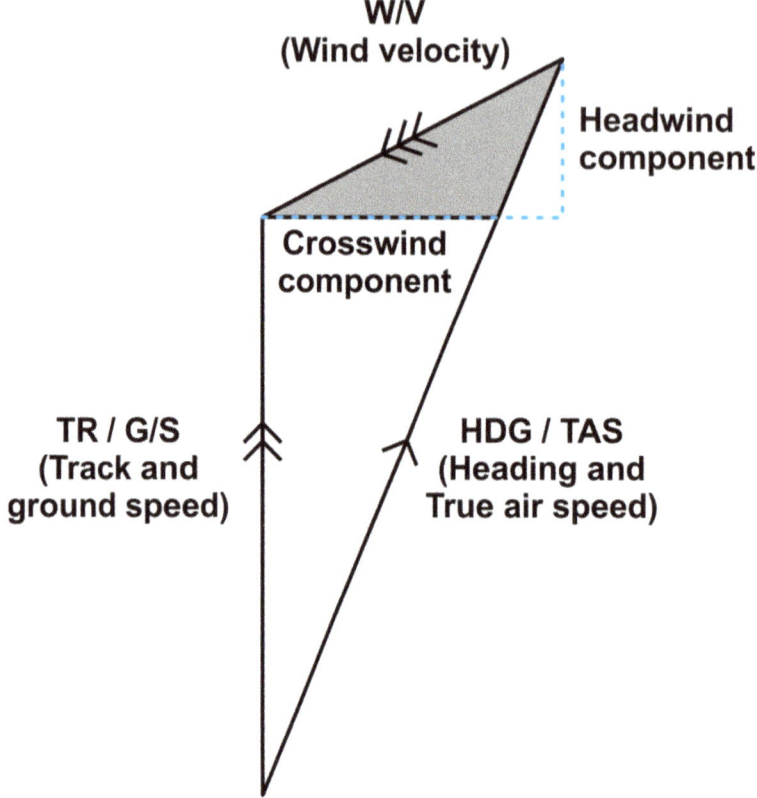

This is the triangle that fits on the backside of the Flight computer.

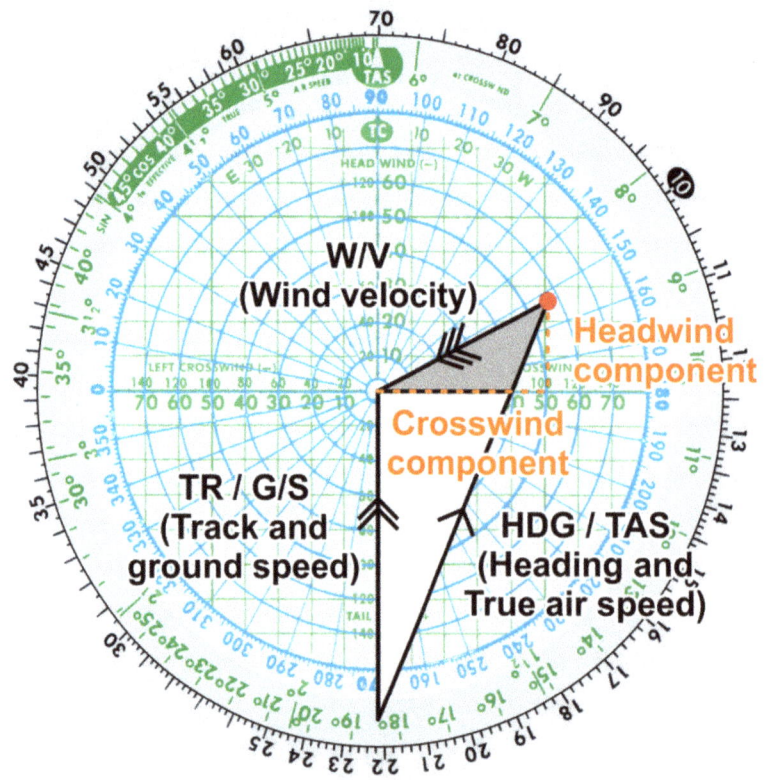

However instead of drawing vectors on the computer, all that is necessary is to place a small pencil mark at the spot that indicates the end of the wind vector.

The backside of the navigation computer has all of the remaining information printed on it so that you then simply have to rotate the transparent slider to line up the remaining information to get a result.

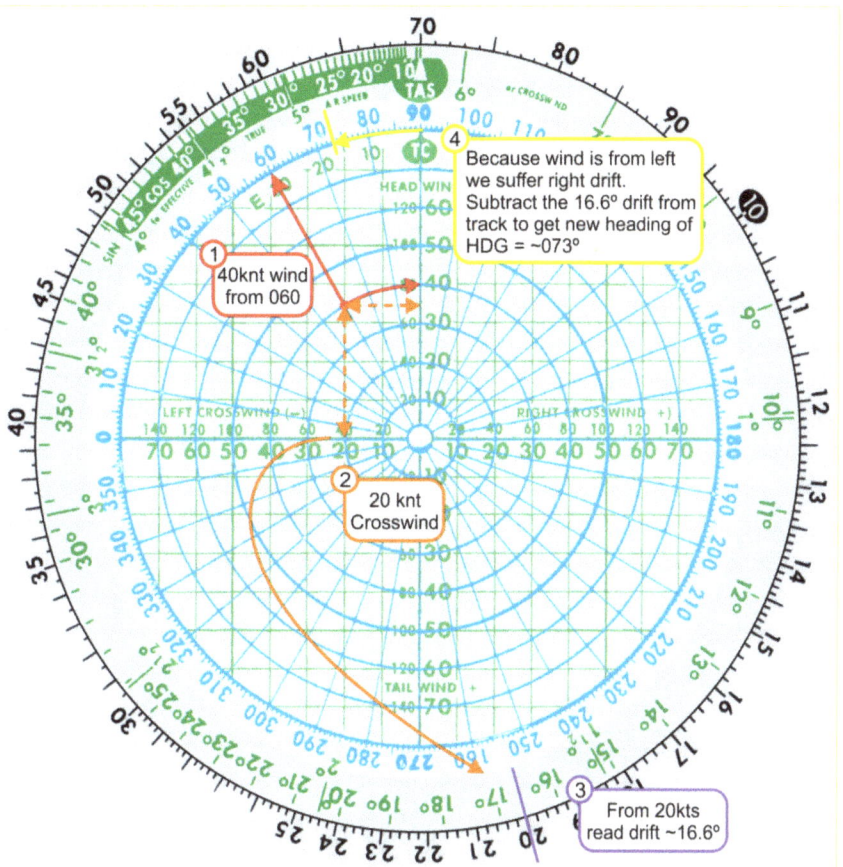

When planning a navigation flight the pilot will have access to the following information:

1. The required magnetic Track calculated from the map.
2. The prevailing W/V obtained from the weather forecast (and converted to magnetic).
3. The helicopter's TAS taken from the Flight Manual.

This information can then be entered on the back side of the Flight Computer in order to calculate the Magnetic Heading and the resulting Groundspeed for the planned flight.

The following exercises will take you through examples on how to use the back side of the Flight Computer and calculate unknown vectors.

Heading and Groundspeed Calculations

Prior to flight it will be necessary to calculate the **Magnetic Heading** and determine the **Groundspeed** for the track flown given the prevailing winds from a forecast.

Remember that all calculations here are done using degrees magnetic (°M) so variation will have to be applied to the wind and the track prior to placing the wind dot on the Flight Computer.

Given a **TAS of 100kts**, a **W/V 050/20 Magnetic** and a **FPT of 360° Magnetic,** calculate the **Heading** and **Groundspeed** using the 'wind side' of the Flight Computer.

Step	Action

FLIGHT COMPUTER BACK SIDE
NAVIGATION
INTERNATIONAL HELICOPTER THEORY

Step	Action
1	Clean any old markings from the transparent slider.
2	Draw a picture of the information on a piece of paper. 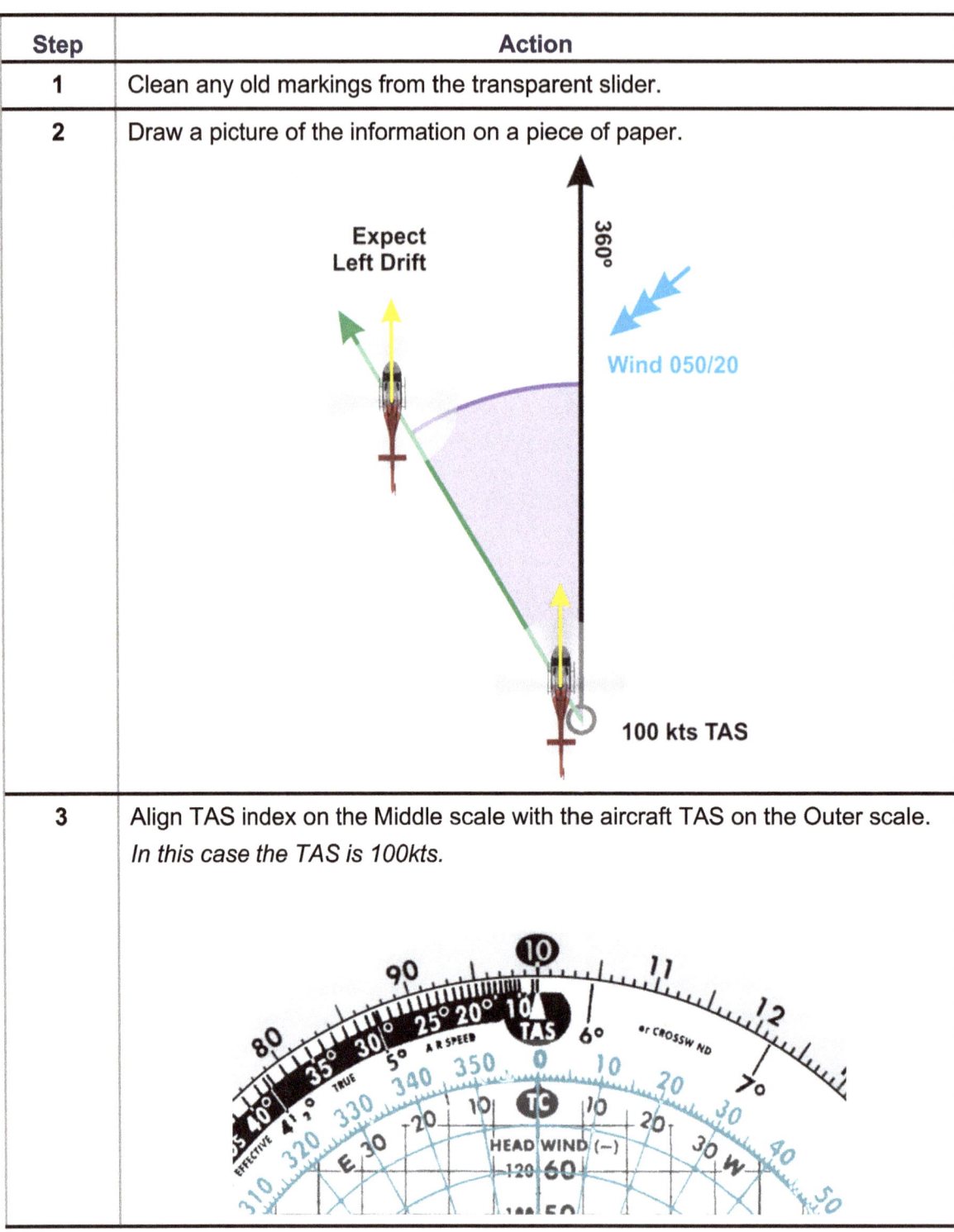
3	Align TAS index on the Middle scale with the aircraft TAS on the Outer scale. *In this case the TAS is 100kts.*

Step	Action
4	Align the Inner transparent wind scale with the TAS index. *In this case wind direction is 050 degrees magnetic.*
5	With a pencil or non permanent fine tip marker, place a dot or cross along the wind line up from the Centre Grommet to the position that corresponds to the given wind speed. *In this case the wind is 20kts.*
6	Rotate the Inner transparent scale until the Flight Planned Track (FPT) is positioned under the TAS index. *In this case the FPT is 360 degrees (shown as 0).*

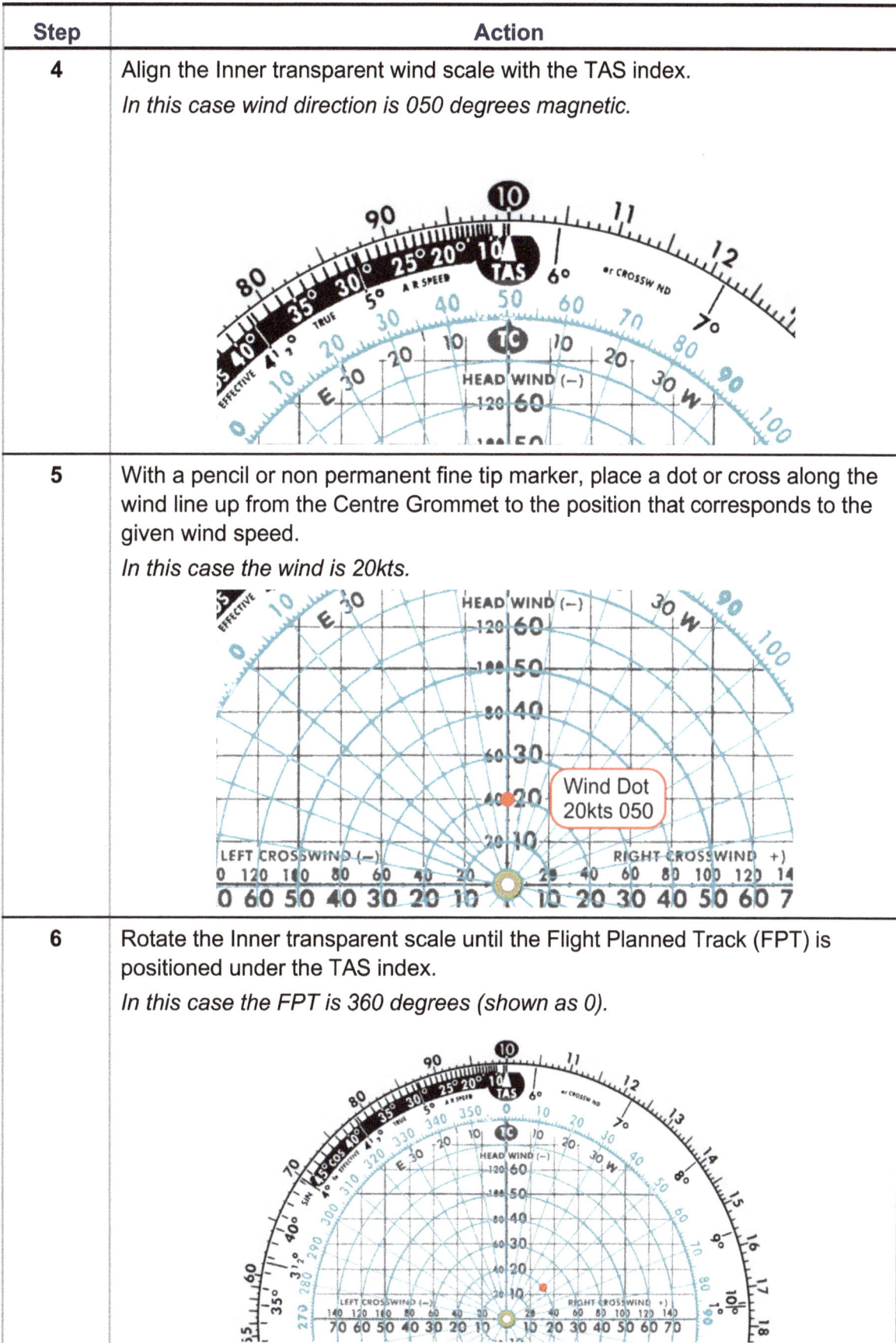

FLIGHT COMPUTER BACK SIDE
NAVIGATION — INTERNATIONAL HELICOPTER THEORY

Step	Action
7	Confirm that the wind on Inner transparent scale matches the wind drawn on your picture. *Expect Left Drift — 360° — Wind 050/20 — 100 kts TAS* In this case the wind is confirmed as coming from the right which will cause the helicopter to drift to the left.
8	To calculate G/S: Note the Headwind or Tail wind component. This is indicated on the Inner transparent scale where the pilot will interpolate between the grids. Anything above the Centre Grommet will be a headwind, anything below the Centre Grommet will be a tailwind. *In this case there is an approximate 12kt headwind component.* To calculate the G/S: TAS 100kts - 12kt headwind = **G/S 88kts**

Step	Action
9	To calculate the HDG: Note the drift and crosswind component.
	The crosswind component is indicated on the Inner transparent scale where the pilot will interpolate between the grids.
	Anything to the right (+) of the Centre Grommet will be indicating a **right** crosswind component and shall be added (+) to the FPT.
	Anything to the left (-) of the Centre Grommet will be indicating a **left** crosswind component and shall be taken away (-) from the FPT
	In this case there is a 15kt crosswind.
10	The drift component is indicated on the Middle scale.
	It is found by the pilot locating the crosswind component on the Outer scale and then looking inside to the Middle scale to note the degrees of drift.
	In this case there is a 15kt crosswind component which aligns with 8.75 degrees of drift. This is then rounded up to 9 degrees of left drift.

FLIGHT COMPUTER BACK SIDE
NAVIGATION — INTERNATIONAL HELICOPTER THEORY

Step	Action
11	With 9 degrees of drift with the wind on the right (+) of the Centre Grommet means the pilot must add (+) the drift to the FPT in order to obtain the new HDG. This logically agrees with the picture you have drawn. *In this case FPT360 + 9 Drift = new HDG009.*

Wind Velocity Calculations

Once airborne there may come a time where the pilot has to determine the Wind Velocity (W/V) as it may be different to that given in the weather forecast that your planning was relying on.

Given a **TAS** of **100kts**, a **TMG of 360°M**, a **G/S of 88kts** and **9 degrees Left drift**. Calculate the unknown **Wind Velocity** using the 'wind side' of the Flight Computer.

Step	Action
1	Clean any old markings from the transparent slider.
2	Draw a picture of the information on a piece of paper. 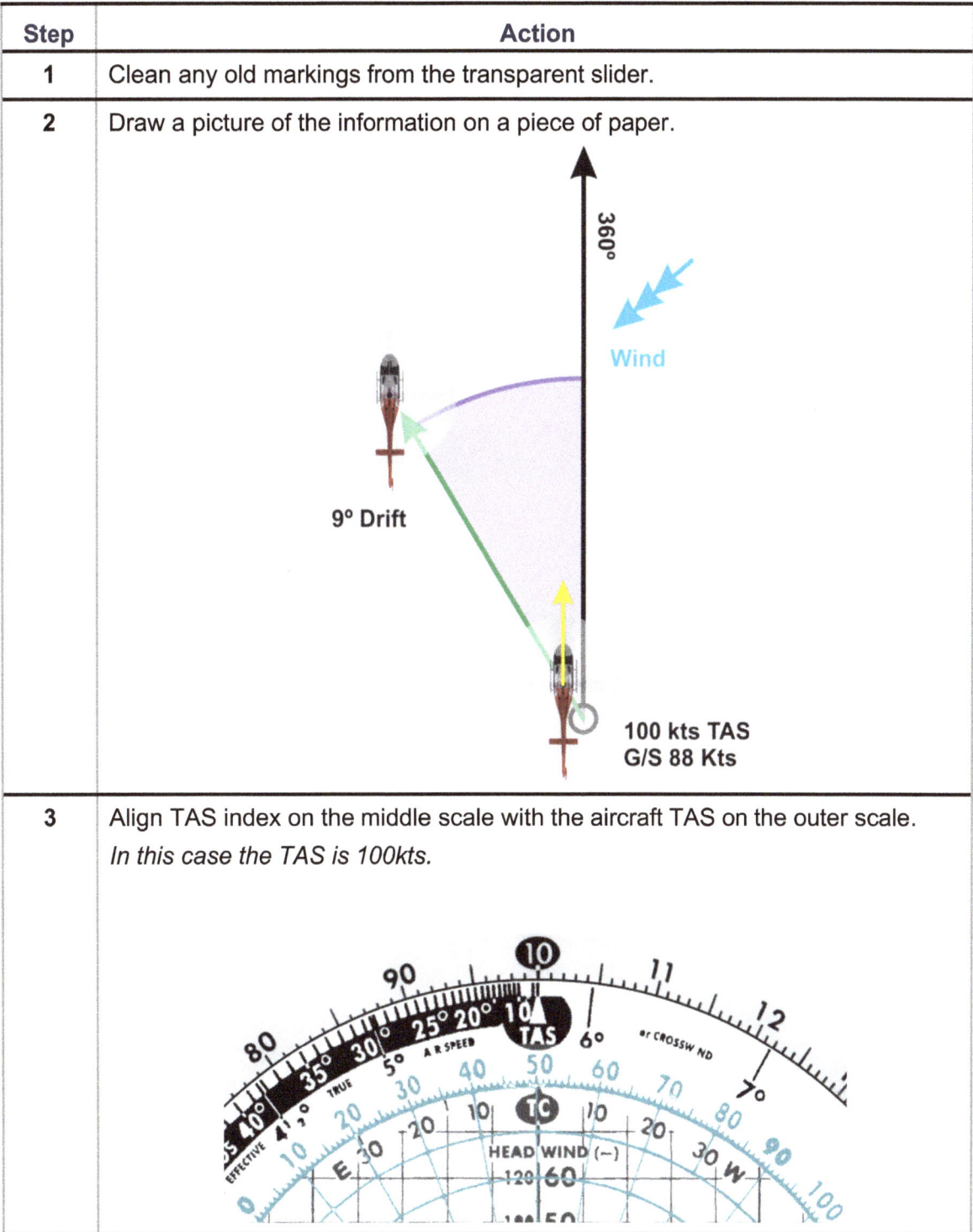
3	Align TAS index on the middle scale with the aircraft TAS on the outer scale. *In this case the TAS is 100kts.*

FLIGHT COMPUTER BACK SIDE
NAVIGATION — INTERNATIONAL HELICOPTER THEORY

Step	Action
4	Rotate the Inner scale until the Track Made Good (TMG) is positioned under the TAS index. *In this case the TMG is 360 degrees.*
5	To mark the unknown wind on the Inner scale, complete the following steps: (5) Calculate the headwind or tailwind component by adding or subtracting the G/S from the TAS. In this case given TAS100kts and G/S88kts. 100 – 88 = 12kts of headwind. (6) Calculate the crosswind component by referencing the known drift. In this case locate 9 degrees of drift on the Middle scale and look out to the Outer scale. This will indicate 15.8kts which is rounded up to 16kts of crosswind. 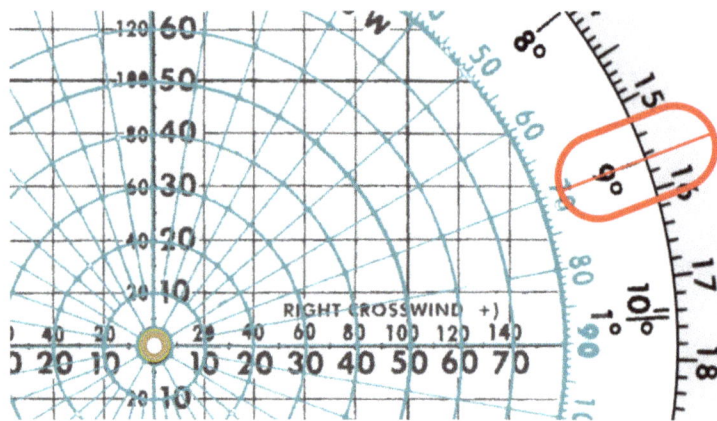 Note: If the 9 degrees of Left drift is causing the helicopter to drift left of the FPT then the wind must be from the **right!**

Step	Action
6	The unknown wind can be found at the intersection of the 12kt headwind and 16kt crosswind values on the Inner scale. Draw a line horizontally from the 12kt mark to the right of the Centre Grommet. Draw a line vertically up from the 16kt mark to the right of the Centre Grommet.
7	Rotate the Inner transparent scale until the new wind dot is aligned under the TAS index. In this case this will now indicate a known wind of 050/20kts.

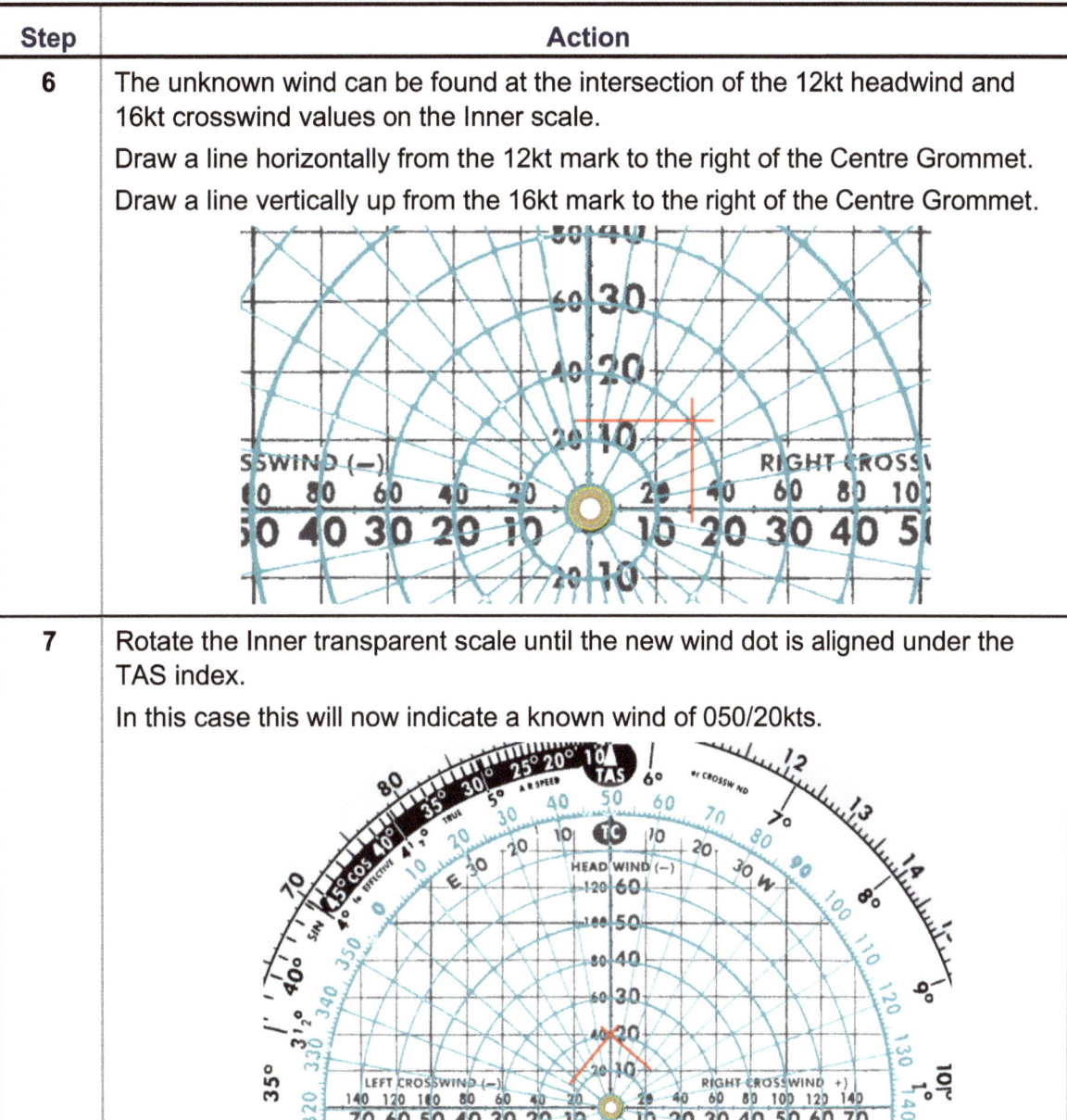

6 Vertical Measurement

In aviation pilots rely on accurate information with regards to altitudes, heights and elevations for flight planning and safety. It is important therefore that the pilot is able to differentiate between them.

The following table revises the terms used in vertical measurement.

Definitions

Term	Definition
Altitude	The vertical distance of an aircraft measured in feet or meters **A**bove **M**ean **S**ea Level (**AMSL**).
Height	The vertical distance of an aircraft measured in feet or meters **A**bove **G**round **L**evel (**AGL**)
Elevation	The vertical distance of the ground measured in feet or meters **A**bove **M**ean **S**ea level (**AMSL**).
QNE	QNE represents the Pressure Altitude for the day. By selecting 1013Mb on the Altimeter subscale, the Altimeters main scale will display Pressure Altitude.
QNH	QNH represents the pressure at MSL for the day. When entered into the Altimeter subscale, the Altimeters main scale will display Altitude.
QFE	QFE represents the pressure at the current elevation for the day. When entered into the Altimeter subscale, the Altimeters main scale will read zero (0) on the ground at the location the QFE is set for and then height above that elevation when flying.
Flight Level	At higher altitudes (above 10,000 feet) all aircraft will operate at a Flight Level and not an Altitude. To determine a Flight Level, on passing through 10,000 feet on the Area QNH the pilot will alter the Altimeters subscale to read 1013Mb. Once above 11,000 feet all subsequent Flight Levels will now be separated based on Pressure Altitude and not actual Area QNH. Flight Levels are not normally used by helicopters as they do not fly that high.

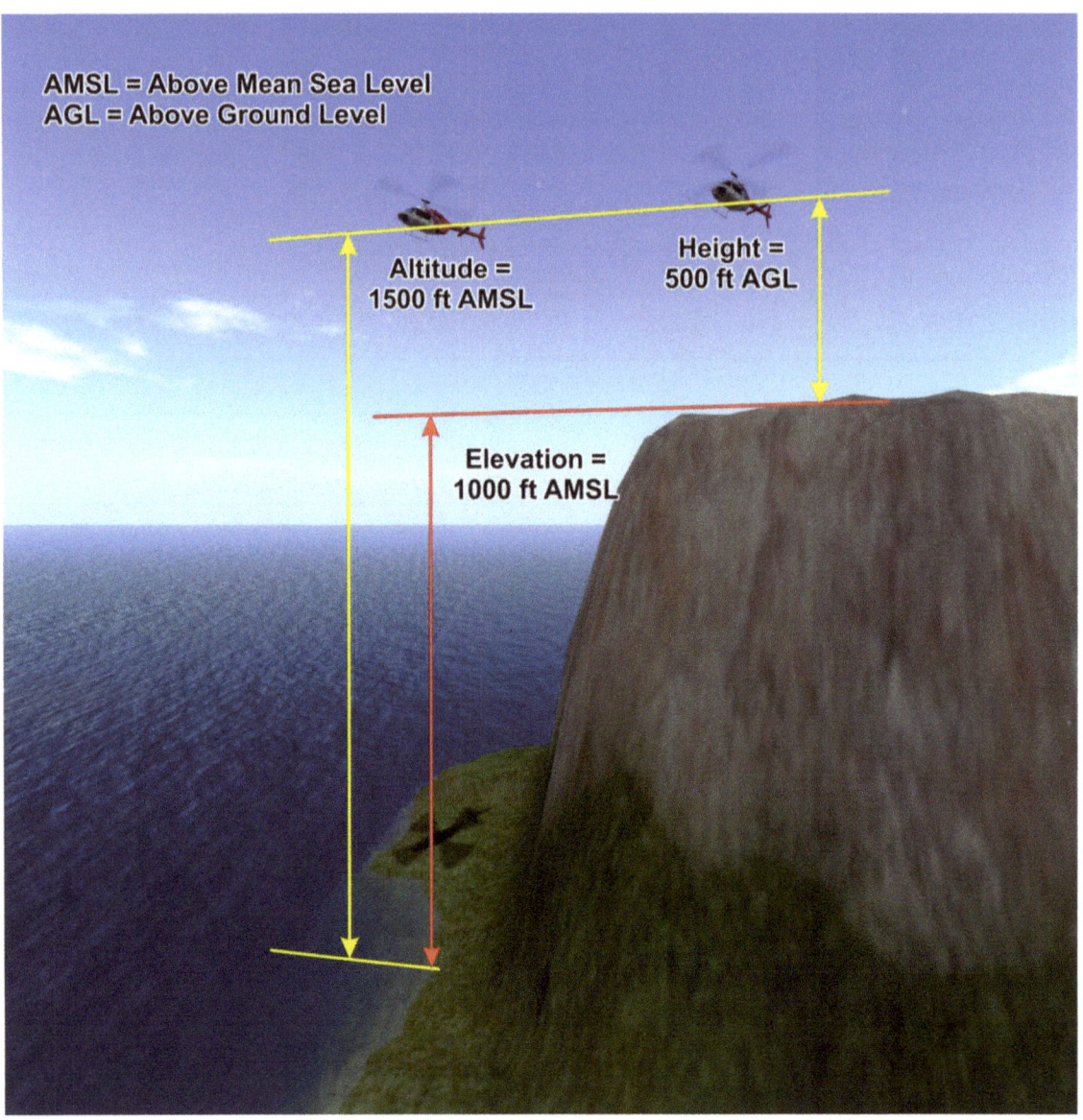

Altimetry Problems

Navigating a helicopter is done in the three dimensional space. This means that not only does the pilot need to know the direction and speed the helicopter is travelling but also how far from the surface of the earth it is.

This is important so the pilot can manage:

1. Terrain clearance
2. Separation from other aircraft and
3. Helicopter performance

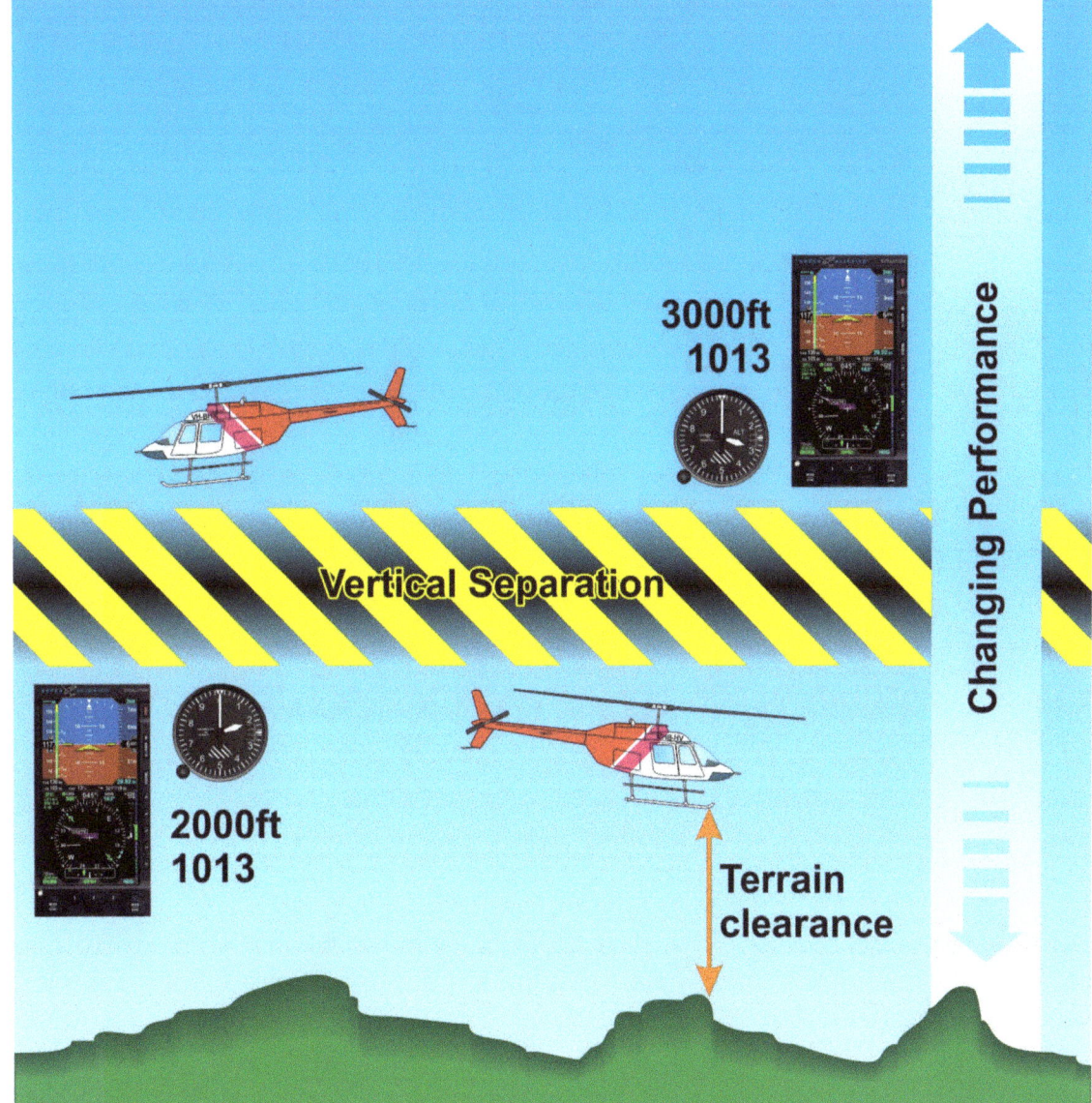

Variations Mean Sea Level Pressure

The standard atmospheric pressure at Sea Level according to the **I**nternational **S**tandard **A**tmosphere (**ISA**) is 1013Mb with an Outside Air Temperature (OAT) of 15 degrees Celsius.

Unfortunately, these conditions very rarely exist as pressure systems move across the country. This means that atmospheric pressure and temperature can change rapidly and often. What the pressure and temperature was five (5) minutes, one (1) hour or one (1) day ago may be different to what it is now.

Below are several synoptic charts showing the pressure changes across Australia over a 24-hour period.

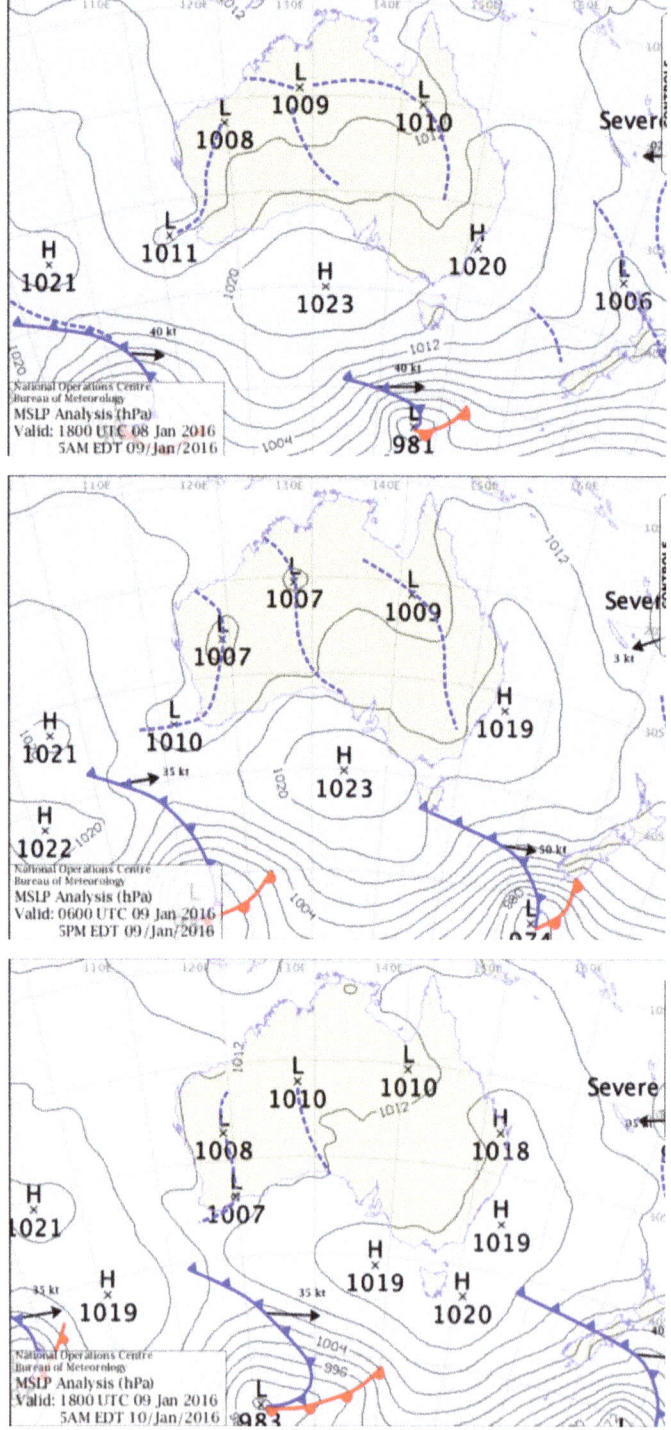

This means that the Altitude displayed on the Altimeter can vary for the same Height Above Mean Sea Level unless the pilot alters the QNH subscale on the Altmeter to take into account for the variations in atmospheric pressure.

Adjusting Analogue Altimeter QNH

Adjusting Aspen Altimeter Barometric scale

Example
Consider Gympie Airport located in Queensland Australia. Gympie Airport has an Elevation Above Mean Sea Level of 260 feet.
If the helicopter is sitting on the ground at Gympie Airport and the QNH for the day is 1013Mb then the Altimeter will show 260 feet.

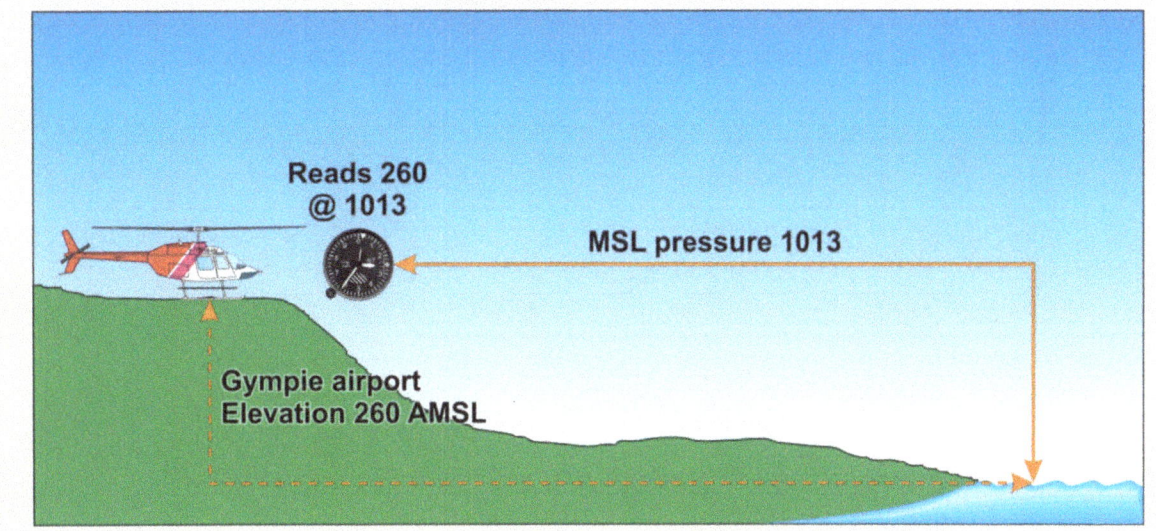

As the pressure system moves across Gympie then the prevailing pressure may change. Lets assume that the pressure drops to 1009Mb as an area of low pressure moves across Gympie.

Pressure changes from 1013Mb

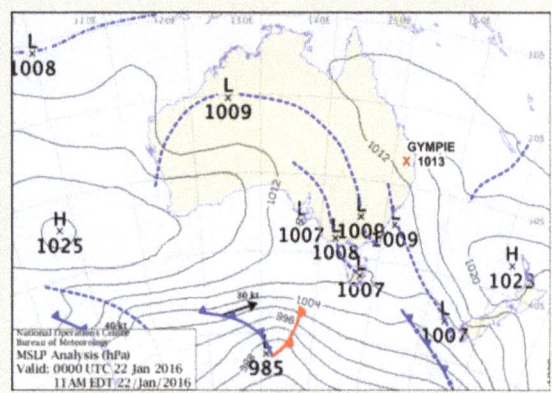

Drops to 1009Mb

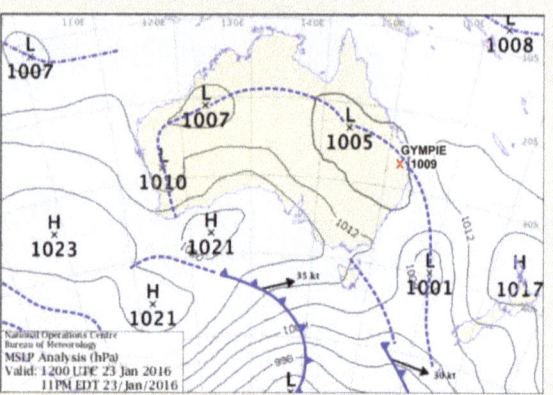

This means the Altimeter will no longer read correctly unless it is adjusted for the new MSL pressure of 1009.

If the actual pressure is 1009Mb, and with 1013 still set on the subscale, height shows 380ft

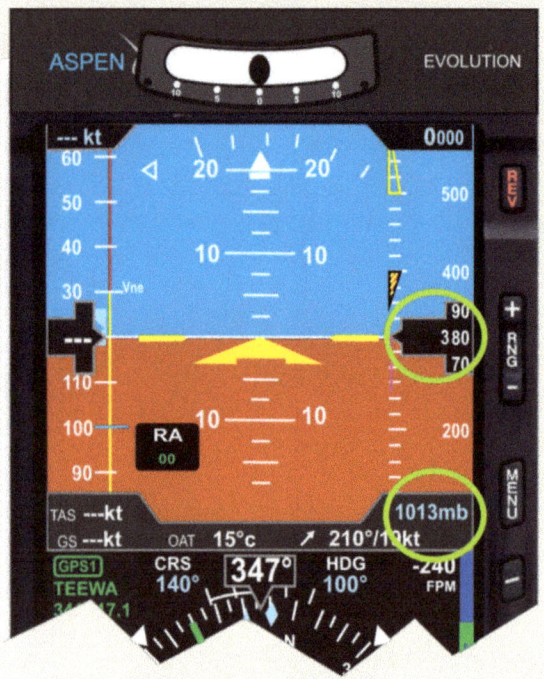

With 1009 set on the subscale, height shows 260ft

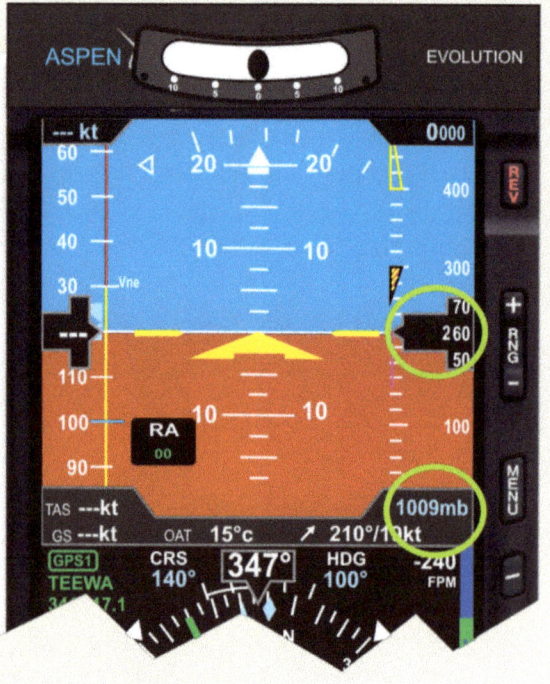

Effects of variation in MSL Pressure

The greatest safety we have when flying an aircraft is *vertical* separation. Therefore, it is important that we understand what may affect the reading of the altimeter and what may happen if we have a different setting on our altimeter subscale compared to another aircraft.

Pilots should be aware that changes in atmospheric conditions will effect the reading of the altimeter to the pilot.

Example
You depart Sunshine Coast Airport (YBSU) where the local QNH is 1015. You now fly to Hamilton Island which is approximately 500NM away where the local QNH is 1005.
In effect you have flown from an area of high pressure to an area of lower pressure. Your altimeter, if not reset to the new local subscale setting at Hamilton Island, will give an incorrect reading of your actual altitude at Hamilton Island.

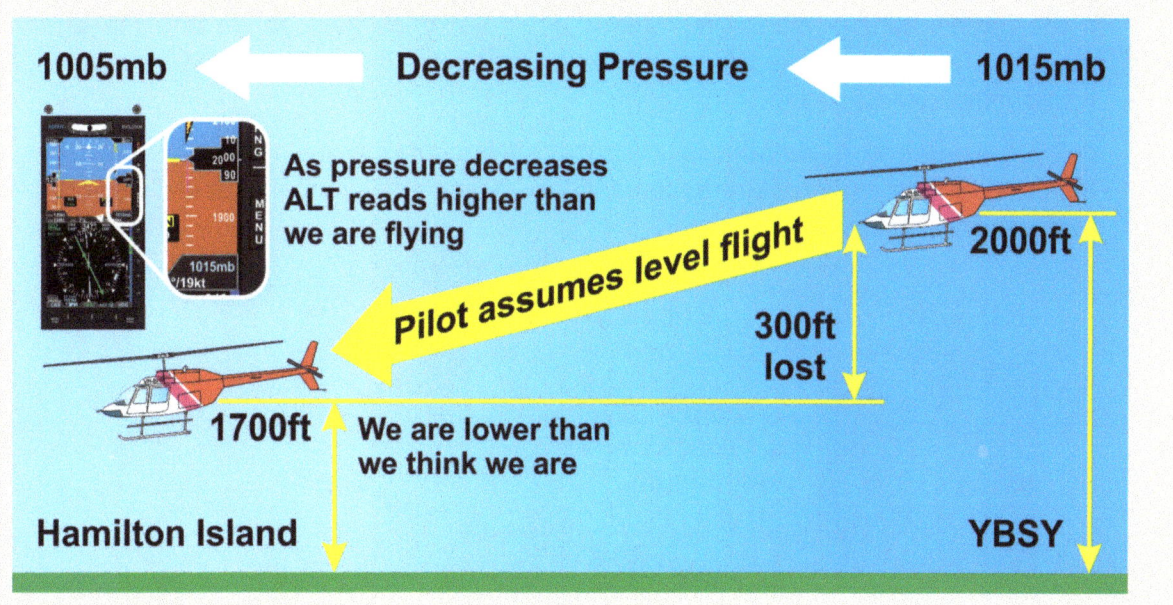

The rule to remember is

If flying from an area of high pressure to an area of low pressure (without adjusting your subscale setting) your altimeter will overread and therefore you will slowly be decending in order to maintain a constant altimeter setting. (In effect, you will phsyically be lower than what the altimeter is telling you because it is no longer set to the correct pressure setting.)

If flying from an area of low pressure to an area of high pressure (without adjusting your subscale setting) your altimeter will underread and therefore you will slowly be climbing in order to maintain a constant altimeter setting. (In effect, you will physically be higher than what the altimeter is telling you because it is no longer set to the correct pressure setting.)

Remember the 2 Chinese gentlemen Hi Lo Hi and Lo Hi Lo they stated:

From Hi to Lo look out below because the altimeter will be reading Hi.

From Lo to Hi lookout high because the altimeter will be reading Lo.

Knowing this rule allows the pilot to guesstimate your answer and then cross check the actual answer to confirm that you have gone the right way.

Example
If going from an area with a QNH (pressure) of 1010hPa (low pressure) to an area with a QNH of 1015 (Higher pressure) and you do not adjust the altimeter subscale but you maintain a constant altimeter reading (for example 1000ft) then the altimeter will actually be under reading. You will actually be climbing in order to maintain the constant 1000ft altimeter setting. Therefore you are going to be Hi.

The Effect of Temperature on Pressure

Temperature will affect pressure as if the helicopter was actually changing altitude.

If the temperature is increasing, then the air becomes less dense and the pressure will decrease. As the temperature increases the helicopter "thinks" it is actually going higher and performance will decrease.

If the temperature is decreasing, then the air becomes more dense and the pressure will increase. As the temperature decreases the helicopter "thinks" it is actually going lower and performance will increase.

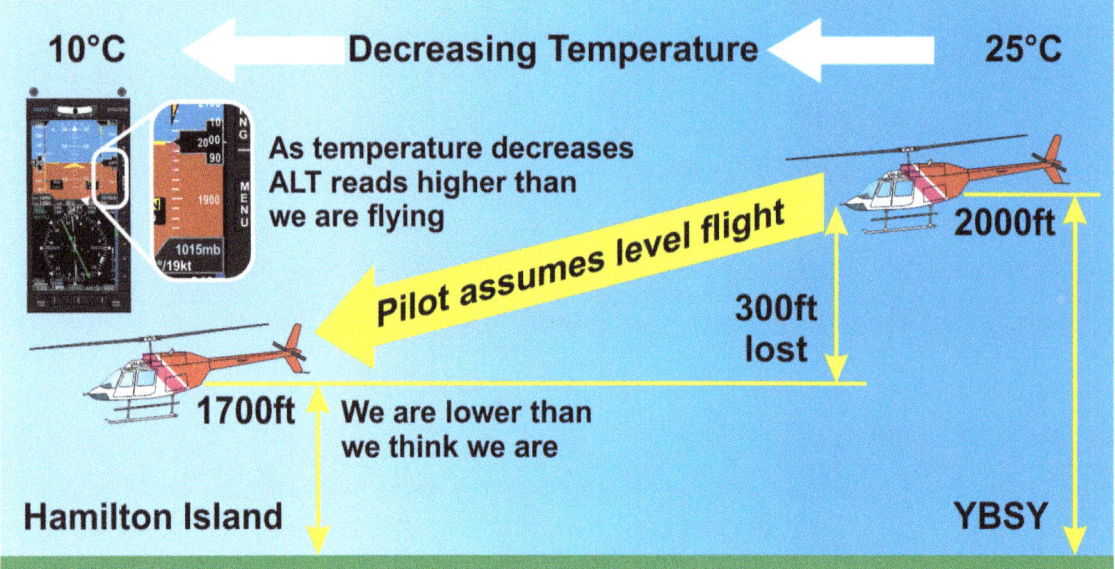

Because temperature affects pressure, the same Hi to Lo and Lo to Hi rule can be assumed for changes in temperature.

That is:

From Hi (temperature) to Lo (temperature) look out below because the altimeter will be reading Hi.

From Lo (temperature) to Hi (temperature) lookout high because the altimeter will be reading Lo.

Adjusting the Subscale of an Altimeter

Given an elevation of 1000ft and a local QNH of 1005hPa, calculate the reading on the altimeter if the altimeter subscale setting is adjusted to 1010hPa.

Step	Action
1	How many hPa does the pilot need to adjust the subscale on the altimeter to make it read the new setting?
	The original local QNH setting of 1005hPa gave an altimeter reading of 1000ft
	If the altimeter subscale is wound **UP** 5hPa it will now read 1010hPa
2	What happens to the altimeter if the subscale is adjusted?
	If the subscale winds UP the altitude goes UP
	If the subscale winds DOWN the altitude goes DOWN
	In this example the subscale was wound UP so the Altitude indication increases showing a higher altitude.
3	For each hPa the subscale is adjusted, the altimeter reading will change by 30ft.
	If the original elevation was 1000ft then 5hPa x 30ft/hPa = 150ft
	1000+150 equals the new altimeter reading of 1150ft
	The following formula describes this:
	((Subscale Setting - Local QNH) X 30') + Elevation=New altimeter reading

Pressure Height (Altitude)

Refer to Performance and Loading course for detailed information.

According to the ISA we know that at MSL, the pressure is equal to 1013hPa.

Because atmospheric conditions vary from day to day influencing our helicopter's performance, we are constantly referring to what we call **Pressure Height, or Pressure Altitude.** This is the height or altitude where the pressure 1013hPa is said to exist. Also known as QNE.

Density Heights (Altitude)

Refer to Performance and Loading course for detailed information.

According to the ISA we know that at MSL, the temperature is equal to 15°C.

Density Height or Density Altitude is the Pressure Height corrected for temperature variances away from ISA conditions of 15°C.

7 Advanced Calculations

Introduction

Before and during a flight there may come a time when the pilot is required to make some advanced calculations in order to ensure:

- a helicopter can safely make a landing site,
- the correct climb and descent profiles are maintained when operating:
  - within or close to controlled airspace,
  - at an aerodrome and having to comply with runway directions, and
- crosswind components can be applied to performance calculations.

The advanced calculations covered include:

1. The 1 in 60 rule
2. Runway crosswind components
3. Rate of Climb and Rate of Descent
4. Equal Time Point (ETP) / Critical Point (CP)
5. Point of No Return (PNR)

The 1 in 60 Rule

The 1 in 60 rule is a technique used by the pilot to determine a new heading to regain the flight planned track once it is discovered that the helicopter is off track. It is a handy and easy to use method able to be applied while in flight.

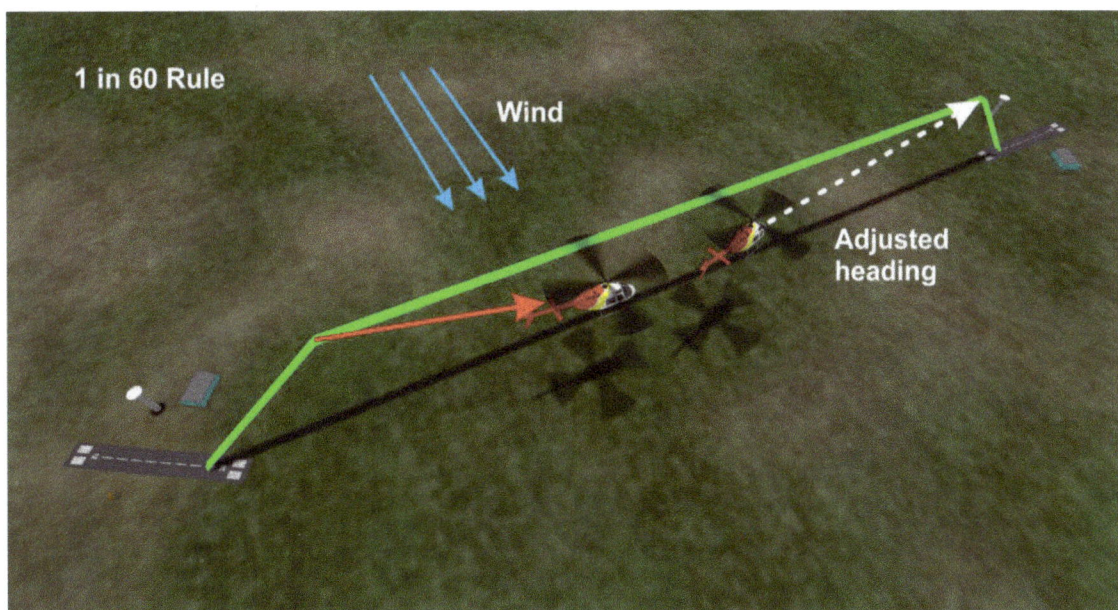

Runway crosswind components

When taking off and landing onto a runway the helicopter pilot may not have a choice but to manage a crosswind or a tail wind component. Understanding how this affects performance will require the calculation of the crosswind component. Although not commonly used, as helicopters typically are able to manoeuvre to maintain a headwind component, it is a requirement to have an understanding of the calculation when flying larger helicopters.

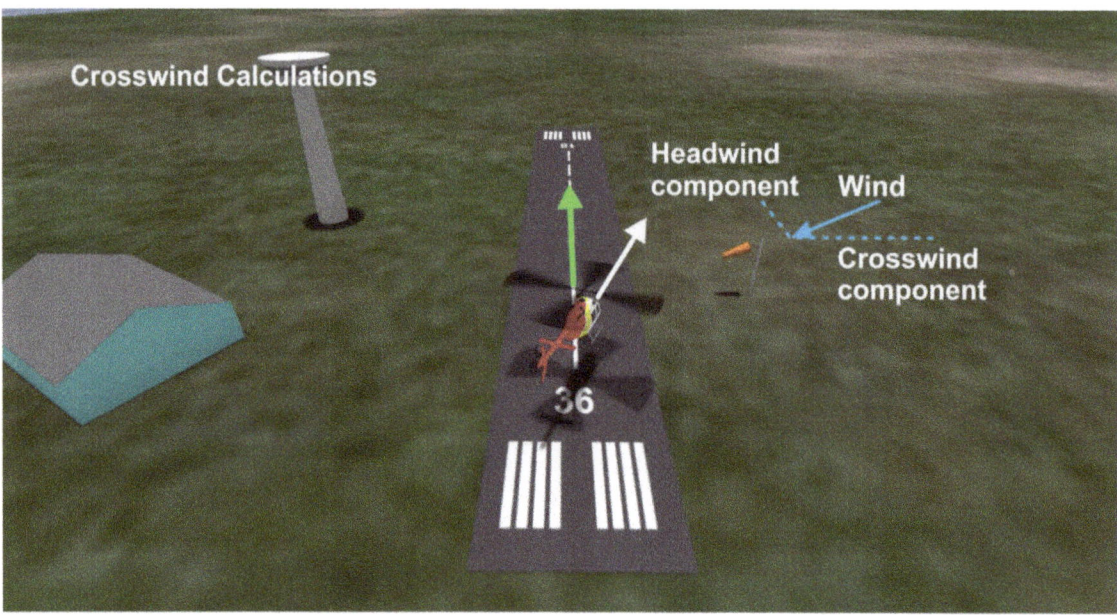

Climbs and Descents

When operating in or around controlled airspace it is important that you are able to adhere to the clearances given by ATC. When climbing and descending there will come a time when the helicopter will be in close proximity to the DME or Controlled Airspace Steps.

Being able to calculate a Rate of Climb (ROC) or a Rate of Descent (ROD) that keeps the helicopter within 500 feet of the Controlled Airspace steps is an important calculation to be able to make.

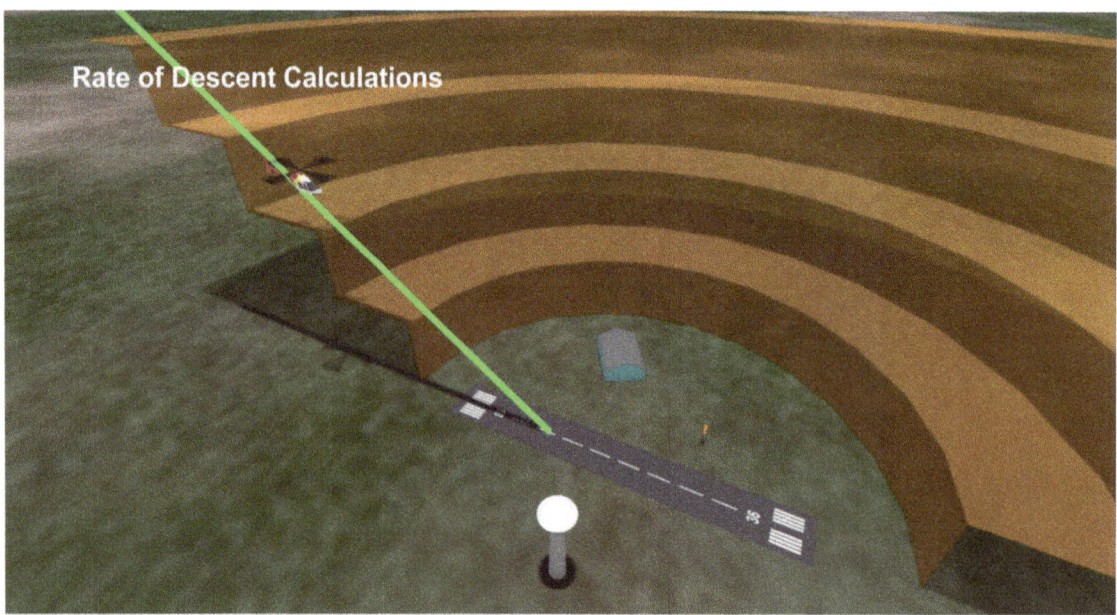

Equal Time Point

Also referred to as the Critical Point (CP), it is a calculation that is handy on very long flights. The pilot will need to calculate where along the Flight Planned Track (FPT) the helicopter is, at a point that, going on to the destination will take the same amount of time as turning around and returning to the departure point.

This helps the pilot make quick decisions in an emergency as prior to reaching the Equal Time Point he knows it is faster to turn around and go home. If past the Equal Time Point then he knows that it is faster to continue on to the destination.

This calculation will be affected by wind so the Equal Time Point has nothing to do with the distance travelled across the ground but everything to do with the amount of time in the air.

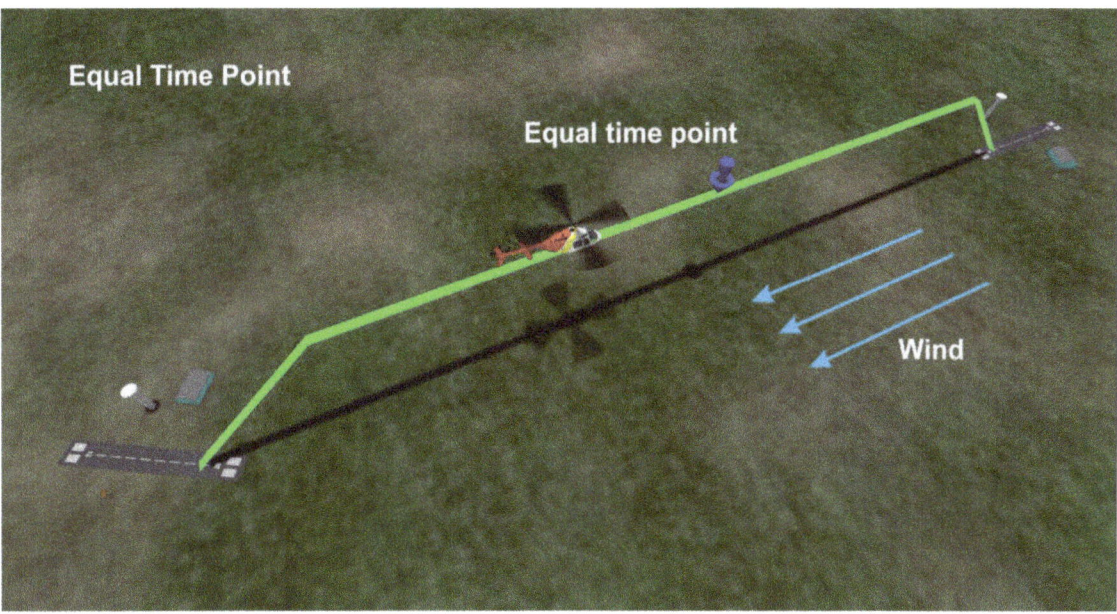

Point of No Return (PNR)

The Point of No Return (PNR) is very handy on long flights. It is the furthest distance the helicopter can travel away from its departure point before having to return to the same point or another airfield with all reserve fuel and holding fuel intact. The PNR calculation is all about fuel management.

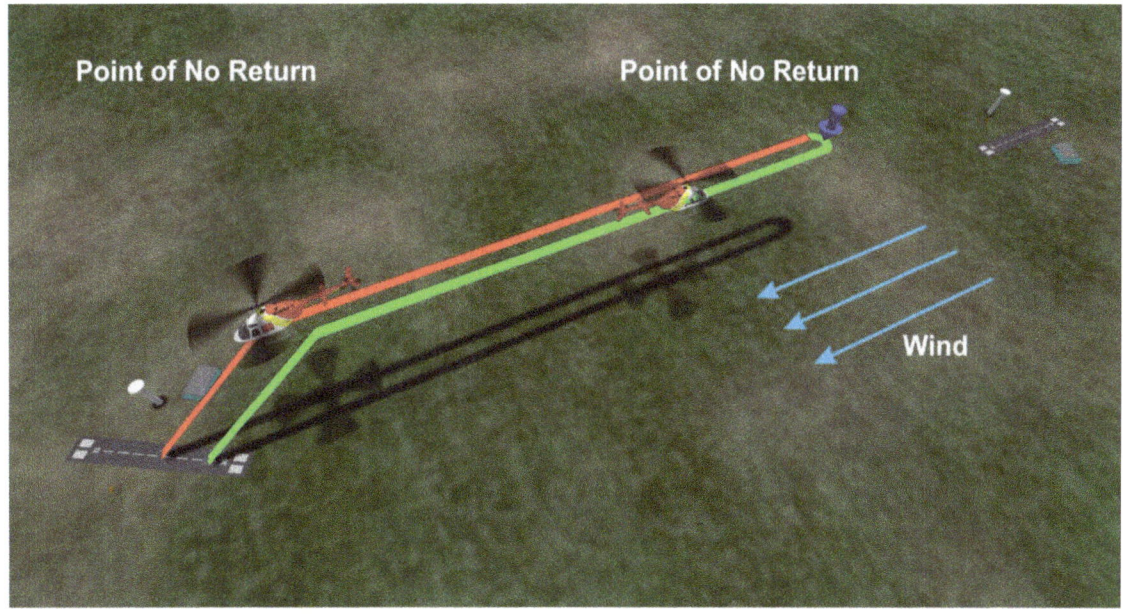

8 The 1 in 60 Rule

What is the 1 in 60 Rule

The 1 in 60 Rule is a simple method of **estimating angles** and using some basic geometry and math to quickly and easily calculate heading changes when navigating.

Calculating Heading Changes

Prior to the use of Radio Navigation Aids (GPS, VOR, NDB) and particularly on long haul flights only using Dead Reckoning (DR) navigation techniques; pilots and navigators would have to manually calculate a new Heading (HDG) using the following information:

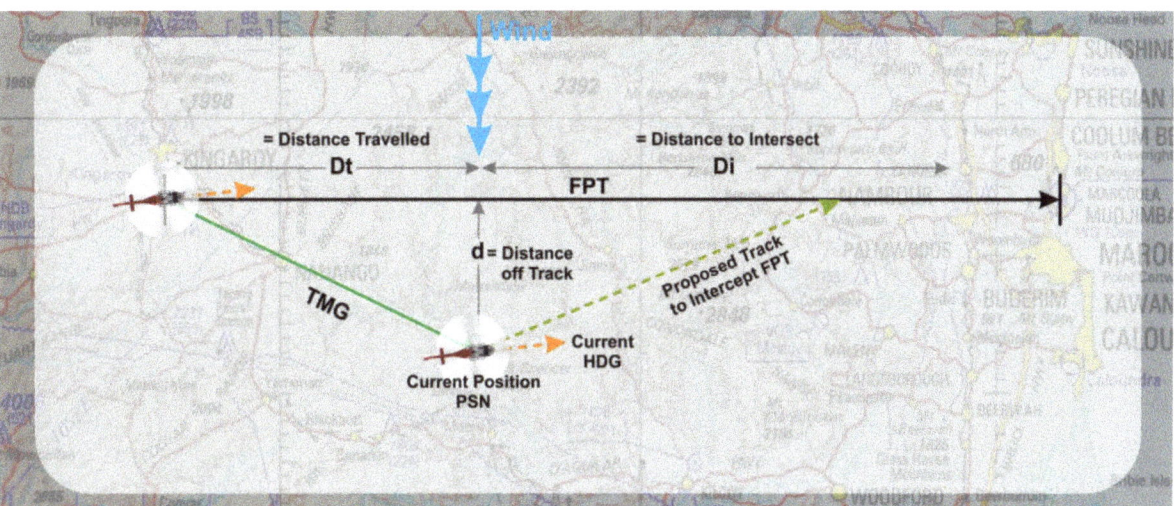

1. The Flight Planned Track (**FPT**) which can be obtained from the map or Flight Plan
2. The helicopters current position (**PSN**). This is done by making a positive position fix on the map.
3. The equivalent distance travelled (**Dt**) from the Departure point 90 degrees to the FPT from the helicopters current position.
4. The distance (**d**) of the helicopter off the original FPT
5. The equivalent distance to go to intercept the FPT (**Di**) taken 90 degrees to the FPT from the helicopters current position.
6. The current compass **HDG** being maintained by the pilot while trying to maintain the original FPT.

Using this information, and by applying the 1 in 60 Rule, a pilot is able to then calculate heading changes.

What is the 1 in 60 Rule

The 1 in 60 Rule is based on an assumption that:

*Over a distance of **60NM**,
if the helicopter is off track by **1NM**,
then the Track Error (TE) angle will be equal to **1°**.*

*If the helicopter is off track by **1NM**,
and the helicopter flies a Closing Angle (CA) equal to **1°**
then the helicopter will intercept the FPT at **60nm**.*

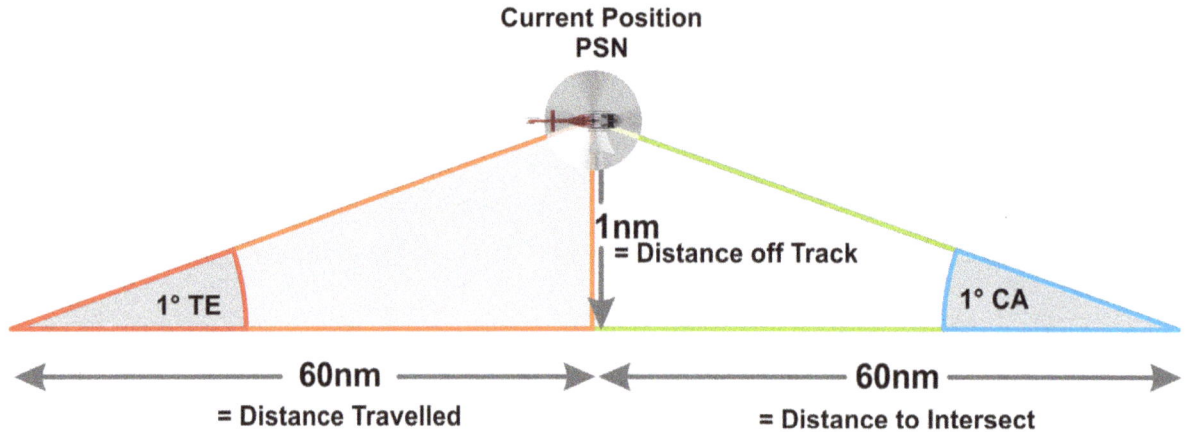

Hence the term 1 in 60:

The 1 in 60 Rule

1NM off track will equal 1 degree of angle in 60NM

Extending the 1 in 60 Rule of Thumb

It follows then that if the helicopter is off track by

- 5NM over a distance of 60NM the TE will equal 5°
- 10NM over a distance of 60NM the TE will equal 10°
- 15NM over a distance of 60NM the TE will equal 15° and so on.

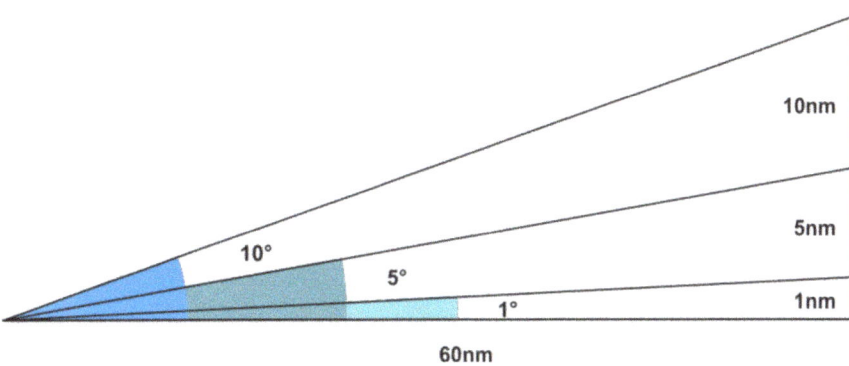

Additionally, it follows that if the helicopter is off track by

- 5NM and there is still 60NM to go to the destination the CA will equal 5°
- 10NM and there is still 60NM to go to the destination the CA will equal 10°
- 15NM and there is still 60NM to go to the destination the CA will equal 15° and so on.

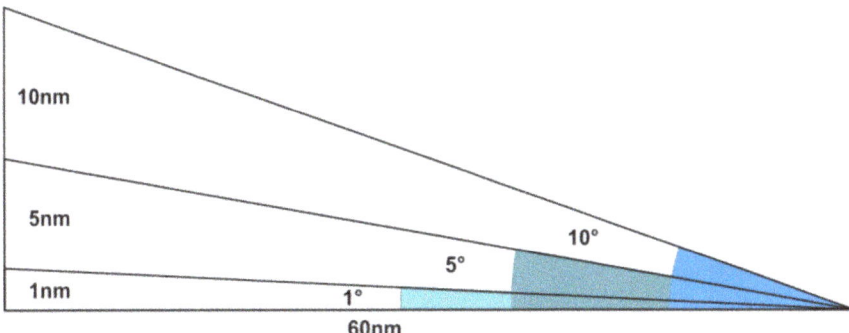

THE 1 IN 60 RULE

Applying Ratios to the 1 in 60 Rule

A pilot can apply ratios to the 1 in 60 Rule.

For example, if the helicopter is 4NM off track and has 30NM to go to arrive at the destination that would be the same as 8NM off track in 60NM which gives a Closing Angle (CA) of 8°.

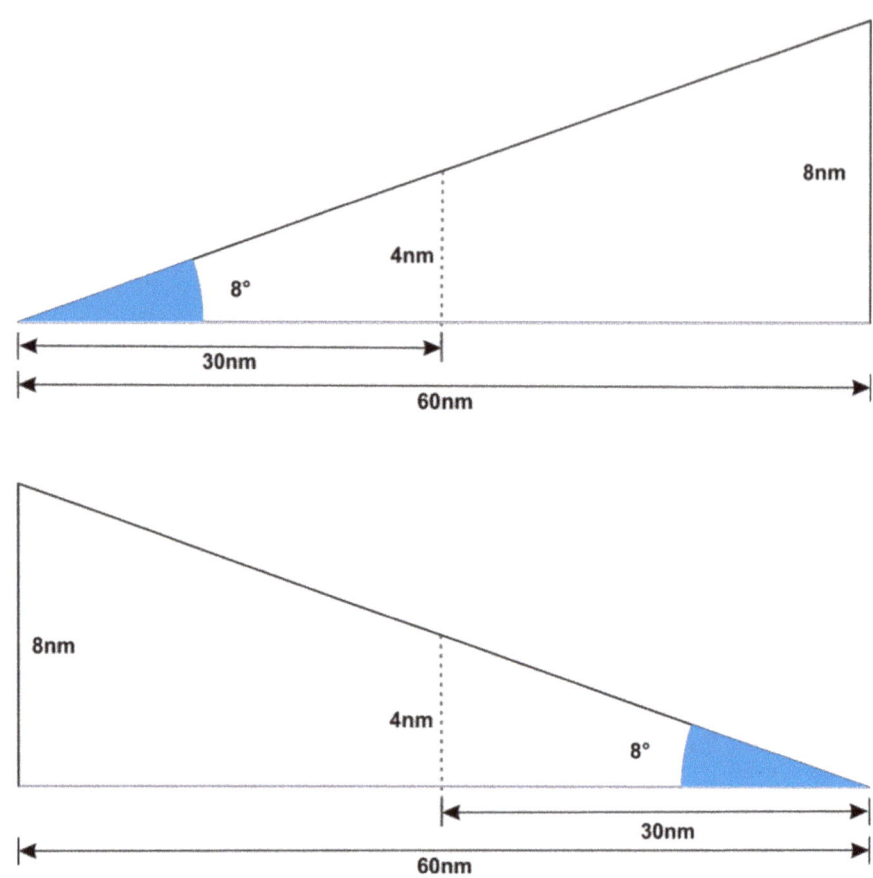

It follows then that if the helicopter is off track by:

- 5NM over a distance of 30NM the TE will equal 10°
- 2NM over a distance of 15NM the TE will equal 8°
- 8NM over a distance of 30NM the TE will equal 16°
- 4NM over a distance of 30NM the TE will equal 8°
- 4NM over a distance of 40NM the TE will equal 6°

Applying the 1 in 60 Rule

Using the 1 in 60 Rule, we can calculate:

- A heading correction (Track Error) to counter drift allowing the helicopter to now parallel the FPT, and
- A heading correction (Closing Angle) to close in and return to the original FPT.

A summary is shown in the diagram below.

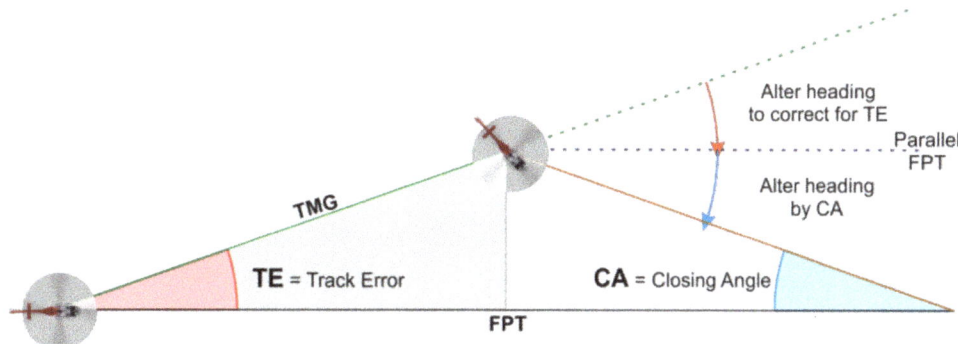

Changing the size of the Closing Angle will change where the helicopter will intercept the FPT.

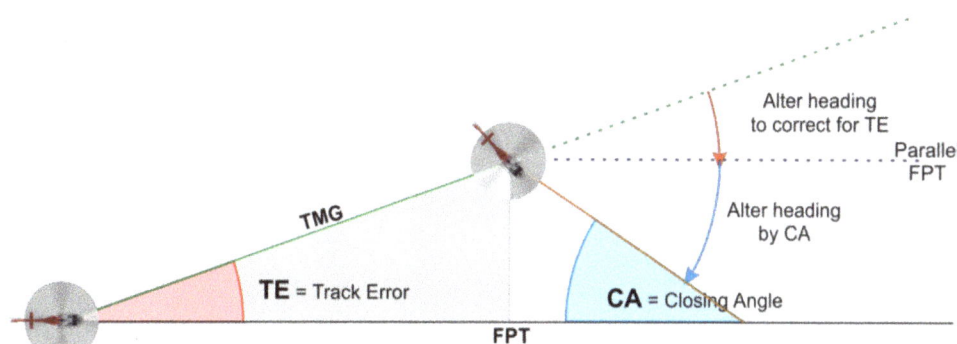

Applying the 1 in 60 Rule: A Simple Example

Example:

A pilot planned a flight with a FPT of 090. Wind was forecast from the left, and the pilot planned a HDG of 085 to counter the effect of wind, to maintain a track of 090.

However, after travelling for 30 NM, the pilot has drifted to the right due to a stronger wind than planned for.

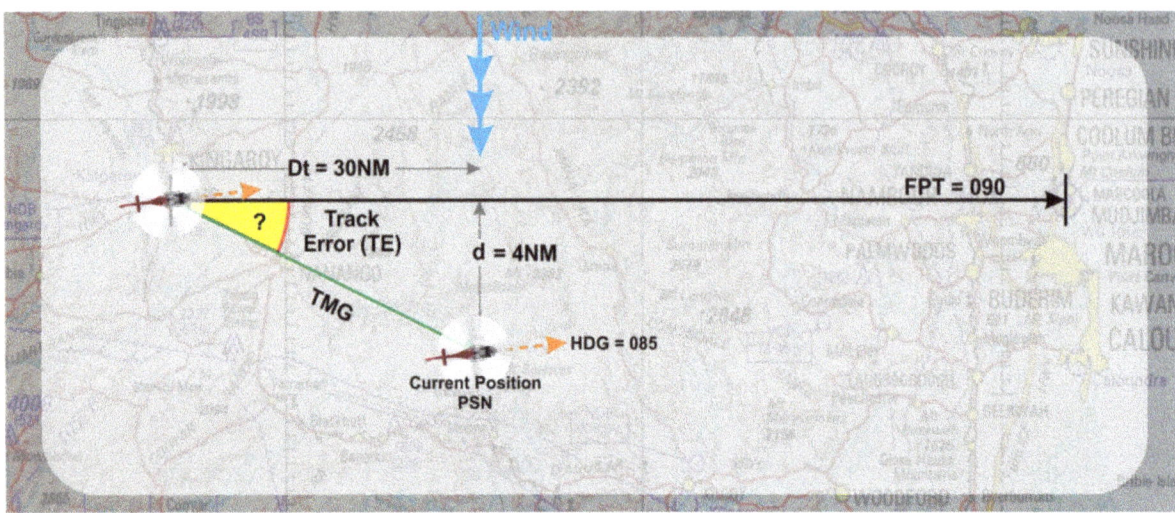

The pilot needs to calculate:

- **Track Error (TE)** – to give the HDG correction required to counter the DFT caused by the stronger wind, and
- **Closing Angle (CA)** - the HDG correction required to close in on and intercept the FPT, to get back on track.

Calculating Track Error

The helicopter is 30NM along the FPT, and is 4NM off track. Therefore, using the 1 in 60 Rule we can estimate **Track Error** (TE) to be **8 degrees**.

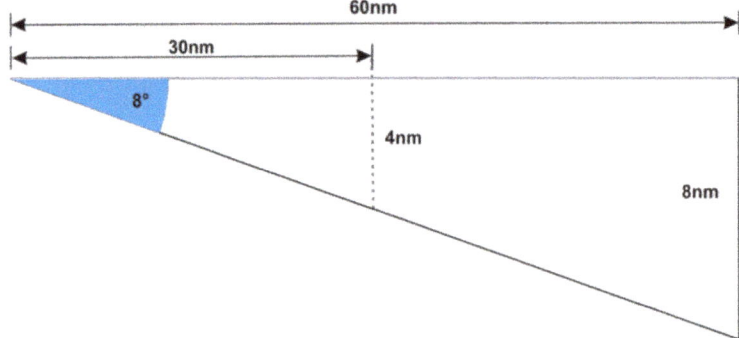

Applying the Track Error Correction

If the pilot adjusts the HDG by 8 degrees to a new HDG of 077, this will correct for the increased DFT. Notice, that once you have corrected for drift, the helicopter will maintain a track parallel to the FPT.

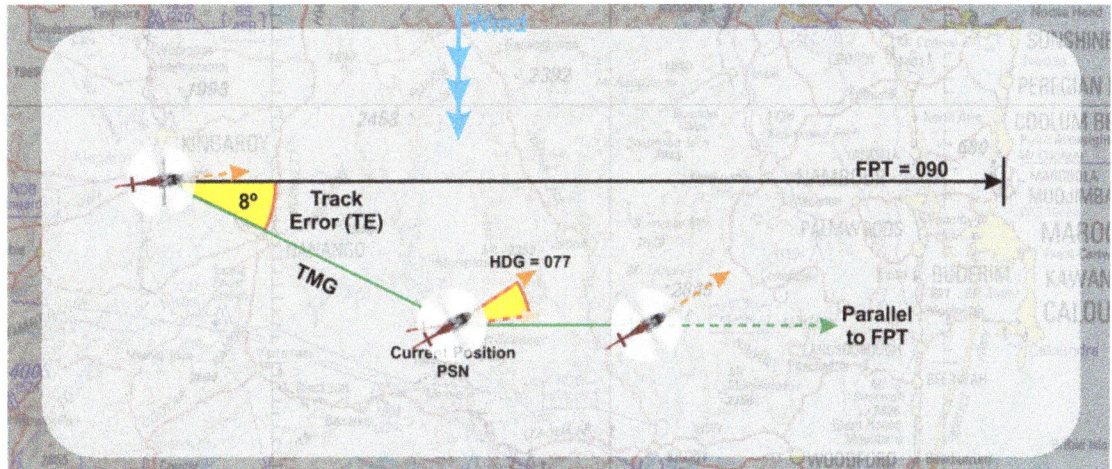

It is not enough to correct for the Track Error, the pilot must also apply a closing angle so the pilot can close in on, intercept and regain the FPT.

Calculating the Closing Angle

In our example, the helicopter is 4NM off track, and the pilot has decided to intercept the FPT at a point 40NM from the current position.

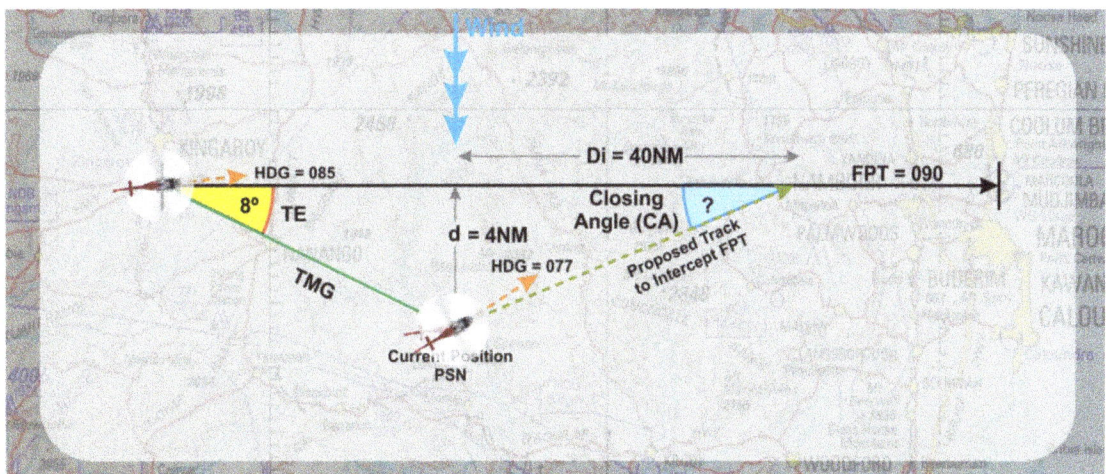

Using the 1 in 60 Rule we can estimate a **Closing Angle (CA)** of 6 degrees.

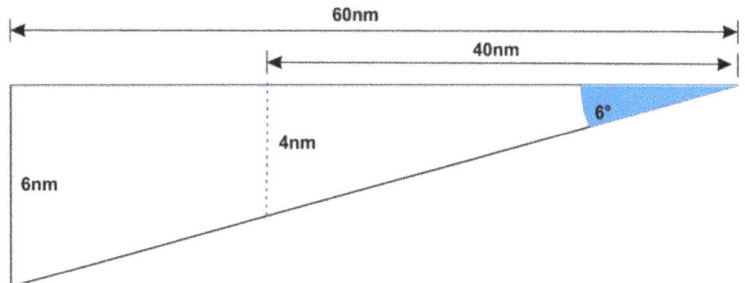

Heading Correction Amount

The total amount of the HDG change in order to stop the drift and then intercept the FPT is referred to as the **HDG Correction Amount (HCA)**. The HDG Correction Amount is the sum of the **Track Error (TE)** and the **Closing Angle (CA)**.

HDG Correction Amount (HCA) = TE + CA

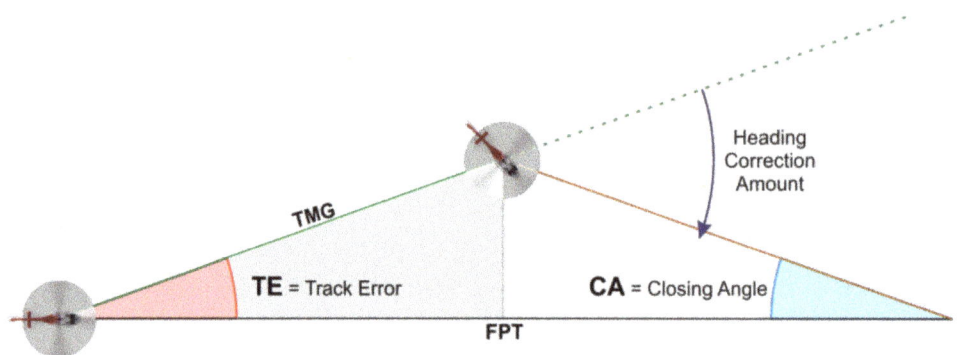

Calculating the HDG Correction Amount

Continuing our example, the pilot needs to make a HDG Correction of 14 degrees.

TE (8°) + CA (6°) = HCA (14°)

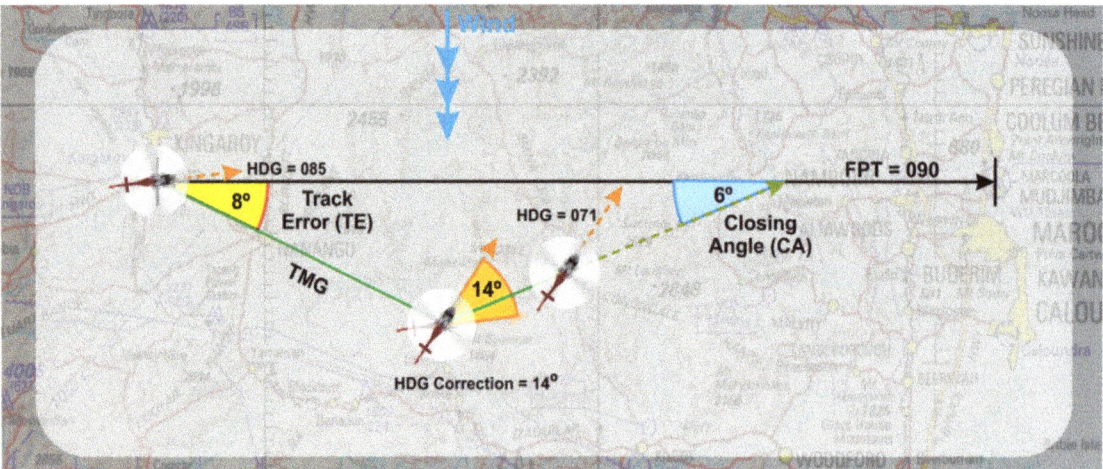

Heading Correction Amount

Adding the estimated TE and CA together would give the pilot a HDG Correction Amount (HCA) that can then be added or subtracted to the current HDG depending on whether the helicopter is left or right of the FPT.

If the helicopter is left of the FPT the HDG correction amount will always be added to the original HDG

If the helicopter is right of FPT the HDG correction amount will always be subtracted from the original HDG

For example:

Consider a helicopter flying a HDG of 090 degrees and it is left of the FPT. It will have to turn right so the HDG Correction Amount (HCA) will be added to the original HDG.

If the helicopter is flying a HDG of 090 degrees and it is right of the FPT. It will have to turn left so the HDG Correction Amount (HCA) will be subtracted from the original HDG.

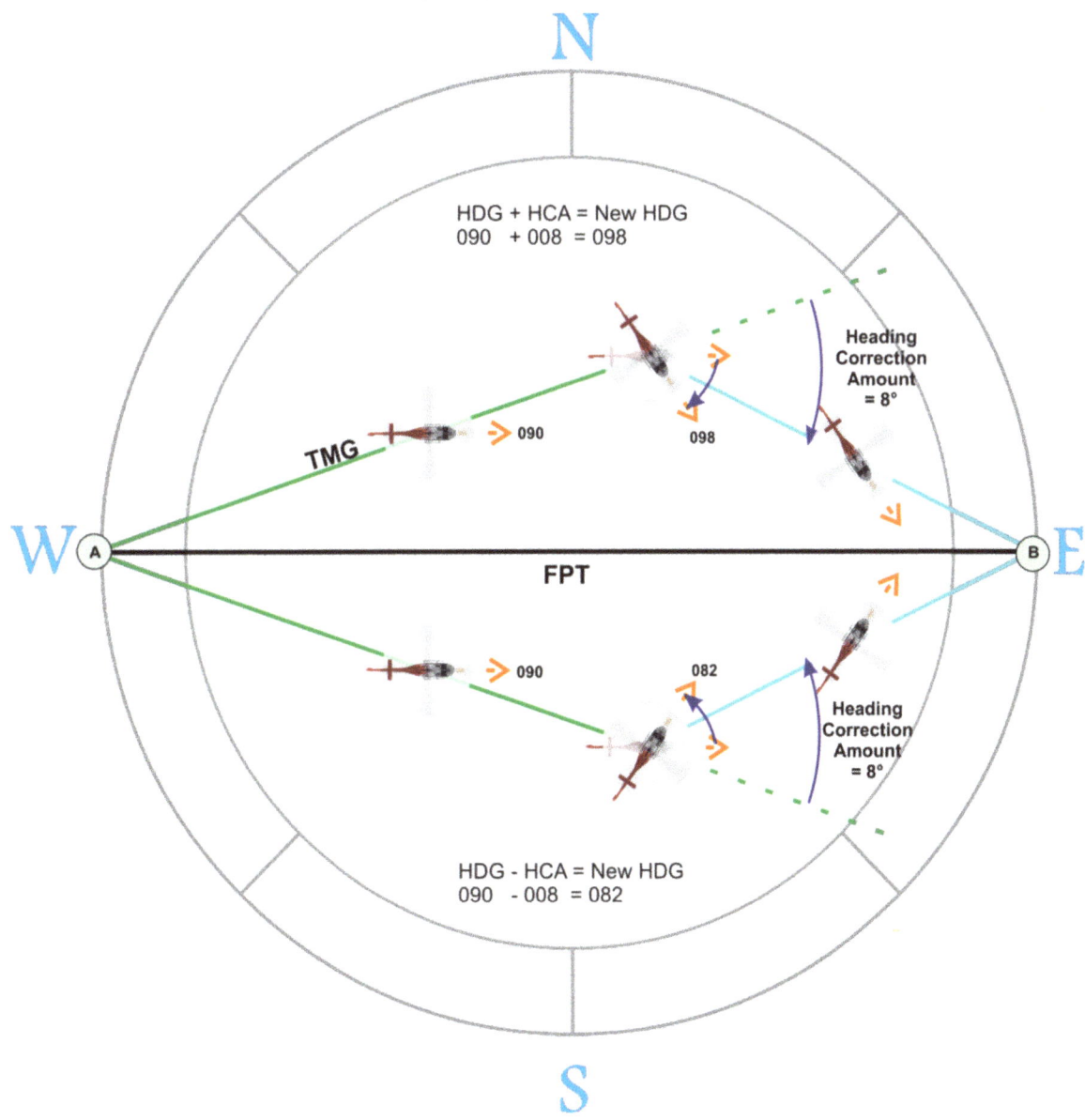

Intercept and Regain the FPT

Once the pilot has made the required corrections and has reached the FPT, the pilot now has to consider another HDG change, otherwise the helicopter will simply fly right through the FPT and then be off track again on the other side.

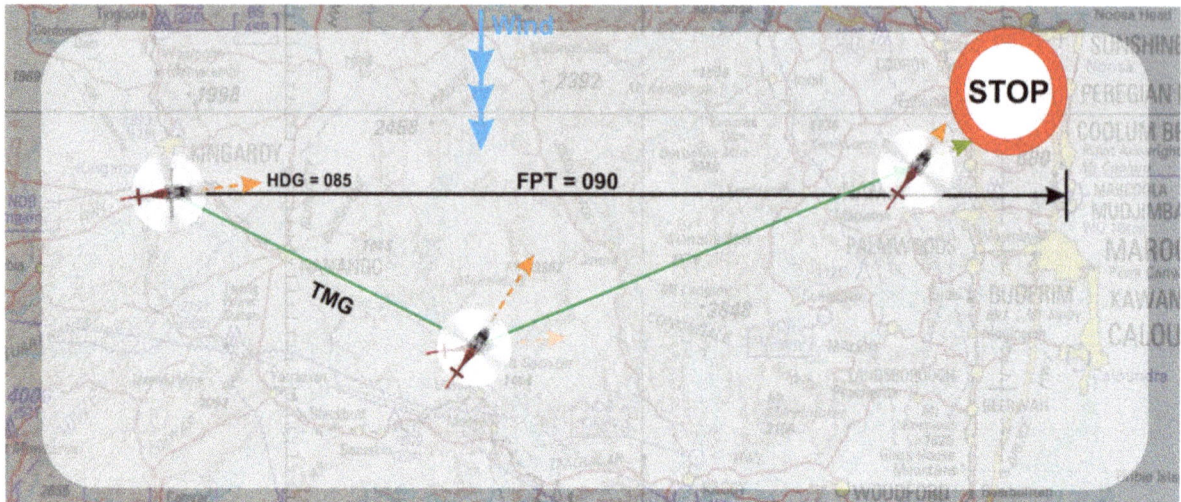

To regain the FPT, the pilot alters the HDG by adding or subtracting the Closing Angle (CA).

Example showing Right Drift

If the helicopter had experienced **right DFT**, then the CA would be **added** to the HDG to adjust the HCA amount and allow the helicopter to now maintain the FPT while still correcting for the DFT.

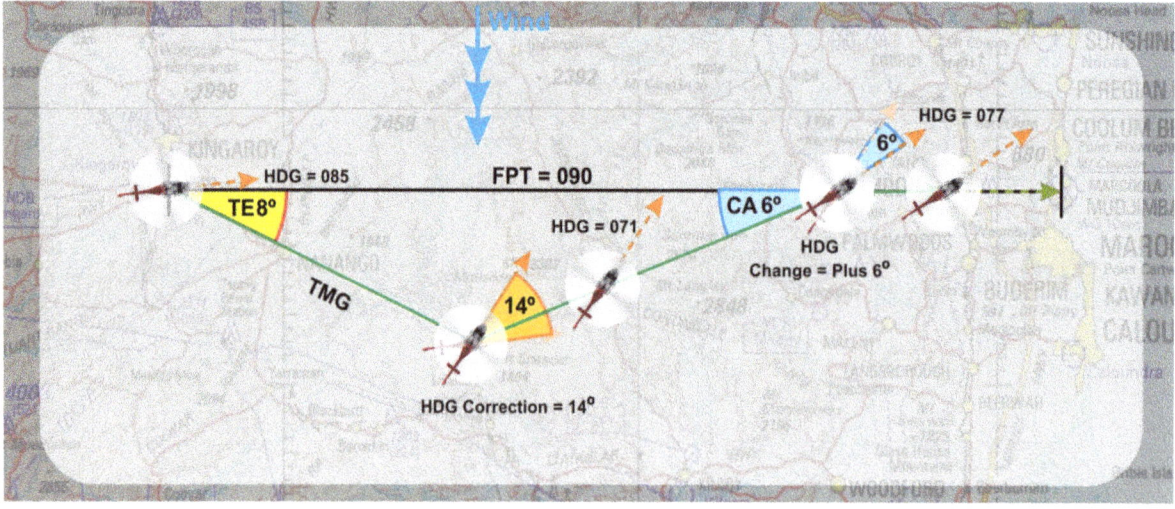

Example showing Left Drift

If the helicopter had experienced **left drift** and the pilot was intercepting the FPT then the CA would be SUBTRACTED from the HDG to adjust the HCA amount and allow the helicopter to now maintain the FPT while still correcting for the DFT.

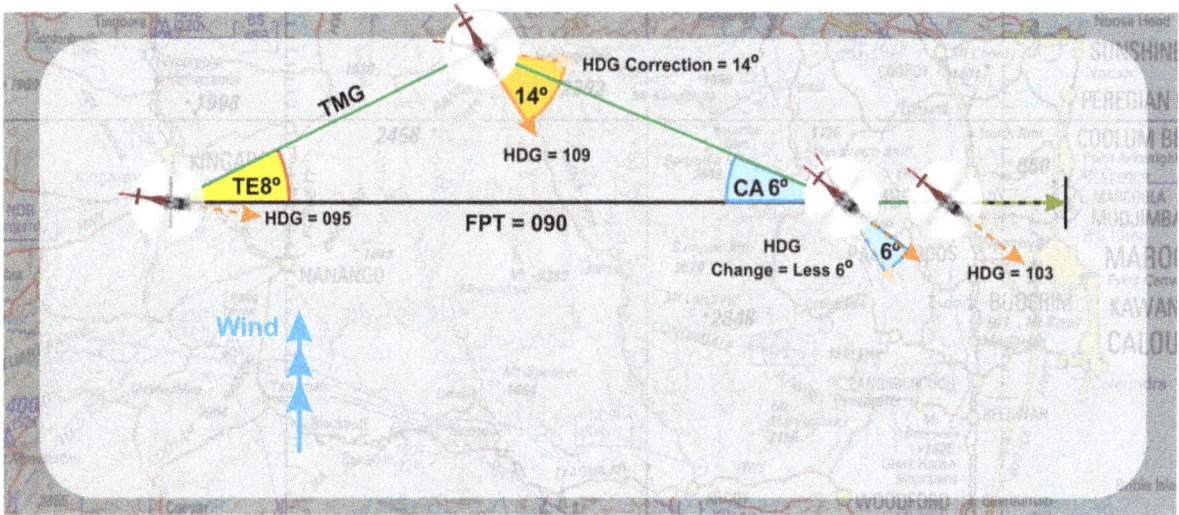

Reasons for Being Off Track

Because the Helicopter was off track for a reason the pilot needs to consider that reason.

If the reason was because the wind was stronger or weaker than forecast and planned for, then the 1 in 60 rule can be used.

If the reason was because the pilot was unable to maintain a constant HDG, or deliberately flew off track, then the 1 in 60 rule cannot be used.

The TE correction accounts for any wind that has caused the helicopter to DFT off track and this represents the HDG to counter any unplanned for DFT.

The CA represents the amount of HDG change that was required to regain or intercept the FPT. Therefore, on regaining the FPT the pilot does not need to maintain the CA amount and simply has to take away the amount of HDG change that was required for the CA but keep the HDG change that was required for the TE and the helicopter should then fly a HDG that will maintain the FPT and counter for the extra wind and DFT.

Different Methods of Applying the 1 in 60 Rule:

There are different ways the 1 in 60 Rule may be used.

Using Estimation A pilot can use the 1 in 60 rule with some quick mental arithmetic to estimate an approximate new HDG.

This is usually good enough when the HDG changes are less than 15 degrees.

This is normally the method used by a single pilot while in flight where the use of his/her hands is limited to manipulating the flight controls and not available for using the Flight Computer or concentrating on writing on a map or piece of paper.

Using a Flight Computer Rather than doing the math in his/her head, a pilot can use the Flight Computer to make the required calculations to apply the 1 in 60 rule

This is normally the method used in a multi crew environment where the Pilot Monitoring (PM) is able to take the time and accurately enter the information into the Flight Computer and advise the Flying Pilot (FP) of the new HDG to steer to ether intercept the FPT or arrive at the destination.

Using Maps and Mathematical Formulas If you have the time and space, a pilot (or navigator) can use a map and apply the 1 in 60 formulas to calculate a new HDG.

While this may be appropriate in larger fixed wing aircraft, this is not a practical method for a helicopter pilot while in flight.

---

[18] http://vw1assoc.tripod.com/connie_laposta19_r1.jpg

Using Navigational Aids

In today's helicopter environment, most modern helicopters have sophisticated navigation equipment and radio navigation aids, (especially the GPS). This means the 1 in 60 rule for all intents and purposes has become obsolete as the navigation equipment will do the calculations for the pilot.

In the basic training phase of VFR DR Navigation, it is an important principle to understand and learn in the path to becoming a qualified professional aviator. It will also be helpful when applying instrument flying techniques later on in the course as it helps the pilot learn and work with Drift, Track Error and Closing angles onto desired tracks. For this reason, the 1 in 60 Rule and how it is applied is a useful tool and is covered here in detail.

Using 1 in 60 Formulas

Sometimes the math can be too difficult to do in your head. Sometimes it helps to have formulas, and to use calculators or Flight Computers to help with the calculation.

If using long handed mathematical formulas the pilot can expand the use of the 1 in 60 Rule to also calculate, without the aid of a map or the Flight Plan, the FPT, TMG, Distance travelled, Distance to go and Distance off track.

To do this at least two (2) components within the calculation need to be known so that the other one (1) can be calculated.

Because we operate in a flying environment, the pilot will usually have pre-planned the flight and will have a map, Flight Plan or GPS available so the FPT, TMG, Distance travelled, Distance to go and Distance off track will be readily accessible and not have to be manually calculated.

Additionally, the Flight Computer can be used to enter in the relevant information, again negating the requirement to do these calculations long hand.

For this reason, even though the formulas are listed below, you will not be expected to use them long hand in this course.

The 1 in 60 Rule Formulas are summarised in the table below:

Item to Calculate	Action
Track Error (TE)	$TE = \dfrac{60}{Dt} \times d$
Closing Angle (CA)	$CA = \dfrac{60}{Di} \times d$
Distance along track (Dt)	$Dt = \dfrac{60}{TE} \times d$
Distance off track (d)	$d = \dfrac{Dt \times TE}{60}$

Using 1 in 60 Formulas: An example

The pilot can select the point at which to intercept the FPT.

Continuing our previous example, the pilot chooses to intercept the FPT at the **destination**, instead of at a point along the FPT.

To do this, the pilot simply calculates the distance to the final destination, and applies the 1 in 60 Rule to calculate the required Closing Angle.

For example

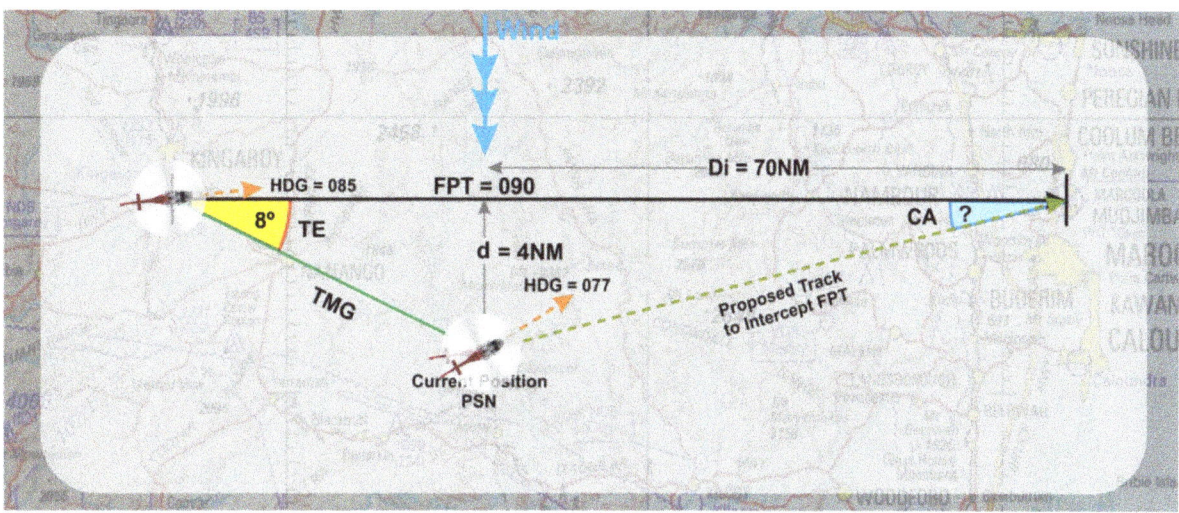

Applying the 1 in 60 Rule, you can calculate the Closing Angle using the following formula:

$$CA = \frac{60}{Di} \times d$$

CA = 60 / 70 x 4 = 3.42

Rounded to the nearest degree = 3 degrees

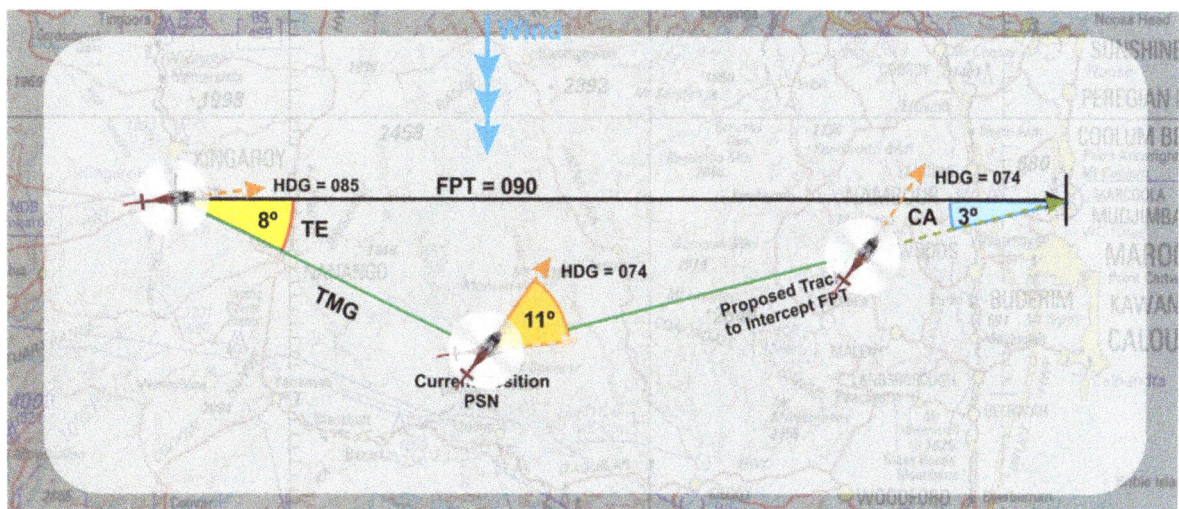

Therefore, with a TE of 8 degrees and a CA of 3 degrees the HDG Correction Amount is 11 degrees.

The Flight Computer method

When flying a helicopter as a single pilot, it can be very difficult, if not impossible to let go of the controls and mathematically calculate the Track Error (TE) and Closing Angle (CA) on a piece of paper to come up with the HDG Correction Amount (HCA).

If the 1 in 60 calculations are complicated and the estimation method cannot be used, then the Front Side of the Flight Computer can be used one handed to enter the relevant information and come up with a 1 in 60 solution.

Alternatively, if flying as part of a Multi Crew operation the Pilot Monitoring (PM) is able to use the Flight Computer to come up with an accurate answer and pass this onto the Pilot Flying (PF).

Calculating Track Error (TE)

To determine the TE using the Flight computer the pilot needs to obtain from the map:

1. The Distance travelled (Dt) and
2. The Distance off track (d)

Knowing this information, the pilot can use the Flight Computer to calculate the TE:

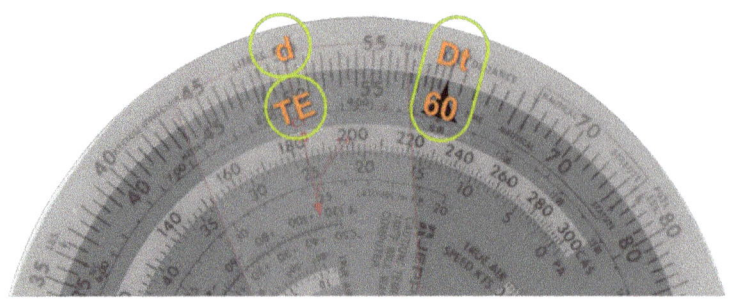

Procedure

To calculate the Track Error (TE) using the Flight Computer (Whiz wheel) complete the following steps:

Step	Action
1	Turn to the Front Side of the Flight Computer.
2	Rotate the Inner scale so the True Index (Black Triangle) representing 60 is under the Distance travelled (Dt) on the Outer scale.
3	Look around the Outer scale until identifying the distance off track (d). (Optional: Align the Cursor Hairline marker to the distance off track on the outer scale)
4	Look directly below the distance off track (d) to the Inner scale to read the Track Error (TE).

Example:

Example
Scenario:
In the previous example, we used the 1 in 60 rule to calculate the track error when:
▪ Distance travelled (Dt) was 30NM; and
▪ Distance off track (d) was 4NM.
And we estimated the **Track Error** (TE) to be **8 degrees**.
We can do the same calculation using the Flight Computer.

Step	Action
1	Turn to the Front Side of the Flight Computer.
2	Rotate the Inner scale to align True Index (60) underneath 30NM on the Outer scale.
3	Look around the Outer scale until reaching 4 (40, you will have to interpolate values remember).
4	Look to the Inner scale for the Track Error (TE) which in this case is **8 degrees.**

Calculating Closing Angle (CA)

To determine the CA using the Flight Computer the pilot needs to obtain from the map:

1. The Distance to go to intercept track or arrive at the destination (Di) and
2. The Distance off track (d)

Knowing this information, the pilot can use the Flight Computer to calculate the Closing Angle (CA).

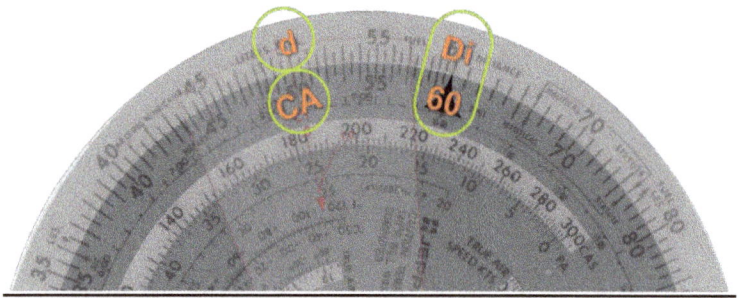

Procedure

To calculate the Closing Angle (CA) using the Flight Computer (Whiz wheel) complete the following steps:

Step	Action
1	Turn to the Front Side of the Flight Computer.
2	Rotate the Inner scale so the True Index (Black Triangle) representing 60 is under the Distance travelled (Di) on the Outer scale.
3	Look around the Outer scale until identifying the distance off track (d). (Optional: Align the Cursor Hairline marker to the distance off track on the outer scale)
4	Look directly below the distance off track (d) to the Inner scale to read the Closing Angle (CA).

Example:

Example	
Scenario: Distance to Intercept the FPT (Di) = 70NM Distance off Track (d) = 4 NM	
Step	Action
1	Turn to the Front Side of the Flight Computer.
2	Rotate the Inner scale to align True Index (60) underneath 70NM on the Outer scale.
3	Look around the Inner scale until reaching 4 (40, you will have to interpolate values remember).

4	Look to the Outer scale for the Closing Angle (CA) which in this case is **3.42 degrees**
	This is then Rounded up to the nearest whole number. 3°.

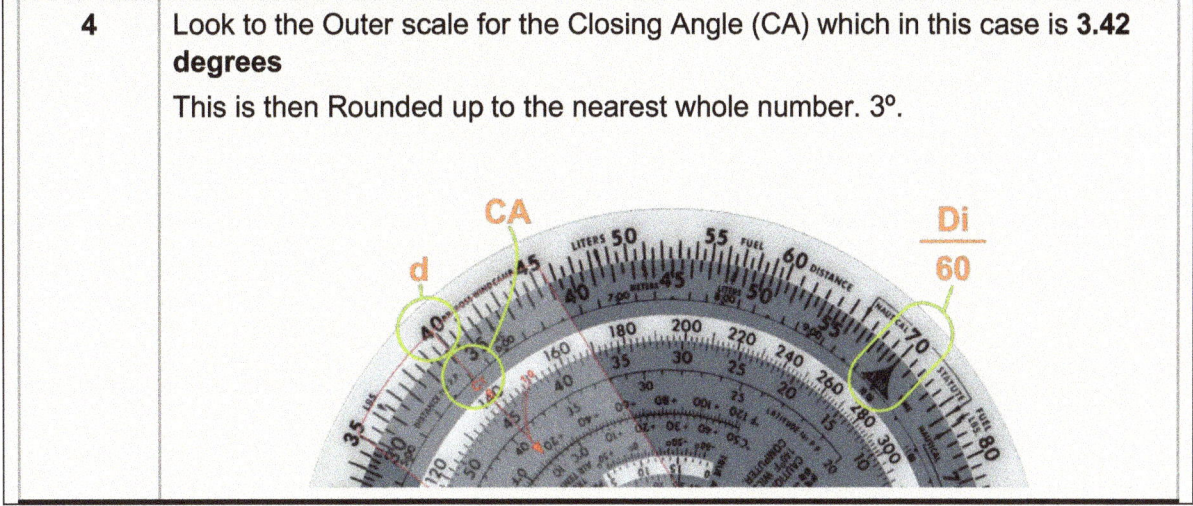

THE 1 IN 60 RULE

Applying the HDG Correction Amount

Once the TE and CA have been calculated it is a simple matter for the pilot to add them together in order to calculate the HDG Correction Amount (HCA).

The HCA is then either **ADD**ed to the HDG or **SUBTRACT**ed from the HDG based on the helicopter being left or right of the FPT.

TE + CA = HDG Correction amount (HCA)

Procedure

To determine the HDG Correction Amount (HCA) complete the following steps:

Step	Action
1	TE + CA = HCA
2	Determine if the helicopter is experiencing Left or Right Drift. If the helicopter is: - Right of the FPT, then the helicopter is experiencing Right Drift - Left of the FPT, then the helicopter is experiencing Left Drift.
3	If the helicopter is experiencing: - **Right** Drift, then **SUBTRACT** the HCA from the current HDG - **Left** Drift, then **ADD** the HCA to the current heading to obtain the new HDG
4	Once the FPT has been intercepted make a HDG adjustment cancelling out the CA - **Right** Drift, then **ADD** the CA to the current HDG - **Left** Drift, then **SUBTRACT** the CA from the current HDG

Example

Scenario:

- Heading = 090
- TE calculated = 5°
- CA calculated = 3°
- Direction of Drift = Right of Track

Step	Action
1	5° TE + 3° CA = 8° HCA
2	Right Drift so SUBTRACT the HCA from the HDG
3	090 − 8 = new HDG of 082° to steer
4	Right Drift so on intercepting the original FPT ADD back in the CA 082° + CA of 3° = new HDG of 085°

1 in 60 Summary

When the helicopter is off track, the pilot needs to be able to calculate a new HDG to regain track and then on regaining the track have to adjust HDG again to maintain the FPT.

The 1 in 60 calculation is a simple method of **estimating angles** and, therefore, estimating HDG changes that can be easily determined in flight.

The 1 in 60 Rule

1NM off track will equal 1 degree of angle in 60NM

Applying the 1 in 60 Rule

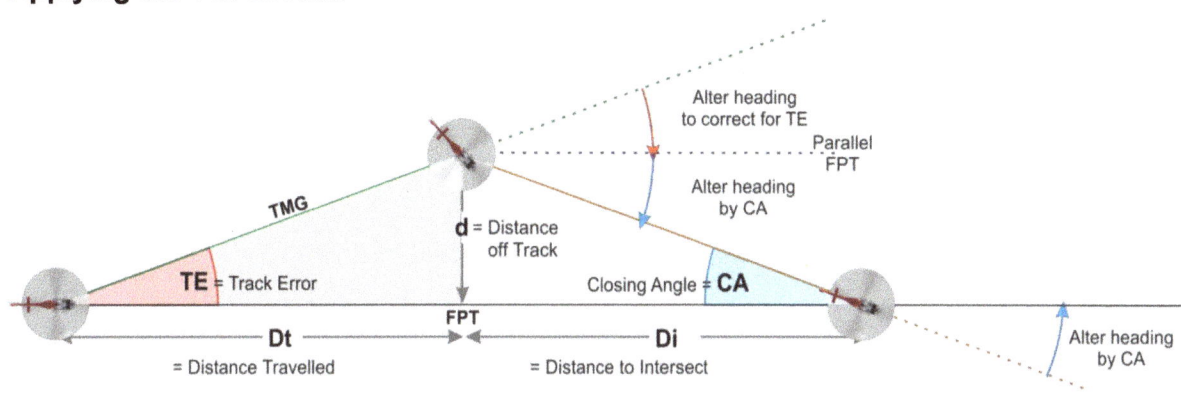

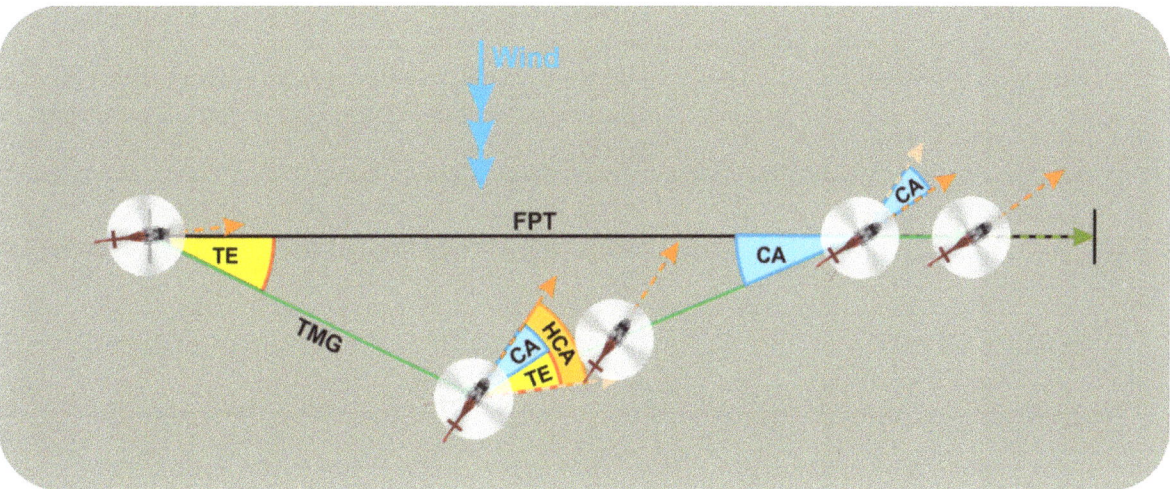

Definitions Summary

Term	Abbrev	Description
Flight Planned Track	**FPT**	The Track the pilot has planned to fly and represents the line drawn on the map.
Track Made Good	**TMG**	The Track the helicopter actually flies over the ground.
Heading	**HDG**	The direction the nose of the helicopter is pointing and is displayed on the magnetic compass or HIS.
Drift	**DFT**	The difference in degrees between HDG and TMG. Drift is *always* measured from the HDG to TMG in degrees Left or Right.
Track Error	**TE**	The difference in degrees between FPT and TMG. Track Error is measured from FPT to TMG and expressed in degrees Left or Right of FPT.
Closing Angle	**CA**	The difference in degrees between TMG and FPT. Closing Angle is measured from TMG to FPT and expressed in degrees Left or Right of TMG.
Heading Correction Amount	**HCA**	The sum of the TE and CA This represents the total heading change required to intercept the FPT or arrive over the destination.
Distance travelled	**Dt**	The equivalent distance travelled along the FPT from the departure point to 90 degrees abeam the current position.
Distance to intercept	**Di**	The equivalent Distance yet to travel from 90 degrees abeam the FPT at the current position to intercept the FPT.
Distance off track	**d**	The distance of the helicopter from its current position 90 degrees to the FPT.

9 Calculating the Effect of Wind on a Runway

Introduction

Wind is always given in the direction it is blowing *FROM*, therefore as a pilot you will always want to be landing *INTO* the wind.

The number on the runway represents the magnetic compass bearing of the runway direction rounded to the nearest 10° and reduced to a two figure grouping.

This grouping is referred to as the "*Runway designator*" and can be any whole number between 01 and 36.

Runway directions should therefore correspond to wind direction and the way the nose of the helicopter is pointing when on final approach to the runway.

For example, if the wind is blowing from 120° magnetic it is safe to assume that Runway 12 will be in use as the pilot will want to be landing INTO the wind therefore will be flying in the 120° magnetic compass direction on finals.

Note the compass heading in the image.

Wind

Any wind blowing directly down the runway onto the nose of the helicopter is referred to as a **Headwind**. This is the ideal takeoff and landing scenario for any aircraft.

Any wind blowing in the opposite direction of the runway onto the tail of the helicopter is referred to as a **Tailwind**. This is the worst takeoff and landing scenario for any aircraft.

Any wind blowing across the runway onto the side of the helicopter is referred to as a **Crosswind**. Each aircraft type will be limited to the amount of crosswind that can be accepted and the pilot may have to vary the takeoff and landing technique.

Obviously the wind can vary at any time during the day so the pilot can calculate how much headwind, crosswind or tailwind needs to be considered for takeoff and landing.

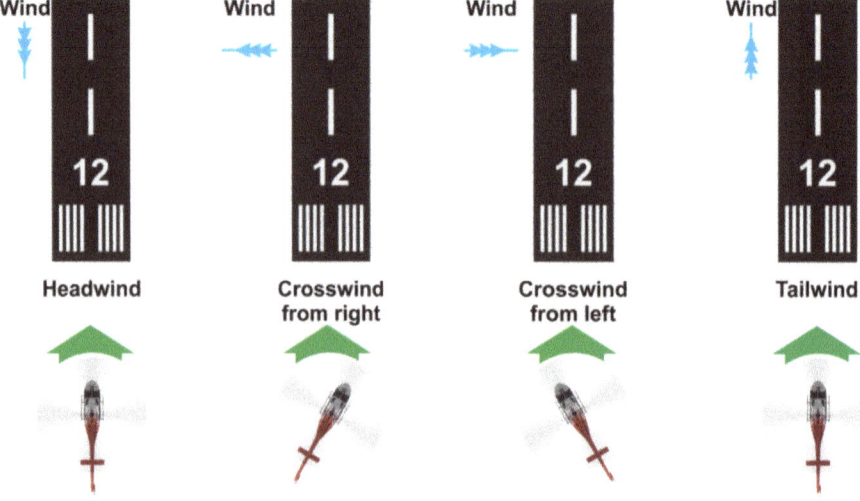

Wind components

As the wind backs or veers away from the runway direction, the wind will be divided into two (2) components.

1. The wind component still giving some advantage and providing some headwind. This is referred to as the **H**ead **W**ind **C**omponent (**HWC**)
2. The wind component that is starting to blow across the runway. This is referred to as the **C**ross **W**ind **C**omponent (**XWC**)

The more the wind moves away from the runway direction, the greater the **C**ross **W**ind **C**omponent (**XWC**) until finally not only is there a **XWC** but there will also now be a **T**ail **W**ind **C**omponent (**TWC**) as the wind is coming from behind the aircraft and there is no longer any **HWC**.

At the point that a Tail Wind Component (TWC) is evidenced, the runway in use and therefore the runway direction, should be changed so that the pilot is again landing into wind.

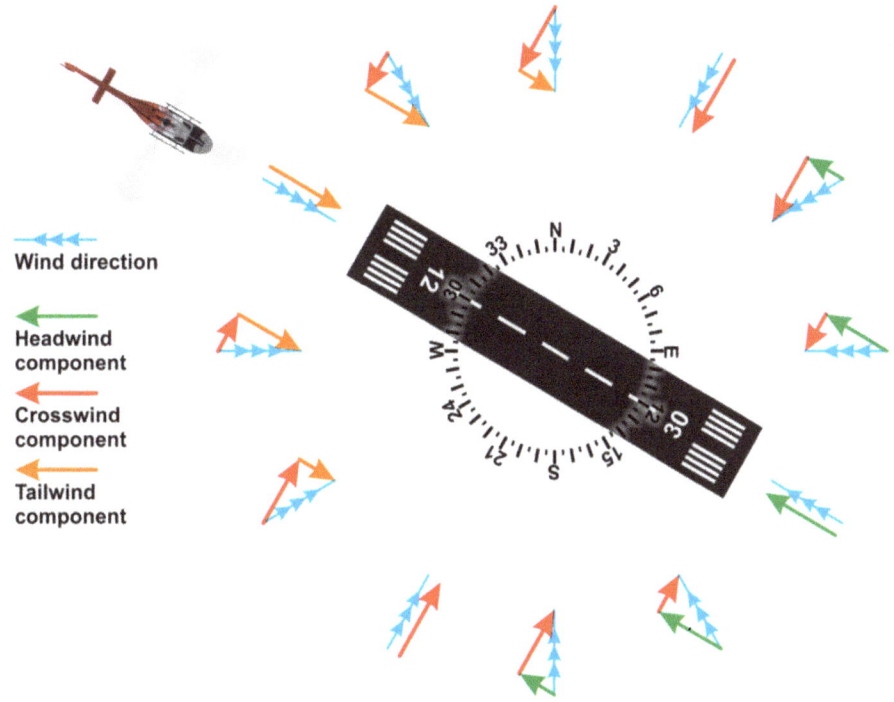

All aircraft can only handle limited amounts of crosswind, which is determined by the wind's direction and speed in relation to the runway. This limit will be stated in the LIMITATIONS section of the aircraft's Flight Manual and may restrict a pilot using a particular runway if the wind direction and speed is greater than the aircraft can safely manage.

It is important, therefore, that the pilot is able to take the Head Wind, Cross Wind and Tail Wind components into consideration, preferably at the planning stages of a flight, to determine the suitability of the runway for use and the performance requirements of the aircraft.

Fixed wing pilots are obviously affected much more than helicopter pilots because helicopters have the option of not using the runway but being able to take-off and land into wind regardless of its direction because helicopters do not need to use the runway to take-off and land.

Take off into wind

---

[20] By Arcturus - Own work, CC BY-SA 3.0, https://commons.wikimedia.org/w/index.php?curid=2915539

Because winds are a limiting factor for take-offs and landings, as a pilot you need to be able to work out the Cross Wind (XWC), Head Wind (HWC) or Tail Wind (TWC) components prior to take-off and landing. This is will be tested in the theory exams, even for helicopter pilots.

Calculating the effect of wind on a runway

Given a particular runway direction and a given Wind Velocity (W/V) the pilot is able to calculate the amount of Head Wind Component (HWC), Cross Wind Component (XWC) and Tail Wind Component (TWC) to determine if the helicopter can land within its limitations if having to do so while aligned with the runway direction.

The beauty of a helicopter of course, is that they do not need a runway, however, in larger helicopters or if required to do so by ATC it is necessary to be able to work out the wind components and apply them as required.

Wind Component Tables

Wind components can be calculated by either referencing the Wind Component Table located in the ERSA GEN – CON – 6 or it can also be calculated using the Flight Computer.

At Becker Helicopters we utilise the Wind Component Table found in the ERSA for all HWC, XWC and TWC calculations.

WIND COMPONENT TABLE

For Crosswind Component
Angle Between Wind Direction and Runway Heading

		10	20	30	40	50	60	70	80	90
W	5	1	2	2	3	4	4	4	5	5
I	10	2	3	5	6	7	8	9	9	10
N	15	3	5	7	9	11	13	14	14	15
D	20	3	7	10	13	15	17	18	19	20
	25	4	8	12	16	19	22	23	24	25
S	30	5	10	15	19	23	26	28	29	30
P	35	6	12	17	22	26	30	32	34	35
E	40	7	14	20	25	30	35	37	39	40
E	45	8	15	22	29	34	39	42	44	45
D	50	9	17	25	32	38	43	47	49	50
	55	10	19	27	25	42	48	52	54	55
K	60	10	20	30	38	46	52	56	59	60
N	65	11	22	32	42	50	56	61	64	65
O	70	12	24	35	45	54	60	66	69	70
T	75	13	26	37	48	57	64	70	73	75
S	80	14	27	40	51	60	69	75	78	80
		80	70	60	50	40	30	20	10	0

For Headwind Component
Angle Between Wind Direction and Runway Heading

Calculating Head Wind Component (HWC)

To calculate the Head Wind Component (HWC) complete the following steps:

Step	Action
1	Draw a picture of the situation so that you have a mental picture of what to expect.
2	Calculate the difference in degrees between the wind direction and runway direction.
3	Refer to the Wind Component table in ERSA GEN CON - 6
4	Calculate the HWC. Locate the difference in degrees between the wind direction and the runway direction at the **bottom** of the table. Locate the wind speed on the left of the table and move horizontally to the right until intersecting the cross wind value vertically **up** from the difference in the wind direction and runway heading. Read the HWC from the table.

Example		
Given Runway 12 and a W/V of 050/15 calculate the HWC		
Step	Action	
1	Draw a picture	
2	Calculate the difference in degrees between the wind direction and runway direction. *In this case 120° runway direction - 050° wind direction = 070° difference*	
3	Refer to the Wind Component table in ERSA GEN – CON - 6	

4	Locate 070° at the **bottom** of the table.
	Locate 15kts wind speed on the left of the table.
	Note the value where 070° (moving vertically **up**) and 15kts (moving horizontally to the right) meet.
	Read the HWC from the table.
	In this case it is a 5kt HWC

WIND COMPONENT TABLE

For Crosswind Component
Angle Between Wind Direction and Runway Heading

		10	20	30	40	50	60	70	80	90
W	5	1	2	2	3	4	4	4	5	5
I	10	2	3	5	6	7	8	9	9	10
N	15	3	5	7	9	11	13	14	14	15
D	20	3	7	10	13	15	17	18	19	20
	25	4	8	12	16	19	22	23	24	25
S	30	5	10	15	19	23	26	28	29	30
P	35	6	12	17	22	26	30	32	34	35
E	40	7	14	20	25	30	35	37	39	40
E	45	8	15	22	29	34	39	42	44	45
D	50	9	17	25	32	38	43	47	49	50
	55	10	19	27	25	42	48	52	54	55
K	60	10	20	30	38	46	52	56	59	60
N	65	11	22	32	42	50	56	61	64	65
O	70	12	24	35	45	54	60	66	69	70
T	75	13	26	37	48	57	64	70	73	75
S	80	14	27	40	51	60	69	75	78	80
		80	70	60	50	40	30	20	10	0

For Headwind Component
Angle Between Wind Direction and Runway Heading

Calculating Cross Wind Component (XWC)

To calculate the Cross Wind Component (XWC) complete the following steps:

Step	Action
1	Draw a picture of the situation so that you have a mental picture of what to expect.
2	Calculate the difference in degrees between the wind direction and runway direction.
3	Refer to the Wind Component table in ERSA GEN CON - 6
4	Calculate the XWC. Locate the difference in degrees between the wind direction and the runway direction at the **top** of the table. Locate the wind speed on the left of the table and move horizontally to the right until intersecting the cross wind value vertically **down** from the difference in the wind direction and runway heading. Read the XWC from the table and determine if it is from the right or the left.

Example	
Given a Runway direction of 12 and a W/V of 050/15 calculate the XWC	
Step	**Action**
1	Draw a picture
2	Calculate the difference in degrees between the wind direction and runway direction. *In this case 120° runway direction - 050° wind direction = 070° difference*
3	Refer to the Wind Component Table in ERSA GEN – CON - 6

4	To work out the XWC
	Locate 070° at the **top** of the table.
	Locate 15kts wind speed on the left of the table.
	Note the value where 070° (moving vertically **down**) and 15kts (moving horizontally to the right) meet.
	Read the XWC from the table.
	Refer to the picture drawn above and determine if it is a left or a right cross wind.
	In this case it is a 14kt XWC from the left.

WIND COMPONENT TABLE

For Crosswind Component
Angle Between Wind Direction and Runway Heading

		10	20	30	40	50	60	70	80	90
W	5	1	2	2	3	4	4	4	5	5
I	10	2	3	5	6	7	8	9	9	10
N	15	3	5	7	9	11	13	14	14	15
D	20	3	7	10	13	15	17	18	19	20
	25	4	8	12	16	19	22	23	24	25
S	30	5	10	15	19	23	26	28	29	30
P	35	6	12	17	22	26	30	32	34	35
E	40	7	14	20	25	30	35	37	39	40
E	45	8	15	22	29	34	39	42	44	45
D	50	9	17	25	32	38	43	47	49	50
	55	10	19	27	25	42	48	52	54	55
K	60	10	20	30	38	46	52	56	59	60
N	65	11	22	32	42	50	56	61	64	65
O	70	12	24	35	45	54	60	66	69	70
T	75	13	26	37	48	57	64	70	73	75
S	80	14	27	40	51	60	69	75	78	80
		80	70	60	50	40	30	20	10	0

For Headwind Component
Angle Between Wind Direction and Runway Heading

Calculating Tail Wind Component (TWC)

To calculate the Tail Wind Component (TWC), complete the same steps as if it was for a Head Wind Component (HWC) but reverse the runway direction in the steps.

Once the HWC has been calculated then use the result as the TWC.

To calculate the Tail Wind Component (TWC) complete the following steps:

Step	Action
1	Draw a picture of the situation so that you have a mental picture of what to expect.
2	Reverse the Runway given so that the calculation is as if there is a Head Wind Component (HWC). This is done by adding or subtracting 180 degrees from the given runway direction.
3	Calculate the difference in degrees between the wind direction and new runway direction.
4	Refer to the Wind Component table in ERSA GEN CON - 6
5	Calculate the HWC. Locate the difference in degrees between the wind direction and the runway direction at the **bottom** of the table. Locate the wind speed on the left of the table and move horizontally to the right until intersecting the cross wind value vertically **up** from the difference in the wind direction and runway heading. Read the HWC from the table.
6	Reverse the Head Wind Component (HWC) and call it a Tail Wind Component (TWC).

Example

Given Runway 12 and a W/V of 360/10 calculate the TWC.

Step	Action
1	Draw a picture
2	Reverse the runway direction to get a head wind component. *In this case 120° runway direction + 180 degrees = a new runway direction of 300° (Runway 30)*
3	Calculate the difference in degrees between the wind direction and runway direction. *In this case 300° runway direction - 360° wind direction = 060° difference*
4	Refer to the Wind Component table in ERSA GEN – CON - 6

CALCULATING THE EFFECT OF WIND ON A RUNWAY

5	Locate 060° at the **bottom** of the table.
	Locate 10kts wind speed on the left of the table.
	Note the value where 060° (moving vertically **up**) and 10kts (moving horizontally to the right) meet.
	Read the HWC from the table.
	In this case it is a 5kt HWC

WIND COMPONENT TABLE

For Crosswind Component
Angle Between Wind Direction and Runway Heading

		10	20	30	40	50	60	70	80	90
W	5	1	2	2	3	4	4	4	5	5
I	10	2	3	5	6	7	8	9	9	10
N	15	3	5	7	9	11	13	14	14	15
D	20	3	7	10	13	15	17	18	19	20
	25	4	8	12	16	19	22	23	24	25
S	30	5	10	15	19	23	26	28	29	30
P	35	6	12	17	22	26	30	32	34	35
E	40	7	14	20	25	30	35	37	39	40
E	45	8	15	22	29	34	39	42	44	45
D	50	9	17	25	32	38	43	47	49	50
	55	10	19	27	25	42	48	52	54	55
K	60	10	20	30	38	46	52	56	59	60
N	65	11	22	32	42	50	56	61	64	65
O	70	12	24	35	45	54	60	66	69	70
T	75	13	26	37	48	57	64	70	73	75
S	80	14	27	40	51	60	69	75	78	80
		80	70	60	50	40	30	20	10	0

For Headwind Component
Angle Between Wind Direction and Runway Heading

5	Reverse the HWC and call it a TWC
	In this case using Runway 12 there is a 5kt TWC

10 Equal Time Point (ETP)

The **Equal Time Point (ETP)**, also referred to as the *Critical Point (CP)*, is that point along the Flight Planned Track from which it would take the same amount of *TIME* to continue *ON* to the destination (or continue *OUT* from the departure point – same thing), as it would take to return *HOME* to the original departure point.

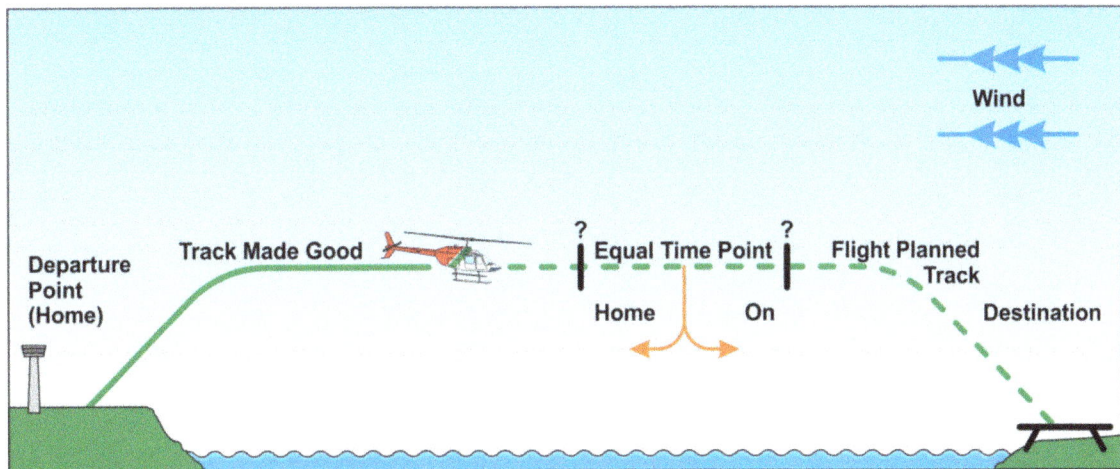

It is usually applied when making sea crossings or flying over jungles, mountains or deserts where there are no other landing sites.

If there is a problem enroute, such as an engine failure (assuming you have 2 engines), a hydraulic failure, a sick passenger or some other problem that necessitates that the aircraft get back on the ground, and the closest landing area was either the *departure point* or the *destination,* the pilot will need to know, quickly, which one it is and therefore it would be best to work it out before departing.

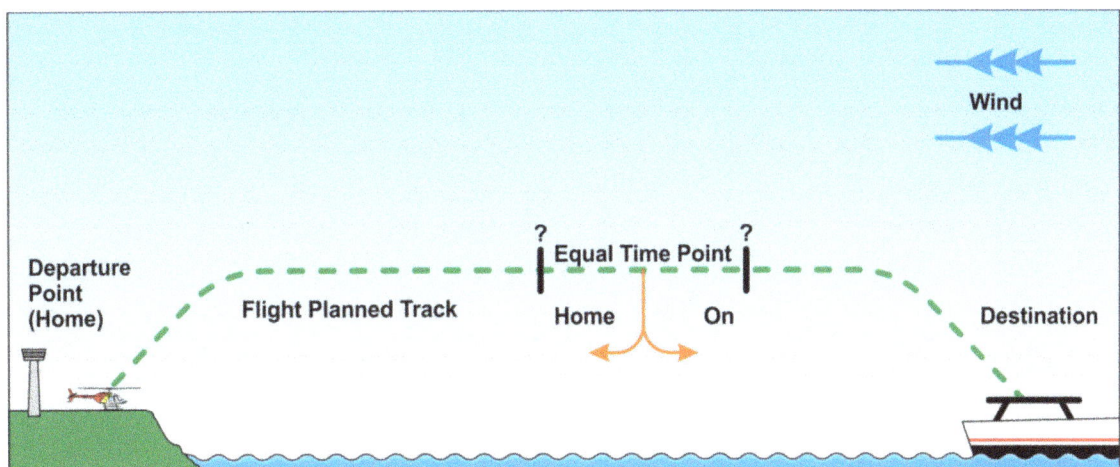

The Equal Time Point is primarily dependant on the distance between the departure and destination and the amount of *time* it will take to travel to the closest landing position. The amount of fuel onboard (the safe endurance) should play no part in the calculation as the helicopter should already have sufficient fuel onboard to complete the original task.

To calculate the position of the ETP use the following formula:

$$\frac{\text{TOTAL DISTANCE} \times \text{G/S HOME}}{\text{G/S OUT} + \text{G/S HOME}} = \text{Distance to ETP (NM)}$$

The G/S used in the ETP formula is always the speed that would apply if actually at the ETP trying to decide if you should go **ON** to the destination (continuing Out from the departure) or **HOME** to the departure aerodrome.

TOTAL DISTANCE is the measured distance between the departure point and the destination.

G/S OUT is the groundspeed used from the ETP when continuing **OUT** from the departure point towards the destination.

G/S HOME is the groundspeed used to return **HOME** to the departure aerodrome from the ETP.

Remember the ETP **always moves upwind (into wind)** when compared to the halfway distance position. It is important to remember this fact as it can be used to make a very easy check of your calculation to ensure you have gone the right way!

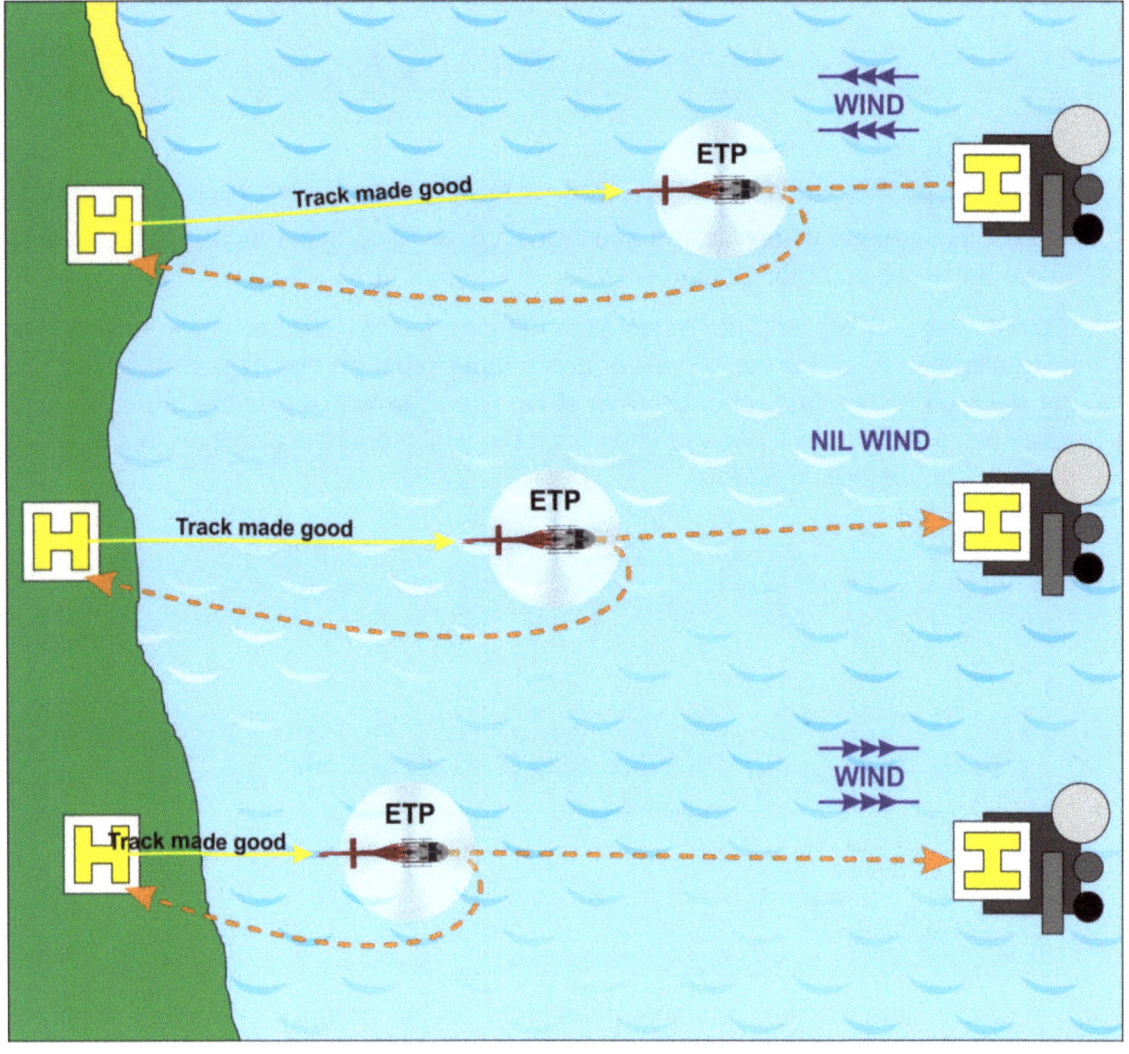

EQUAL TIME POINT (ETP)
NAVIGATION

To calculate Distance and Time to the ETP complete the following steps:

Step	Action
1	Determine the Groundspeed **OUT** from the ETP (This will require a calculation using the Flight Computer considering Track, W/V and TAS to determine a HCW or a TWC)
2	Determine the Groundspeed **HOME** from the ETP (This will require a calculation using the Flight Computer considering Track, W/V and TAS to determine a HWC or a TWC)
3	Measure The **TOTAL DISTANCE** between the departure and destination points
4	Draw a picture and determine which side of the half-way point the ETP will be based on the known wind
5	Enter the above information into the formula to determine the **Distance** to the ETP from the departure point: $$\frac{\text{Total Distance} \times \text{G/S HOME}}{\text{G/S OUT} + \text{G/S HOME}} = \text{Distance to ETP}$$
6	Calculate the **Time** to the ETP Using the Front Side of the Flight Computer enter the G/S OUT under the True Index and look on the Outer scale to the Distance to the ETP. Look down to the Inner scale to read the time.

Example

Given the following information calculate the ETP

The Total Distance between the departure and destination is 150NM,

130kts TAS, the wind is a 10kt HWC Out and 10kt TWC Home

Step	Action
1	Determine the Groundspeed **OUT** from the ETP *In this case* *130kts TAS − 10kt HWC = 120kts G/S OUT*
2	Determine the Groundspeed **HOME** from the ETP *In this case* *130kts TAS + 10kt TWC = 140kts G/S HOME*

3	The Total Distance between departure and destination *In this case 150NM*
4	Draw a picture ![diagram showing GS Out 130 kts, GS Home 140 kts, Half way, ETP?, 150 NM, Dept., Dest.]
5	Apply the formula to calculate the **distance** to the ETP *In this case* $$\frac{150NM \times 140kts\ HOME\ (21,000)}{120kts\ OUT + 140kts\ HOME\ (260)} = 80.77NM$$ *80.77 is rounded to* **81NM Distance to ETP**
6	Calculate **Time** to ETP from the departure point *In this case* 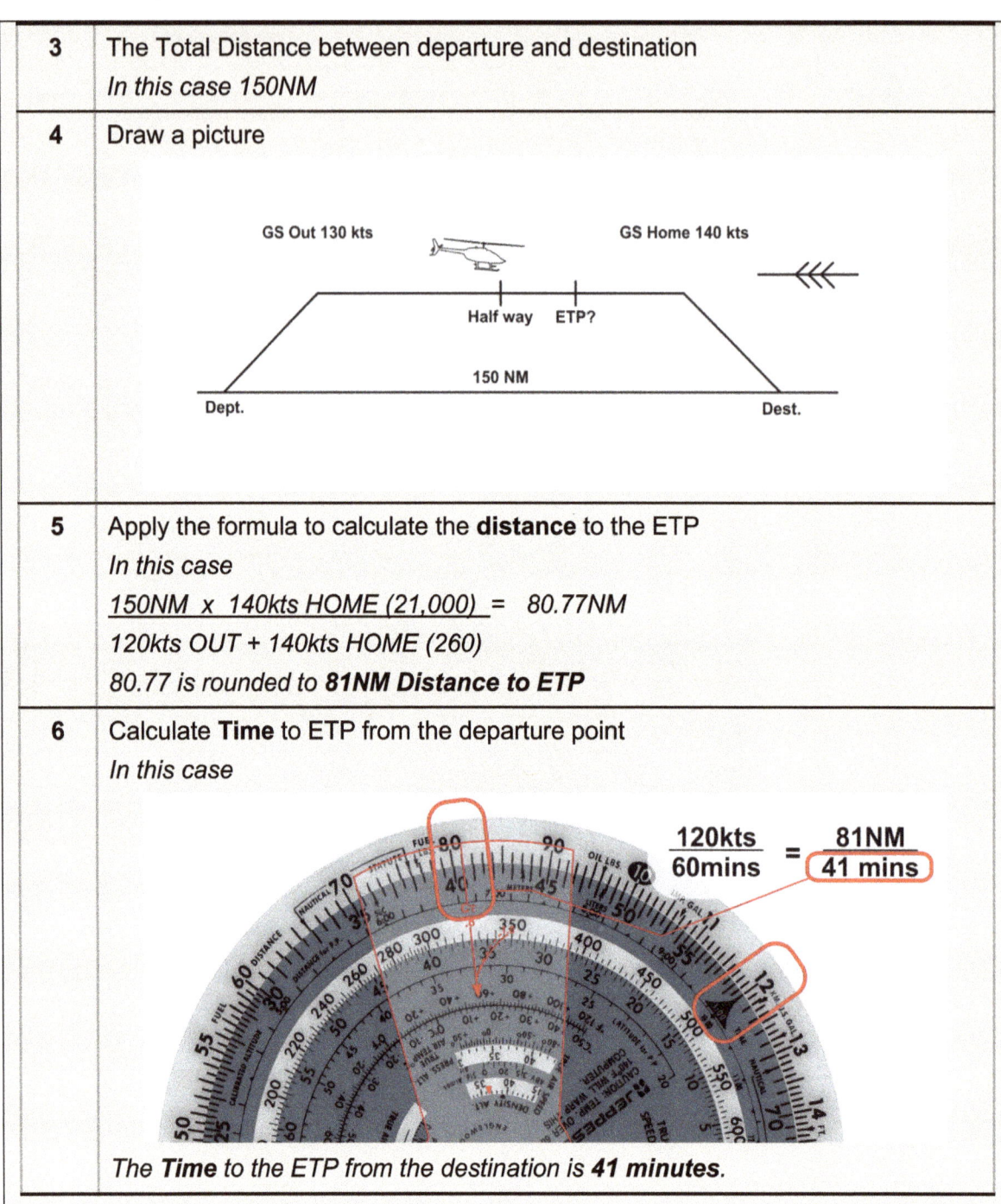 $$\frac{120kts}{60mins} = \frac{81NM}{41\ mins}$$ The **Time** to the ETP from the destination is **41 minutes**.

11 Calculating Rates of Climb And Descent

Introduction

When operating in and around controlled airspace, if asked to by ATC or due to an operational requirement (there may be a mountain in front of you or you may need to calculate the Top of Descent Point prior to an instrument approach) being able to work out a **R**ate **O**f **C**limb (**ROC**) and **R**ate **O**f **D**escent (**ROD**) over a given distance is a useful and necessary calculation to be able to make.

This is particularly valuable when operating under the **I**nstrument **F**light **R**ules (**IFR**) at higher levels and being sequenced with other aircraft while maintaining a distance from any Controlled Airspace steps.

Calculating the Rate of Climb or Rate of Descent

To calculate the ROC or ROD the pilot needs to know how much **Altitude** has been gained or lost over a particular period of **Time**.

The total Altitude *gained* or *lost* is then divided by the *time* taken to change the Altitude change in order to calculate the *rate of change*.

Example
Consider a helicopter that has increased 1000 feet of Altitude in 5 minutes.
1000ft divided by 5 minutes equals 200 feet per minute (fpm) Rate of Climb (ROC)

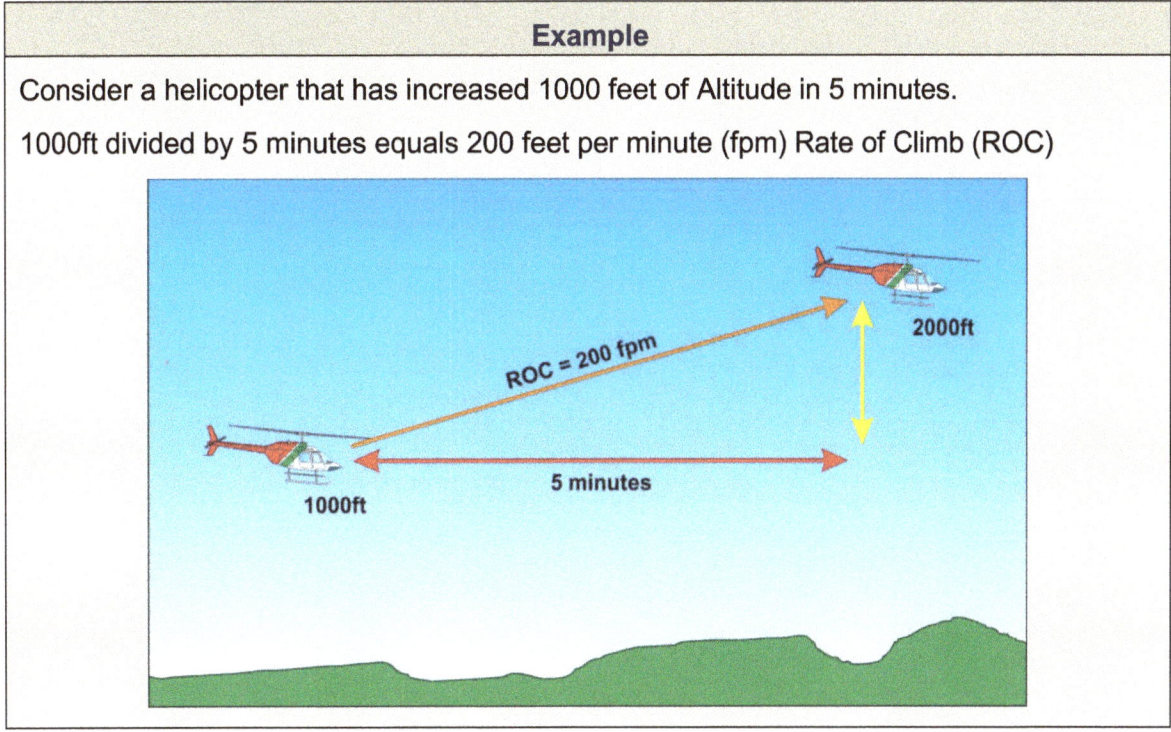

CALCULATING RATES OF CLIMB AND DESCENT

Example

Consider a helicopter that has decreased 500 feet of Altitude in 5 minutes.

500ft divided by 5 minutes equals 100 feet per minute (fpm) Rate of Descent (ROD).

Revision of the variables to calculate ROC or ROD

In order to calculate the ROC or ROD the pilot will need to know:

- The actual Altitude gained or lost
- The timeframe it has taken to gain or lose the Altitude

If the time is not given in a particular theory exam question then knowing the *Groundspeed* and *Distance* will allow time to be calculated by dividing the Distance by Groundspeed on the Flight Computer.

The following table summarises the Flight Computer formulas and the information needed to calculate a ROC or ROD.

To calculate	Formula
The amount of Altitude change	Note the change on the Altimeter over a period of time. ALT (altimeter)
Time	As viewed on a clock or Divide the Distance Travelled by the Groundspeed on the Flight Computer.

To calculate	Formula
Groundspeed	As viewed on the GPS or EFIS display or Multiply Time by the Distance travelled on the Flight Computer TAS/GS (true air speed ground speed)
Distance	As viewed on the map, GPS or Multiply the Groundspeed by Time on the Flight Computer

To calculate the ROC or ROD complete the following steps:

Step	Action
1	Obtain the relevant information available - Altitude increase or decrease from the Altimeter - Time elapsed from the clock or - Distance divided by Groundspeed to obtain Time
2	Draw a picture to visualise the calculation
3	Divide the Change in Altitude by Time to find the ROC or ROD

Example
Given an Altitude increase of 4500ft over a Distance of 15NM with a G/S of 60kts calculate the ROC

Step	Action
1	Obtain the relevant information you do have: - Altitude has **increased** by 4500ft - Time is not given but Distance travelled and Groundspeed has, so *In this case 15NM divided by 60kts G/S = **15 minutes***
2	Draw a picture 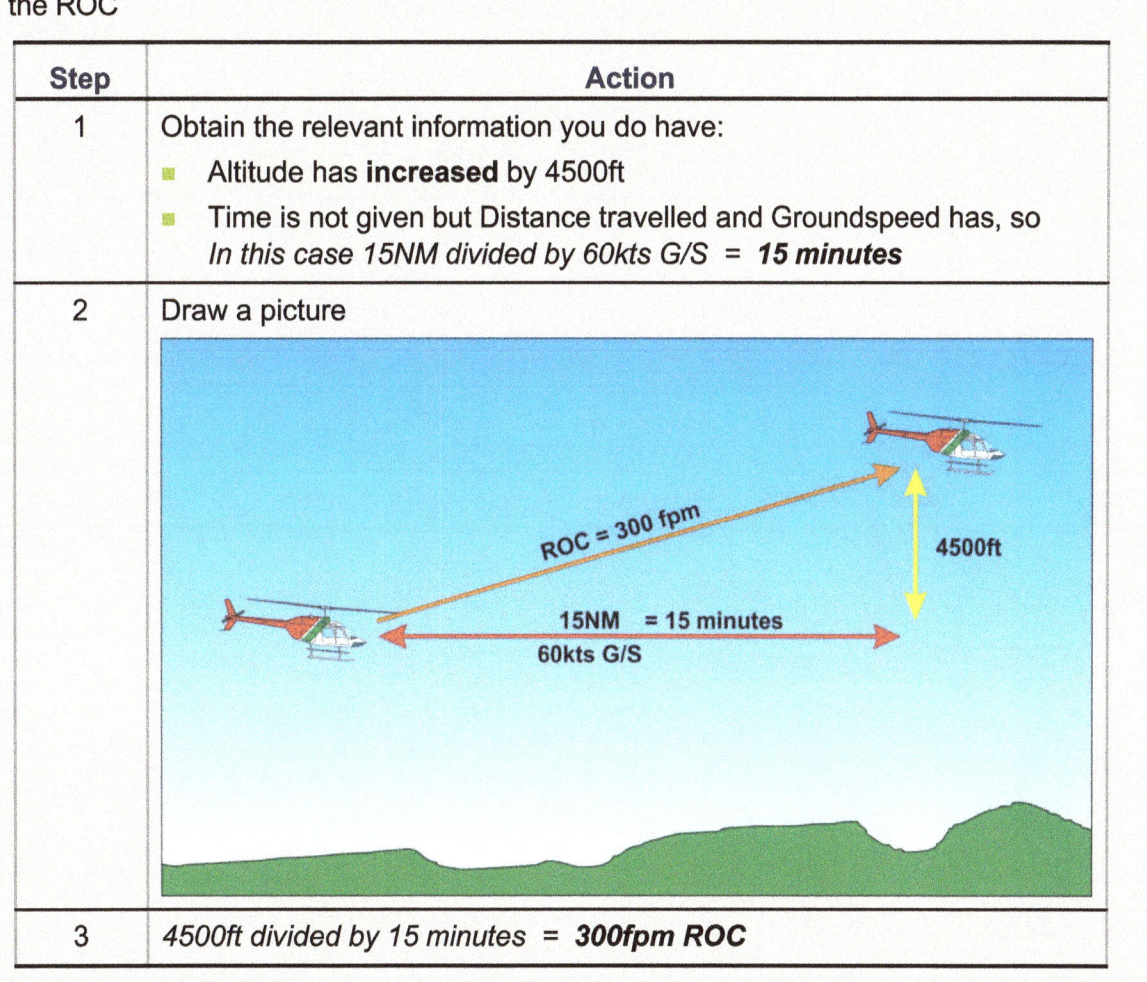
3	*4500ft divided by 15 minutes = **300fpm ROC***

Example

Given an Altitude decrease of 5000ft over a Distance of 20NM with a G/S of 100kts calculate the ROD

Step	Action
1	Obtain the relevant information you do have: ■ Altitude has **decreased** by 5000ft ■ Time is not given but Distance travelled and Groundspeed has, so *In this case 20NM divided by 100kts G/S =* **12 minutes**
2	Draw a picture 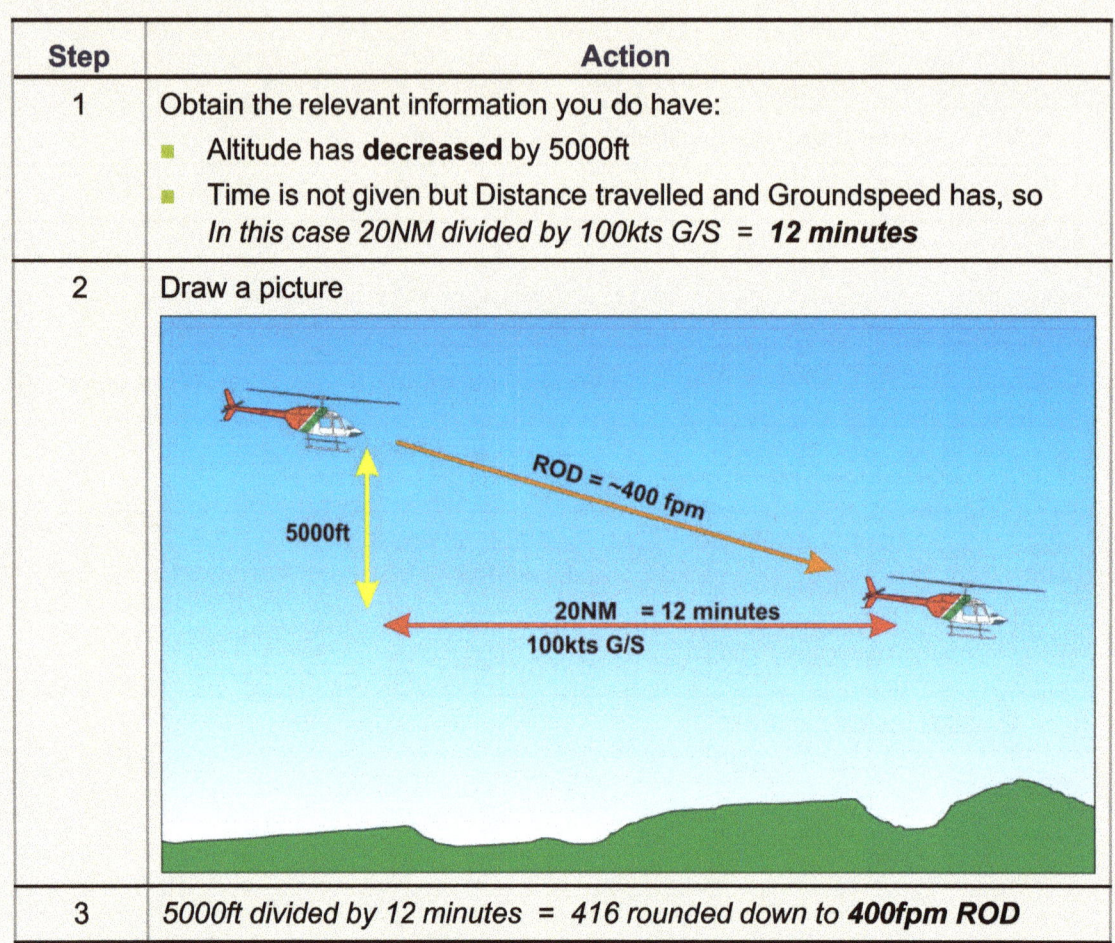
3	*5000ft divided by 12 minutes = 416 rounded down to* **400fpm ROD**

The **Rate** of climb or descent in a helicopter can be displayed on the **V**ertical **S**peed **I**ndicator (**VSI**). This is a pressure instrument and shows the change in pressure as the helicopter climbs or descends.

Aspen VSI

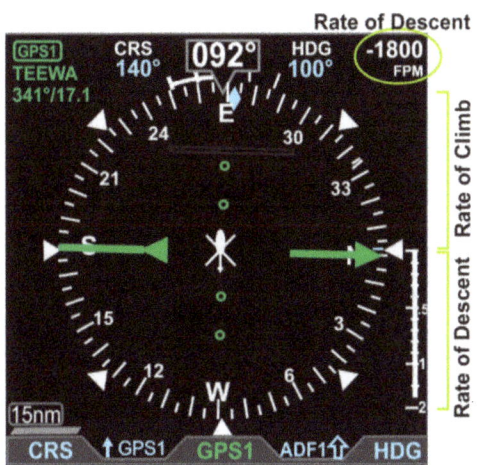

Analogue VSI

Climb and Descent Gradient

A "*Climb or a Descent Gradient*" shows the relationship between the height gained or lost over a distance travelled and is then normally expressed as a percentage (%) or as a degree of glideslope (°).

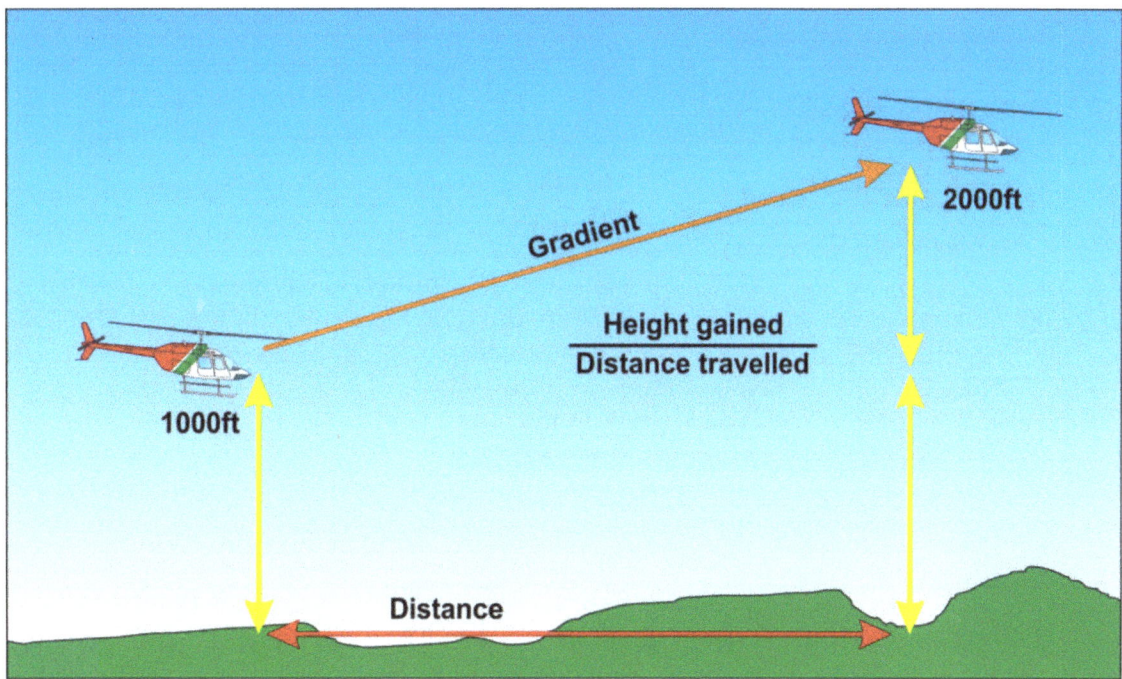

Climb and descent gradients are useful in determining whether an aircraft is going to be able to maintain a particular climb or descent to clear a particular obstacle that may be on track or to manage airspace requirements.

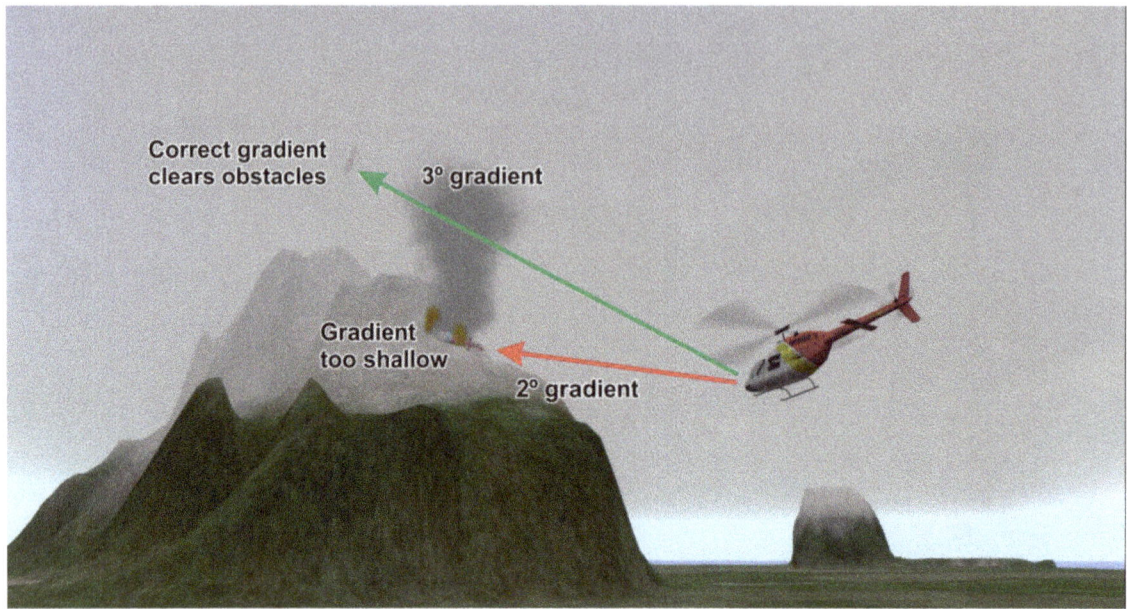

Each licenced aerodrome will have a Runway Distance Supplement found in the ERSA.

This not only gives the distances of the runways available for takeoff and landing but also gives any required climb gradients required in order to maintain obstacle clearance when using that runway direction.

Although this is mainly applicable to fixed wing operations, helicopters also have to abide by them if operating under the Instrument Flight Rules (IFR) or at night.

```
RUNWAY DISTANCE SUPPLEMENT          12-Nov-2015                          RDS S - 1

SUNSHINE COAST
RWY   (CN)    TORA          TODA              ASDA          LDA
12    (1)     650 (2133)    710 (2329) (4.43%)  650 (2133)    650 (2133)
30    (1)     650 (2133)    710 (2329) (2.15%)  650 (2133)    650 (2133)
      Slope 0.1% down to NW. RWY WID 18 RWS WID 90
18    (3)     1797 (5896)   1857 (6092) (2.71%) 1797 (5896)   1797 (5896)
36    (3)     1797 (5896)   1857 (6092) (2.22%) 1797 (5896)   1797 (5896)
      Transition SFC infringed by apron lights on W side. APCH SFC survey based on 150M inner edge
      WID.
      Slope Level. RWY WID 30 RWS WID 150
SUPPLEMENTARY TAKEOFF DISTANCES
RWY18 -   995(3264)(1.9)  1715(5627)(2.2)  1805(5922)(2.5)
RWY36 -   1535(5036)(1.6) 1718(5636)(1.9)  1854(6083)(2.2)
```

A Climb and Descent Gradient is commonly used in describing the glideslope required to maintain a particular instrument approach and will be stated on the Instrument Approach Plate (IAP).

In the example below, the descent profile required on final approach is 3°. This will require a combination of ROD and G/S to achieve a 3° glideslope.

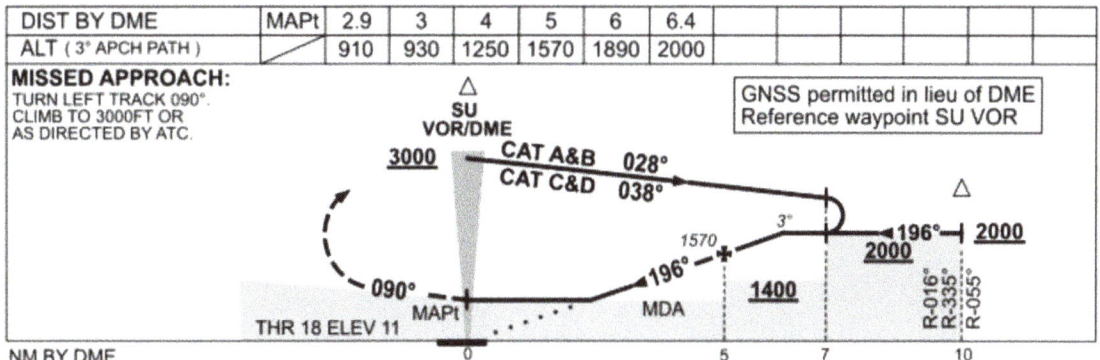

There are three (3) methods to calculate the Climb or Descent Gradient and the associated ROC or ROD and G/S to achieve it, they are:

1. In Flight Method
2. Pre-Flight Planning Method
3. Long Method

In Flight Method

The In-flight method uses a simple formula that can be calculated in your head (or on a calculator) while flying.

In general, every instrument approach normally has a descent gradient of 3°.

By multiplying the current G/S by five (5) this will equal the ROD required to achieve a 3° glideslope.

The formula to calculate a ROD to achieve a 3° Glideslope is:

$$G/S \times 5 = \text{ROD to achieve a 3° Glideslope}$$

Example
1. Consider a helicopter with a G/S of 100kts requiring a 3° Glideslope for an approach: 100 x 5 = ROD 500fpm required to achieve the 3° Glideslope
2. Consider a helicopter with a G/S of 85kts requiring a 3° Glideslope for an approach: 85 x 5 = ROD 425fpm required to achieve the 3° Glideslope
3. Consider a helicopter with a G/S of 120kts requiring a 3° Glideslope for an approach: 120 x 5 = ROD 600fpm required to achieve the 3° Glideslope

The same calculation can be made to calculate a 3° Climb Gradient which may be a requirement on some departures due to obstacles or noise abatement.

Typically, a helicopter is able to maintain at least a 6° climb gradient under normal operations so this calculation is not normally used unless flying a twin engine helicopter and having to calculate the climb gradient after one engine has failed as the ROC will significantly be different.

By multiplying the current G/S by five (5) this will equal the ROC required to achieve a 3° Climb Gradient.

The formula to calculate a ROC to achieve a 3° Climb Gradient is:

G/S x 5 = ROC to achieve a 3° Climb Gradient

Example
1. Consider a helicopter with a G/S of 100kts requiring a 3° Climb Gradient for departure: 100 x 5 = ROC 500fpm required to achieve the 3° Climb Gradient
2. Consider a helicopter with a G/S of 85kts requiring a 3° Climb Gradient for departure: 85 x 5 = ROC 425fpm required to achieve the 3° Climb Gradient
3. Consider a helicopter with a G/S of 120kts requiring a 3° Climb Gradient for departure: 120 x 5 = ROC 600fpm required to achieve the 3° Climb Gradient

 This shortcut to calculating the ROD or ROC required to achieve a 3° Glideslope or Climb Gradient is a handy tool for the pilot to memorise and use later on in instrument flying.

---

[21] By Lance Cpl. Robert R. Carrasco [Public domain], via Wikimedia Commons / https://upload.wikimedia.org/wikipedia/commons/5/53/A_U.S._Army_HH-60M_Blackhawk_medical_evacuation_%28medevac%29_helicopter_of_Army_Task_Force_Lift_%22Dust_Off%22%2C_Charlie_Company_1-171%2C_Aviation_Regiment%2C_departs_for_mission%2C_Forward_Operating_Base_Edinburgh%2C_Helmand_111209-M-CL319-178.jpg

Pre-Flight Planning Method

The Pre-Flight Planning method using the *Gradient Rate Nomograph* found in AIP DAP 2-1 (Departure and Approach Plates used in IFR) allows the pilot to quickly calculate the required ROC or ROD based on a G/S to achieve the desired Climb or Descent profile.

This graph allows the pilot to use a ruler to align a groundspeed with a ROC or ROD on the Gradient Rate Nomograph in order to determine either the Climb or Descent Gradient as a percentage (%), as a degree (°) of glideslope or in feet per nautical mile or (Ft/NM).

Example
Common Descent Profile
Consider a helicopter with a G/S while on descent of 100kts. In order to maintain a 5% Descent Gradient (which is the same as a 3 degree glideslope, which is the same as 318 feet per nautical mile) the ROD would have to be maintained at 500fpm.
Common Climb Profile
If the helicopter was departing on a climb at 60kts with a ROC of 600fpm the Climb Gradient would be equal to 6.5°.
Using the Nomograph
Using the aircraft's performance graphs to determine the available ROC or ROD for the day, given the aircraft's current AUW and then applying this information to the Nomograph allows the pilot to cross check the result with the Takeoff profile required for a particular runway in the ERSA.

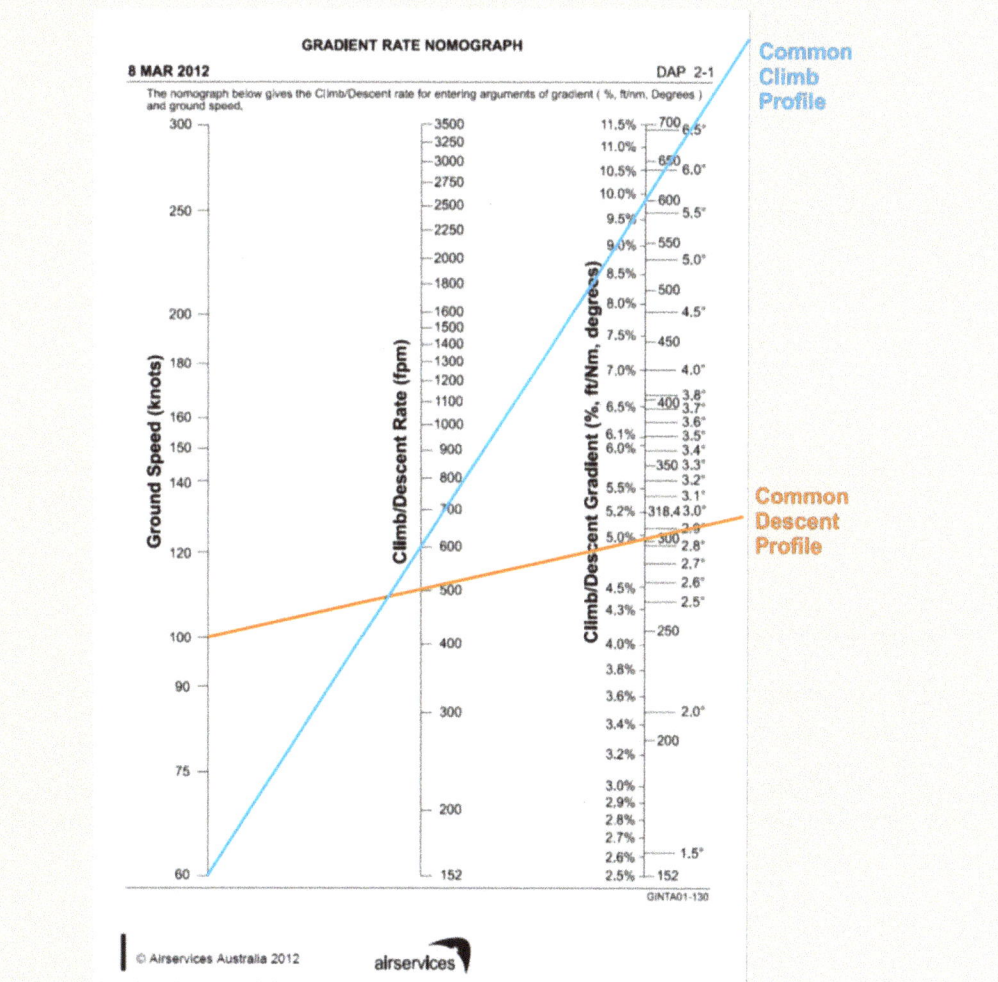

Long Method

The long method of doing a mathematical calculation.

To calculate the "*Climb Gradient,*" use the following formula:

$$\text{Gradient as a \%} = \frac{\text{ROC (fpm)}}{\text{Groundspeed}}$$

To calculate the "*Descent Gradient,*" use the following formula:

$$\text{Gradient as a \%} = \frac{\text{ROD (fpm)}}{\text{Groundspeed}}$$

To calculate the Climb or Descent Gradient complete the following steps:

Step	Action
1	Obtain the ROC or ROD
	Obtain the Groundspeed (G/S)
2	ROC or ROD divided by the Groundspeed (G/S) equals the Gradient

Example	
Given a ROC of 300 fpm and a G/S of 100kts, what is the climb gradient?	
Step	**Action**
1	Obtain the ROC
	In this case the ROC is 300fpm
	Obtain the Groundspeed (G/S)
	In this case the G/S is 100kts
2	Divide ROC by G/S
	In this case 300ROC divided by 100kts G/S = 3% Gradient

Airspace Protection

When operating within Controlled Airspace (CTA) there may be times, particularly on climb or descent, where the helicopter will get close to the airspace boundary.

On the other side of that boundary there may be another aircraft operating **O**utside **C**ontrolled **A**irspace (**OCTA**) that is not being controlled by ATC. This means the two aircraft may inadvertently get close to each other without even knowing it.

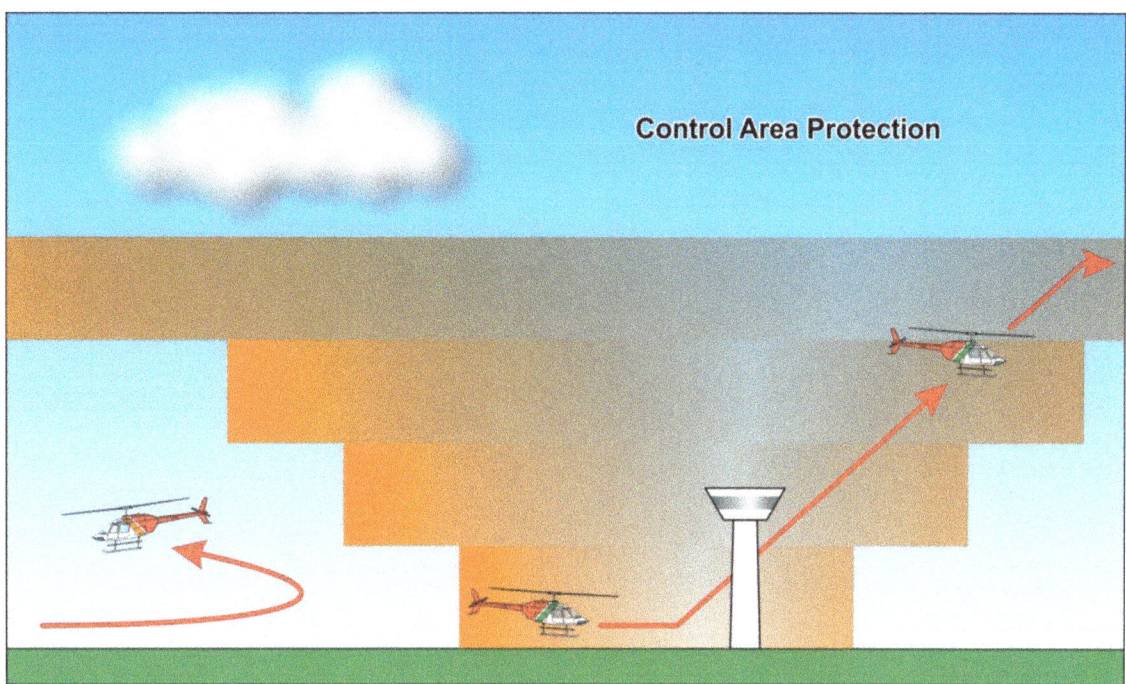

In order to maintain a safe distance from the airspace boundary the pilot will need to calculate a ROC or ROD that gives a 500 foot buffer. This is referred to as "*Airspace Protection*."

If the pilot desires to retain Airspace Protection during a climb or descent in Class D or C Airspace then the helicopter shall be flown to maintain at least 500ft above the lower limit of the CTA steps as shown in the diagram below.

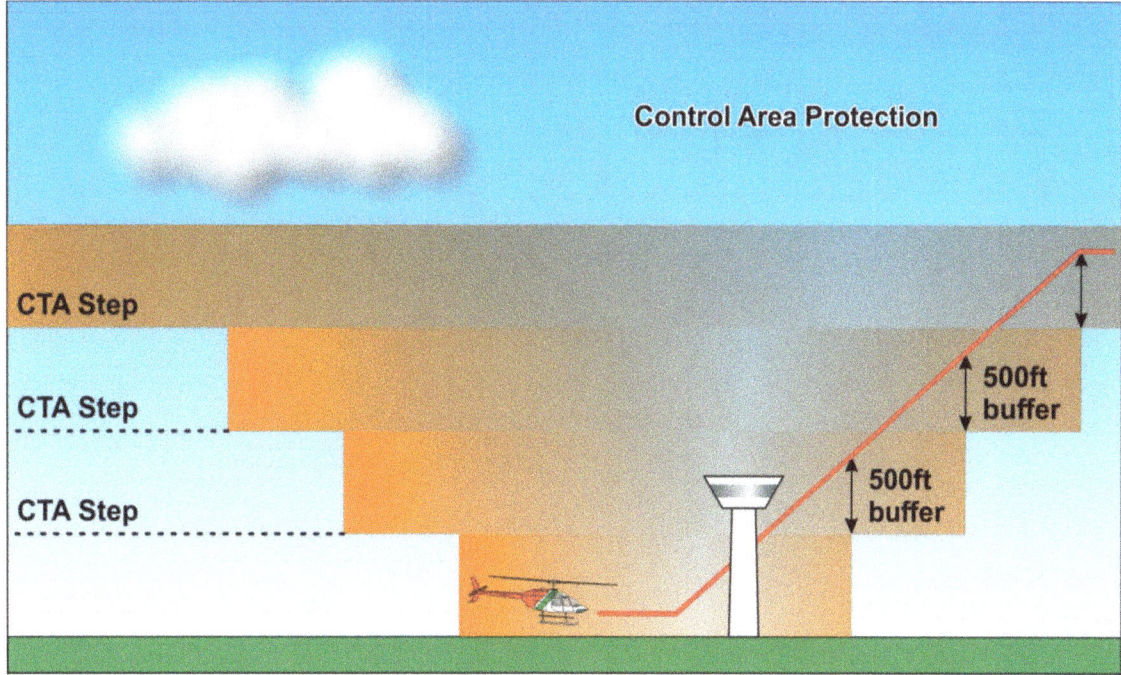

CALCULATING RATES OF CLIMB AND DESCENT

Review of CTA Steps

When making an approach into, or a departure from, a controlled airport it is common for the controlled airspace to be in steps radiating out from the centre of the controlled airport. These are referred to as **C**ontrolled **A**rea steps (**CTA** Steps).

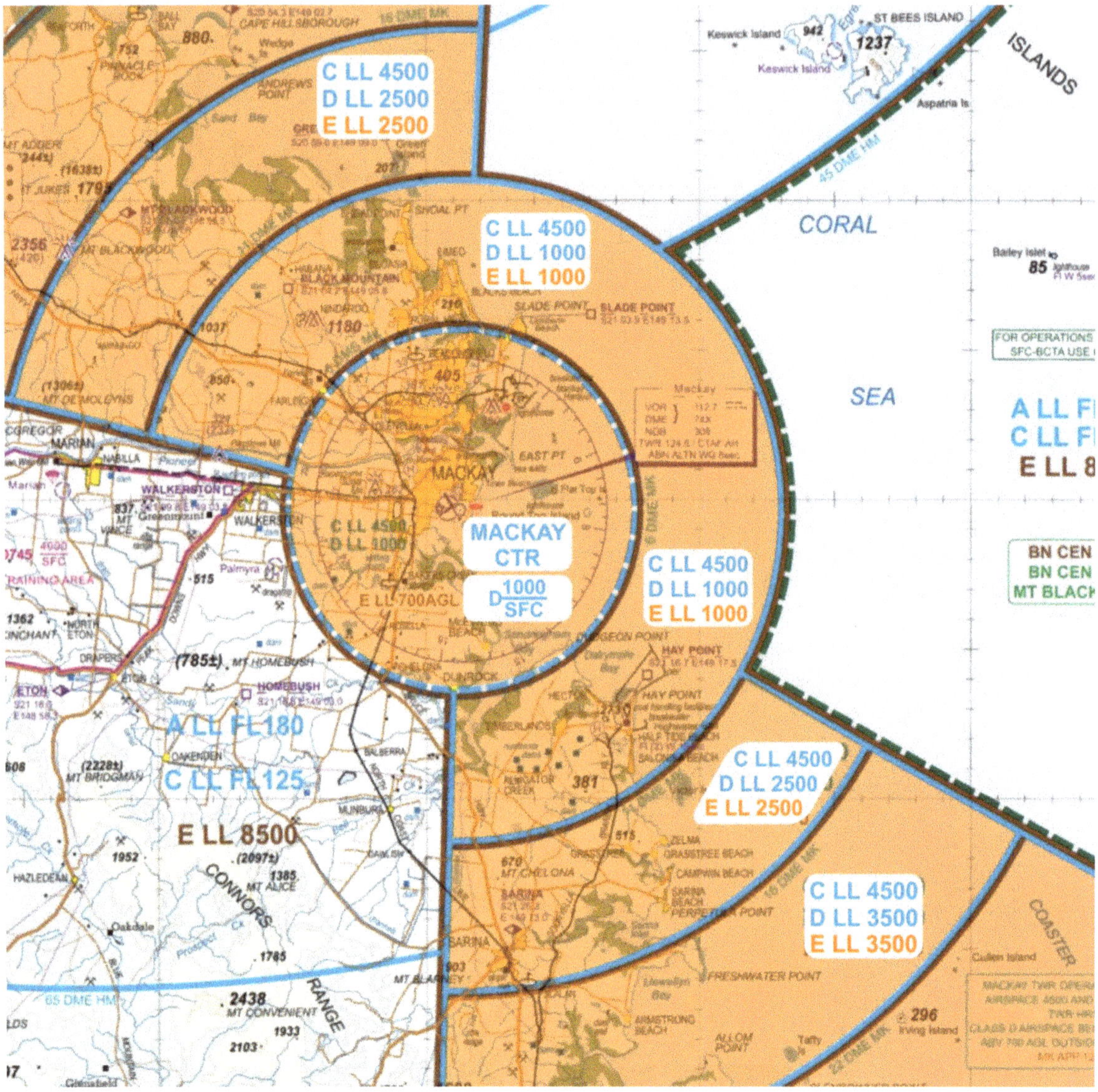

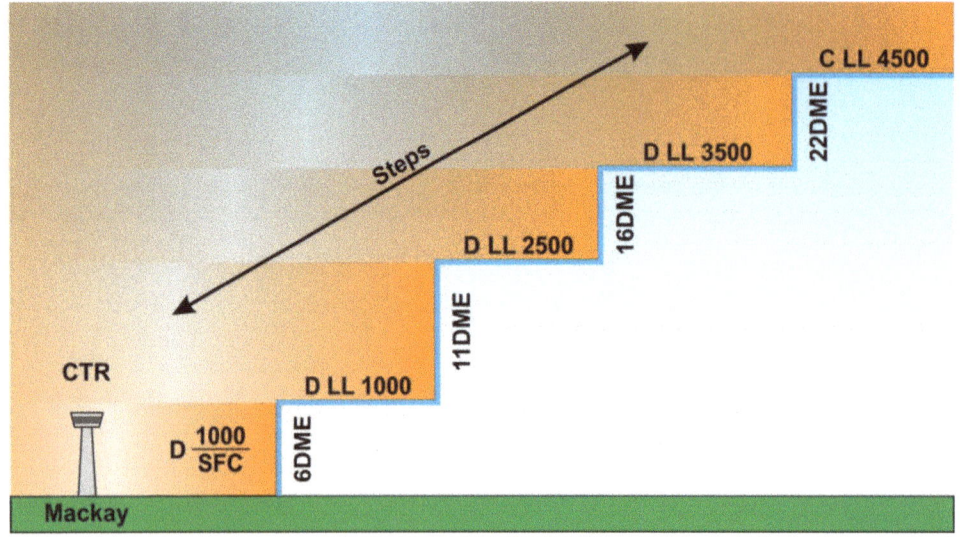

This assumes that the further away from the airport, the higher the helicopter will be, and the closer to the airport, the lower the helicopter is going to be.

Because ATC like to be "*controlling*" larger passenger carrying aircraft, controlled airspace will go in steps measured by distance from an airport and marked on detailed maps.

A CTA step is a blue line drawn on a VTC, VNC, ERC or TAC that shows a distance from a reference aerodrome and a **L**ower **L**evel (**LL**) where the height of the controlled airspace starts.

These steps are often referred to as an upside down wedding cake because when drawn as a side view it is obvious to see the steps.

In the image below *C LL 4500* refers to the Lower Level of C airspace starting at 4500ft and *D LL 3500* refers to the Lower Level of D airspace starting at 3500ft.

The distance is given as a number followed by either NM or DME. For example, in the image above *16 DME MK* refers to the CTA Step starting at 16 DME from Mackay.

The terms NM, DME and GPS are generically referred to as being the same but the reality is there are slight differences in how each of these is determined.

NM obviously refers to **N**autical **M**iles and is measured in feet from a reference point on a map.

DME refers to **D**istance **M**easuring **E**quipment and is measured by radio signals so has some inherent errors.

GPS refers to **G**lobal **P**ositioning **S**ystem and is mathematically measured by cross referencing multiple satellites with the GPS receiver with little or no significant error.

The DME is an older generation radio navigation instrument. When installed it provides the aircraft's distance from an associated transmitter when within range. The pilot can therefore easily and accurately read off the distance from the transmitter.

The DME has been replaced by the GPS, however, maps and charts still describe the distance as a DME distance when discussing CTA steps.

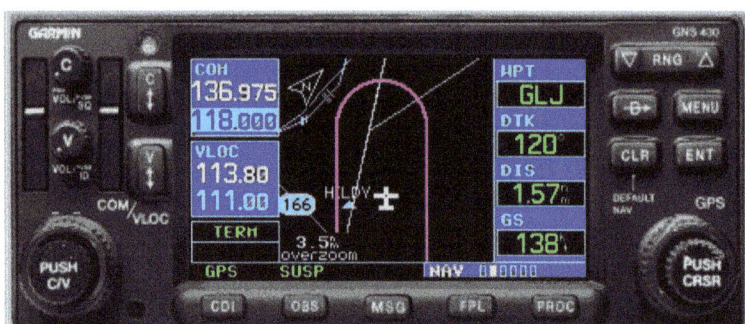

Over time this will change but in the meantime a pilot can use both the DME (if installed) or the GPS to state distance. The only requirement is when talking to ATC, the pilot must state which instrument was referenced for the distance, as the two instruments can give differing distances due to design errors in the DME.

If using the GPS as a reference for distance, then when talking to ATC the pilot should phrase the distance in miles followed by the words GPS.

If using the DME as a reference for distance, then when talking to ATC the pilot should phrase the distance in miles followed by the words DME.

Example
If 10NM from the airfield and this information was obtained from the GPS then the pilot would say "*10 GPS*" to ATC.
If 10NM from the airfield and this information was obtained from the DME then the pilot would say "*10 DME*" to ATC.
If a LL step is referred to as a distance in NM then it is the same as GPS but not the same as DME.
(This will be covered in more detail during the Instrument Rating Course)

Calculating a ROC/ROD to Maintain CTA Protection

Climbs

To calculate the ROC to maintain a 500 foot buffer from the CTA steps, and therefore maintain *Airspace Protection*, complete the following steps:

Step	Action
1	Collect the following information: • What is the helicopter's current distance and Altitude from the reference aerodrome? • At what distance and altitude does the helicopter cross the next CTA step?
2	Draw a picture to orientate yourself to the problem Exam questions will normally provide the following picture of the CTA steps 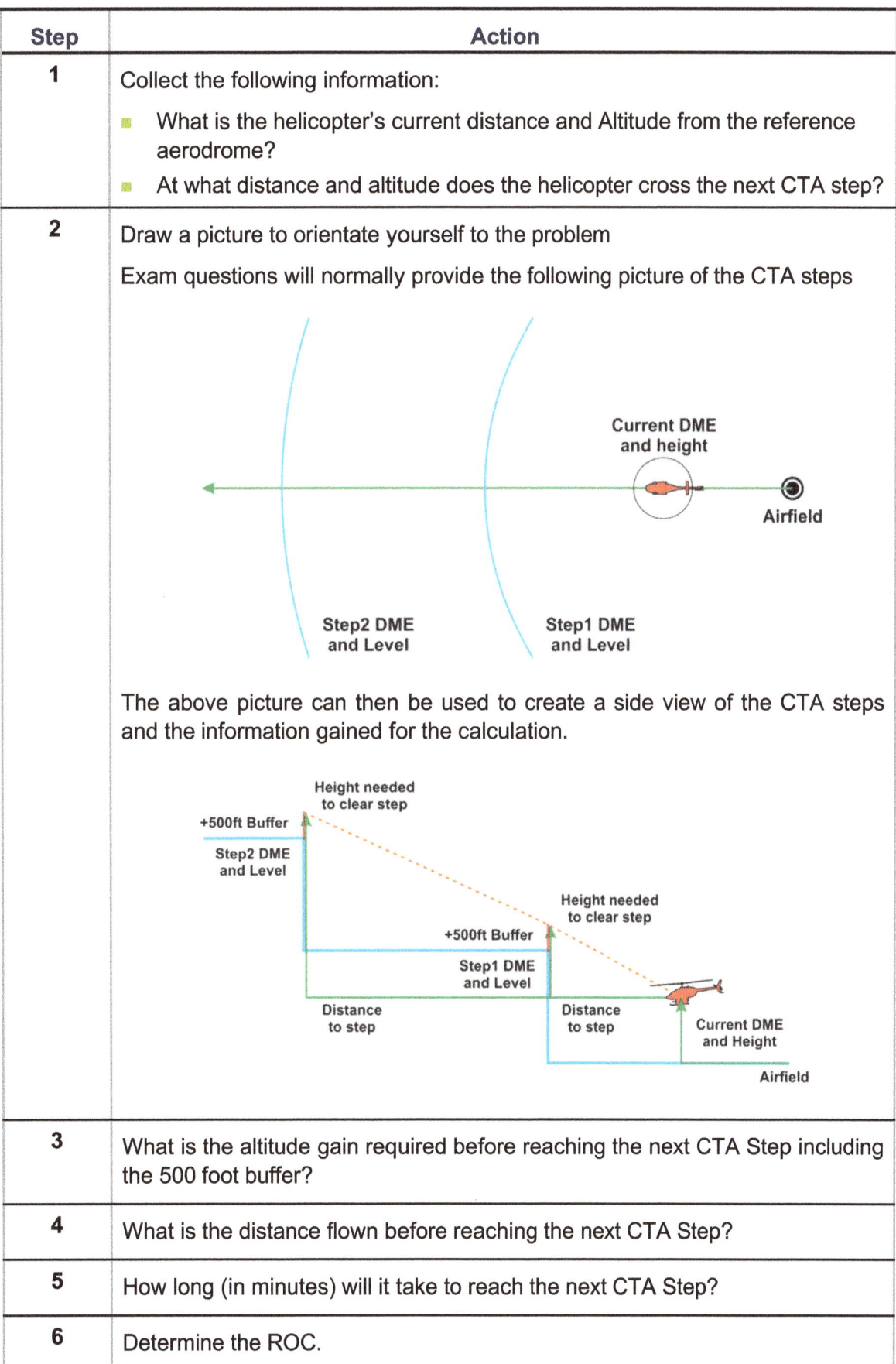 The above picture can then be used to create a side view of the CTA steps and the information gained for the calculation.
3	What is the altitude gain required before reaching the next CTA Step including the 500 foot buffer?
4	What is the distance flown before reaching the next CTA Step?
5	How long (in minutes) will it take to reach the next CTA Step?
6	Determine the ROC.

CALCULATING RATES OF CLIMB AND DESCENT

NAVIGATION — INTERNATIONAL HELICOPTER THEORY

Step	Action
7	Confirm that the ROC calculated will also be sufficient to cross the next CTA Step with a 500 foot buffer. (This will require repeating the above steps assuming the helicopter is now at the first CTA Step tracking towards the next CTA Step).

Example

Given the CTA steps are centred on YBHS and the helicopter is positioned at 3500ft AMSL and 20NM out from YBHS. A climbing G/S has been calculated of 120kts.

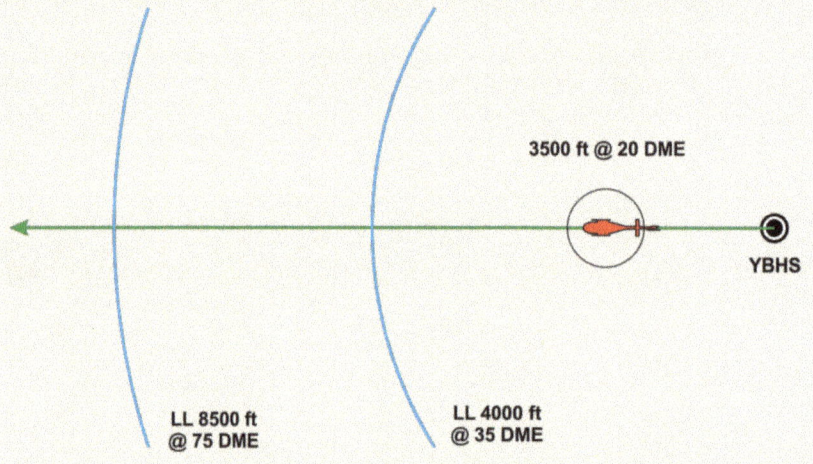

If controlled airspace protection of at least 500ft above the CTA Lower Level step (LL 4000 35 DME) is desired what is the minimum constant ROC for a continuous climb on track from the helicopters current position?

Step	Action
1	What is the helicopters current distance and Altitude from the reference aerodrome? *In this case 20DME from YBHS at 3500ft* At what distance and altitude does the helicopter cross the next CTA step? *In this case 35 DME from YBHS at 4500ft (LL 4000ft + 500ft buffer = 4500ft)*
2	Draw a picture

Step	Action
3	What is the altitude gain required before reaching the next CTA Step including the 500 foot buffer? *In this case the helicopter is currently at 3500ft and must climb to 4500ft therefore the Altitude gain is **1000ft** (4500 – 3500 = 1000)*
4	What is the distance flown before reaching the next CTA Step? *In this case the helicopter is currently at 20 DME from YBHS and has **15 DME to go** to reach the 35 DME step. (35 – 20 = 15DME)*
5	How long (in minutes) will it take to reach the next CTA Step? Using the Front Side of the Flight Computer do a Distance x G/S calculation to determine time *In this case 15 DME to go at 120kts G/S = 7.5 minutes* $$\frac{120kts}{60mins} = \frac{15NM}{7.5 mins}$$
6	Determine the ROC *In this case 1000ft of Altitude gain in 7.5 minutes = ROC 133fpm*

The reason for calculating the first CTA step is to ensure the 500ft buffer is achieved at the first step. Once that is confirmed then the pilot can calculate the next CTA step. As long as the ROC for the next CTA step is bigger than the first CTA step then the bigger ROC is the answer.

Descents

To calculate the ROD to maintain a 500 foot buffer from the CTA steps, and therefore maintain *Airspace Protection*, complete the following steps:

Step	Action
1	Collect the following information: - What is the helicopters current distance and Altitude from the reference aerodrome? - At what distance and altitude does the helicopter cross the next CTA step?

Step	Action
2	Draw a picture to orientate yourself to the problem Exam questions will normally provide the following picture of the CTA steps 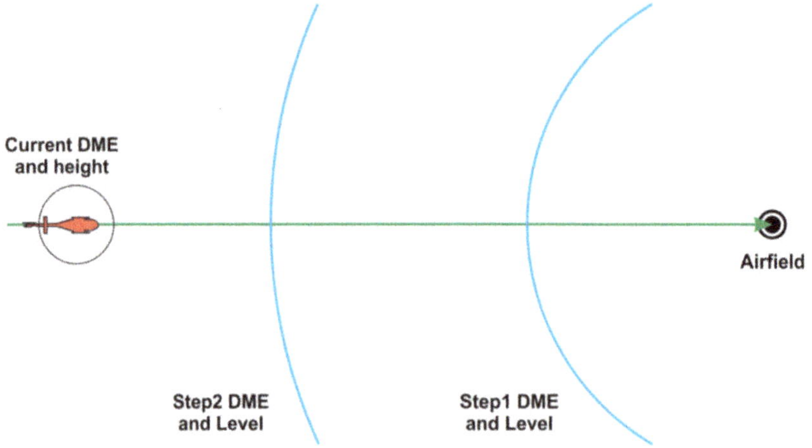 *[Diagram: top-down view showing Current DME and height on the left, with two arc lines representing Step2 DME and Level and Step1 DME and Level, with Airfield on the right]* The above picture can then be used to create a side view of the CTA steps and the information gained for the calculation. 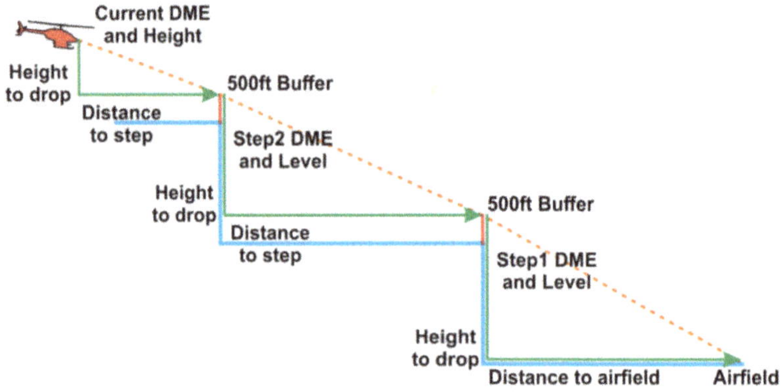 *[Diagram: side view showing stepped descent profile with Current DME and Height at top, then Height to drop / Distance to step / 500ft Buffer down to Step2 DME and Level, then again down to Step1 DME and Level, then Height to drop / Distance to airfield to Airfield]*
3	What is the altitude **loss** required before reaching the next CTA Step including the 500 foot buffer?
4	What is the distance flown before reaching the next CTA Step?
5	How long (in minutes) will it take to reach the next CTA Step?
6	Determine the ROD.
7	Confirm that the ROD calculated will also be sufficient to cross the next CTA Step with a 500 foot buffer. (This will require repeating the above steps assuming the helicopter is now at the first CTA Step tracking towards the next CTA Step).

CALCULATING RATES OF CLIMB AND DESCENT

NAVIGATION

Example

Given the CTA steps are centred on YBHS and the helicopter is at positioned at 80DME from YBHS at 9000ft AMSL. A descending G/S has been calculated of 130kts.

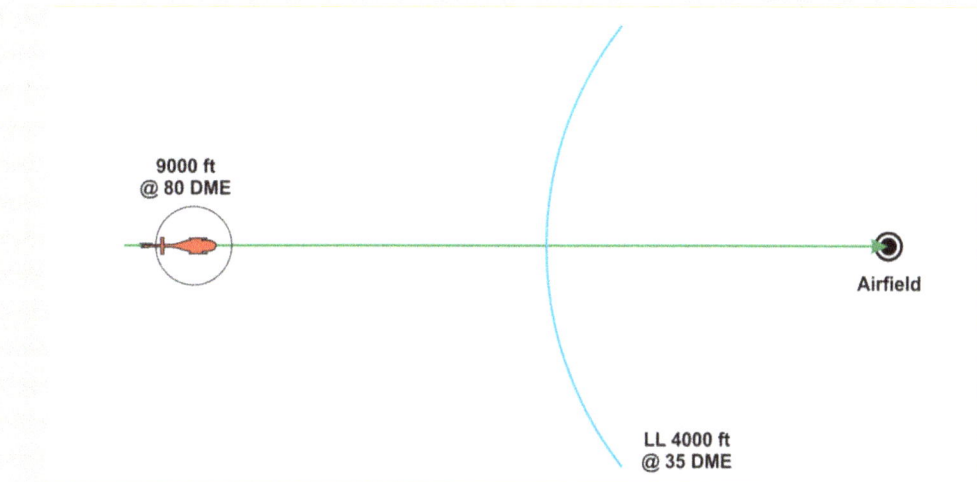

If controlled airspace protection of at least 500ft above the CTA Lower Level step (LL 4500 at 35DME) is desired what is the minimum ROD for a continuous descent on track from the helicopter's current position?

Step	Action
1	What is the helicopters current distance and Altitude from the reference aerodrome? *In this case 80DME from YBHS at 9000ft* At what distance and altitude does the helicopter cross the next CTA step? *In this case 75DME from YBHS at 9000ft (LL 8500ft + 500ft buffer = 9000ft)*
2	Draw a picture 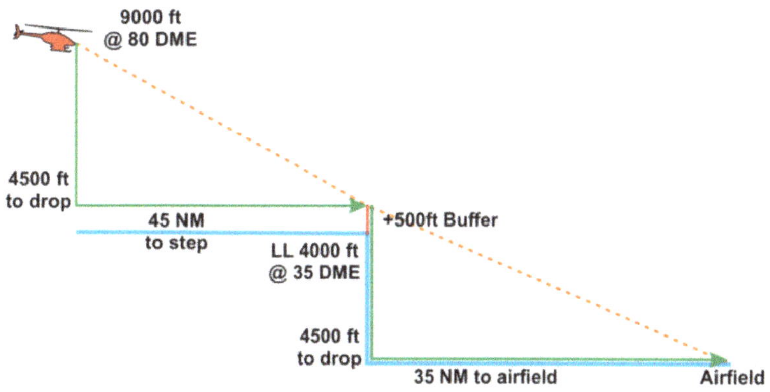
3	What is the altitude loss required before reaching the next CTA Step including the 500 foot buffer? *In this case the helicopter is currently at 9000ft and must descend to 4500ft therefore the Altitude loss is **4500ft** (9000 – 4500 = 4500)*

4	What is the distance flown before reaching the next CTA Step? *In this case the helicopter is currently at 80DME from YBHS and has **45DME to go** to reach the 35 DME step. (80 – 35 = 45DME)*
5	How long (in minutes) will it take to reach the next CTA Step? Using the Front Side of the Flight Computer do a Distance x G/S calculation to determine time *In this case 45DME to go at 130kts G/S = 20.8 minutes* ![flight computer]
6	Determine the ROD. *In this case 4500ft of Altitude loss in 20.8 minutes = ROD 216.34fpm rounded to ROD 216fpm*
7	Confirm that the ROD calculated will also be sufficient to cross the next CTA Step with a 500 foot buffer. *In this case there are no other CTA steps to consider so the calculation ends here*

Theory Exam

If a question:

- states that airspace protection is **desired** then it is up to the pilot to know to add 500ft clearance from the lower limit (LL) of the DME step (as shown in the above examples).

- **does not state** that airspace protection is desired then the pilot need not make allowance for the extra 500ft (then simply delete 500ft buffer from the calculations above).

12 Point of No Return (PNR)

The **P**oint of **N**o **R**eturn (**PNR**) is an essential requirement of flight planning for helicopter crews flying offshore on long-range flights.

The PNR is the furthest distance an aircraft can travel away from its departure point before having to return to the same point or another airfield with all reserve fuel and holding fuel intact.

Unlike the ETP, the PNR is dependent on the fuel endurance of the aircraft.

The PNR may not be a point along a track but a *Time* before having to return to the planned destination.

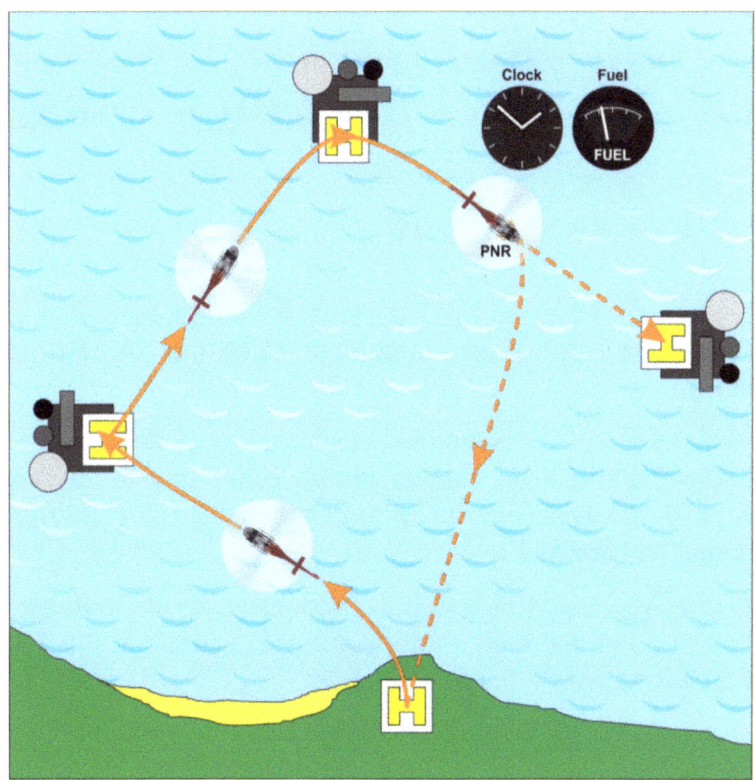

POINT OF NO RETURN (PNR)

Example

Consider a helicopter departing to an oilrig or a ship 300NM offshore.

The ETP in nil wind conditions may be 150NM along track but the helicopter may have enough fuel onboard to get all the way to the oil rig or ship but upon arrival discover that bad weather and visibility is going to prevent a landing.

If the pilot has calculated the PNR as a time, then he may know that the helicopter can hold for another 45 minutes before reaching the point at which the helicopter cannot return to the departure aerodrome because of lack of fuel (PNR) at which point the helicopter must either land at the oil rig or ship or immediately return to its departure point.

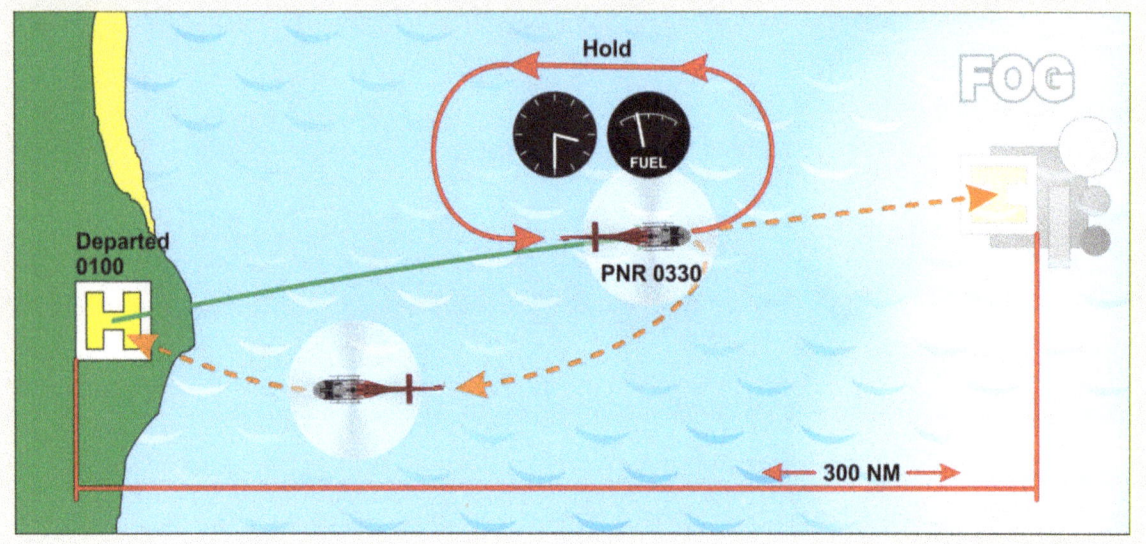

To calculate the PNR use the following formula:

$$\frac{\text{Total Safe Endurance (in minutes)} \times \text{G/S HOME}}{\text{G/S OUT} + \text{G/S HOME}} = \text{Time to PNR (in minutes)}$$

G/S OUT is the groundspeed used when continuing out from the departure point towards the destination and taking into account any HWC or TWC and applying that to the TAS.

G/S HOME is the groundspeed used to return to the chosen landing point, this may be the destination, departure point or an alternate. It will be the TAS for that leg corrected for any HWC or TWC.

Total Safe Endurance (TSE) is the maximum amount of *Time* that can be spent flying out to the PNR position, and still be able to return to the original departure point (or alternate landing point) taking into account all of the necessary *fuel requirements* including reserve fuel, holding fuel, and taxi fuel.

To calculate the TSE, work backwards and remove the operational fuel requirements, (reserves, holding, and taxi fuel), so they are not included in the TSE calculations but kept aside and therefore remain in the fuel tank!

When calculating the TSE, as shown below, it is important to remember that all fuel requirements are to be stated in minutes.

Fuel is calculated as follows:

	Fuel considerations	**Example**
	Total fuel onboard the aircraft at start up	300mins
Minus	Fuel allowance for taxi	15mins
Minus	Fixed reserves as required for the flight	30mins
Minus	Any holding fuel required at the departure point (remember you are working this out on returning to your base so if it requires holding you have to allow for it)	60mins
Equals	Cruise fuel plus the 15% variable reserve	195mins
Minus	15% variable reserve (divide the cruise fuel by 1.15 to remove the variable reserve)	15%
Equals	Total Safe Endurance (TSE)	169mins

Variable fuel is often a legal or Company or Unit requirement to allow for variations in fuel consumption. As such the 15% value may be changed or not required at all. If the variable amount is different to 15% as given in the above example simply change that part of the calculation.

For example: If the Variable Reserve is given as 10%, then divide the cruise fuel by 1.10 instead.

POINT OF NO RETURN (PNR)

Calculating Time to the PNR

To calculate the *Time* to the PNR complete the following steps:

Step	Action
1	Determine the Groundspeed **OUT** from the departure point. (This will require a calculation using the Flight Computer considering Track, W/V and TAS to determine a HCW or a TWC)
2	Determine the Groundspeed **HOME** from to the departure point. (This will require a calculation using the Flight Computer considering Track, W/V and TAS to determine a HWC or a TWC)
3	Draw a picture G/S out towards PNR G/S home from PNR Departure Point (Land back at the departure airport with all fuel reserves intact) — Destination
4	Calculate the Total Safe Endurance (TSE)
5	Enter the above information into the formula to determine the *time* to the PNR $$\frac{\text{Total Safe Endurance (in minutes)} \times \text{G/S HOME}}{\text{G/S OUT} + \text{G/S HOME}} = \text{Time to PNR (in minutes)}$$

Example

Given the following information, calculate the **Time** to the PNR.

Fuel on board at start-up	150 minutes
Taxi Fuel	5 minutes
Fixed Reserve	20 minutes
Holding Fuel at departure	30 minutes
Variable Reserve	15%
TAS	120kts
Wind Components	15kts Headwind OUT, 15kts Tailwind HOME

Step	Action
1	Determine the Groundspeed **OUT** from the departure point *In this case* *120kts TAS − 15kts HWC = 105kts G/S OUT*

POINT OF NO RETURN (PNR)
NAVIGATION

INTERNATIONAL HELICOPTER THEORY

2	Determine the Groundspeed **HOME** from to the departure point *In this case* 120kts TAS + 15kts TWC = 135kts G/S HOME
3	Draw a picture G/S out towards PNR G/S home from PNR Departure Point (Land back at the departure airport with all fuel reserves intact) Destination

4	Calculate the TSE (Total safe endurance):
	In this case:
	
	    150 minutes Fuel on board at start-up
	− 5 minutes Taxi Fuel
	− 20 minutes Fixed Reserve
	− 30 minutes Holding fuel for return to departure
	= 95 minutes Cruise Fuel including the variable reserve
	    95 minutes Remove variable reserve
	    ―――――――
	    1.15
	= **83 minutes** **Total Safe Endurance (TSE)**

5	Enter the information into the formula: *In this case* $$\frac{83 \text{ minutes} \times 135\text{kts G/S HOME (11205)}}{105\text{kts G/S OUT} + 135\text{kts G/S HOME (240)}} = 46.68 \text{ minutes}$$ Rounded to **47 minutes** to the PNR from the departure point

Point of No Return (PNR)

Calculating Distance to the PNR

Once the PNR has been calculated using the above steps, the result will always be in minutes therefore the position of the PNR from the departure point will be in MINUTES FROM the departure point.

If the pilot is now required to convert the minutes from the departure point to the PNR into a distance of the PNR from the departure point then use the Front Side of the Flight Computer to complete a simple Time multiplied by G/S to calculate a distance.

Example
Given the following information, calculate the **Distance** to the PNR.
Using the same example as above, simply add one extra step (step 6) to the process to calculate distance:

Fuel on board at start-up	150 minutes
Taxi Fuel	5 minutes
Fixed Reserve	20 minutes
Holding Fuel at departure	30 minutes
Variable Reserve	15%
TAS	120kts
Wind Components	15kts Headwind OUT, 15kts Tailwind HOME

Step	Action
1	Determine the Groundspeed **OUT** from the departure point *In this case* *120kts TAS − 15kts HWC = 105kts G/S OUT*
2	Determine the Groundspeed **HOME** from to the departure point *In this case* *120kts TAS + 15kts TWC = 135kts G/S HOME*
3	Draw a picture

4	Calculate the TSE (Total safe endurance):
	In this case:
	    150 minutes Fuel on board at start-up
	 - 5 minutes Taxi Fuel
	 - 20 minutes Fixed Reserve
	 - 30 minutes Holding fuel for return to departure
	 = 95 minutes Cruise Fuel including the variable reserve
	     $\dfrac{95 \text{ minutes}}{1.15}$ Remove variable reserve
	 = **83 minutes** **Total Safe Endurance (TSE)**

5	Enter the information into the formula: *In this case* $$\dfrac{83 \text{ minutes} \times 135\text{kts G/S HOME (11205)}}{105\text{kts G/S OUT} + 135\text{kts G/S HOME (240)}} = 46.68 \text{ minutes}$$ Rounded to **47 minutes** to the PNR from the departure point
6	Using the Flight Computer convert the ***Time*** OUT to the PNR, to the ***Distance*** OUT to the PNR *In this case* $$\dfrac{105\text{kts}}{60\text{mins}} = \dfrac{82\text{NM}}{47 \text{ mins}}$$ The Distance to the PNR is 82NM

It is very important to note that calculating a Distance to the PNR only works if flying in a straight line on a long leg. If the helicopter has sufficient fuel on board, if the flight plan takes the helicopter to multiple destinations or if the helicopter has to hold or divert then a distance calculation will not work.

Calculating a Time to PNR is the most accurate way to measure a PNR.

13 Radio Navigation

Introduction

The VFR pilot is able to use Radio Navigation aids to **supplement** (assist) VFR navigation. This is often referred to as a **secondary** means of navigating.

For the VFR pilot the **primary** means of navigating is by applying Dead Reckoning navigation techniques using a map, compass and clock.

However, in modern helicopters, the use of Radio navigation aids is encouraged and is used to make sure that your Dead Reckoning navigation is correct.

Remember the goal of navigating is to actually get from one place to another, so any help you can get in doing that, the easier and more accurate the navigation will be.

The Radio Navigation aids available to use as a supplement to VFR navigation include the:

- NDB
- VOR, and
- GPS.

For the VFR pilot only a basic understanding of these aids is required as they will not be used for making instrument approaches.

Instead the VFR pilot simply needs to be able to:

1. Point to and name each aid in the cockpit,

2. **Turn** the aid ON,

3. **Tune** (select) the appropriate frequency,

4. **Identify** that it is the correct frequency,

5. **Test** the aid to make sure it is receiving the correct signal, and

6. Use the aid to help determine the current position or confirm where the destination is.

What is a Radio Navigation Aid

A radio navigation aid is a system that transmits a radio signal from either a ground based station or a satellite in space to a receiver in the helicopter.

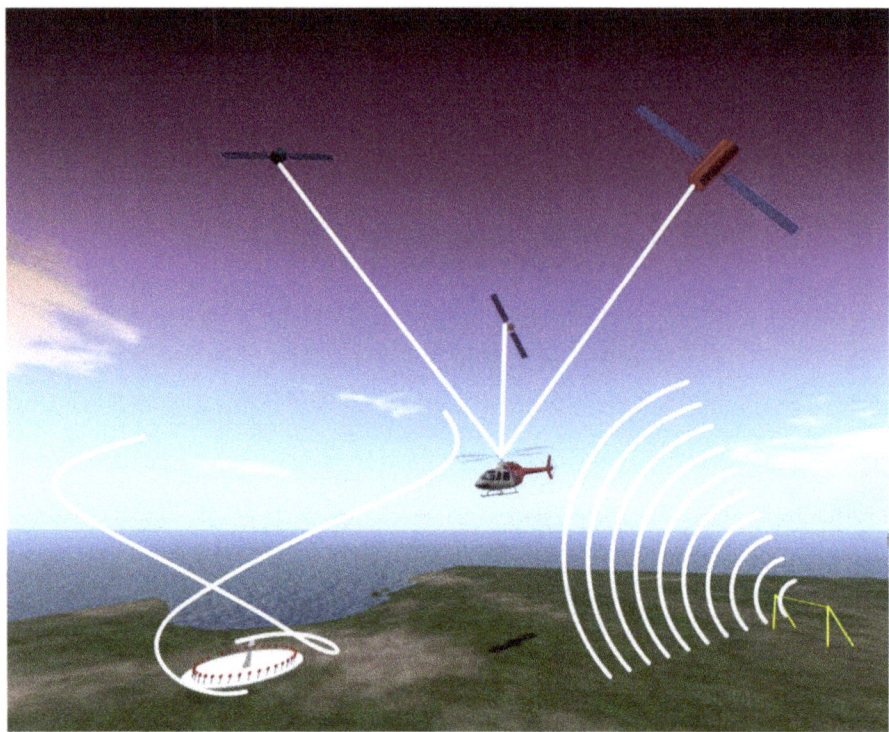

This receiver will then display the information onto an instrument in the cockpit in various different ways depending on the design of the instrument and the type of information transmitted.

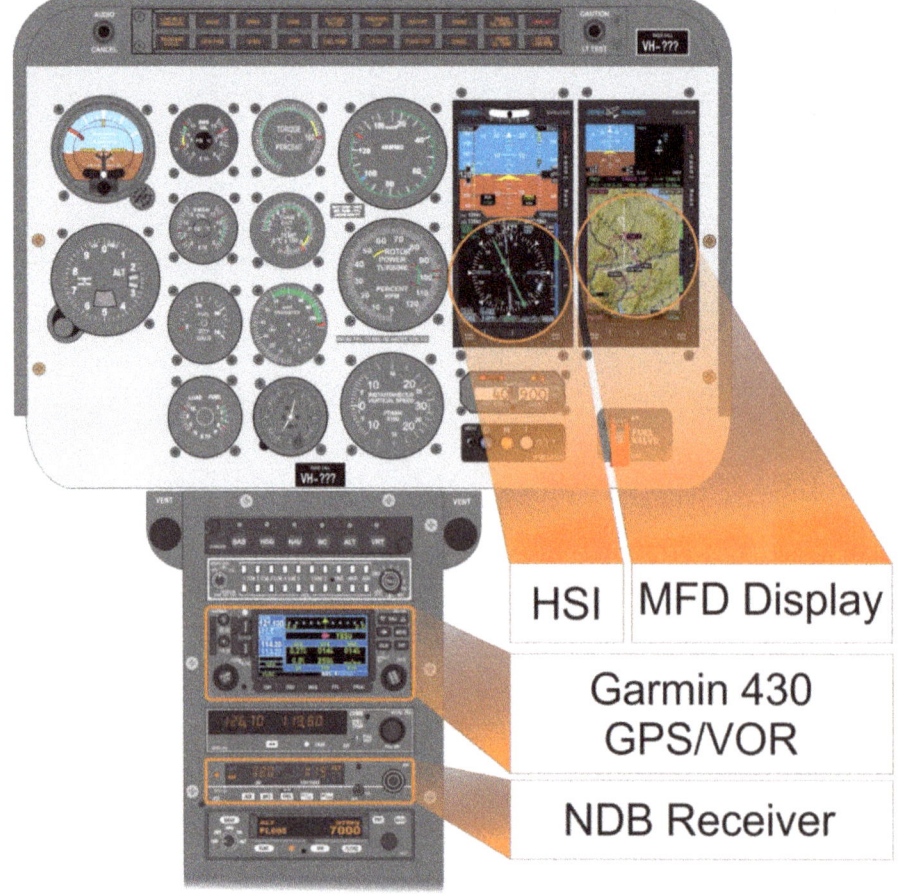

How the Information is Displayed

There are four (4) ways that the Radio Navigation aid may display its information in the cockpit to the pilot. They are:

1. Written Information
2. Multi-Function Display (MFD)
3. Azimuth indicator
4. Course Deviation Indicator (CDI)

Written Information

Written information may be displayed on a screen in the cockpit. This is relevant to the GPS which is a device that has a built in database of all airports and registered waypoints.

Waypoint

A "waypoint" is defined as a reference point in physical space for the purpose of navigation. Before the introduction of GPS all waypoints were two (2) dimensional; given in terms of latitude and longitude. More often than not, the term "landmark" or "navigational point" was used.

GPS has the ability to also give altitude information so that a three (3) dimensional position can be created. This is collectively called a "waypoint". The term waypoint is now commonly used in navigation to mean any identifiable position that is available within the GPS database.

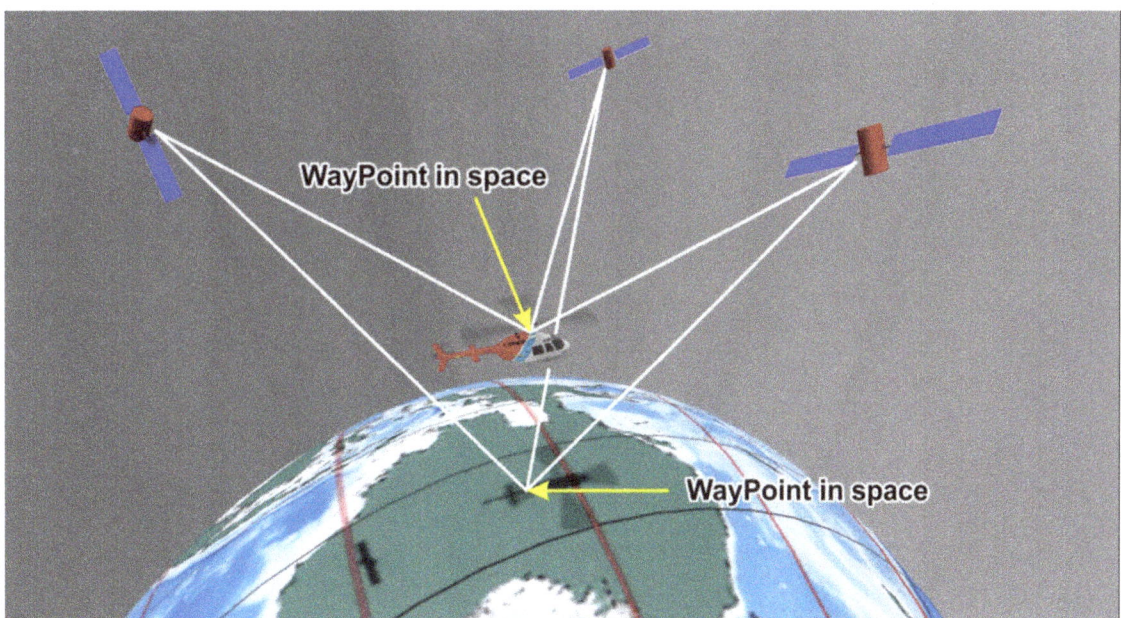

The radio signals from the satellites allow the GPS to determine where it is and then through internal mathematical calculations is able to project or "reckon" where it is going automatically and display information such as current ground speed, heading, altitude, distance, ETI and ETA for the pilot to read.

The GPS has the ability to do much, much more as it is a very powerful instrument, but the VFR pilot only needs a rudimentary (basic) knowledge of how to use it.

The GPS has multiple pages that the pilot can scroll through and use, with different information contained on each page. It will take some time and practice to understand how to get the best out of it and how to use its various features.

More detailed information can be found in the Becker Helicopters "Pilot Equipment Quick Reference Guide" or the full Garmin "GNS 430 Reference Guide".

Pilot Equipment Quick Reference Guide

Garmin GNS 430 Reference Guide

Multi-Function Display (MFD)

The radio navigation aid may be a picture shown on a screen, called a Multi-Function Display or MFD for short.

A MFD will take information from a GPS and display an overlay of a map and a picture of the helicopter so that the pilot can see exactly where they are and where they are going.

The map will move with the helicopter and the MFD has the ability to also display airspace boundaries, terrain and navigation waypoints such as towns, cities and in some cases even weather.

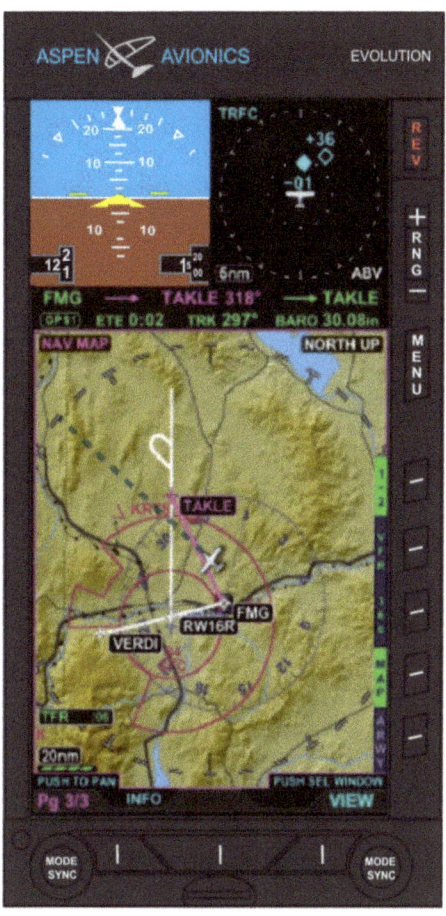

Azimuth Indicator

The radio navigation aid may be an Azimuth indicator. The word azimuth is Arabic meaning "directions".

All radio navigation aids can display information onto an azimuth (directions) indicator. In its simplest form, this consists of a pointed needle overlaid on a compass ring that points to the relevant navigation aid or destination.

Often referred to as a homing needle, the pilot can use the azimuth indicator to point to where they are going and then follow it to get "home".

In modern helicopters, the azimuth indicator is overlaid on to the Horizontal Situation Indicator (HSI). In Glass cockpit displays the pilot may be able to bring up multiple needles all pointing to different radio navigation aids or destinations.

In this case it can sometimes be confusing as the pilot receives too much information. It is best to use only what you need to determine your position or where you are going, rather than cluttering up the screen with multiple needles all pointing in different directions.

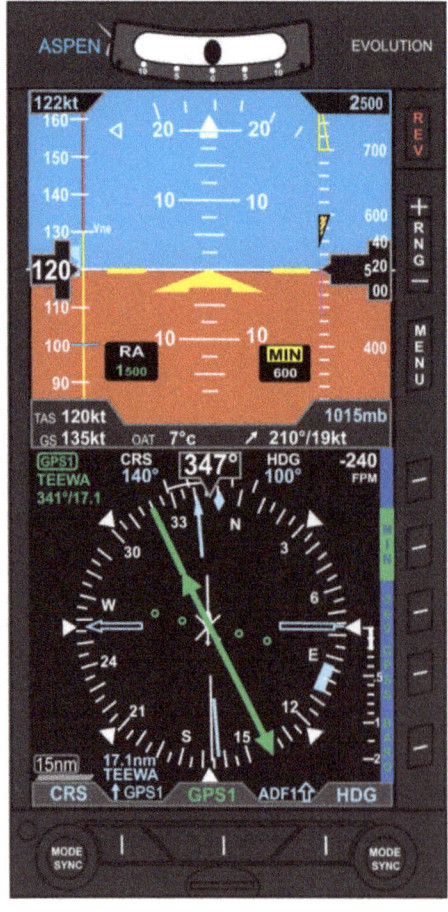

[23] http://i.ebayimg.com/00/s/NDUyWDUwNQ==/$(KGrHqZ,!gwE9T96KBrmBPc7S4Cj0Q~~60_35.JPG

Course Deviation Indicator (CDI)

Lastly, the radio navigation aid may be a Course Deviation Indicator or CDI for short.

This is only available to the VOR and GPS. In its simplest form it is a modified azimuth indicator that can split so that the pilot can see, in graphic form, where the desired track is compared to where the helicopter currently is. A CDI allows the pilot to determine the helicopter's lateral (left or right) position relative to the desired course.

Right of track

If the helicopter is to the right of the desired course then the CDI bar within the azimuth needle deflects to the left.

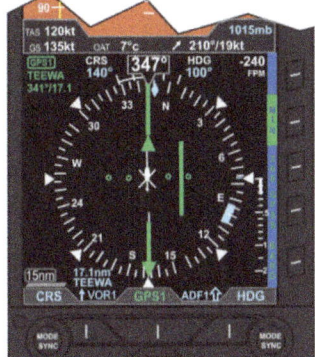

Left of track

If the helicopter is to the left of the desired course then the CDI bar within the azimuth needle deflects to the right.

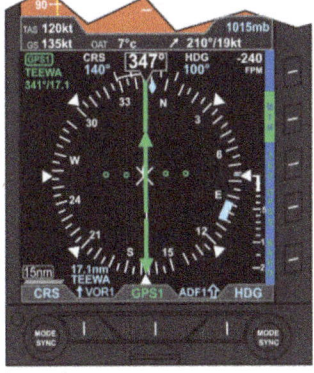

On Track

If the helicopter is exactly on course then the CDI needle will be in the middle.

In modern helicopters the CDI indicator can be overlaid on the HSI within the Glass display.

It is also possible to have both the Azimuth and the CDI displayed at the same time.

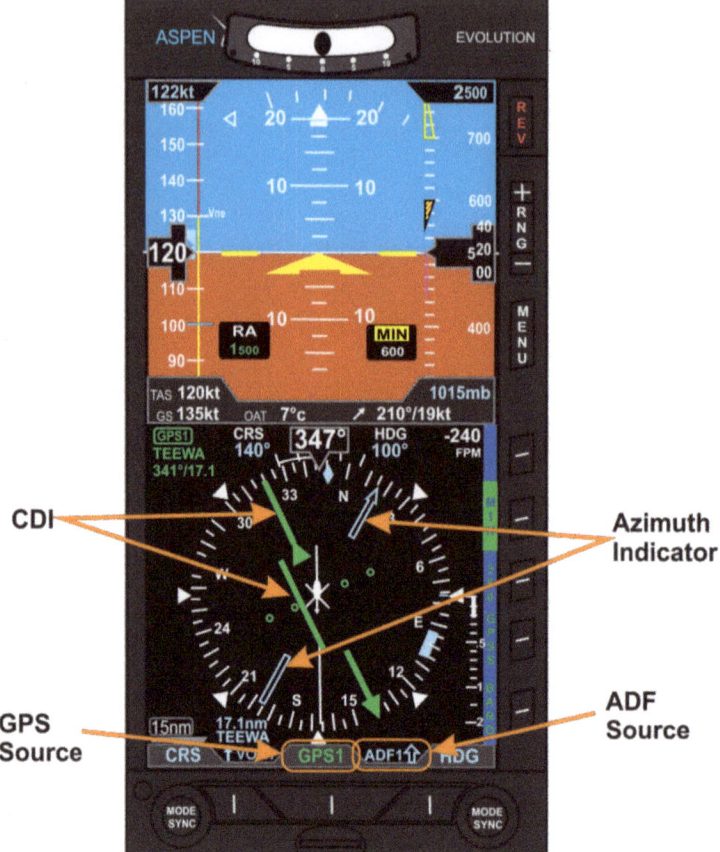

The NDB

The **Non Directional Beacon (NDB)** Radio Navigation aid is made up of two principal components:

- the ground station component called the **NDB**, and
- the helicopter installed component called the **ADF** which stands for Automatic Direction Finder. The ADF has a receiver and frequency selection panel and a separate Azimuth indicator.

Note: In some texts it may also be referred to as the Airborne Direction Finder or Helicopter Direction Finder

It can be referred to by the pilot as either the NDB or the ADF. Both terms are interchangeable and are taken to mean the same thing.

The ADF allows the pilot to identify where a NDB station is and then determine the position of the helicopter relative to the station by interpreting the Azimuth needle on the ADF indicator.

ADF receiver   **ADF indicator**

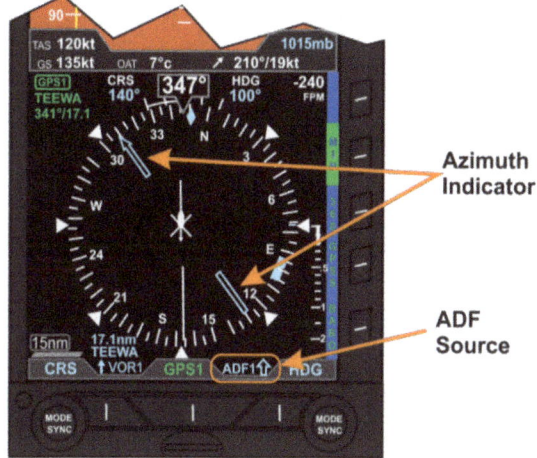

RADIO NAVIGATION

The VFR Pilot Needs to

Point to	Point to the ADF on the instrument panel and know how to select and adjust the indicator.  
Turn	Turn the ADF receiver in the cockpit ON. This is done by rotating the combined ON/OFF/VOLUME control to the right. 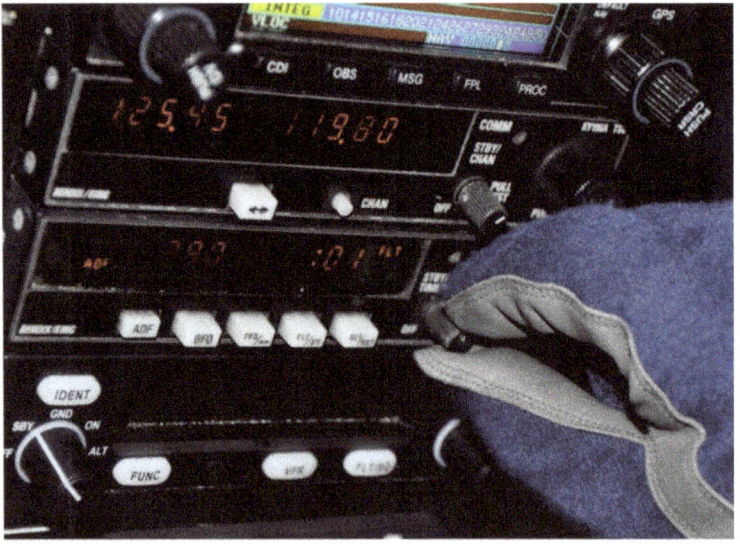
Tune	Selecting or "tuning" the right frequency. To tune the frequency, the pilot turns the frequency knobs then selects the FREQ button to USE the required frequency.  ### Finding the Right Frequency NDB frequencies can be found in the ERSA. Additionally, the ADF will receive signals from any AM radio station. Many

towns and cities have their own local radio station that can be received by the ADF which allows the azimuth needle to point to where the radio station transmitter tower is located.

LEIGH CREEK
AVFAX CODE 5102

ELEV 856

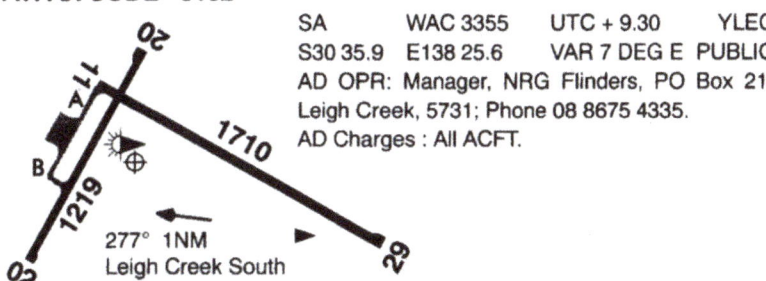

SA   WAC 3355   UTC + 9.30   YLEC
S30 35.9   E138 25.6   VAR 7 DEG E   PUBLIC
AD OPR: Manager, NRG Flinders, PO Box 21, Leigh Creek, 5731; Phone 08 8675 4335.
AD Charges : All ACFT.

RUNWAY PHYSICAL CHARACTERISTICS
02/20   023   40a Unrated. Sealed gravel   RWY WID 18
11/29   114   56a PCN 11/F/A/580(84 PSI) /U Sealed gravel   RWY WID 30

AERODROME AND APPROACH LIGHTING
RWY 11/29   LIRL PAL 120.6 SDBY PWR AVBL PTBL.
RWY 11   AT-VASIS Left side GP 3DEG 51FT
RWY 29   AT-VASIS Left side GP 3DEG 49FT
ABN   FLG W 6 SEC
Note: AT-VASIS post located 99M from clearway end, offset 58M to the left, height 8FT.

ATS COMMUNICATIONS FACILITIES
FIA   Melbourne Centre   121.2   On Ground

RADIO NAVIGATION AND LANDING AIDS
VOR   LEC   117.8   S30 35.8 E138 25.7
NDB   LEC   287   S30 35.9 E138 26.5   125/1.6 Range 150; HN 85.

CTAF
126.7

UNICOM
126.7   Leigh Creek Unicom. HR as per Refueller.

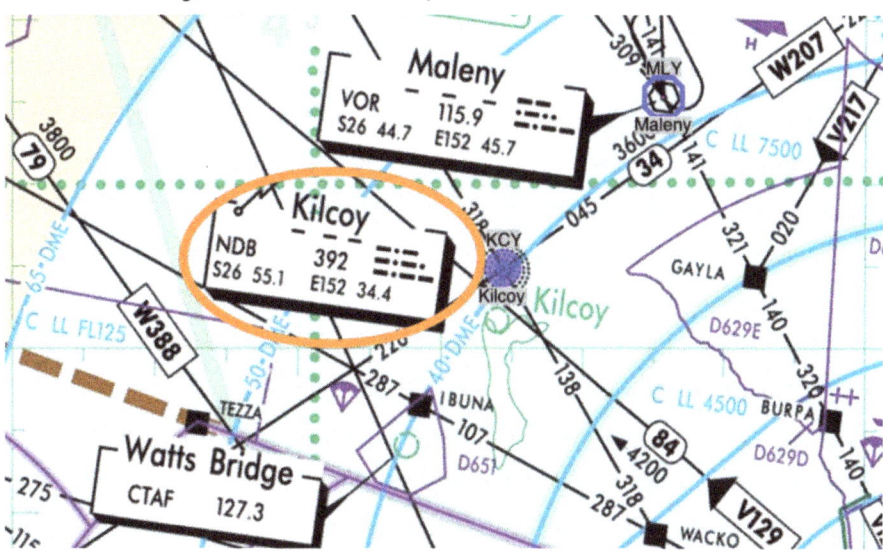

The location of the transmitters is shown on the WAC (World Aeronautical Chart) and the frequency numbers can be found in the ERSA under the heading Broadcasting Stations.

Gympie shown on the WAC

RADIO NAVIGATION

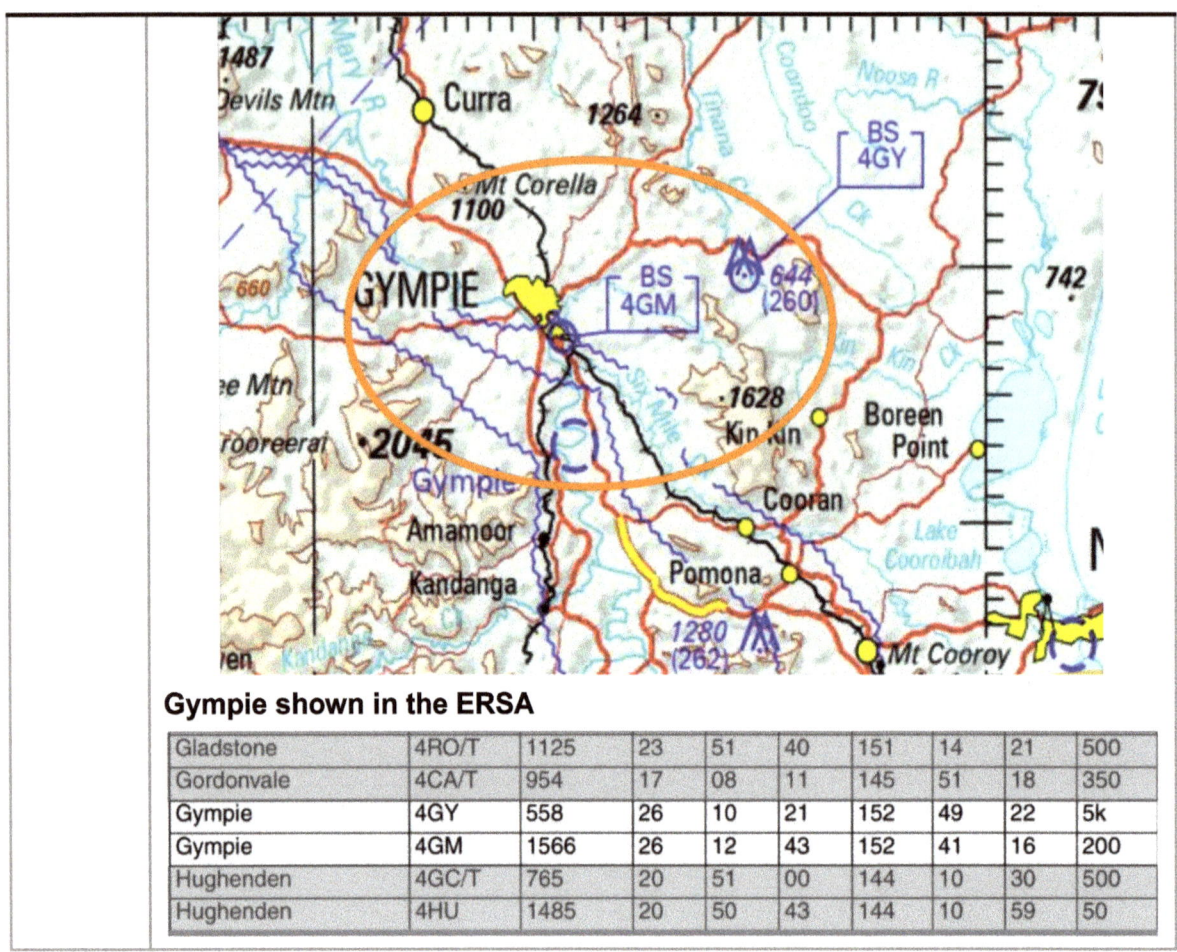

Gympie shown in the ERSA

Gladstone	4RO/T	1125	23	51	40	151	14	21	500
Gordonvale	4CA/T	954	17	08	11	145	51	18	350
Gympie	4GY	558	26	10	21	152	49	22	5k
Gympie	4GM	1566	26	12	43	152	41	16	200
Hughenden	4GC/T	765	20	51	00	144	10	30	500
Hughenden	4HU	1485	20	50	43	144	10	59	50

Identify	Once the correct frequency is selected the pilot needs to confirm that the displayed frequency is indeed the one wanted. Each NDB will give out a morse code signal which can be found in the ERSA on a VNC, VTC or ERC. Each Broadcasting Station must identify themselves several times every hour so the pilot needs to listen. 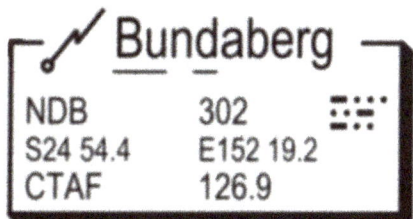 To identify, select the audio panel ADF button and press it IN. If necessary, adjust the volume and the pilot now must wait and listen for the signal. Once it is positively identified, the audio panel button can be selected OUT. (So you do not have to keep listening to the morse code or the Country and Western music!) 

| **Test** | Once the ADF is correctly tuned and it is receiving a signal, the azimuth needle should be pointing to the station.

To check that the azimuth needle is working properly the pilot can deselect OUT the ADF button.

This will rotate the helicopter's ADF antenna so the signal will be cleaner but the azimuth needle will not work. Instead, the needle should rotate to the 90-degree right position. This is known as its resting position.

Once it is in the Resting Position press the ADF button back IN. The needle should then again point to the station. This performs a functional check on the ADF azimuth indicator.

Use	The Radio Navigation aid is now available for you to use to help:
	▪ Confirm your current position (known as a position fix)
	▪ Confirm your destination
	▪ Point to a waypoint enroute
	▪ Help you maintain track
	▪ Help you intercept another new track
	All of these options will be demonstrated to you in the helicopter during a navigation training sortie.

NDB Summary

NDB 1

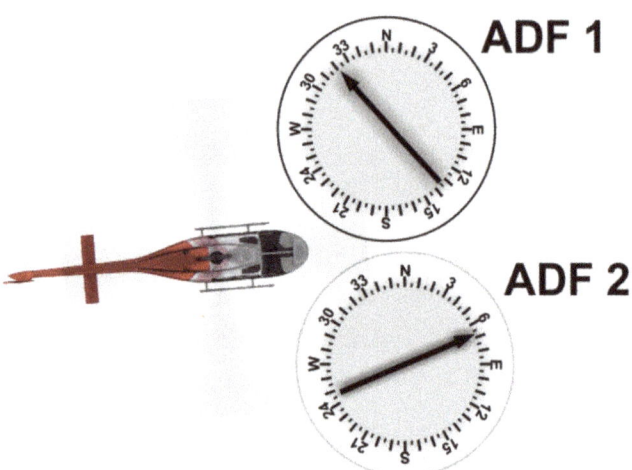
ADF 1
ADF 2

NDB 2

The VOR

The **VHF Omni-directional Radio (VOR)** Radio Navigation aid is made up of two principal components:

- the ground station component called the **VOR** transmitter, and
- the helicopter installed component called the **VOR** receiver. The helicopter installed component has a receiver and frequency selection panel and a separate CDI indicator.

The VOR allows the pilot to determine the magnetic track (also referred to as a "*radial*") TO or FROM the VOR station. The CDI bar can also indicate to the pilot if the helicopter is to the LEFT, RIGHT or ON the selected radial.

VOR Receiver

VOR Source

CDI Indicator

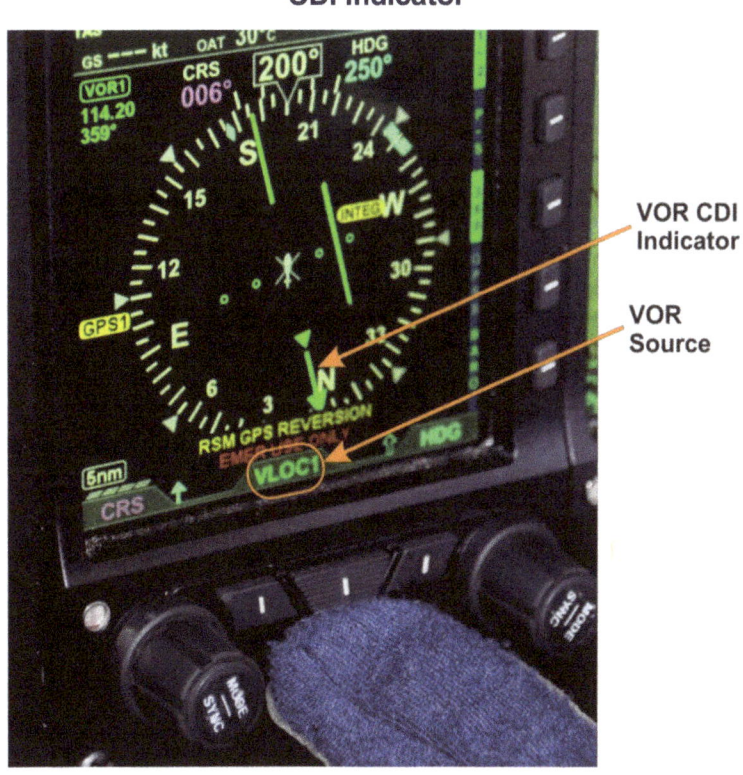

VOR CDI Indicator

VOR Source

The VFR Pilot needs to

Point to	Point to the VOR on the instrument panel and know how to select and adjust the indicator.
	Being VHF, the VOR radio navigation selection panel is often co-located with another VHF radio used for communicating. The two when combined are then called a NavCom (Navigation and Communication unit).
	Below are two common cockpit NavCom receiver installations. One with just a VHF radio, the other with a GPS and a VHF radio.
	### King NavCom 
	### Garmin GPS NavCom 
	### ASPEN PFD
	The picture below shows the pilot pointing to the VOR indicator which forms part of the HSI on the Aspen PFD. 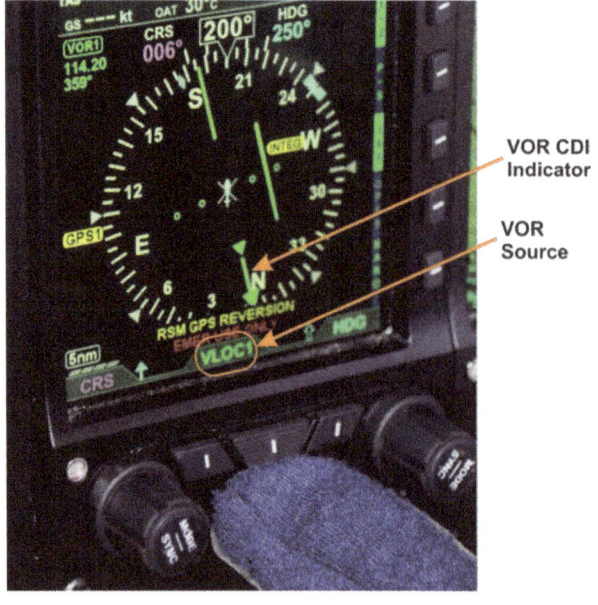

Turn	Turn the VOR receiver in the cockpit ON. This is done by rotating the combined ON/OFF/VOLUME control to the right. 
Tune	Selecting or "tuning" the right frequency. **Finding the VOR Frequency** VOR frequencies can be found in the ERSA or on the VNC, VTC or ERC 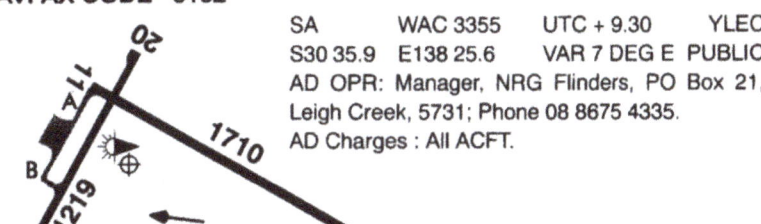

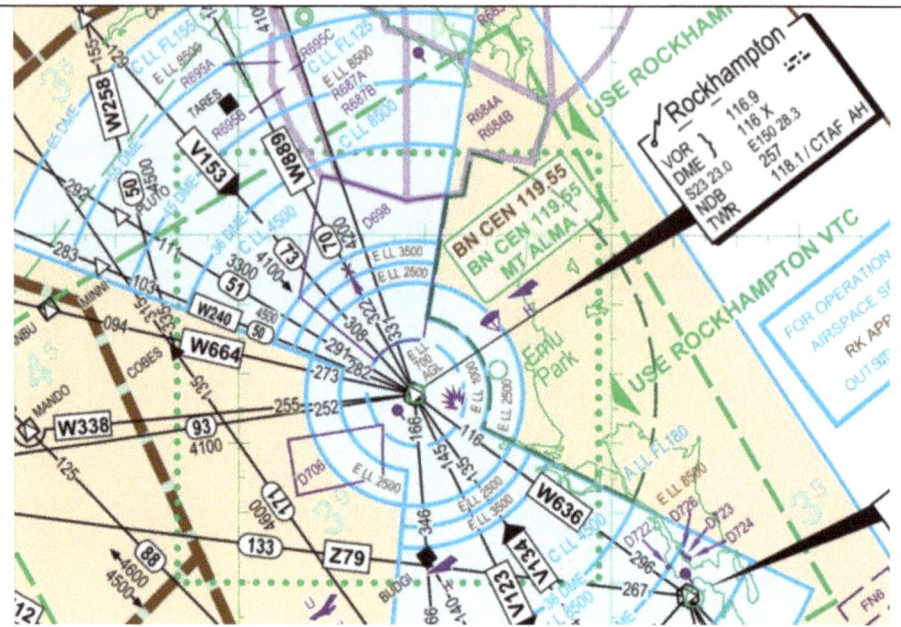

Tuning to the frequency:

To tune the frequency:

(7) Press the C (double arrow button) to move the cursor to the VOR window on the Garmin unit.

(8) Rotate the big Push C/V knob to selects the desired frequency.

(9) Once the frequency is selected, select the V (double arrow) to move the new frequency from the standby to the active position.

(10) The volume can be adjusted by rotating the small V button on the left.

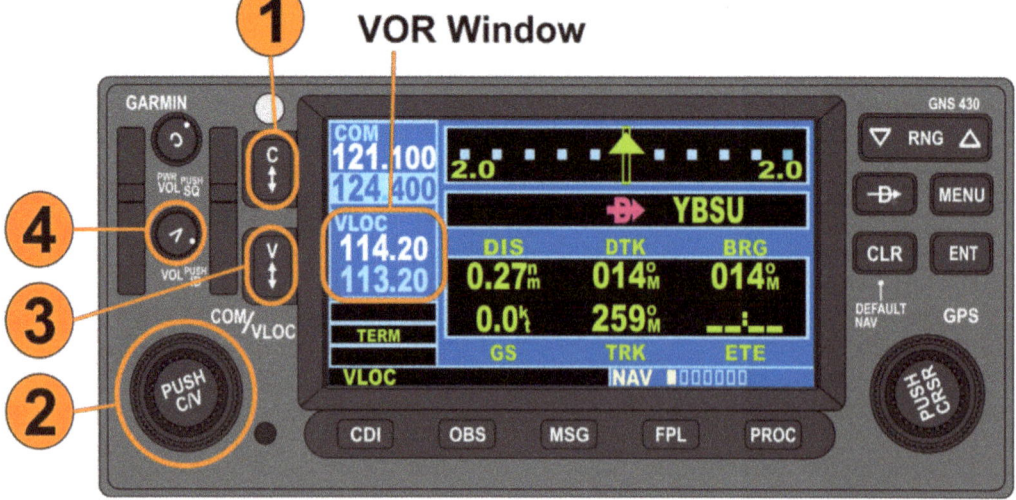

Identify	Once the correct frequency is selected the pilot needs to confirm that the displayed frequency is indeed the one wanted.
	Each VOR will give out a Morse code signal which can be found in the ERSA on a VNC, VTC or ERC. Additionally, many VORs also broadcast the ATIS or AWIS if it is installed for the aerodrome.

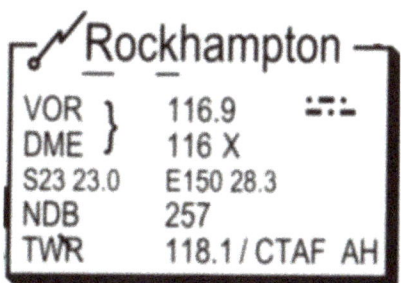

To identify, select the audio panel NAV button and press it IN.

If necessary, adjust the volume on the VOR and the pilot now must wait and listen for the signal. Once it is positively identified the audio panel button can be selected OUT.

Test	Testing the VOR receiver is easy.
If it is receiving a signal and the CDI needle comes alive with a TO or FROM indication, then it is working.
The pilot can now do a functional check by rotating the Omni Bearing Selector knob (OBS) which will rotate the CDI needle until the needle and bar are aligned.
Once aligned move the OBS knob 10 degrees to the right. The CDI bar should move out to the left by 10 degrees.
Then move the OBS 20 degrees left. The CDI bar should move so it is now 10 degrees out to the right.

CDI needle and bar aligned	CDI bar out to the left	CDI bar out to the right
	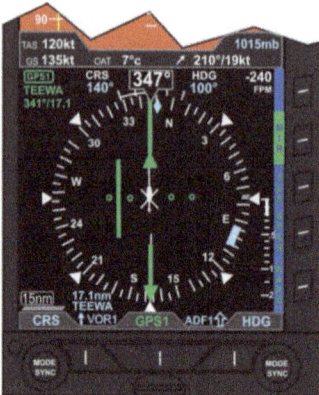	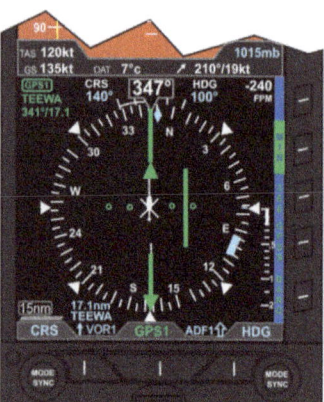

 |
| **Use** | The Radio Navigation aid is now available for you to use to help

- Confirm your current position (known as a position fix)
- Confirm your destination
- Point to a waypoint enroute
- Help you maintain track
- Help you intercept another new track

All of these options will be demonstrated to you in the helicopter during a navigation training sortie. |

INTERNATIONAL HELICOPTER THEORY

RADIO NAVIGATION
NAVIGATION

VOR Summary

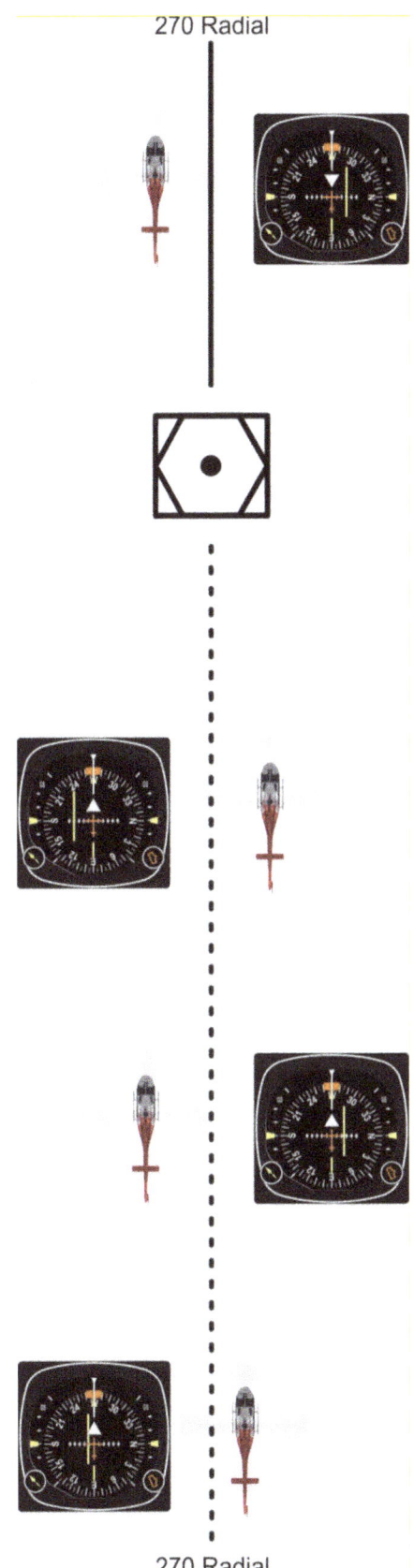

Position Fix Using the VOR/NDB
Refer to AIP ENR 1.1-31 Para 17.4.6

You can confirm your position by one or more of the following methods:

- Station passage over (passing directly over the top) the NDB or VOR station.
- By the intersection of two or more position lines that intersect at an angle of **not less than 45°** and which are obtained from NDB or VOR stations in any combination.

A position line must be within the rated coverage of the selected aids with the exception that if a fix is determined entirely by NDB's, the lines must be within a range of **30nm** from each of the NDB's.

In gaining a position line simply determine your magnetic bearing from each of the stations then draw these lines on a map. Where the two lines intercept is your current position.

Example
Let's consider a pilot determining his position by using a NDB and a VOR, both within their rated coverage and their intersecting lines are greater than 45°.
Let's put the helicopter on a magnetic heading of 280° with a relative bearing from the NDB station of 180°. Rotating the OBS of the VOR until a FROM flag shows and the CDI (needle) is in the middle the VOR will show the helicopter on a radial from the station of 010°. If the pilot now transposes this information onto a map with the two navigation aids as your points of reference, then where the two lines meet is your current position.

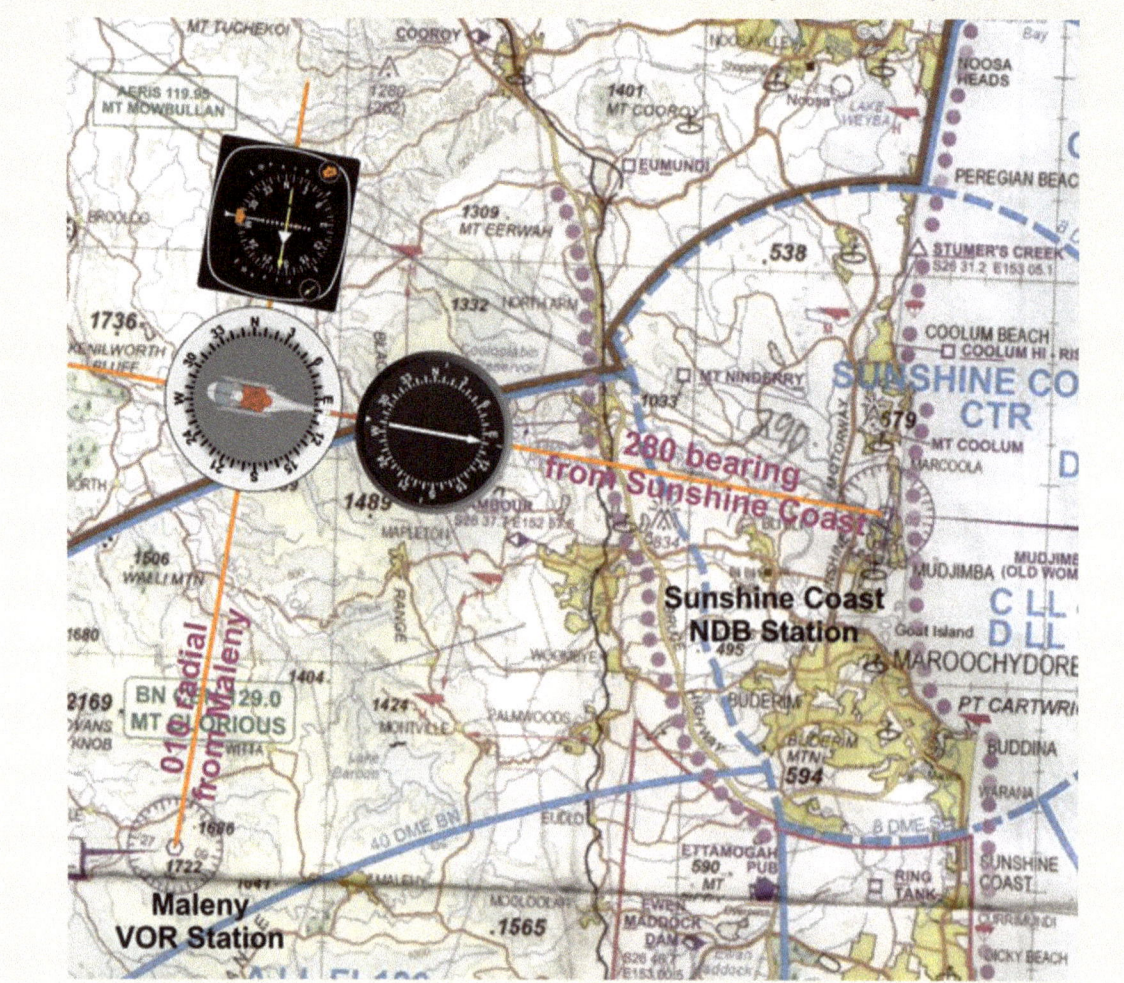

The GPS

The **Global Position System (GPS)** Radio Navigation aid is made up of two principle components:

- the satellites system orbiting in space around the earth called the **G**lobal **N**avigation **S**atellite **S**ystem referred to as **GNSS** and
- the helicopter installed component called the **GPS** receiver. The helicopter installed component has a receiver with a built in database and various different functions including a waypoint selection page and the ability to display this information in several different ways including:
    - on a selection of different pages and screens within the receiver unit
    - projected onto a Multi-Function Display (MFD)
    - connected to either both an azimuth or CDI indicator or both at the same time.

The GPS is the most powerful navigation tool the pilot has available and is now commonly used and integrated into most aircraft systems worldwide.

GPS systems are slowly replacing all other navigation systems so that in time the VOR and NDB will no longer be in use.

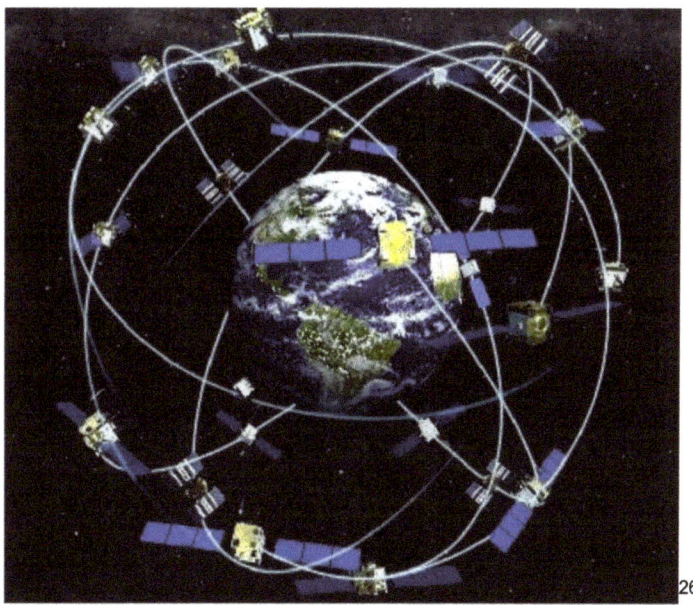

[26]

Garmin 430 GPS/NavCom Receiver Unit

---

26 http://njnnetwork.com/njn/wp-content/uploads/2009/05/spac_gps_navstar_iia_iir_iif_constellation_lg.jpg

It is important to note that there are several different GNSS systems operational in space.

The original was created by the USA and was called the **G**lobal **P**ositioning **S**ystem (**GPS**).

This is the system that we all typically use in aviation today and is where the term GPS originated.

As other Countries then started to launch their own GPS satellites, they each gave their system a unique name.

Currently the following GNSS systems are operational:

Country	GNSS Name	Use
USA	GPS	Military and civil
Russia	Global Navigation Satellite System (GLONASS)	Military and civil
Europe	Galileo	Military and civil
Japan	Quasi-Zenith Satellite System (QZSS)	Civil
China	Chinese Regional Satellite System called Beidou	Military

The VFR Pilot needs to

Point to	Point to the GPS on the instrument panel and know how to select and adjust the indicator or display. Because the GPS unit itself is such a sophisticated piece of equipment, manufacturers have designed units that can replace various other instruments in the one unit. Below is the most widely used commercially approved GPS. The Garmin 430. Because it has a VHF radio for communications, a VOR and a GPS receiver all part of the one unit, it is referred to as the **GPS/NavCom.** 
Turn	Turn the GPS receiver in the cockpit ON. This is done by rotating the combined ON/OFF/VOLUME control to the right 

| Tune | Selecting or "tuning" the right frequency.

There are no "frequencies" to enter into a GPS but there are waypoint details or latitude and longitude references.

Because the GPS unit has a worldwide data base built into it, all the pilot has to do is enter the correct abbreviation for the desired waypoint and then enter that into the GPS.

The GPS will then do all of the hard work and be continually making calculations based on satellite referencing and data in order to indicate to the pilot which way to go.

Waypoint information can be found in the ERSA or on the VNC, VTC or ERC

SUNSHINE COAST   **ELEV 15**
AVFAX CODE 4005
QLD   UTC +10   YBSU
S 26 36.2   E 153 05.5   VAR 11 DEG E   CERT
AD OPR Sunshine Coast Regional Council - Locked Bag 72, Nambour, QLD, 4560. PH 07 5453 1500. ARO 0419 658 272. PH AH 07 3830 5251. FAX 07 5453 1511.

To select a waypoint:

(11)   Press the CLR button  to go to the main navigation page.

(12)   Rotate the lower right knob (PUSH CRSR)   to enter in the waypoint designator.

(13)   Once entered press the Direct to button.

(14)   Press Enter to   button accept the waypoint, and the GPS will then start giving directions.

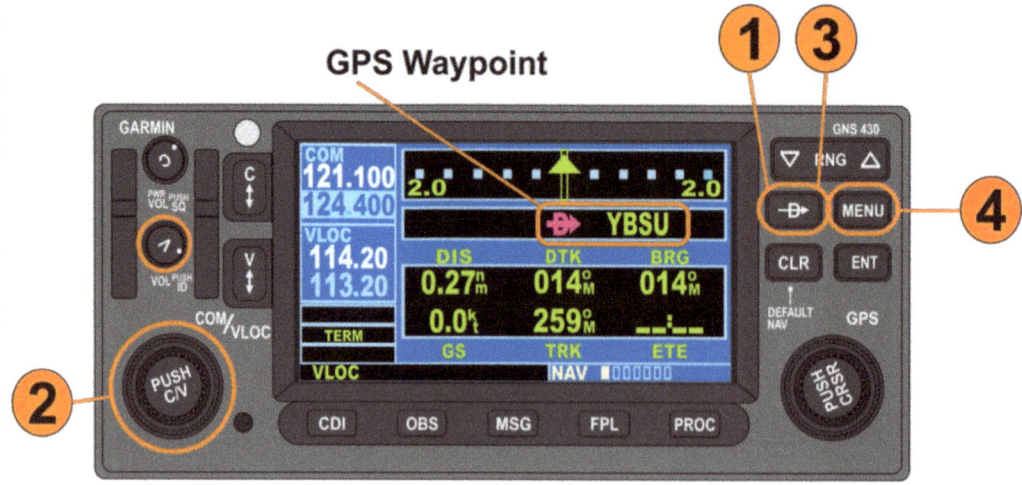 |
|---|---|
| **Identify** | Identifying the waypoint is done during the tuning phase.

Once the waypoint is entered, the GPS will ask you to check the waypoint details before you press Enter for the last time. |

Test	Testing the GPS receiver. The GPS relies on a minimum of 6 satellites to be very accurate and be able to continually self-test itself for faults. If there is an error or if it cannot receive signals from enough satellites it will give the pilot a warning. This does not mean that it cannot give position information but it is a warning that the GPS accuracy may not be as good as needed. This self-testing is referred to as **Receiver Autonomous Integrity Monitoring** or **RAIM** for short. If a pilot needs to ensure the GPS is not going to have a RAIM outage during the flight (not enough satellites) then this can be checked by selecting the RAIM page in the GPS and asking the GPS, based on the data it has received from the satellites, if there is going to be a problem at any time during the flight. 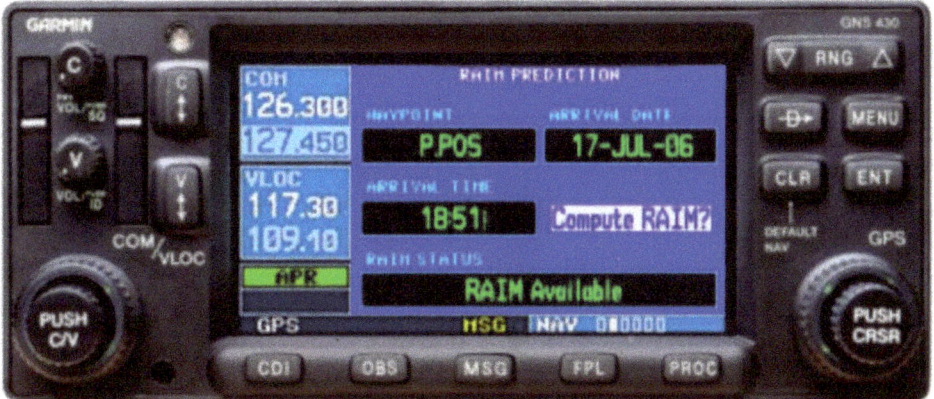 This is not normally done by VFR pilots but is an important check for IFR pilots.
Use	The Radio Navigation aid is now available for you to use to help: - Confirm your current position (known as a position fix) - Confirm your destination - Point to a waypoint enroute - Help you maintain track - Help you intercept another new track All of these options will be demonstrated to you in the helicopter during a navigation training sortie.

GPS Summary

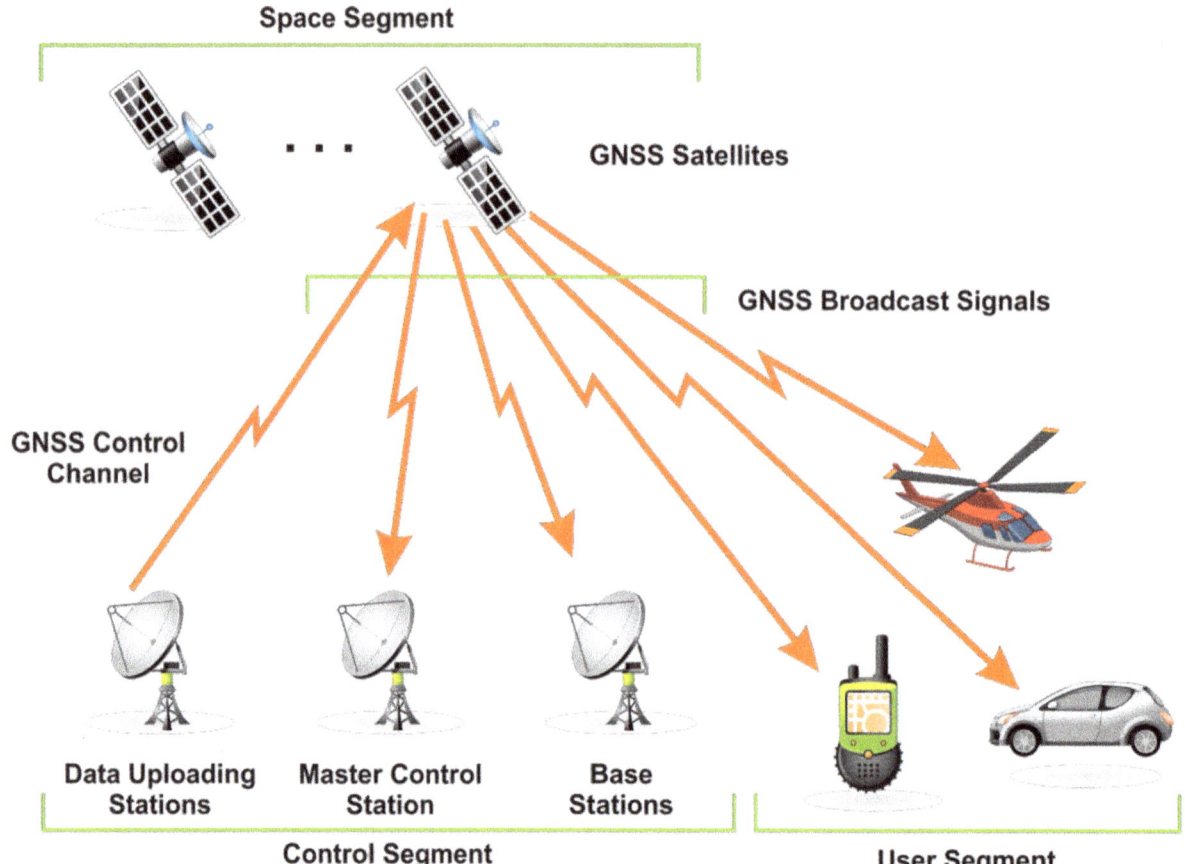

14 Creating a Flight Plan

Introduction

The operation or mission the helicopter is tasked to complete is not likely to be located at its base; therefore to get from the helicopter's base to the place of operation will require some form of navigation planning.

The planning phase of the navigation takes time to complete accurately and requires careful study of the maps, airspace, route selection, applying the weather and NOTAMS, fuel planning, performance planning and anything else that can be done prior to the flight in the preparation phase.

On completion of the previous chapters in the Foundation Theory for Navigation it is time to bring all this new knowledge together in creating a plan for the flight referred to as a **Flight Plan**.

Tools Required

To accurately plan a VFR cross country flight (navigation) the following tools are required:

Item	Image
Maps relevant to the area being flown	
The **ERSA** The **E**n**R**oute **S**upplement **A**ustralia (**ERSA**) contains all the detailed information of most airports commonly used in Australia as well as other useful Flight Planning information.	

Item	Image
The VFRG The **V**isual **F**light **R**ules **G**uide (**VFRG**) is a condensed vision of the relevant rules and regulations normally found in the AIP or CASRS for VFR flight in Australia. It can be accessed electronically at http://vfrg.casa.gov.au It is recommended that this document is downloaded and available to all trainees to use as guidance and reference material.	
Scale ruler To measure distance	
Protractor To determine the true tracks on a map	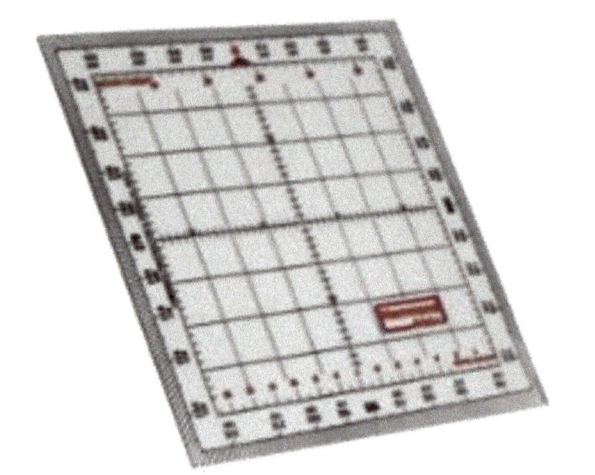
Flight computer Sometimes referred to as the "wiz-wheel" it is a manual circular slide rule that can be taken on the flight. Understanding how to use the Flight Computer is part of being an aviator.	

Item	Image
Pencil and eraser A pencil is important as you will make mistakes so it is easier to rub them out, compared to starting again if you were using a pen.	
Access to an **iPad, Tablet or computer**. Flight planning programs, weather information, NOTAMs and Google earth information is all available to help you and is now readily available through the internet accessed via an iPad, Tablet or computer.	
The use of **Applications** (**APPS**) Using APPS such as Oz-Runways, NAIPS and the E6B electronic "wiz wheel" is encouraged, as: ■ it will improve proficiency in these new technologies and ■ the use of technology will assist in the learning process and will ultimately be used in real life.	

CREATING A FLIGHT PLAN

Item	Image
| **Weather Briefing and NOTAMS**<br><br>This can be viewed electronically on an iPad, Tablet or computer.<br><br>This information can also be printed via the AVFAX system (becoming obsolete).<br><br>When first learning to create a flight plan, it is better to print the information so it can be seen as a whole, written on and referenced. | ```
1513 UTC 08/11/15         AIRSERVICES AUSTRALIA
                          AREA BRIEFING

PREPARED FOR: MIKEBECKER
VALID FROM 1513 UTC NOV 08, 2015 TO 1513 UTC NOV 09, 2015

                    WEATHER INFORMATION
                    -------------------
AREA40 (40)
   AREA QNH 13/16
   AREA 40: S OF YMLS/YGAY/YBSU 1016,
   REST 1013

AMEND AREA FORECAST 081216 TO 082300 AREA 40.

AMD OVERVIEW:
ISOLATED SHOWERS AND THUNDERSTORMS, CHIEFLY E OF DAG/YMTO/YLIS.
SHOWERS TENDING SCATTERED E OF YBUD/YGAY/YLIS, THIS AREA SHIFTING N
TO BE E OF YBTR/YMTO/YBBN BY 18Z. BROKEN LOW CLOUD IN LAND AREAS E OF
YBTR/YGAY/YSPE, EXTENDING TO LAND E OF YRLL/YTAM/YXTX BY 16Z,
CLEARING BY 22Z. ISOLATED FOG PATCHES DEVELOPING CHIEFLY NW OF
YROM/YGLA FROM 16Z, CLEARING BY 21Z. AREAS OF SMOKE BELOW 8000FT,
LOCALLY THICK NEAR FIRES. MODERATE LOW LEVEL TURBULENCE SE OF
YBUD/YTFD, CHIEFLY SEA/COAST, CONTRACTING TO E OF YBRK/YKRY/YBNA BY
22Z.
``` |
| **Load Data Sheet** for the helicopter being flown.

One of the tasks to complete when creating a Flight Plan is to check the helicopter's weight and balance.

To do this the pilot needs to know the exact Empty Weight and ARM of the helicopter being flown. This is found in the helicopter Flight Manual installed in the cockpit.

For training purposes, a generic Load Data sheet is provided within the Trainee's B206 Trainee Flight Manual. | 
 |
```

Item	Image
Flight Log form This is a critical element in successfully managing the flight. It provides an easy place to record all the calculations with regards to Altitude, track, wind, times and headings in one place and will be used during the flight in order to update the information as it changes.	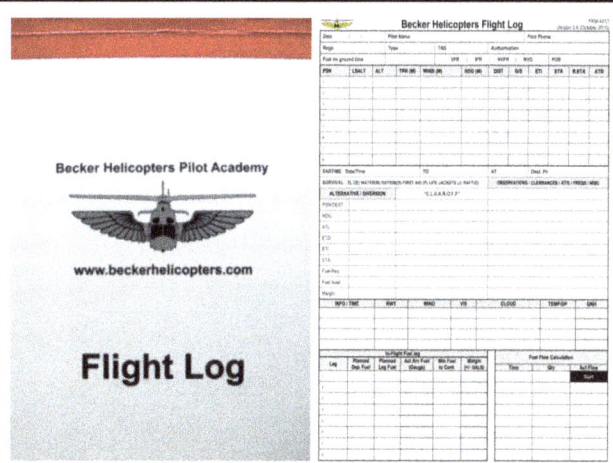
Fuel Flow figures for the helicopter used. Each helicopter model will have a different fuel flow figure and this figure can vary depending on the helicopter's configuration at the time and what altitude it is flying at. Manufacturers do not normally put fuel flow figures in the Flight Manual, instead the Company or Military Unit will have a database of information on the fuel flows based on their experience. The fuel flow figures are therefore given. They will be stated in Operations Manuals, Standard Operating Procedures, or Standing Orders. Opposite is an example of the information found in the Becker Helicopters Operations Manual Part B.	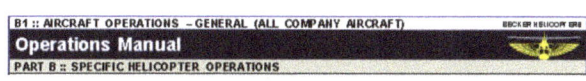 | Type	TAS	Airwork	Nav	Holding	Sling
---	---	---	---	---	---
B206B	100	100L/ph	100L/ph	100L/ph	110L/ph
	100	24G/ph	24G/ph	24G/ph	26G/ph	

Introducing the Flight Log

The Flight Log is simply a form that has been created in order for the pilot to easily and logically place all the information collected and calculated during the navigation planning stage. They can come in different shapes, sizes and formats depending on the Company or Military unit who has created it.

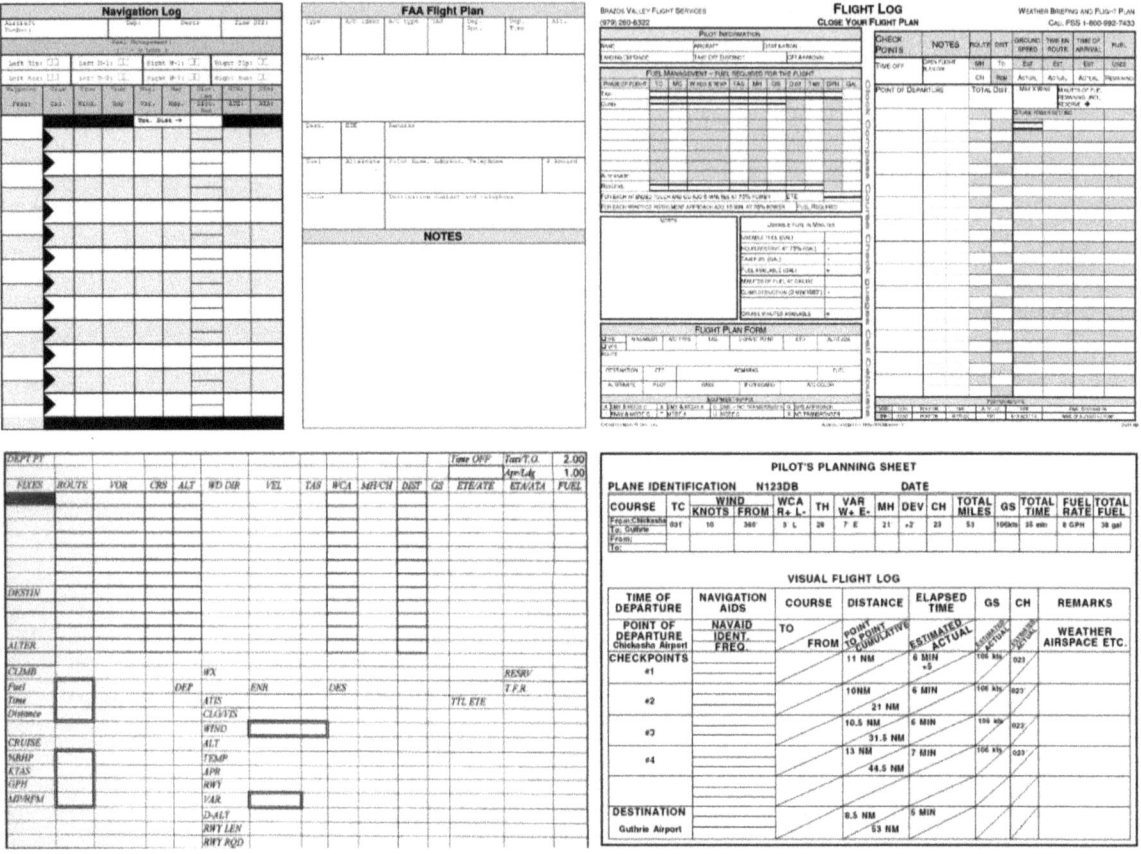

In general, they all try to make the pilot's job easier by having a place to put information about the flight in one place.

Each Flight Log may be different as each Company or Military Unit may have a different focus on information they may deem important or a specific type of operation that may require the collating of specific information. Sometimes pilots design their own Flight Logs based on how they like to record the information.

Becker Helicopters Flight Log

The Becker Helicopters Flight Log is divided into two (2) segments.

The front side of the Flight Log, and the back side of the Flight Log.

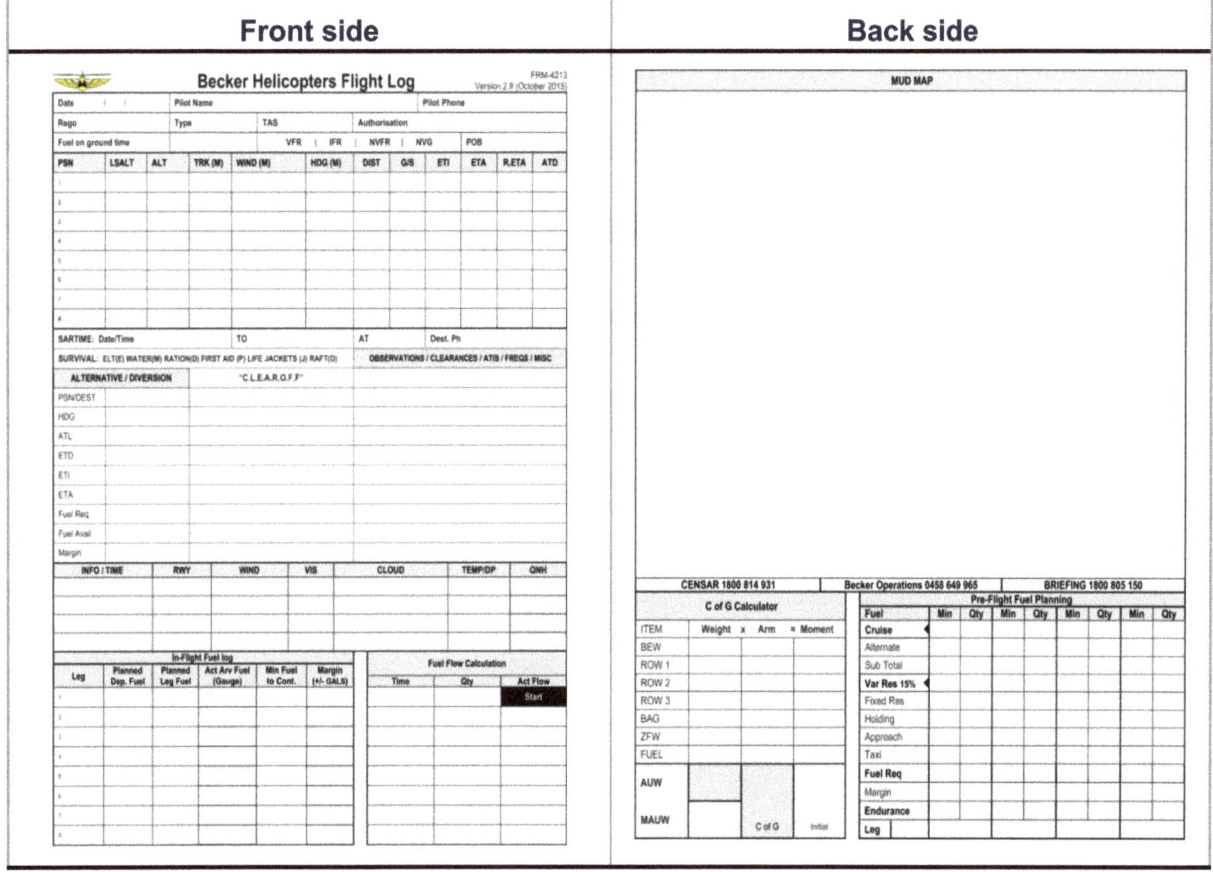

The front side is designed for the pilot to use during the flight and make continuous additions and changes as the flight progresses. It also has all the relevant information that will be needed to set the helicopter on its next course.

The back side of the Flight Log has pre-flight planning detail to confirm the amount of fuel required and the helicopter's Weight and Balance calculation.

It also has an area where the pilot can draw out a rough "mud-map" to help the pilot remain orientated to the navigation and easily access important information that may be useful to have instead of looking through the ERSA and AIP during the flight.

Creating a Flight Plan

The Front Side

The Front Side of the Flight Log is divided into four (4) areas.

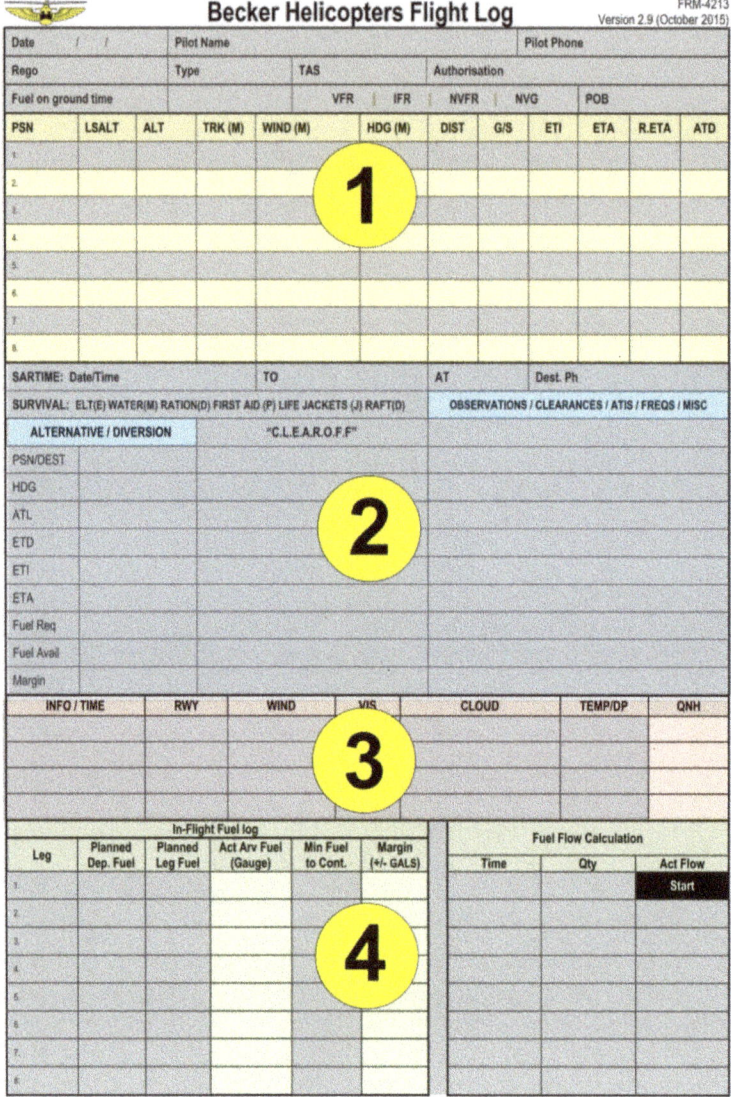

1. Route information

Route information is where the pilot will place all the relevant detail obtained from the aircraft, maps, weather forecasts, altitudes, etc and place them all in one easy place for reference during the flight. This section is where departure times, distance and HDGs are all placed.

Becker Helicopters Flight Log FRM-4213 Version 2.9 (October 2015)

Date: 28/1/16 Pilot Name: M. Becker Pilot Phone: 0415 555 555
Rego: WCF Type: B206 TAS: 100 Authorisation: ✓
Fuel on ground time: (VFR) | IFR | NVFR | NVG POB: 3

PSN	LSALT	ALT	TRK (M)	WIND (M)	HDG (M)	DIST	G/S	ETI	ETA	R.ETA	ATD
1. YBSU											
2. YKRY		A045	260	030/11	263	67	110	36			
3.											
4. YGYM		A035	060	030/13	060	50	90	33			
5.											
6. YBSU		A035	123	030/13	117	28	95	18			
7.											
8.											

2. Alternate and notes

There will come a time when the pilot has to divert from their planned route and go somewhere else. This may be due to weather, a change in plans or a technical issue. This is the area where any relevant information for a diversion can be placed during the flight.

Additionally any other observations, clearances or notes can also be placed here.

SARTIME: Date/Time	TO	AT	Dest. Ph
SURVIVAL: ELT(E) WATER(M) RATION(D) FIRST AID (P) LIFE JACKETS (J) RAFT(D)		OBSERVATIONS / CLEARANCES / ATIS / FREQS / MISC	
ALTERNATIVE / DIVERSION	"C.L.E.A.R.O.F.F"	KRY AWIS	
PSN/DEST		CTAF	
HDG			
ATL		GYM CTAF 126.9	
ETD			
ETI		SU ATIS 119.8 GND 121.1	
ETA		TWR 124.4	
Fuel Req			
Fuel Avail			
Margin			

3. ATIS

At many airports there will be an **A**erodrome **T**erminal **I**nformation **S**ervice (**ATIS**) or **A**erodrome **W**eather **I**nformation **S**ervice (**AWIS**). As the pilot tunes into the correct radio frequency and listens to this recorded information it can be written down so it does not have to be memorised and can be referred to later if required.

INFO / TIME	RWY	WIND	VIS	CLOUD	TEMP/DP	QNH
SU A 0830	18	L/V	10K	FEW 020	25/16	1018
KRY AWIS 0850		020/10	10K	NCD	18/15	1016

CREATING A FLIGHT PLAN
NAVIGATION
INTERNATIONAL HELICOPTER THEORY

4. Fuel Log and Fuel Flow

During the flight it is essential the pilots monitor the fuel usage and confirm at regular intervals that there is still enough fuel available in the fuel tanks to continue with the flight.

Simply calculating the amount of fuel prior to departure is no guarantee that there will *remain* sufficient fuel in the tank to complete the flight. This is because consumption rates can vary depending on the atmospheric conditions, the helicopter may have had to divert due to weather or unforeseen circumstances, the fuel tank may have a leak or the power settings may be different and the helicopter's engine may simply be using more.

The majority of the **Fuel Log** can be filed out prior to departure leaving only the shaded areas to be completed in flight.

Prior to each leg the pilots can confirm that they have the minimum amount of fuel available to conduct the next leg over and above what is actually remaining in the tank.

Leg	Planned Dep. Fuel	Planned Leg Fuel	Act Arv Fuel (Gauge)	Min Fuel to Cont.	Margin (+/- GALS)
1. SU	90	34	79	58	+21
2. KRY	79	32	60	26	+34
3. GYM	60	26			
4. SU					
5.					
6.					
7.					
8.					

Fuel Flow Calculation		
Time	Qty	Act Flow
0830	90	Start
0900	77	26g
1000	62	30g

On arrival at each leg they can determine if they are burning exactly what was expected, burning more (where they will have less fuel than expected (-)) or burning less (where they will have more fuel than expected (+)).

Example

Consider a helicopter departing with 90USGs in the fuel tank. The fuel required for the leg is only 34USGs. The minimum amount of fuel required to be in the tanks over the next waypoint in order to complete the rest of the flight is 58USGs. On arrival, and looking at the fuel gauge, the pilot notes there is 79USGs indicating on the gauge. This means there is a margin of an extra 21USGs available in the tank to use as a margin or as an extra reserve.

Leg	Planned Dep. Fuel	Planned Leg Fuel	Act Arv Fuel (Gauge)	Min Fuel to Cont.	Margin (+/- GALS)
1. SU	90	34	79	58	+21
2. KRY	79	32	60	26	+34
3. GYM	60	26			
4. SU					
5.					
6.					
7.					
8.					

The **Fuel Flow calculation** allows the pilot to determine just what the fuel consumption rate has been, based on what the fuel gauge is displaying and the time the helicopter has been flying.

To use the Fuel Flow table at some point in the flight, simply note the time and fuel quantity.

At another time (there is no set amount of time but it is better to wait at least 30 minutes to get a more accurate result) again note the time and the fuel gauge amount, then by doing a simple calculation on the Flight Computer the pilot can determine the current fuel consumption rate. This should be done at least once on each leg over 30 minutes.

Example

Consider departing a HLS at 0830 with 90USGs on-board.

At 0900 the fuel gauge is indicating 77USGs. Using the Flight Computer, the consumption rate can be calculated as 26USG per hour.

Fuel Flow Calculation		
Time	Qty	Act Flow
0830	90	Start
0900	77	26g
1000	62	30g

CREATING A FLIGHT PLAN

The Back Side

The Back Side of the Flight Log is divided into three (3) areas.

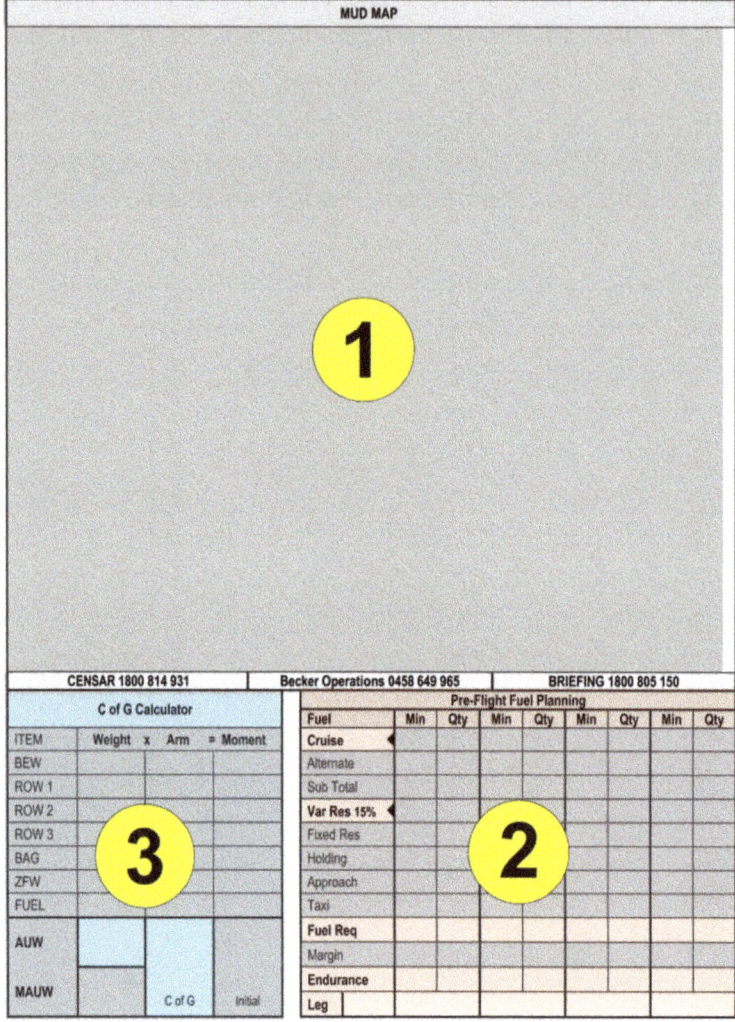

1. Mud Map

A mud map is a simplified drawing of the route being flown. It often has relevant information such as the departure and destination points with the runway designations and circuit directions, altitudes being flown. The high terrain points are marked in their approximate locations as are obvious navigation points and hazards such as wires, towns and mountains. Distances to ATC areas and radio frequencies, Pilot Activated Lighting (PAL) frequencies, LSALTS and much more or much less can be placed on a mud map depending on what each individual pilot wants to be reminded of during a flight.

As such, a mud map can have more or less detail on it. There are no set rules, it is simply there as an aid for the pilot to use at his discretion. It is most useful when flying at night, as looking at a map in full colour is not really helpful in the dark.

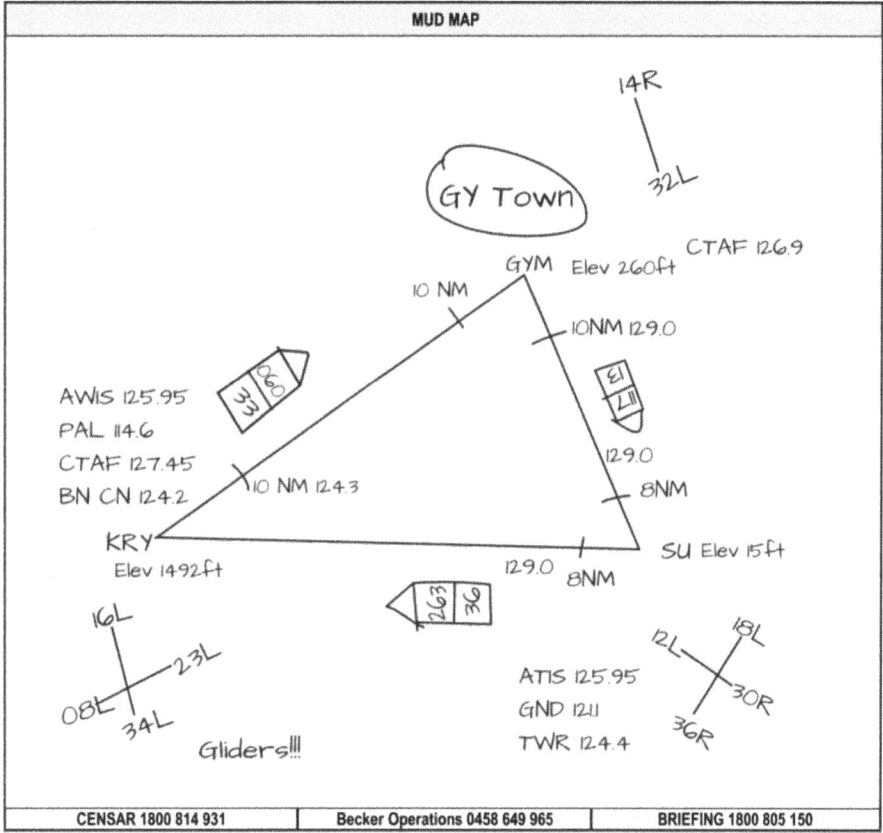

CREATING A FLIGHT PLAN

2. Pre-Flight Fuel Planning

Once the Flight Log information on the front side has been determined the pilot will know:

1. The ETI between each waypoint
2. The forecast weather and if there are any Operational Requirements such as:
   (a) Holding fuel
   (b) Alternate fuel
   (c) Approach fuel (instrument approaches)
3. Taxi fuel requirements
4. Fixed reserve requirements
5. Variable fuel requirements

The Pre-Flight Planning area allows the pilot to place in all the relevant fuel information to determine the minimum fuel required, prior to commencing each separate leg.

Pre-Flight Fuel Planning								
Fuel	Min	Qty	Min	Qty	Min	Qty	Min	Qty
Cruise	36	16	33	14	18	8		
Alternate								
Sub Total	36	16	33	14	18	8		
Var Res 15%								
Fixed Res	30	13	30	13	30	13		
Holding								
Approach								
Taxi	-	5	-	5	-	5		
Fuel Req	66	34	63	32	48	26		
Margin	134	56	110	47	80	34		
Endurance	200	90	173	79	128	60		
Leg	SU		KRY		GYM		SU	

As a general rule, if the helicopter is not landing at a particular waypoint but is only over flying it, then the fuel calculation for the next leg is included within the previous leg as if it was one flight.

If the plan is to land at a waypoint, then an entirely new fuel calculation shall be made as if the next leg was a stand-alone flight.

Example

If flying a helicopter from YBSU-YKRY-YGYM-YBSU and the helicopter was only going to overfly YKRY and not land, then the pilot can calculate the fuel based on a flight as if the YBSY –YKRY-YGYM was only one leg and not two.

Pre-Flight Fuel Planning								
Fuel	Min	Qty	Min	Qty	Min	Qty	Min	Qty
Cruise	69	30	18	8				
Alternate								
Sub Total	69	30	18	8				
Var Res 15%								
Fixed Res	30	13	30	13				
Holding								
Approach								
Taxi	-	5	-	5				
Fuel Req	99	48	48	26				
Margin	101	42	80	47				
Endurance	200	90	128	60				
Leg	SU		GYM		SU			

There are several points to consider when calculating fuel:

1. The consumption rate can vary depending on the Altitude and the Power being used by the pilot. The pilot may have to consult the performance charts and the fuel flow charts if available in the Flight Manual, otherwise the Company or Military unit will give known fuel flow figures based on historical data.
2. The consumption rates may vary depending on the heicopter's configuration.
   For example, a helicopter typically burns more fuel on a navigation with a consistently high power setting as opposed to a helicopter in a low speed low power holding configuration. Again, this data may be available through the Company or Military Unit.
3. The requirement for a Variable Reserve and the amount of the Fixed Reserve can be dependent on legal or Company or Unit requirements.

Description of each fuel item

Item	Image
Cruise fuel	Is the amount of fuel required to climb to the cruise altitude and arrive at 1500 feet over the destination (including the descent). In some Flight Logs the Fuel Planning section has separate fields for climb and descent. This is usually a concern for larger aircraft climbing to high altitudes where there is a significant difference in the climb and descent fuel consumption rate compared to the high altitude cruise. In helicopters, the difference in climb and descent fuel is minimal as they typically operate below 10,000 feet. At Becker Helicopters the climb and descent fuel is all inclusive within the "cruise" fuel.
Alternate fuel	is that required to get to the planned Alternate destination (if required) at the cruise configuration.
Variable reserve (Var Res) fuel	is an amount nominated to take into account unplanned consumption rates. It is not required for VFR flights. It is often a requirement for IFR flights.
Fixed reserve (Fixed Res) fuel	is the legal minimum amount of fuel that shall be remaining in the helicopter's fuel tank upon arrival at the destination. The fixed reserve can vary depending on Company or Military Unit requirements. In Australia the legal minimum for a helicopter is 20 minutes. At Becker Helicopters we have a requirement for a **30 minute fixed reserve** and this is what shall be used.
Holding fuel	is that required if planning to hold due to weather (INTER or TEMPO) or if there is an operational requrimnet at a particular airport that holding fuel must be carried. For example If visiting Brisbane or Sydney airport there is often a requirement to carry 30 minutes holding fuel due to the high amount of aircraft traffic.
Approach fuel	is that required to conduct any specific VFR or instrument approach. It includes the fuel required to conduct sector entries, any holding and then the instrument approach procedure. This amount of fuel may vary depending on how long the approach procedure is.
Taxi fuel	is the amount of fuel required to start, run-up and taxi to the departure point ready for take-off. Taxi fuel is not considered fuel that is available for the flight, this is because taxi fuel is burnt off prior to departure. For this reason then, the taxi fuel will be a nominated amount that the pilot can expect to burn and will not form part of the endurance (airbourne) fuel.
Fuel Required (Fuel Req)	is the total *minimum* fuel required to be in the fuel tank prior to departure.

Item	Image
Margin fuel	is the difference between the minimum fuel required for the flight compared to the total amount of fuel actually in the tank at start up.
Endurance fuel	is the total amount of fuel actually in the fuel tank and available for flight once airbourne.

3. C of G Calculator

Once the pilot has determined the amount of fuel that is to be loaded onboard the helicopter he can then work out how much payload (passengers and cargo) can also be loaded onboard. This will require the pilot to calculate the All Up Weight (AUW) and then confirm a Centre of Gravity (C of G) calculation with the Centre of Gravity Envelope in the Limitations Section of the Flight Manual.

C of G Calculator			
ITEM	Weight x	Arm	= Moment
BEW	1898	116	220,168
ROW 1	344	65	22,360
ROW 2	132	104	13,728
ROW 3			
BAG	30	148	4,440
ZFW	2404		
FUEL	603	110.6	66,691.8
AUW	3007	108.8	327387.8
MAUW	3200	C of G	Initial

This simple reference calculator allows all the relavant information from the helicopter's Load Data sheet and the specific weights of the fuel, pilots, passengers and cargo to be in one place and then signed off by the Pilot in Command (PIC).

Creating a Flight Plan

Creating a Flight Plan and conducting a VFR Navigation is all about using *Dead Reckoning* principles and this is what will be focused on in this chapter.

This requires the pilot to determine the navigation waypoints to be flown over or to, calculating a compass heading corrected for any known wind, determining a safe altitude and allowing for any bad weather **before** actually flying the route.

To create a Flight Plan complete the following steps:

Step	Action
1	Clear an area on a desk and have available the "*Tools*" as described above
2	Determine the departure and destination points and any waypoints in between. For planning purposes during training this information will normally be given to you by the Instructor. For example: *Plan a flight from YBSU to Imbil township to YGYM (land) and return to YBSU.* *The planned departure time is 0830 local time. The TAS is 100kts and the fuel consumption rate is 25USGS per hour. The Helicopters Basic Empty Weight is 1800lbs at 115 inches aft of the datum.* Having been given this information the rest is now up to you to determine.
3	Select the relevant Map and draw a line between all the various waypoints.
4	Determine an Altitude to fly based on the height of the terrain and the ICAO heights for headings table. The height must be at a minimum 500ft above the highest terrain or obstacle enroute (1000ft is preferred).
5	Obtain a weather forecast for the area being flown over and read it. Apply the weather to the route being flown and determine if there is any adverse weather or cloud that may cause you to select another route or a different Altitude. Write the relevant W/V for each leg on the Flight Log. Remember that the wind is always given in Degrees True so before determining the wind direction for the Flight Log add or subtract the Magnetic variation from the True Wind to calculate the Magnetic Wind.
6	Using the protractor, determine the True Tracks to each of the waypoints.
7	Add or subtract the Magnetic Variation from the True Tracks and determine the Magnetic Tracks between the waypoints and write these down on the Flight Log.
8	Using a ruler measure the distance between each waypoint and write these down on the Flight Log.
9	Using the Back Side of the Flight Computer (wind side) calculate the Magnetic Heading (HDG) and G/S for each leg. Write the answers in the Flight Log under the HDG and G/S headings as appropriate.

Step	Action
10	Using the Front Side of the Flight Computer calculate the **E**stimated **T**ime **I**nterval (**ETI**) between each leg by using Distance measured and G/S calculated. Write each ETI into the Flight Log.
11	Complete the Pre-Flight Fuel Planning form on the back side of the Flight Log.
12	Complete the In-Flight Fuel Log on the front side of the Flight Log in preparation for the flight.
13	Complete the C of G calculator form on the back side of the Flight Log.

Example
Consider a helicopter departing the Sunshine Coast (YBSU) at 0830 local time for Kingaroy (YKRY) and landing before departing to Gympie (YGYM) for another landing and then returning to the Sunshine Coast (YBSU). The TAS is 100kts and the Fuel consumption rate is 26US GALS per hour. The Helicopter's Basic Empty Weight is 1898lbs at 116 inches aft of the datum. Complete the Flight Log for this flight.

Step	Action
1	Clear an area on a desk and have available the "*Tools*" as described above

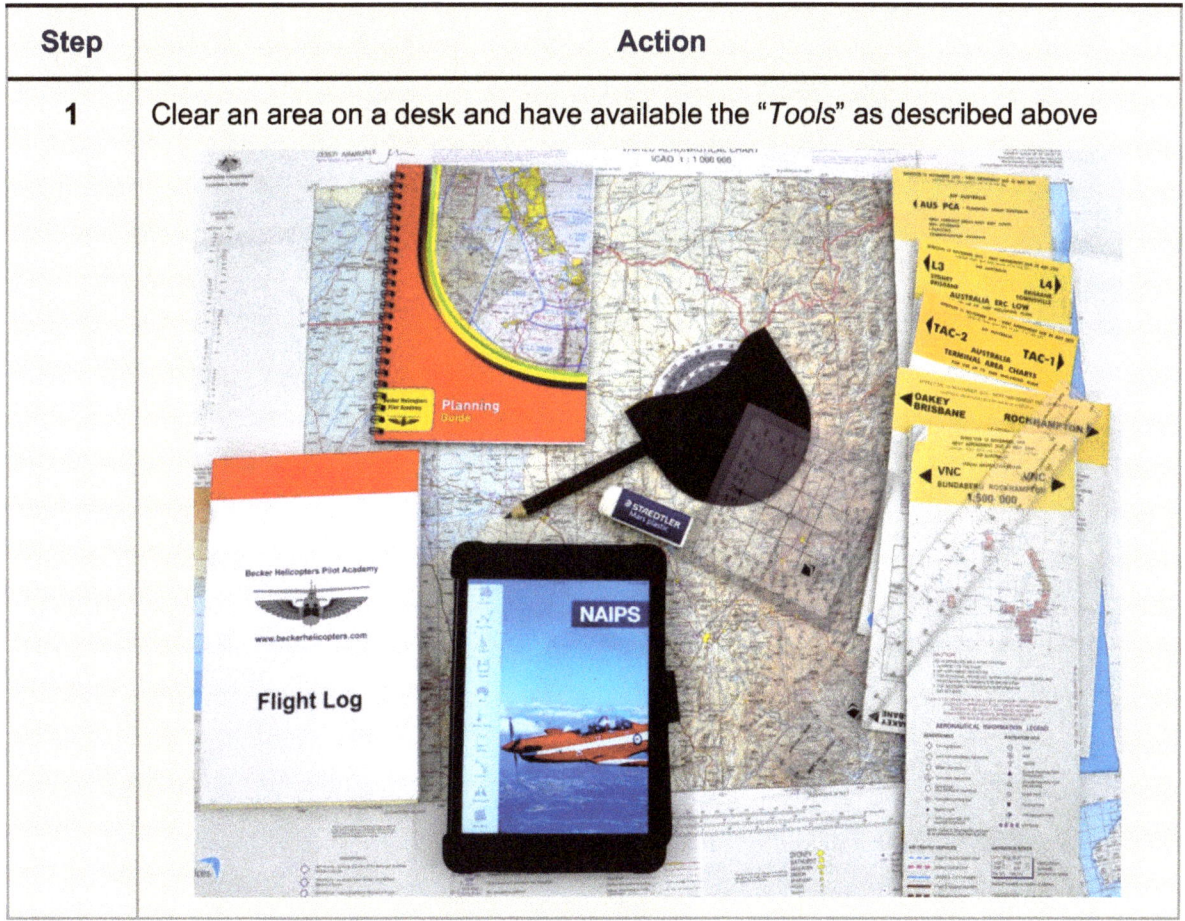

CREATING A FLIGHT PLAN

Step	Action
2	Determine the departure and destination points and any waypoints in between from the information given. *In this case* *Depart YBSU at 0830 local* *Track direct to YKRY and land, then* *Track direct to YGYM and land, then* *Return home to the YBSU.*
3	Select the relevant Map and draw a line between each of the various waypoints. *In this case the Bundaberg VNC has been selected as the most appropriate map to use and a line drawn between the waypoints (YBSU – YKRY – YGYM – YBSU)*

Step	Action
4	Determine an Altitude to fly based on the height of the terrain and the ICAO heights for headings table. *In this case:* *YBSU to YKRY the highest terrain is 2848ft therefore the best altitude to fly will be above that. A westerly HDG will require flying at even thousands plus 500ft (ICAO Altitudes for HDG)* *Therefore the best Altitude to fly this leg will be 4500ft, 6500ft or 8500ft*  YKRY to YGYM the highest terrain is 2458ft therefore the best altitude to fly will be above that. An easterly HDG will require flying at odd thousands plus 500ft Therefore, the best Altitude to fly this leg will be 3500ft, 5500ft or 7500ft.

Step	Action
	YGYM to YBSU the highest terrain is 1401ft therefore the best altitude to fly will be above that. An easterly HDG will require flying at odd thousands plus 500ft Therefore the best Altitude to fly this leg will be 3500ft, 5500ft or 7500ft 
| 5 | Obtain a weather forecast for the area being flown over and read it.<br>Make a final determination on the Altitude for each leg based on the wind and the cloud.<br>*In this case the weather is given as:*<br><br>```
AREA FORECAST 252200 TO 261000 AREA 40

OVERVIEW:
SCATTERED SHOWERS SEA AND COAST, ISOLATED AREAS OF SMOKE
BELOW 8000FT INLAND, LOCALLY THICK NEAR FIRES.

WIND:
2000     5000     7000     10000
040/15   040/10   VRB/10   240/15 PS08

CLOUD:
FEW CU/SC 4000/8000
SCT ST 1000/2000 NEAR SWRS

WEATHER:
NIL SIG

VISIBILITY:
10K REDUCING TO 8000M IN FU
``` |
```

Step	Action
| | *Based on the Terrain and interpretation of the weather the best altitudes to fly would be:*<br><br>YBSU – YKRY 4500ft<br>YKRY – YGYM 3500ft<br>YGYM – YBSU 3500ft<br><br>*These will be written on the Flight Log in the ICAO format as:*<br>4500ft is written as **A**045 (**A**ltitude 4500ft)<br>3500ft is written as **A**035 (**A**ltitude 3500ft)<br><br>| PSN | LSALT | ALT | TRK (M) | WIND (M) | HDG (M) | DIST | G/S | ETI | ETA | R.ETA | ATD |<br>|---|---|---|---|---|---|---|---|---|---|---|---|<br>| 1 YBSU | | | | | | | | | | | |<br>| 2 YKRY | | A045 | 260 | 030/11 | 263 | 67 | 110 | 36 | | | |<br>| 3 | | | | | | | | | | | |<br>| 4 YGYM | | A035 | 060 | 030/13 | 060 | 50 | 90 | 33 | | | |<br>| 5 | | | | | | | | | | | |<br>| 6 YBSU | | A035 | 123 | 030/13 | 117 | 28 | 95 | 18 | | | |<br>| 7 | | | | | | | | | | | |<br>| 8 | | | | | | | | | | | |<br><br>When interpreting the wind at each of these heights the pilot will have to use some judgement based on the altitude being flown and interpolate between the levels and W/V's given.<br><br>For example if given:<br><br>```
WIND:
2000      5000       7000
040/15   040/10     VRB/10
```<br><br>The pilot will have to interpolate what the wind may be if flying at an altitude that is not shown on the forecast.<br><br>| Given | Interpolate | Interpolate | Given | Interpolate | Given |<br>|---|---|---|---|---|---|<br>| 2000 | 3000 | 4000 | 5000 | 6000 | 7000 |<br>| 040/15 | 040/13 | 040/12 | 040/10 | 040/5 | VRB/10 |<br><br>In this case:<br>*YBSU – YKRY A045 the wind can be planned at 040/11T*<br>*YKRY – YGYM A035 the wind can be planned at 040/13T*<br>*YGYM – YBSU A035 the wind can be planned at 040/13T* |
```

CREATING A FLIGHT PLAN
NAVIGATION — INTERNATIONAL HELICOPTER THEORY

Step	Action
	Remember the wind will still be in degrees True so a Magnetic Variation calculation will also have to be done. *In this case the Magnetic Variation is 10°East* YBSU – YKRY A045 040/11T - 10E = 030/11M YKRY – YGYM A035 040/13T - 10E = 030/13M YGYM – YBSU A035 040/13T - 10E = 030/13M | PSN	LSALT	ALT	TRK (M)	WIND (M)	HDG (M)	DIST	G/S	ETI	ETA	R.ETA	ATD
---	---	---	---	---	---	---	---	---	---	---	---
1. YBSU											
2. YKRY		A045	260	030/11	263	67	110	36			
3.											
4. YGYM		A035	060	030/13	060	50	90	33			
5.											
6. YBSU		A035	123	030/13	117	28	95	18			
7.											
8.											
6	Using the protractor, determine the True Tracks to each of the waypoints.  *In this case the True Track between each leg is* *The True Track from YBSU to YKRY is 270°T* *The True Track from YKRY to YGYM is 070°T* *The True Track from YBGYM to YBSU is 133°T*

Step	Action
7	Add or subtract the Magnetic Variation from the True Tracks and determine the Magnetic Tracks between the waypoints and write these down on the Flight Log. *In this case the Magnetic Variation for this area is 10.5° East* *Round it down to 10° to make the calculation simple.*  *East is Least so the Magnetic Variation shall be taken away from the True Track* YBSU – YKRY 270°T - 10E = 260°M YKRY – YGYM 070°T - 10°E = 060°M YGYM – YBSU 133°T – 10E = 123°M | PSN	LSALT	ALT	TRK (M)	WIND (M)	HDG (M)	DIST	G/S	ETI	ETA	R.ETA	ATD
---	---	---	---	---	---	---	---	---	---	---	---
1 YBSU											
2 YKRY		A045	260	030/11	263	67	110	36			
3											
4 YGYM		A035	060	030/13	060	50	90	33			
5											
6 YBSU		A035	123	030/13	117	28	95	18			
7											
8												

CREATING A FLIGHT PLAN
NAVIGATION — INTERNATIONAL HELICOPTER THEORY

Step	Action
8	Using a ruler with the scale that matches the map, measure the distance between each waypoint and write these down on the Flight Log. *In this case the map used is a VNC with a scale of 1:500,000.* *The middle scale of the ruler is scaled to measure NM on a 1:500,000 map.*
	In this case the Distance between each leg is: YBSU – YKRY 67NM · YKRY – YGYM 50NM · YGYM – YBSU 28NM

PSN	LSALT	ALT	TRK (M)	WIND (M)	HDG (M)	DIST	G/S	ETI	ETA	R.ETA	ATD
1. YBSU											
2. YKRY		A045	260	030/11	263	67	110	36			
3.											
4. YGYM		A035	060	030/13	060	50	90	33			
5.											
6. YBSU		A035	123	030/13	117	28	95	18			
7.											
8.											

Step	Action
9	Using the Back Side of the Flight Computer (wind side) calculate the Magnetic Heading (HDG) and G/S for each leg.

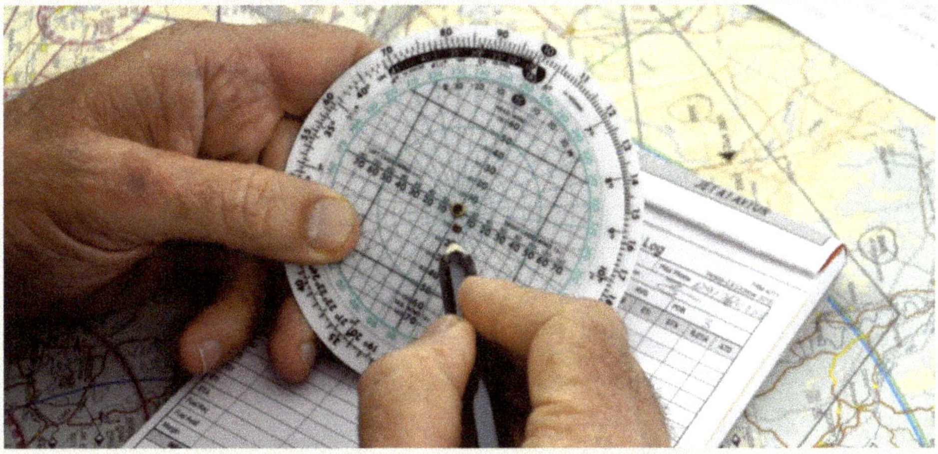

In this case the HDG and G/S for each leg is:

YBSU – YKRY 263°M

YKRY – YGYM 060°M

YGYM – YBSU 117°M

PSN	LSALT	ALT	TRK (M)	WIND (M)	HDG (M)	DIST	G/S	ETI	ETA	R.ETA	ATD
1. YBSU											
2. YKRY		A045	260	030/11	263	67	110	36			
3.											
4. YGYM		A035	060	030/13	060	50	90	33			
5.											
6. YBSU		A035	123	030/13	117	28	95	18			
7.											
8.											

CREATING A FLIGHT PLAN

Step	Action
10	Using the Front Side of the Flight Computer calculate the **E**stimated **T**ime **I**nterval (**ETI**) between each leg by using Distance measured and G/S calculated. *In this case the ETI for each leg is:* YBSU – YKRY 36 minutes YKRY – YGYM 33 minutes YGYM – YBSU 18 minutes

PSN	LSALT	ALT	TRK (M)	WIND (M)	HDG (M)	DIST	G/S	ETI	ETA	R.ETA	ATD
1. YBSU											
2. YKRY		A045	260	030/11	263	67	110	36			
3.											
4. YGYM		A035	060	030/13	060	50	90	33			
5.											
6. YBSU		A035	123	030/13	117	28	95	18			
7.											
8.											

Step	Action
11	Complete the Pre-Flight Fuel Planning form on the back side of the Flight Log. *In this case with a fuel consumption rate of 26USGs per hour the Fuel Planning would look as follows:*

Pre-Flight Fuel Planning								
Fuel	Min	Qty	Min	Qty	Min	Qty	Min	Qty
Cruise	36	16	33	14	18	8		
Alternate								
Sub Total	36	16	33	14	18	8		
Var Res 15%								
Fixed Res	30	13	30	13	30	13		
Holding								
Approach								
Taxi	-	5	-	5	-	5		
Fuel Req	66	34	63	32	48	26		
Margin	134	56	110	47	80	34		
Endurance	200	90	173	79	128	60		
Leg	SU		KRY		GYM		SU	

Step	Action
12	Complete the In-Flight Fuel Log on the front side of the Flight Log in preparation for the flight. *In this case the helicopter is departing with full fuel (90USGs). The shaded areas will be filled out during the flight. The unshaded fields can be filled in from data taken from the Pre-Flight Fuel Planning form.*

In-Flight Fuel log					
Leg	Planned Dep. Fuel	Planned Leg Fuel	Act Arv Fuel (Gauge)	Min Fuel to Cont.	Margin (+/- GALS)
1. SU	90	34	79	58	+21
2. KRY	79	32	60	26	+34
3. GYM	60	26			
4. SU					
5.					
6.					
7.					
8.					

Remember that all going well the reserve fuel will NOT be used so will be in the tank on departure from the next waypoint. The Planned departure fuel reflects what is expected to be in the fuel tank.

Step	Action
13	Complete the C of G calculator form on the back side of the Flight Log. *In this case with a Basic Empty Weight (BEW) of 1898lbs and an arm of 116 inches aft of the datum.* The two (2) pilots in Row 1 each weigh 75kg (convert to lbs) 1 passenger in Row 2 weighing 60kgs (convert to lbs) There is no Row 3 Baggage in the aft baggage compartment is 30lbs Total fuel on board at start-up is 90USGs. 		C of G Calculator		
		ITEM	Weight x	Arm	= Moment
		BEW	1898	116	220,168
		ROW 1	344	65	22,360
		ROW 2	132	104	13,728
		ROW 3			
		BAG	30	148	4,440
		ZFW	2404		
		FUEL	603	110.6	66,691.8
		AUW	3007	108.8	327387.8
		MAUW	3200	C of G	Initial

Step	Action
	Remember to calculate the C of G add up the total of the moments and divide by the AUW. *In this case 327,387.8 divided by 3007 = C of G 108.8 inches aft of the datum.* *Cross reference the result with the C of G Envelope in the Limitations Section of the Flight Manual.* 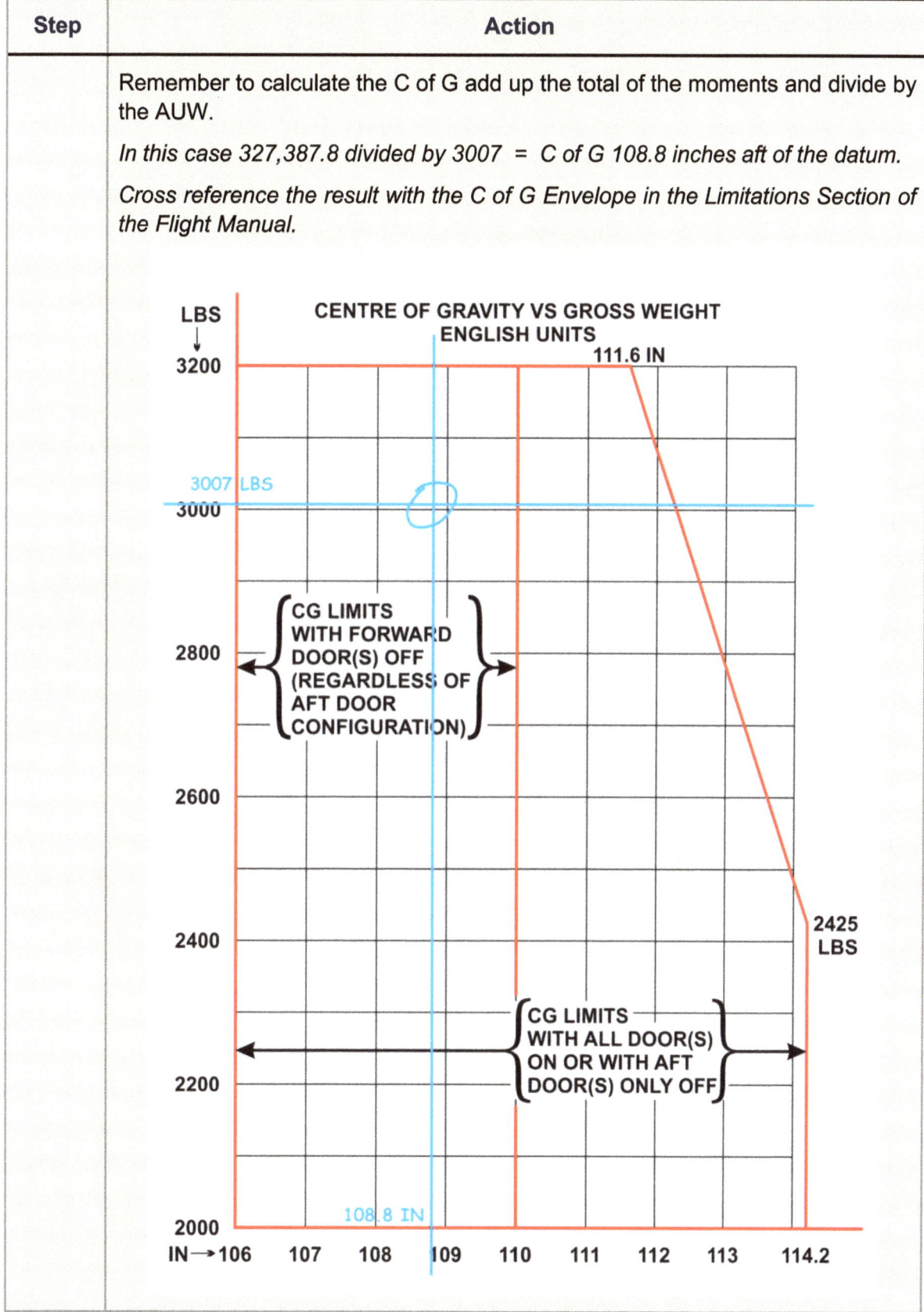

On completion of the Flight Log the pilot is now able to transpose some of the relevant detail on to the topographical map and mud map for easy reference in the cockpit while in flight (covered later in the VFR Navigation Pilot Handling Notes).

Transposing information onto the topographical map

There are several conventions (expected way of doing things) when marking detail from the Flight Log onto the topographical map.

Convention	Description
Start with a clean map	The map you have will be used many times before it is replaced, therefore it is important to look after it.
	Make sure prior to starting to plan a new cross country flight the map is clean of all old markings and is fit for purpose.
Use a pencil	Because the map will be used again and again you will need to erase any old tracks. By using a pencil this will be easy to do with an eraser.
Draw straight lines	Always try to draw straight lines with a ruler starting from the centre of the departure to the centre of the destination waypoints.
	Do not try to do it freehand. If a long leg has to be broken into smaller segments in order to avoid Controlled Airspace, Restricted Areas, high terrain or for some other reason then again draw smaller straight lines.
Circle waypoints	All waypoints should have a 5NM or 10NM circle drawn around them. This allows the pilot to notice obvious lead in features to help identify the destination.

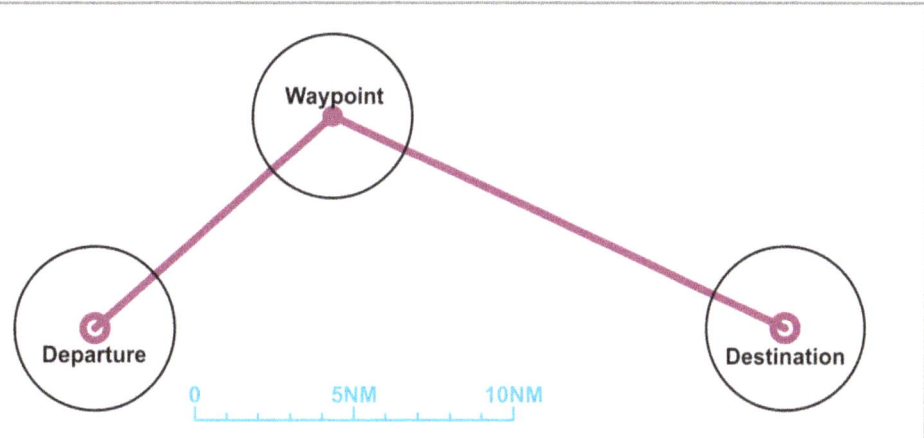

| Proportional markers | Along each leg select obvious navigational features and draw a line through them with an arrow ahead and behind. This is a *proportional marker* and is a navigation reference of how many NM the helicopter has already travelled from the last known position and how many NM are still to go to the destination waypoint.

By convention the arrow on the right of track will be the distance *to the destination* and the arrow on the left will be the *distance already travelled from the last known proportional marker*. (Remember Right on and Left behind!)

At these proportional markers the pilot shall note the current time. This will allow a time, distance and G/S calculation to cross check if the helicopter is behind, ahead or on time of the planned **E**stimated **T**ime of **A**rrival (**ETA**) at the destination.

The proportional marker is also a good indication of whether the helicopter is actually still on track to the destination.

Proportional markers do not have to be a particular distance. The pilot can choose based on the features available. Some may be close, some may be far apart.

If there are no obvious navigation features along a particular leg then using 10NM or 20NM proportional markers will suffice.

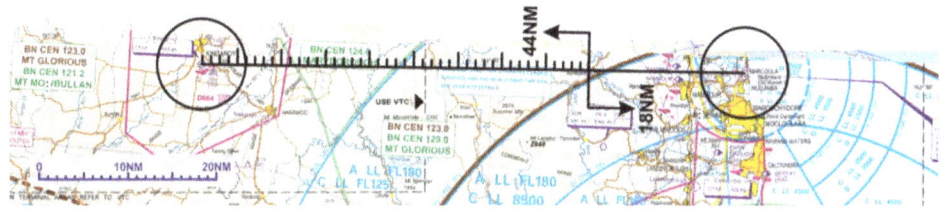 |

Rocket Boxes	A Rocket Box is simply a small table of numbers with an arrow at the top indicating the direction of travel that looks similar to a "rocket".
	Placed alongside the track it can give the pilot quick reference to information about the leg being flown including:
	Magnetic track, Altitude, ETI and the minimum fuel for that leg.
	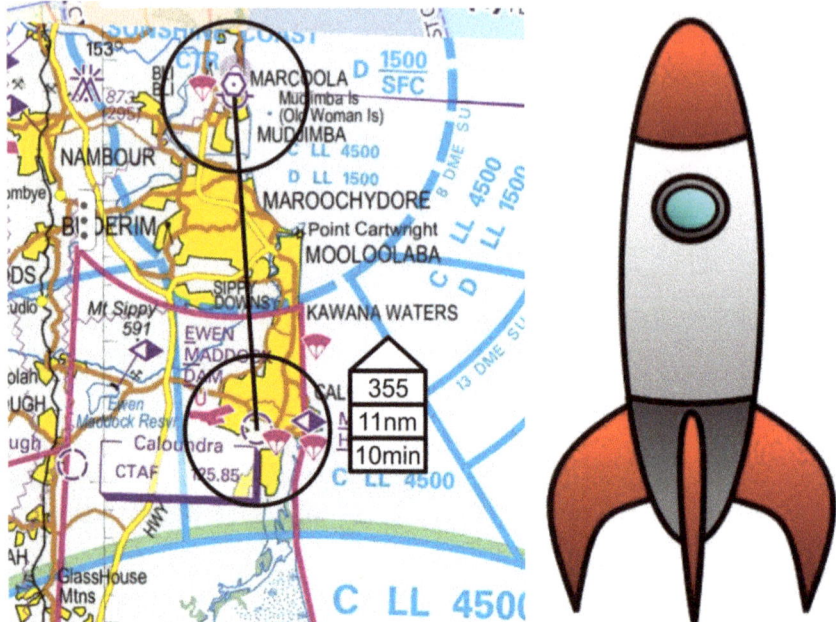
	The pilot can choose to put in more information, less information or different information, depending on what he decides is important to him on that leg.

Summary

Below shows the fully completed Flight Log.

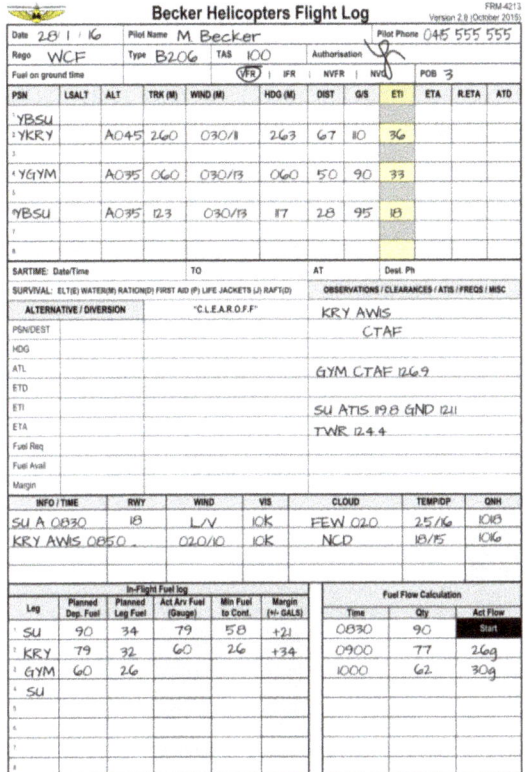
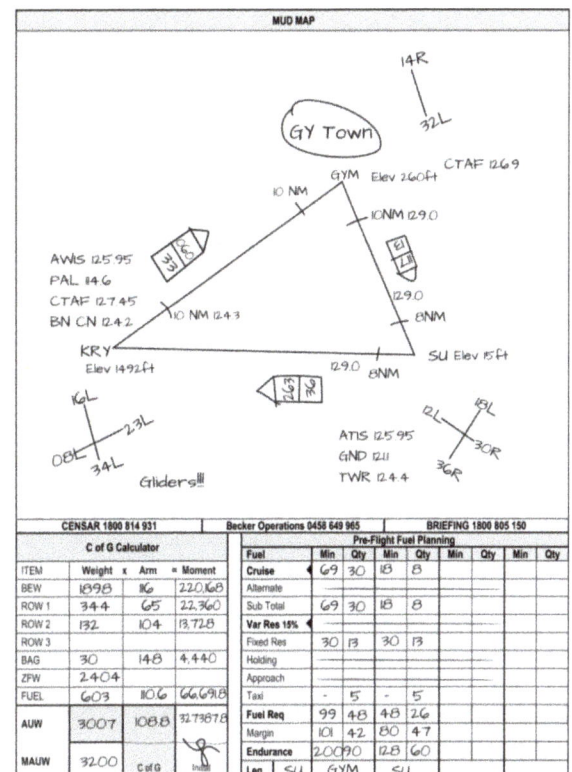

Map Reading 101

There are some basic techniques that can help a pilot read a map and identify features both on the ground and on the map.

Map to Ground and Ground to Map

When flying VFR and particularly by DAY the pilot will rely heavily on map reading skills and the ability to identify key features on the ground.

Map reading is simply the ability to identify a feature on a map and then identify the same feature on the ground. This is referred to as reading *map to ground*.

Alternatively the pilot will need to develop the ability to identify a feature on the ground and then identify the same feature on the map. This is referred to as reading *ground to map*.

Map to Ground ↓ or ↑ Ground to Map

Both skills are required depending on the pilot's awareness of their position and the availability of obvious features.

There are some traps to be aware of when relying solely on a map for VFR navigation.

Maps are made by people based on what was last recorded or seen. This means that sometimes the information on the map is old or simply not accurate. What is on the ground may not actually be on the map.

For example:

Consider the construction of a new road or communications tower or runway. Although you can see them on the ground they may not be on the map.

In the image below the map has no reference to a large bitumen runway that is actually on the ground.

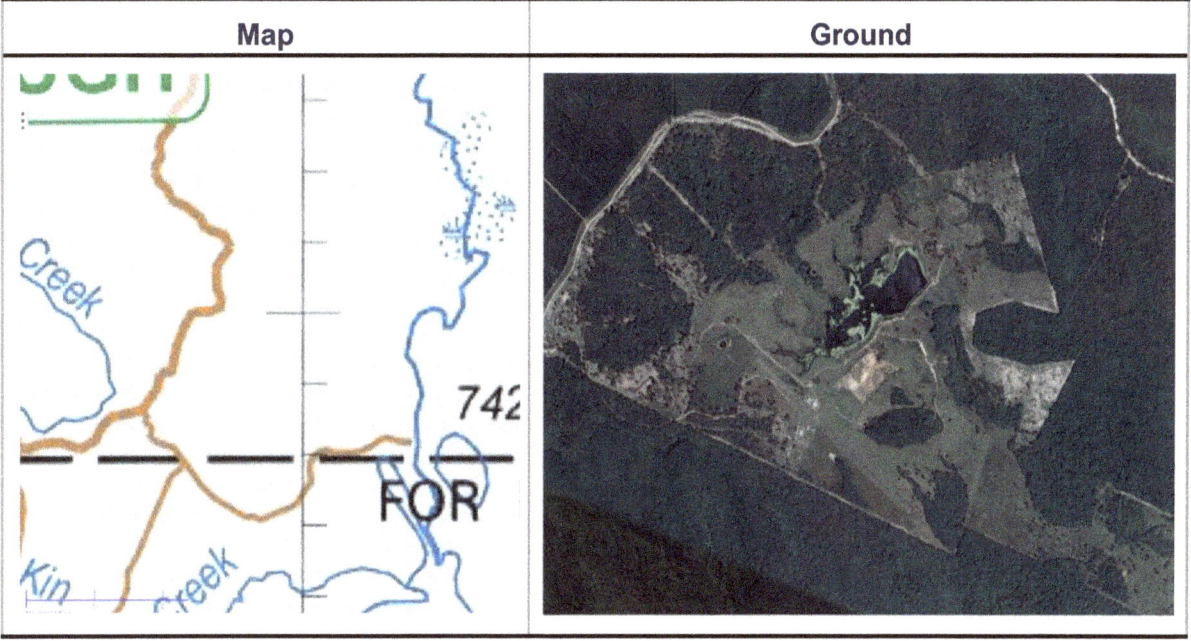

The same applies the other way. Sometimes features on the ground change or disappear. This means that sometimes what is on the map is actually not on the ground.

For example:

Consider a fire tower or a set of power lines or railway lines that have been removed. They may still appear on the map but not be on the ground.

In the image below the map shows a railway line but on the ground the line has been removed and is no longer there (although the railway bridge still remains for historical reasons).

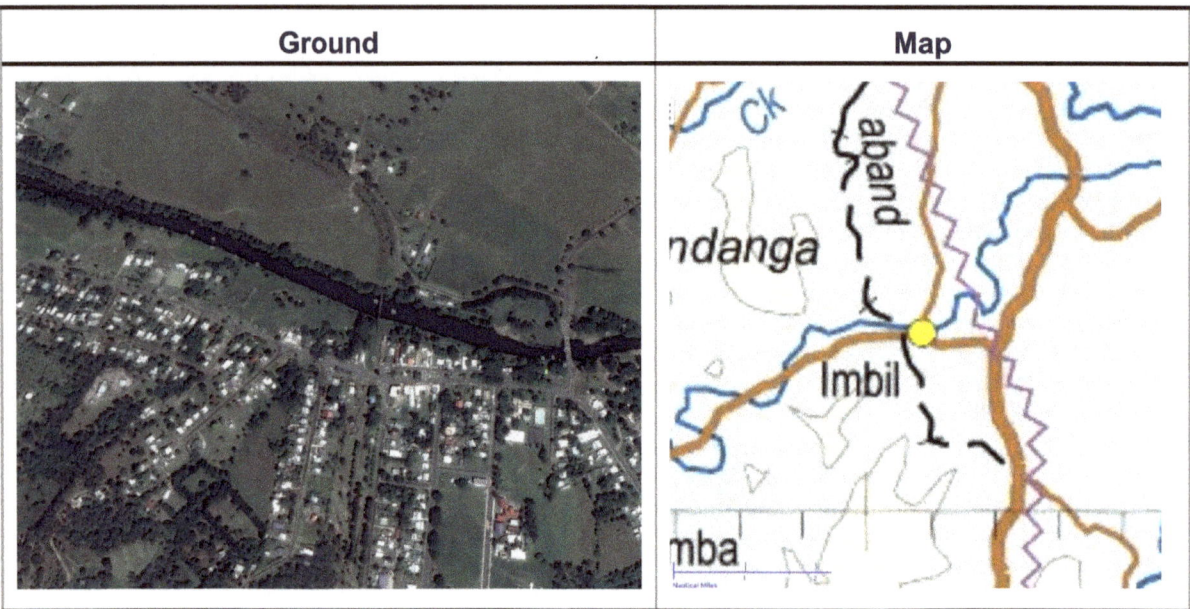

For this reason there are some rules to apply when navigating with reference to a map.

Rules

1. Use the clock code

Use the clock code relative to the helicopter's nose to identify where features are.

This is a very simple method to help keep the pilot orientated and knowing where to look as well as a simple method to communicate to the crew where the pilot is looking relative to the nose of the helicopter.

Imagine a clock superimposed over a helicopter. Each number on the clock will relate to a direction the pilot is looking.

All the pilot has to do now is be able to estimate distance in NMs and give a direction using the clock code to identify where a particular feature is.

Understanding what a Nautical Mile (NM) looks like from the air can take some practice so having a reference distance will help. A simple reference distance can be the length of a known runway.

For example:

Consider Runway 18/36 at the Sunshine Coast, it is approximately 1NM long. Knowing this the pilot can simply ask, how many runways away is the feature? 2 Runways equals 2NM and so on.

So when identifying a feature on the ground the pilot is able to give a direction using the clock code and an estimated distance by referencing a known runway length.

For example:

In the image below the feature is at the 2 o'clock position at approximately 5NM away

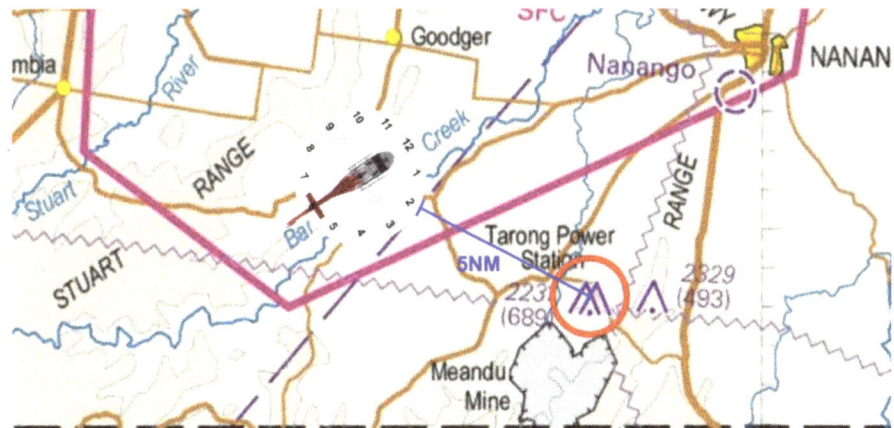

2. Select the right features

Choosing the right features is essential to good map reading skills and the ability to navigate.

Remember the pilot has the ability to:

1. Position fix:
   This is estimating the helicopter's position relative to other identified features on the ground.
   To Position fix, pick at least two (2) obvious features in the distance that are at least 45° apart. Using the clock code draw a line from each feature relative to the helicopter and where they intersect will indicate the helicopter's approximate position on the map.

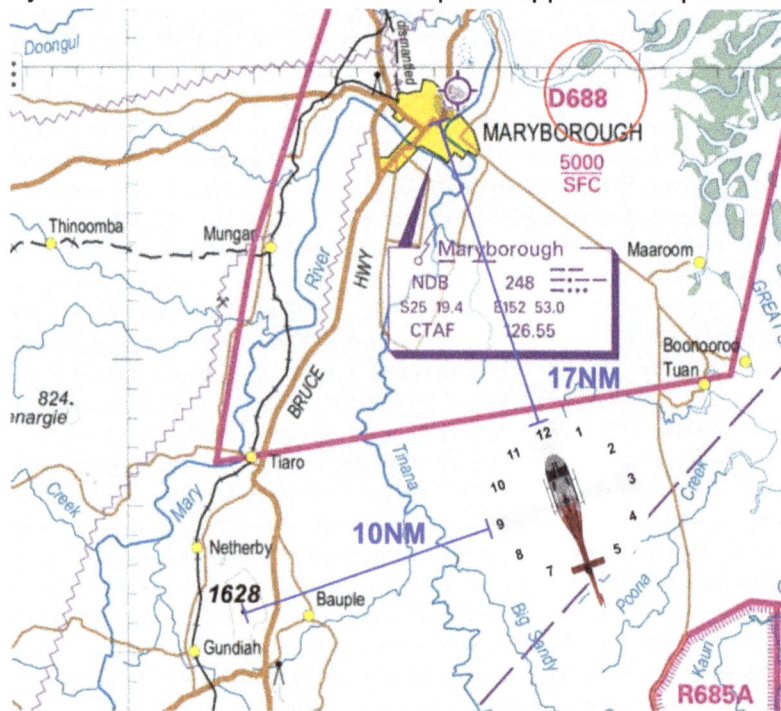

2. Dead Reckon the position of the helicopter which requires the pilot to maintain a constant heading and calculate a distance travelled against a known G/S and time interval.

3. Track crawl:
   Which means the pilot is identifying the position of the helicopter on the map every few minutes and flying from known feature to known feature. This requires looking outside, identifying a feature on the ground and identifying the same feature on the map and determining that it is on the desired track then flying directly to that feature before selecting another feature and repeating the process.

Each of these techniques requires the pilot to identify features. The secret to identifying features is to look for **big obvious features** that are a **distance** away from the helicopter. Never look directly under the helicopter at small features as typically every road or river can look the same and this is how pilots can become lost.

Once identifying one or more **big obvious features** the pilot can start moving the scan closer to the helicopter to look at smaller and smaller features until positively being able to position the helicopter on the map.

In summary, when identifying features on the ground to map or map to ground:

- Look in the distance first
- Look for big features
- Look for natural features first (mountains, valleys, lakes, oceans)
- Look for manmade features second (towns, roads, dams, wires)
- Slowly bring the scan in towards the helicopter going from identified feature to identified feature until looking directly ahead or below.

Example
Consider a helicopter flying between YBSU and YGYM.
If the helicopter was located 1NM SW of Cooroy what big obvious features should you see on the ground?

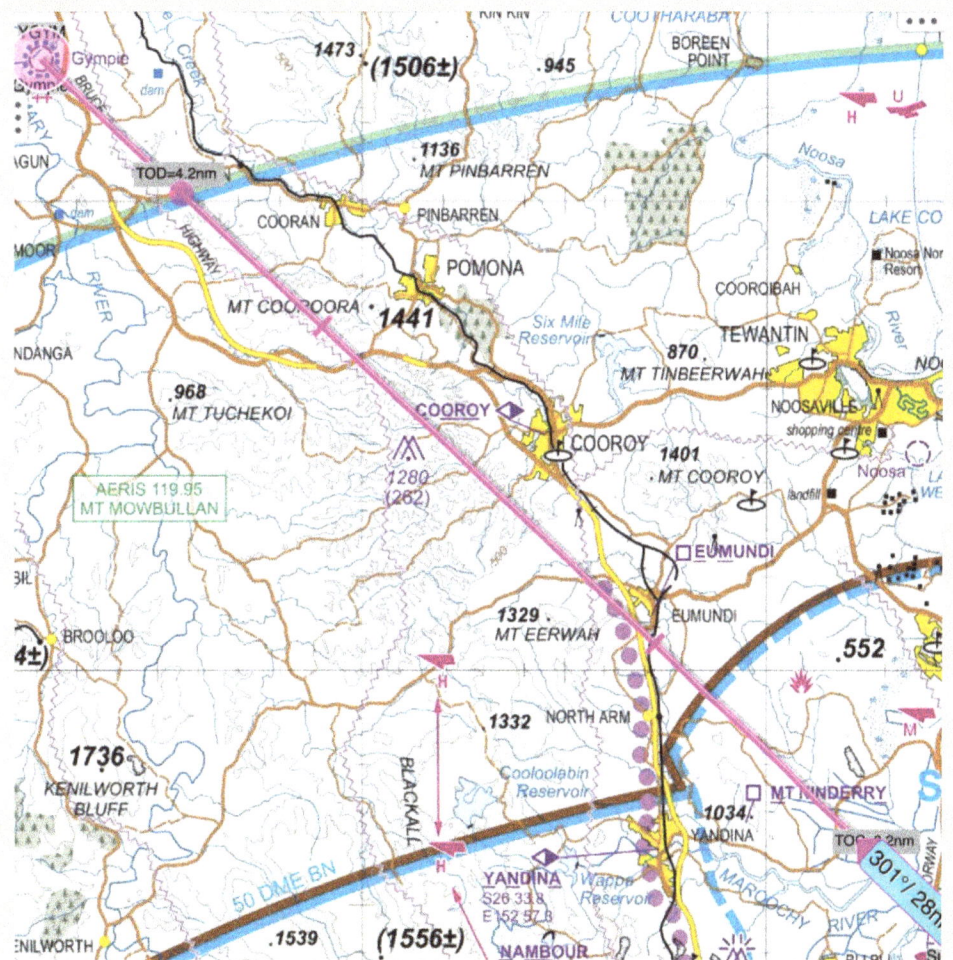

Some of the *big* obvious natural features in the distance would be:

The ocean is behind the helicopter

Lake Cootharaba approximately 10NM at the helicopter's 3 o'clock position

Mt Cooroy at 1401ft 4NM at the helicopter's 4 o'clock position

Mt Cooroora 1441ft 5NM at the helicopter's 1 o'clock position

Kennilworth Bluff at 1736ft approximately 12NM at the helicopter's 9 o'clock position

Rising ground on the left of the helicopter and lower ground on the right

> Six Mile Reservoir 4NM at the helicopter's 3 o'clock position
>
> Some *smaller manmade* features that can be identified on the ground would then be:
>
> The Bruce Highway is on the helicopter's right
>
> Cooroy township is on the right
>
> There are some towers approximately 2NM at the helicopter's 1 o'clock position
>
> There are several sets of power wires that you may be able to identify
>
> Finally you may be able to look under the helicopter and correctly identify which road the helicopter is now flying across.

3. **Map to Ground**

   If the pilot knows the helicopter's current position then identifying a feature on the map then identifying it on the ground should be a simple thing.

   Using the clock code on the map identify a feature and measure the distance in NM then looking outside the helicopter look in the direction (using the clock code) and estimate the distance and the feature should be in its correct place.

   Using Map to Ground is the normal VFR navigating technique to apply.

4. **Ground to Map**

   If the pilot is uncertain of the helicopter's position then first estimate the position on the map by doing a G/S over Time at a constant HDG calculation. This should give the pilot an area of probability of where the helicopter currently is.

   Given an area of probability identify some features on the map that should be able to be identified on the ground.

   Looking on the ground identify at least 2 obvious features at least 45 degrees apart and then identify them on the map.

   Using the position fix technique the pilot should then be able to plot the helicopter's new position.

   Using Ground to Map is normally used when uncertain of your position.

Flight Notification via NAIPS

On completion of the Flight Log a Flight Notification may then be submitted to Air Services Australia through the internet using the **N**ational **A**eronautical **I**nformation **P**rocessing **S**ystem (**NAIPS**).

At the same time the pilot has the choice to nominate a **S**earch **A**nd **R**escue **Time** (**SARTIME**) with Air Services or alternatively a SARTIME can be held by the Company.

NAIPS can be accessed by a computer, iPad or Tablet with internet access.

Using NAIPS directly requires some knowledge of the abbreviations used in each of the fields. Using NAIPS via an APP means some of the hard work is done for you as detail can be taken directly from your electronic flight plan.

For training purposes we allow the use of both methods to file a flight plan through NAIPS.

The most important ability is that you can file a flight plan when required so knowing both systems may be necessary.

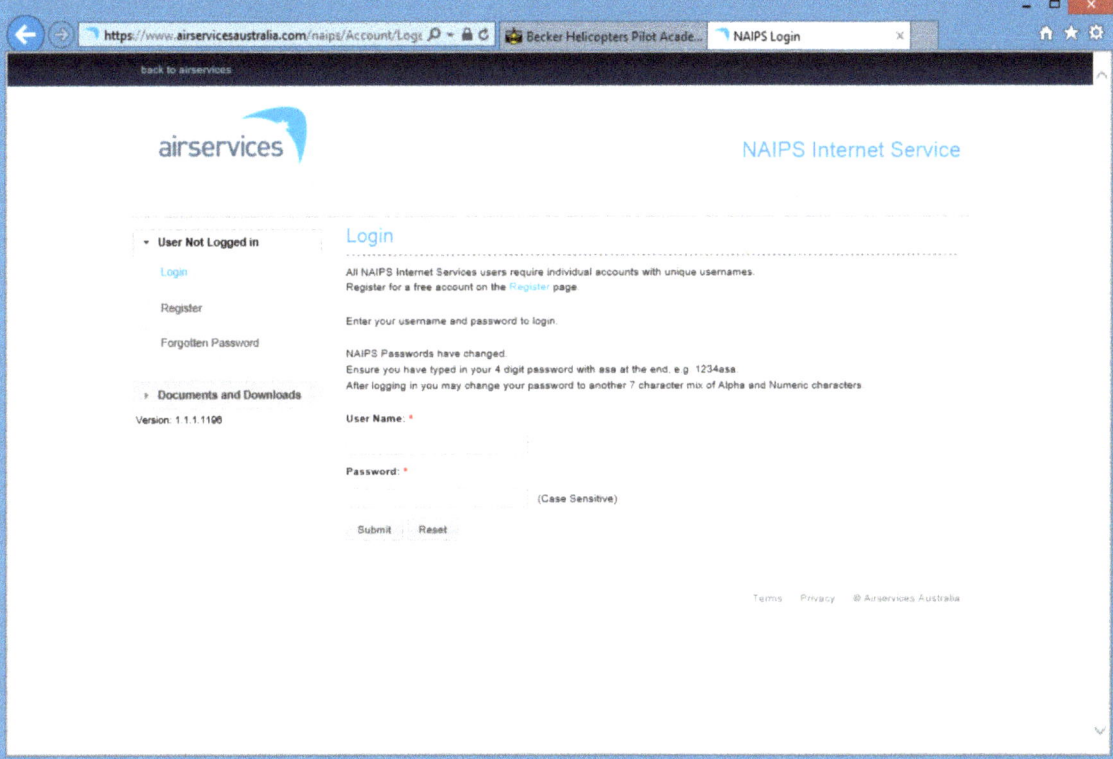

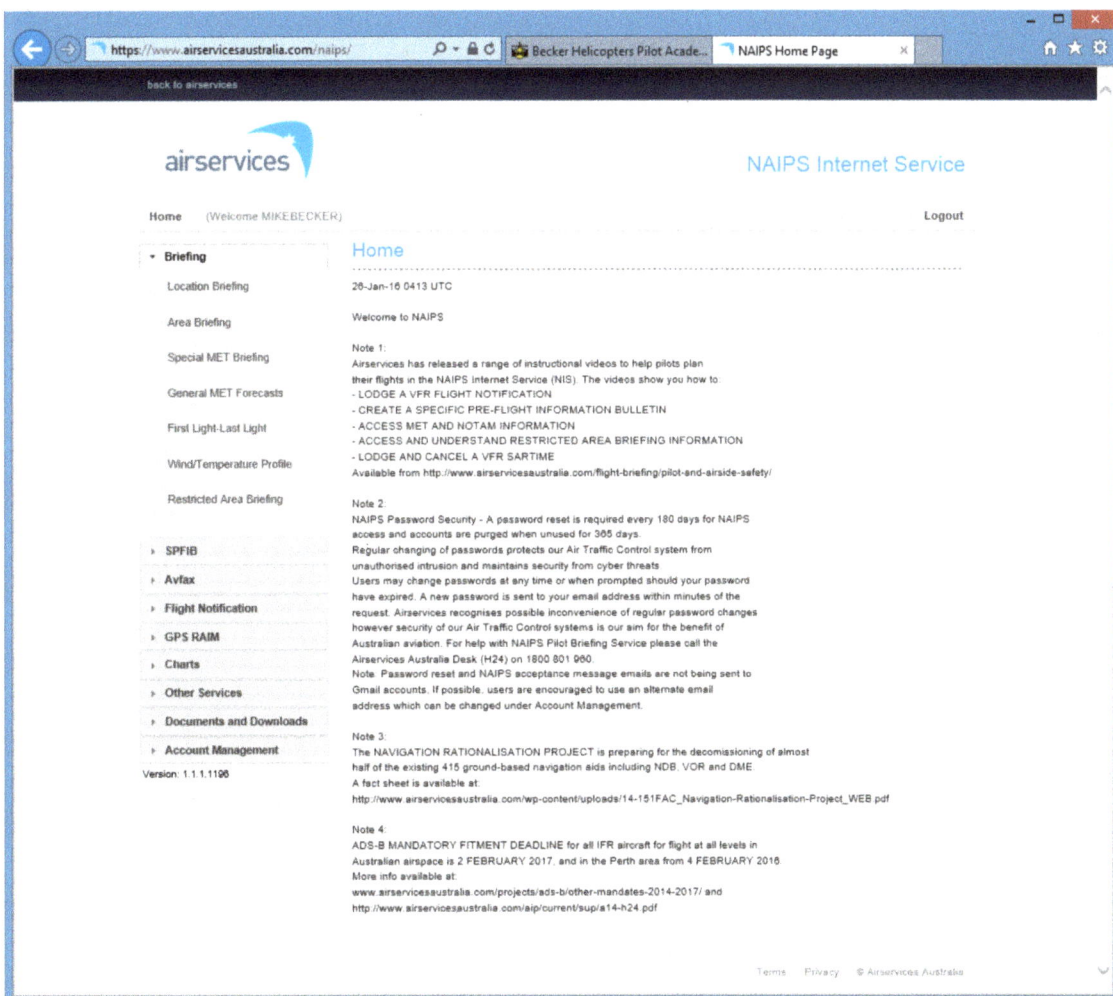

CREATING A FLIGHT PLAN
NAVIGATION
INTERNATIONAL HELICOPTER THEORY

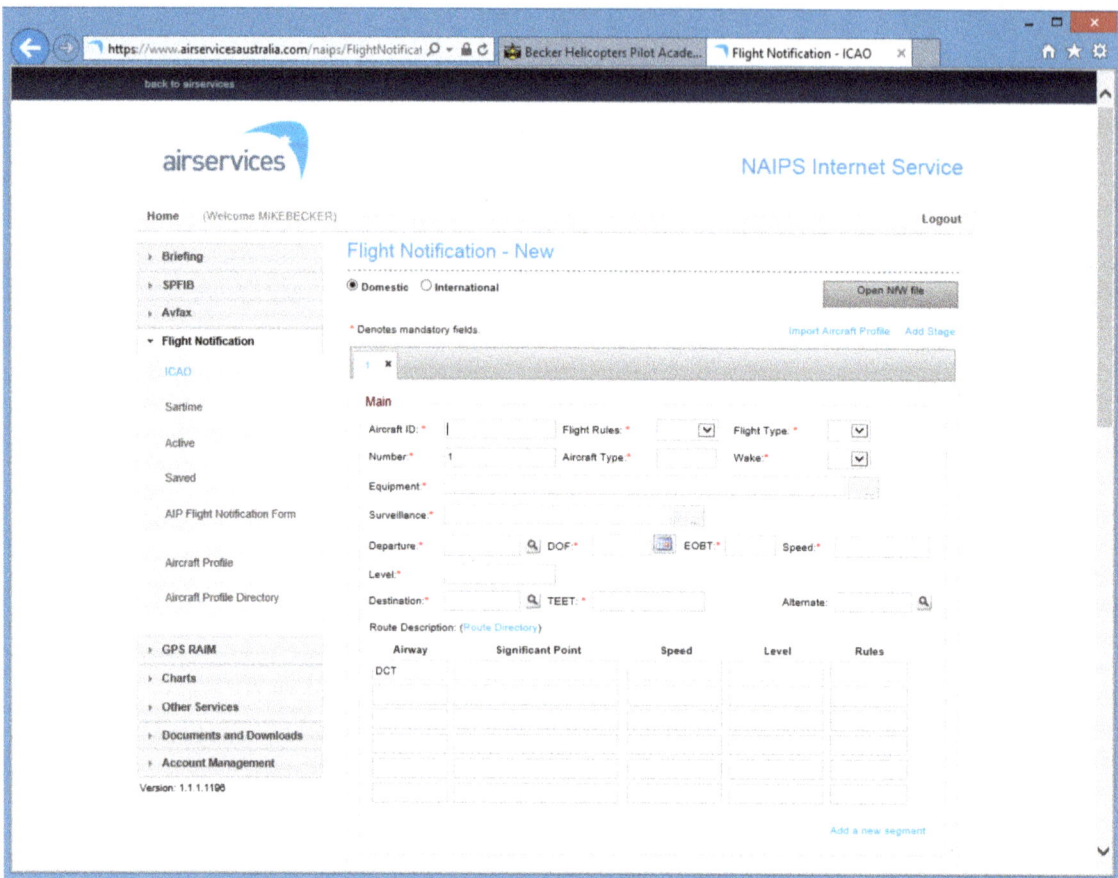

CREATING A FLIGHT PLAN
NAVIGATION

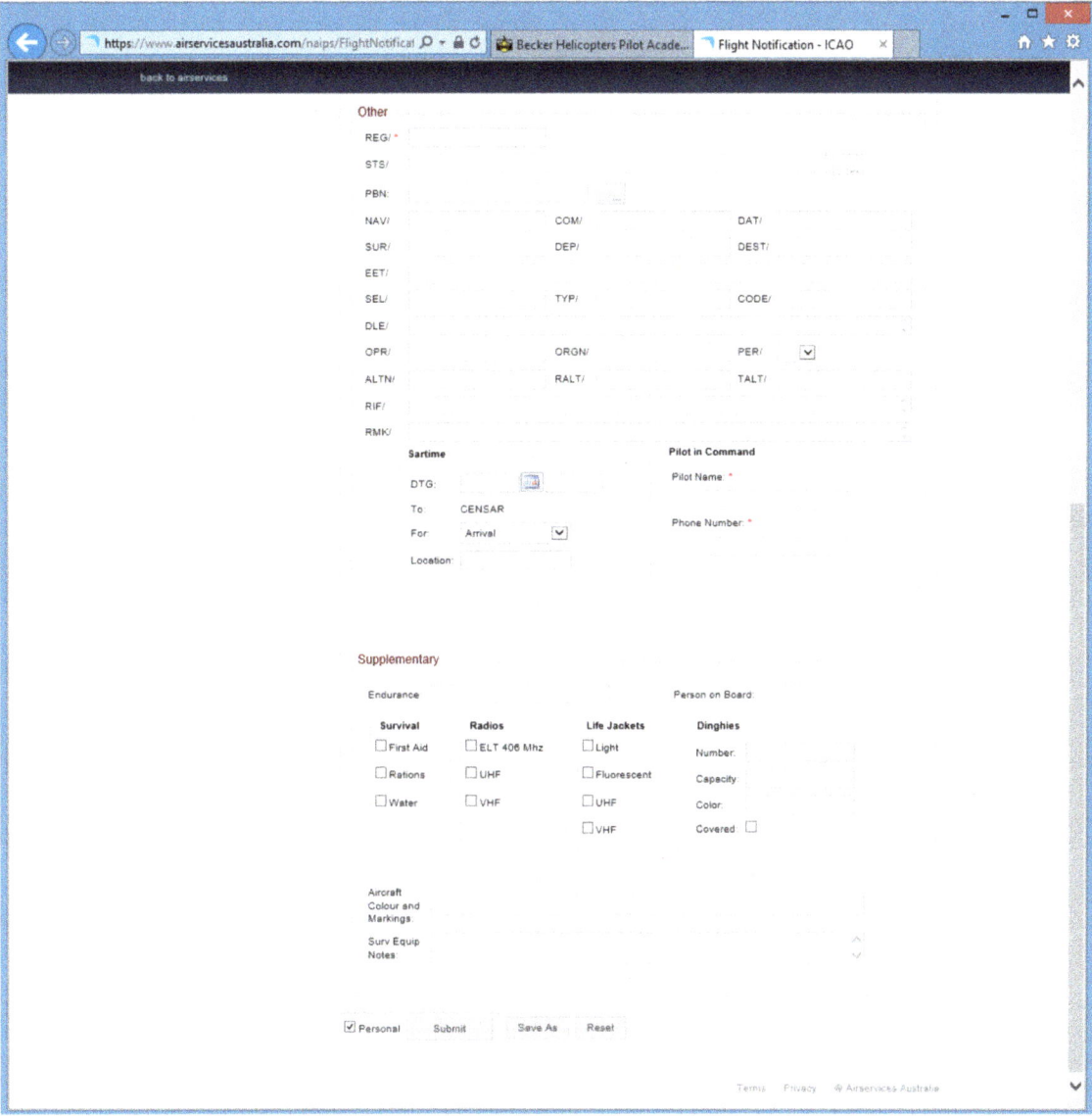